EMPOWERING PEDAGOGY FOR EARLY CHILDHOOD EDUCATION

BEVERLIE DIETZE

OKANAGAN COLLEGE

DIANE KASHIN

RYERSON UNIVERSITY

PEARSON

Toronto

Vice President, CMPS: Gary Bennett
Editorial Director: Claudine O'Donnell
Executive Editor: Lisa Rahn
Senior Marketing Manager: Michelle Bish
Program Manager: Madhu Ranadive
Project Manager: Susan Johnson
Developmental Editor: Christine Langone
Production Services: Niraj Bhatt, iEnergizerAptara®, Inc.
Permissions Project Manager: Erica Mojzes
Photo Permissions Research: Dimple Bhorwal
Text Permissions Research: Phyllis Padula
Cover Designer: iEnergizerAptara®, Inc.
Cover Image: Left: Dzmitry Malyeuski/Fotolia, Middle: milicanistoran/Fotolia, Right: waldemarus/Fotolia

Credits and acknowledgments for material borrowed from other sources and reproduced, with permission, in this textbook appear on the appropriate page within the text.

If you purchased this book outside the United States or Canada, you should be aware that it has been imported without the approval of the publisher or the author.

7 18

Library and Archives Canada Cataloguing in Publication

Dietze, Beverlie, 1957, author
    Empowering pedagogy for early childhood education / Beverlie Dietze, Okanagan College;
Diane Kashin, Ryerson University.
Includes bibliographical references and index.
ISBN 978-0-13-343693-8 (pbk.)
    1. Early childhood education—Study and teaching—Canada.   2. Early childhood education—
Curricula—Canada.   I. Kashin, Diane, author   II. Title.

LB1139.3.C3D54   2015 372.210971   C2014-907175-2

ISBN 978-0-13-343693-8

To my late mother, Eileen Lucy Arthurs; my late father, William Christie Arthurs; and my brothers and sisters, who gave me the foundation in my childhood and influenced me to explore, try new paths, take new journeys, and reflect upon those journeys to discover what was learned and how that new learning could support new adventures.

—Beverlie Dietze

To my late father, Gerald Lackman, whose analytical mind and photographic memory influenced my continual quest for knowledge, and to my mother, Reeva Lackman, whose artistic eye and spirit help me stay connected to the heart of teaching and learning.

—Diane Kashin

Brief Contents

Contents

Preface

The changing nature of childhood in the twenty-first century has led many provinces and territories across Canada to examine public policies and approaches to early childhood education. Debate continues among professionals about how children learn, the theories and models of programming that meet children's needs, and the roles and responsibilities of adults in creating rich environments that support children in their experiences and provide opportunities to play. We recognize that there are no clear answers; rather, there is a need for us to collectively engage in authentic debate and discourse so that we collaboratively think about positive ways to influence children's environments and experiences, which, in turn, will contribute to their development.

Empowering Pedagogy for Early Childhood Education evolved from our desire to advance discussions about what constitutes pedagogy in early learning programs that will empower children and adults to collectively create environments that foster active play; provide space and materials to spark children's creative, imaginative, and symbolic worlds; and reflect children's learning, cultures, and family values. The text situates the discussions of pedagogy and how children learn and develop in early childhood in a Canadian and local perspective. We pay particular attention to relevant legislative and policy developments and draw upon international research and field experiences to bring forth programming models of practice that address how children learn and develop. In order to represent the broad base of concepts that are intertwined in early childhood pedagogy, we examine a review of early childhood curriculum materials used nationally and internationally. With more than eight provinces across Canada either in the process of developing or already having developed curriculum frameworks for early learning programs, we wanted to provide up-and-coming early learning professionals with opportunities to become familiar with curriculum frameworks and begin discussion on how the frameworks are used to conceptualize what constitutes effective early learning environments, experiences, meaning making, relationship building, equity, diversity, and active learning options. As well, we wanted to create a textbook that emphasizes the idea that empowering pedagogy in early childhood programs provides children with equal opportunities to explore, discover, and wonder in both indoor and outdoor environments.

In exploring the image of children and environments and thinking about ways in which pedagogy empowers children to be active and inquisitive learners in early learning environments, this book is intended to create dialogue about how learning and development take place. The text introduces the reader to research and perspectives from many disciplines, and attempts to provide a contemporary view of how early learning programs, when designed to support children's authentic interests and embrace their sense of wonder, can empower children to be inquisitive, lifelong learners.

We hope that by reading this text and, more importantly, discussing, debating, and determining what new knowledge to embrace, collectively we will support our most precious resources in our communities—our children, our families, and our early learning students and professionals.

OUR VISION FOR THIS BOOK

As we began planning for and conducting research for this text, we agreed that we wanted the book to represent early childhood education from a Canadian perspective, while introducing students to international approaches that have influenced or are influencing programming, policies, and directions of early childhood programs. We wanted this book to

- support early childhood education students in exploring the array of topics that are interwoven in early childhood pedagogy;

- create opportunities for readers to question, imagine, think about, reflect upon, and determine how their approach to early childhood pedagogy can empower and influence children's play and learning;

- highlight new research in order to understand the relationship of environments, approaches, materials, and experiences to children's sense of wonderment, exploration, and learning;

- stimulate discussions among early learning professionals and early childhood students as a way to promote meaning making as a visible and meaningful learning experience;

- reinforce the importance of designing early childhood education programs to stimulate children in both the indoor and outdoor environments;

- provide early childhood education students with information about theories, beliefs, and practices that empower children's play and learning and outline how these areas are foundational for creating a working philosophy;

- offer our readers' stories and photos from the field as examples that can be the impetus for discussions, reflections, and "aha" moments;

- stimulate thinking about how the implementation of empowering pedagogy is influenced by children, families, and communities, and about how it may look different in urban and rural settings; and

- contribute to early childhood education students developing a passion for and commitment to children and families.

APPROACH TO THE TEXT

This text is intended to be a user-friendly, valuable resource for early childhood education students during their studies and as they prepare to enter any number of exciting career paths with children and families. Each chapter begins with a story from a child's perspective. These stories are intended to help the reader hear the voices of children and think about how by listening to children, we can develop environments that will empower them to embrace the options and opportunities available. These messages and the application examples in each chapter are intended to support the reader in examining current beliefs and practices and in embracing new ways of knowing and practising based on current research.

Empowering Pedagogy for Early Childhood Education differs from other texts in several ways:

- The chapters provide opportunities for readers to engage in reflective moments related to key messages in the text. The ideas and questions posed are intended to support the reader in thinking about the issues presented in depth so that meaning making occurs and is transferable to working philosophy or practice.

- Research, pedagogical tools, case studies, and ideas are embedded in each chapter to provide opportunities for readers to consider thought-provoking examples and concepts that bring forth multiple perspectives on pedagogy.

- Both Canadian and international content are introduced to the student, including up-to-date information on curriculum frameworks, family structures, and locally appropriate programming.

- The text offers readers opportunities to examine ways to empower pedagogy from multiple perspectives by emphasizing a constructivist and postmodern approach to pedagogy and providing the foundational information that is transferable to a variety of programming approaches and personal philosophies, while maintaining the focus of the child and family as the centre of pedagogy.

- Links are provided that students may use to acquire further information on subjects and help them connect theory to practice, or to expand their sense of curiosity and bring forth more questions and inquiry.

- The text embraces new technologies and the opportunities for professional learning made possible through social media. As early learning professionals worldwide are curating topics of potential interest to our readers, we acknowledge this untraditional source of learning that is revolutionizing and democratizing learning in our profession.

We believe that this text takes a holistic approach that emphasizes listening to the children; creating and using the environment as a "third teacher"; and ensuring that the voices of children, early learning students and professionals, parents, and community are heard and that they all become collective participants in empowering children with rich, inspiring, and unique experiences.

CONTENT AND FEATURES OF THE TEXT

The pedagogical features of this text are designed to support both theory and practice in ways that will meet readers' diverse learning requirements. The pedagogical layout of the text is designed to give readers different points of entry to learning through stories, examples, dialogue, technology, and reflection.

The first five chapters of the text lay the foundation for programming and pedagogy for the reader. Following the introductory chapter, we hope the reader sees that the players, including children, their families, and early learning professionals, are key to any early learning environment. Recognizing and supporting the community, culture, and diversity of the players is foundational to programming and pedagogy. Chapters 4 and 5 give the reader background on models, approaches, and frameworks, both Canadian and international, that can be used to build a program that supports all the players.

Beginning with Chapter 6, we address key programming areas and concepts for early learning students and professionals to consider as they develop their own approaches and philosophies, including relationships, politics, ethics, the environment, materials, and the programming, reflective, and research processes.

Each chapter includes the following features:

Learning Outcomes—A series of learning objectives to help the reader recognize the content presented in the chapters.

A Child's Story—Stories based on our experiences and children we have known, designed to give a child's perspective while illuminating the content.

Opening Quotations—A quotation intended to offer the reader a starting place for thinking about the particular content of that chapter.

A Reflective Moment—Boxes that provide opportunities to pause and reflect deeply on key elements, and to help the reader recognize that the concepts explored in each chapter can be unpacked in a way to expose multiple perspectives.

Programming Bubbles—Connections between theory and practice that arise from the content of each chapter.

Program Design Tables—Tables in Chapters 6 to 12 that are designed to give practical suggestions for programming appropriate for children in various stages of development, including infancy, early childhood, and middle childhood.

Featured Research—Chapter content research that will inspire the reader to continue to explore particular research studies.

Pedagogical Tools—Concrete suggestions to help professionals and students use tools to increase awareness of what is possible in their work with children and families.

Professional Case Study—Opportunities to view the practice of others and to ponder the ethical decisions professionals are required to make every day.

Reflection Questions for Self-Learning—Questions the reader may ponder and reflect on based on the content of the chapter.

Big Ideas for Dialogic Learning—Opportunities to socially construct learning that will support and illustrate the importance of dialogue and the learning that is possible when professionals critically examine professional big ideas.

Vision—Thoughts of how the ideas expressed within the chapter will inspire future learning opportunities.

Making Connections—New technologies in professional practices intended to guide and support the reader to explore the potential for professional learning that is possible when technological connections are made.

Key Terms—Terms defined in the margin and graphically represented in a "wordle" at the end of the chapter.

Summary—Key points that summarize the core concepts of the chapter and reflect the learning outcomes presented at the beginning of the chapter.

For Further Thought—An end-of-chapter feature that provides suggestions for further exploration.

SUPPLEMENTS

Instructor's Manual   The Instructor's Manual includes teaching tips and activities for the classroom. This material is linked to the main sections of each chapter and includes page references back to the textbook. It is available in PDF format from the Pearson Online catalogue to instructors who adopt the textbook.

CourseSmart for Instructors   CourseSmart goes beyond traditional expectations—providing instant, online access to the textbooks and course materials you need. You can save time and hassle with a digital eTextbook that allows you to search for the most relevant content at the very moment you need it. Whether it's evaluating textbooks or creating lecture notes to help students with difficult concepts, CourseSmart can make life a little easier. See how when you visit www.coursesmart.com/instructors.

Pearson Custom Library   For enrollments of at least twenty-five students, you can create your own textbook by choosing the chapters that best suit your own course needs. To begin building your custom text, visit www.pearsoncustomlibrary.com. You may also work with a dedicated Pearson custom editor to create your ideal text—publishing your own original content or mixing and matching Pearson content. Contact your local Pearson representative to get started.

ACKNOWLEDGMENTS

We would like to sincerely thank Pearson Education Canada for providing us with the opportunity to write a second textbook together, one that we believe has many possibilities for post-secondary learning communities across Canada. We are particularly grateful to Pearson's Carolin Sweig for working with us to launch this project. We sincerely extend our thanks and appreciation to Christine Langone, who has worked with us throughout the project to ensure that our text reflects our vision of one that will support educators and students in college and university environments.

We thank a number of researchers and educators, such as Dr. Anna Kirova at the University of Alberta, who allowed us to use or adapt their work for our text, and also the reviewers—Melanie Collett, College of the North Atlantic; Cathy Coulthard, Sheridan College; Kath Gradwell, Georgian College; Debra Harwood. Brock University; Heather Hill, Georgian College; Dale Kern, Mohawk College; Barb Mathieson, Capilano University; Lisa McCaie, Centennial College; Donna Mese, Cambrian College; and others who wish to remain anonymous—whose feedback helped us shape the content and the layout of the text. We continue to be grateful to Ingrid Timmermans for introducing us to each other in 2010.

We are thankful to our students and our colleagues for challenging us and helping us to continuously think about ways to make learning visible, and to all the children, families, colleagues, and early learning centres who have allowed us to use their photos throughout the text. In Nova Scotia, we wish to thank Bora Kim, Angie Brant, and staff at Fox Hollow Child Care Centre; Beverley Williams and Susan Willis at Point Pleasant Child Care; Florence McCarthy and staff at Elmwood Child Care; and Liz Hicks and Tanya Moxley. From In Ontario, we wish to thank Jackie MacDonald and Andrea Boyd from The Village Children's Programs, June Williams from the Seneca College Newnham Lab School, and Rosalba Bortolotti and the wonderful teachers and children from the Acorn School.

This, my third text in eight years, was possible because of the support and encouragement I received from my brothers and sisters; my husband, Peter; and my friend Sue, who collectively have always encouraged me to follow my dreams and aspirations to make a difference for children in early childhood education programs, allowing me to explore and discover new ways of knowing and thinking. Peter, you have always provided me with the support, time, and space I need in my quest to gain new knowledge, and you have been my best critic and partner in learning.

As a new employee at Okanagan College, I would like to thank the leadership team for encouraging me to continue to write and add new knowledge to the field of early childhood education.

—Beverlie Dietze

My family, including my mother, Reeva; my husband, Lorne; my children, Jeremy, Ben, and Dory; and my nephew Brandon, continue to encourage my work and are first and foremost my greatest champions. When opportunity knocks, it is with the confidence of their support that I can take on new challenges in my life. Aside from my family, Beverlie Dietze has been an unwavering ally who has encouraged my professional growth and development. So much has been possible because of her willingness to mentor, and without Beverlie's support, I would never have been able to realize my dream of writing and researching.

I would also like to remember my years at Seneca College, where in 1984, I would become an early childhood educator; in 1988, I would teach my first course; and in 1998, I would be hired to teach early childhood education full time. Ten years later, Seneca College launched the bachelor of child development (BCD) degree program, and I had the opportunity to teach at the degree level. I hold these past six years and all the BCD students I have had the privilege to teach close to my heart.

To all the wonderful educators who are part of my professional learning network, thank you for helping me find a way to bring Reggio home.

—Diane Kashin

Chapter 1
Introduction to Programming in the Early Years

LEARNING OUTCOMES

After exploring this chapter, you should be able to

1. Discuss the relationship between professional roles, the early learning profession, and the cycle of professional practice.

2. Explain why professional skills and pedagogical tools are important components of practice.

3. Explain what is meant by theoretical language and define seven common theoretical language concepts of the early learning profession.

4. Describe how curriculum frameworks, models, approaches, and theories inform practice.

5. Explain what is meant by the term *big ideas* and describe how it relates to dialogic learning.

6. Compare how vision and making connections influence early learning students and professionals in their practice.

A CHILD'S STORY   Benjamin

Ever since we woke up from nap, Marcus, Ethan, and I have been having so much fun building a parking garage in the block centre. Marcus brought his collection of little cars and trucks from home. We need to make room for them so the people can get to the mall to buy food for their children. Marcus has so many cars that we need extra room on the floor to build. Rachel helps us make room and then we count the cars and trucks. There are twenty-seven! Seven are trucks, twenty are cars. There are six red ones. Ethan wants a sign for the garage, so Rachel helps him find stuff from the writing area to make it. I think we need to wash the cars and trucks before they go into the parking lot. We need a car wash. I want to ask Rachel for help, but she is busy talking to Sherene. I find a pail and put all the vehicles in it and go to the water table. Some children are at the water table washing clothes for the dolls. The water is soapy. I pour the cars into the water and it goes splash! Rashid laughs and Becky screams. Water is flying everywhere. I ask them to help me wash the cars and trucks so they are clean for the garage. I notice that Rachel is smiling and nodding her head. I lay down a dry doll blanket and we line up the clean cars. Rachel is taking pictures of us, but we are too busy to smile for the camera. I hear Rachel say to Sherene, "I can't believe what started when Marcus brought in his cars. Can you help me record the children's conversation?" Sherene sounds worried about us. She says, "But they are soaking wet." Rachel says, "We need to get their dry clothes ready, but this is too good to stop." We keep playing. Becky, Rashid, and Bridgitte are starting to make the mall where we will buy the groceries. Sherene has the camera now and she is taking movies! Rachel says that she is going to put them on our secure Facebook site for our parents to see and write about our parking garage on the classroom blog. Then she says she is going to tweet about it! Becky asks Sherene to show us the movie, and Sherene puts it on the big white screen in the classroom. Marcus looks at the screen and has an idea to build a second floor of the parking garage. Sherene says his idea was sparked because he could see it from a different perspective. I'm having so much fun. I think Daddy is coming to get me soon, but I don't want to go home!

Early learning professionals support and encourage children in their play.

Bora Kim

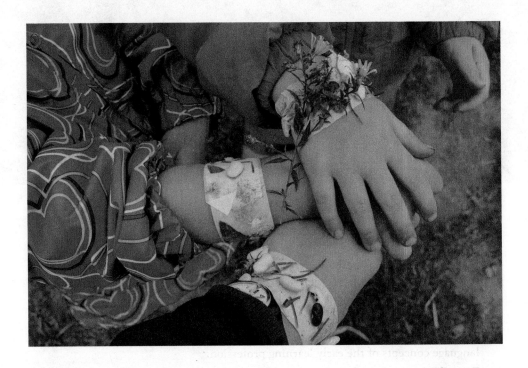

CHAPTER PREVIEW

It is through others that we develop into ourselves.

—LEV VYGOTSKY (1896–1934)

Becoming an early learning professional is a complex process requiring rigorous study, practical experience, and a commitment to continuous improvement in practice. We use the title **early learning professional** to encompass all educators working with young children. It is a broad and encompassing term to reflect a complex profession. There is no magical formula to be followed to become an educator of young children. Early learning professionals are required to have a diverse background of core professional knowledge, as well as occupationally related skills and abilities. Developing the skills and ways of knowing how to support children is highly individual and is influenced by the interplay of context, biography, and values. It involves a process of professional practice that is dynamic and ongoing. We use the metaphor of the journey as a way to describe the lifelong process of early learning professional practice. It is like travelling across a changing landscape with uneven terrain. Some parts of the journey will have a defined destination, with a map; others may be spontaneous and discovered without a plan. Journeys can be both pleasurable and difficult. Wherever you are in your own journey, it is beneficial to reflect on early learning practice.

You will have brought with you at the onset of this journey an idealized image of children, families, and what a good and effective early learning professional looks like. As you travel, you will have the opportunity to examine concepts and ideas from different perspectives, and you will continuously sift through your beliefs and practices. As shown in Figure 1.1, this process of bringing clarity to practice happens when you reflect on, question, and explore your perspectives while applying theoretical concepts or application scenarios. Throughout this process, your image of early learning and practices becomes clearer, more defined, and more refined. As you sift and sort through your values

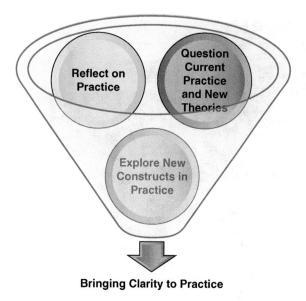

Bringing Clarity to Practice

Figure 1.1 The process of bringing clarity to early learning practice

and beliefs, you will have an opportunity to challenge the images you hold, figure out why you believe what you do, and determine if there are new ideologies that you want to explore. Through sifting, sorting, and perhaps shifting your perspective, you will craft your professional practice.

Your Journey Guides

We, the authors of this textbook, see ourselves as your journey guides. We were once where you are, and with our combined experience, education, and commitment to early learning, we hope to help you navigate the professional landscape that lies ahead. We can't tell you exactly which road you will travel, as it is up to you to find your own path. We serve as an example of a professional collaboration, and our relationship demonstrates that we are in a process of learning together as we move forward on our own journeys. We question and challenge each other while always trying to listen to truly hear each other's perspective. In our work we practise **critical reflection**.

Reflection is the bridge between your cognitive and emotional states, and it is essential to professional practice. Critical reflection involves thinking. According to Jones & Shelton (2011), there are four aspects of thinking that make reflection possible:

1. *Abstract Thinking:* A cognitive process for understanding concepts that cannot be experienced directly through our senses such as friendship and trust.

2. *Complex Thinking:* An ability to see the multiplicity of problems or situations at the same time.

3. *Metacognition:* An awareness of our thinking about our thinking as it relates to a problem or a situation; thinking about thinking.

4. *Pragmatism:* An ability to think logically and apply this thinking to real-life to manage the ambiguity that often accompanies these situations.

Applying these four aspects of thinking to practice will help to build skill, ability, and knowledge—the important ingredients to becoming critically reflective. Critical reflection in practice requires you to embrace a habit of mind—to think deeply—and is a key disposition for professional practice (Jones & Shelton, 2011). Dispositions are

critical reflection Involves deep thinking and is a key disposition for professional practice.

ways in which a person is inclined to behave. To practise critical reflection, let's consider the story that appears at the beginning of this chapter. In what ways would you say
Rachel and Sherene demonstrated abstract thinking in this experience with the
children? Is there an example in the story indicating that Rachel's thinking may have
been more complex, as she could see beyond the immediate situation? What do you
think Rachel and Sherene were thinking during this experience? By thinking about
thinking, you are demonstrating metacognition. In what ways does the story reflect
pragmatic thinking? In the story, Sherene was thinking practically about day-to-day
concerns such as the children getting wet. Pragmatic thinking is important in the
early learning profession, but as we have indicated, it is not the only way to think critically and deeply. Throughout the chapter, ideas will be presented that are intended to
help you explore the broad tenets of thinking and learning associated with being an
early learning professional. Thinking about the role, image, and status of early learning
professionals is important to understanding the complex and compelling journey on
which you have embarked.

YOUR PROFESSIONAL ROLE

According to Hill, Stremmel, and Fu (2005), knowingly or unknowingly, we construct
and reconstruct a personal philosophy or theory of what it means to be an early learning professional. As a student, you have an image of yourself now and an image of who
you wish to become when you complete this part of your journey. As you gain new

The following are sentence completers that you can use to help to define your values and beliefs at this point in your journey. Finish the sentences now. Later in your journey, you can reflect back to see if your values and beliefs have been refined.

1. My vision for working with children is . . .

2. In three years, I see my greatest strengths with children to be . . .

3. I envision the early learning environment as . . .

4. I see children as . . .

5. I view children's families to be . . .

6. I suspect that cultural diversity will . . .

7. I envision my colleagues as . . .

knowledge about early childhood education, images will evolve about how you envision yourself as a professional in the future. One of the first steps in preparing to work with children is to define your current vision. As you gain new insight from your studies, experience, and dialogue with peers, families, and professionals, you can determine how you wish to stretch yourself in new learning and refine your vision (Dietze, 2006). By reflecting upon your beliefs and values, relating them to new ideas, and aligning your vision with varying theoretical perspectives that influence it, you will be able to effectively engage in a cyclical professional practice of continuous learning and improvement.

One of the key attributes to becoming an effective early learning professional is being able to wonder, think, explore, and reflect. You also need to develop a **theoretical language** to describe and discuss your beliefs about programming with families or other professionals you will come into contact with in your practice. Being able to clearly communicate about beliefs and values, beginning as a learner and continuing throughout your professional practice, sets a foundation for being able to adjust your current beliefs and practices with new knowledge. As you learn and communicate, you will expand your theoretical language and be able to relate to the language of others in your profession. You will be introduced to some of the core theoretical language terms later in the chapter.

theoretical language The terms used within a profession.

Let's begin the journey with a visioning exercise. Defining your vision requires you to be introspective. You need to think deeply about who you are and the core values and beliefs that you currently have. When you start moving forward on your professional path, your values and beliefs may be well defined, but they do not have to be static; they will change because of the continuous process of reflecting. To help you think deeply, reflect on this fundamental question: What do you believe is worthy or of great importance in the early learning professional's practice? Your values represent your beliefs about what you think is worthwhile. We would like you take a reflective moment to begin to define your vision. In the Reflective Moment box above, we have provided you with some sentence completers so that you can contemplate your values and beliefs. Values and beliefs are foundational to understanding yourself as a professional and to aligning your inner thoughts with a professional context. Defining these values and beliefs requires an in-depth look at the early learning profession.

THE EARLY LEARNING PROFESSION

Blank (2010) suggested that before examining ways to define quality in working with children, we first need to define the term *profession*. Doyle (1990) defined profession as "public acceptance of the legitimacy of what the occupation asserts about itself" (p. 8). Blank expanded on Doyle's definition by suggesting that "professional work is something the public perceives to serve a significant social need and as work the public cannot conduct on its own" (p. 400). These perspectives would lead educators to "move away from a search for essential characteristics of good teaching that oversimplifies the nature of teaching as a technical practice that can be uniformly applied in order to achieve particular outcomes [and] shifting the emphasis toward the importance of articulating the complex nature of high-quality teaching and learning" (Blank, 2010, p. 400). In other words, the early learning profession is complex, dynamic, and open to change.

The early learning profession can be seen as a profession in process. There have been achievements and progress in the field, but it has a long way to go before all those who practise as early learning professionals in every city and country in the world are viewed as professionals in the true sense of the word. You can act professionally in any occupation; however, in order for the occupation to be deemed a **profession**, a general set of criteria must be met (Feeney, 2012). These criteria include

profession An occupation that meets professional criteria.

- an ongoing commitment to continuous learning;
- recognized and upheld standards of practice;
- an accepted code of ethics to which professionals are accountable;
- a requirement for prolonged training to enter the profession;
- rigorous requirements for entry to training and eligibility to practise;
- commensurate salary (the wage of the profession matches the training required);
- autonomy or self-governance of the profession;
- recognition of the profession (being the only group able to legally practise);
- a commitment to serving a social value; and
- a specialized body of knowledge not normally held by others in society.

professionalization The process of an occupation becoming a profession.

professional A person who has obtained specialized training and competently carries out the work of the profession.

Depending on where you live, where you study, and where you practise, the level of **professionalization**, or the process of early learning becoming a profession, may be different. For the purposes of this textbook, we assume that those practising as early learning **professionals** have obtained or are participating in specialized education that supports them in competently carrying out the work of the profession. Education, practice, continuous learning, and reflection lead to the creation of professional knowledge. When early learning professionals use professional knowledge to serve society in their practice every day, they are exhibiting professionalism.

Professional Roles and Contexts

Starting with rigorous training and education, those who specialize in the professional knowledge related to early learning can find themselves in a variety of careers and contexts. With an early childhood education diploma or related degree, many opportunities will be available to practise and to participate in continuous learning. Early learning professionals include early childhood educators working in child care programs. They may work with children of a range of ages, from infancy to middle childhood. Each program has its own particular context.

Early learning professionals also may work in full-day kindergarten classrooms within public school boards or private schools. Many practise in home environments. They work with adults, as well, in a variety of contexts, such as in parent–child resource centres. Whatever the environment, part of professional practice is a commitment to continuous professional learning. Advanced degrees, diplomas, certificates, and experience offer a wide range of possibilities to you as your journey progresses.

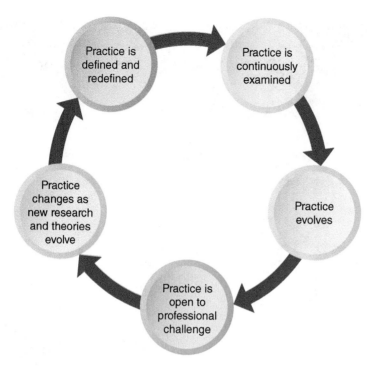

Figure 1.2 The cycle of professional practice

Professional Practice

To be effective in what they do, early learning professionals are continuously focused on learning, improvement, and growth—their practice is cyclical in nature. As an early learning professional, you, like your profession, are in process. Rather than remaining static or stagnant, you will continuously evolve as you respond to the context in which you practise. You will face challenges along the way, and you will need to change and make adjustments. Change is an integral part of your practice. Figure 1.2 represents the cycle of professional practice.

Schön (1983) has clearly articulated the need to think about professional practice as a kind of artistry or craft. From an early learning perspective, professional practice includes a process of making sense of a situation, figuring out what is really happening, and making adjustments to how you practise. To do this, you need to reflect on, critically examine, and reformulate your ideas and practices, and at times shift your philosophical orientation.

Early learning professional knowledge, then, encompasses a model of social justice, local practice, values, experiences, and ethical practices that are best for children (Carter & Curtis, 2010). As you work with children, you will be required to make ethical decisions or judgments based on your professional knowledge. Thus, your professional knowledge will define your practice.

Professional practice is what you do every day when you work with children, families, and colleagues. Within your professional practice, you will be required to adhere to a code of ethics, as outlined in Figure 1.3 on the next page. Ethics are moral principles that professionals apply to their work. As an early learning professional, you will need to reflect on ethical codes of conduct as part of your commitment to ongoing learning.

Ethics are always present, even when they are not recognized. Ethical professionals use codes to support ethical decision making. The recognized codes of ethics in the early learning profession universally refer to the responsibility that you have to the people you work

professional practice What you do every day when you work with children, families, and colleagues.

with, including children, families, and colleagues. As an ethical practitioner, you'll be required to make daily decisions that demonstrate your professional responsibility to others. Ethical practice requires professional knowledge and an ability to make decisions that reflect respect for your profession and for others. You learn to be an ethical practitioner by

In professions where members have power or influence over the lives of others, it is important to have an agreed-upon code of ethics (Newman & Pollnitz, 2002). A code of ethics serves as a guide about what is right and what is moral for a particular profession. Across the country, early learning professionals will find many different codes. The Canadian Child Care Federation provides one that focuses on seven aspects of practice, including

1. promoting the health and well-being of children;
2. enabling children to engage;
3. demonstrating caring;
4. working in partnership;
5. enhancing relationships;
6. pursuing ongoing learning; and
7. demonstrating integrity.

Some provinces and other countries have their own codes for early learning professionals. Here are some examples:

■ Ontario:

www.college-ece.ca/en/Documents/Code_Ethic_English_Web_August_2013.pdf

■ Prince Edward Island:

http://earlychildhooddevelopment.ca/content/ecda-code-ethics

■ British Columbia:

www.ecebc.ca/resources/pdf/ecebc_codeofethics_web.pdf

■ Australia:

www.earlychildhoodaustralia.org.au/code_of_ethics/early_childhood_australias_code_of_ethics.html

Figure 1.3 **Codes of ethics**

New ideas and materials spark a sense of curiosity among children.

Bora Kim

practising. There is no magic formula that will tell you everything you need to know—it is the nature of being a professional. If you can consider yourself as "not as an autonomous subject seeking objective truth," but rather an "ethical actor in relationships with others and located in a particular context" (Dahlberg & Moss, 2005, p. 13), you will have the beginnings of an ethical, professional practice.

Effective early learning professionals must not only know what to do every day when working with children, but also be politically astute and have ideas, interests, good communication skills, and a broad sense of curiosity that is supportive of children and family needs. Early learning professionals engage with and relate to others in a multitude of contexts and are skilled at identifying new learning opportunities and strategies that will facilitate change in practice, perspective, and knowledge creation (Whitebook, Kipnis, Sakai, & Austin, 2012). Early learning professionals are lifelong learners because the professional landscape is complex and evolving. As a result, early learning students and professionals continuously navigate challenging terrain as they define and redefine professional practice. There will be changes, and you will need to take these on as part of the journey. What can you do to prepare yourself for these challenges?

If you find a trusted friend to travel with, you don't have to face these challenges on your own. Bringing a **critical friend** along on your journey will help you achieve your professional goals. A critical friend is a like-minded individual whom you can trust and who will ask you provocative questions, help you see different perspectives, and critique your work (Costa & Kallick, 1993). If you undertake your professional journey with a critical friend, you will be applying a model of collegial inquiry where conversation and collaboration foster individual and collective construction of knowledge (Bullough, Knowles, & Crow, 1991; Cochran-Smith & Lytle, 1991). Having a critical friend will help you take a different view of your professional practice, thus widening your professional knowledge and supporting your work.

critical friend Someone you trust who will ask you provocative questions, provide perspective so that you can examine your practice through another lens, offer critiques of your work, and take the time to try to fully understand the context of your practice.

Core to crafting your professional practice is thinking about fundamental concepts or big ideas both as an individual and collectively with others. These big ideas are changing

Early learning professionals provide children with freedom to explore and information to support their exploration and learning.

Bora Kim

the terrain of the landscape and propelling the new wave of knowledge and skills for early learning professionals in the twenty-first century. In Figure 1.4, we introduce you to key concepts that represent aspects of the theoretical language of the profession. We will expand on these terms later in this introductory chapter and throughout the textbook. We start with the key concept of *constructivism* to represent the central place this theory has in the history, language, and practice of the profession.

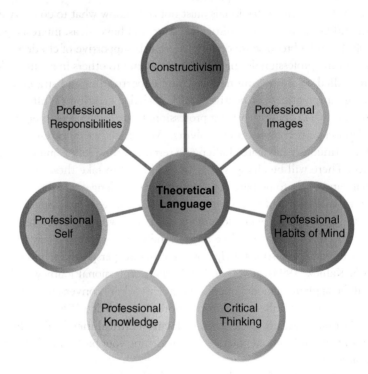

Figure 1.4 Theoretical language of the early learning profession

THE THEORETICAL LANGUAGE OF THE PROFESSION

Constructivism

Constructivism is an educational paradigm that explains the nature of knowledge and how we learn. According to this perspective, knowledge is acquired through active learning (Kashin, 2009). Constructivism is "a particular way of looking at learning and knowing and it is 'at the very heart' of the early learning profession" (Jones & Shelton, 2011, p. 6). It is core to this textbook and to the professional practice of the authors. Knowledge construction is what happens when learners make meaning of concepts or ideas. It is how we believe children should learn, and it has a strong connection to how adults learn. The theory of constructivism was influenced by the work of Friedrich Froebel (1782–1852), John Dewey (1859–1952), Jean Piaget (1896–1980), and Lev Vygotsky (1896–1934). You will read more on constructivism in upcoming chapters. From a constructivist stance, as you engage in new learning, we invite you to work with your critical friends to make meaning of the concepts and ideas presented throughout this text.

Professional Images

Within the paradigm of constructivism, the image of the learner, whether it is the child printing his name for the first time or the adult student learning a new theory or the idea, is one in which the learner is actively involved in making meaning of his world. Images are powerful. They can be positive, giving a person confidence in his thoughts and actions, or negative, making a person doubtful of his capabilities and ideas. The image you have of yourself will influence your professional practice. The image that you have of children will make a difference to the lives of children and their families. We hope that this textbook helps you shape an image for yourself as a strong professional, capable of learning and building your own set of theories. We see the image of the child and the image of the early learning professional as closely aligned.

Professional Habits of Mind

Katz (1993) defined *disposition* as consistent and frequent patterns of behaviour wherein an individual acts intentionally or mindfully. Intentional habits are the opposite of being mindless or not thinking about what you are doing. In professional practice, you are expected to act mindfully. Jones and Shelton (2011) have identified five key habits of mind for early learning professionals, as outlined in Figure 1.5 on the next page.

Let's look more closely at these habits of mind. We ask you to be flexible in your thinking and be open to new and different perspectives. We encourage you to be intellectually curious and to seek to expand your professional knowledge. We also ask you to exhibit perseverance, as some of the concepts and ideas that we introduce throughout this textbook may be new to you or difficult to grasp at first. Exploring new ideas and concepts requires taking some risks. Risk taking is essential for professional growth and development. Above all, we invite you to be critically reflective and engage in critical thinking.

Critical Thinking

To think critically is to examine reality beyond the surface—to see and think more deeply. When you think critically, you ponder questions of who, what, where, when, how, and, most importantly, why. Everyone has the ability to use the power of their mind to integrate

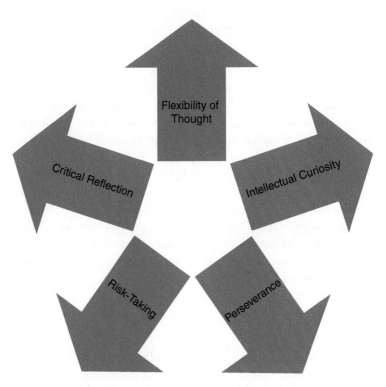

Figure 1.5 **Professional habits of mind**

Source: Adapted from Jones & Shelton, 2011.

thinking and practice. Critical thinking requires a disruption to the status quo—that which has always been done (hooks, 2010). It is your professional responsibility to think deeply and be a disrupter of the status quo!

Professional Knowledge

You will build your professional knowledge as you engage in the habits of mind key to professional practice. Throughout this text, we will share information that should serve as a basis for the development of your professional knowledge. Your professional knowledge will be expressed as you engage in the deliberate intellectual processes of planning effective programs for children and reflecting on your experiences (Dickson, 2007). As your knowledge base grows, we hope your self-esteem and confidence will be enhanced. We hope to inspire you to have a stronger image of your professional self.

Professional Self

Developing your professional self and raising your professional consciousness should be a goal of your practice. To achieve professional status, the early learning sector must overcome issues of self-esteem and confidence (Osgood, 2006). We believe that by socially constructing your professional self, such as by working effectively with others, you will support the profession in its efforts to overcome an identity or image that has been preventing those engaged in early learning from achieving professional status. Paramount to professional status is accepting professional responsibility.

Professional Responsibilities

It is your professional responsibility to develop the dispositions required for your profession and to adhere to its ethical code. Above all, early learning professionals are responsible for considering the well-being of others as their first priority. Building trusting relationships is fundamental to your professional practice. In Chapter 2, we introduce the key players in your professional practice, and in Chapter 6, we expand on the concept of relationship building. According to Dahlberg and Moss (2005), you have a responsibility to the *Other* in your practice. In fact, Others are considered so fundamental to practice that the word is capitalized. Ethics are paramount to respecting the Other.

The need to respect others in your practice makes confidentiality a key professional responsibility. You have a professional obligation to maintain confidentiality of privileged information about children, families, and colleagues that you obtain during the course of your work. Maintaining confidentiality is an important responsibility and a hallmark of every profession. According to Feeney (2012), "nothing destroys a person's trust or a relationship faster than to learn that information given in confidence has been shared" (p. 66). Respecting and maintaining confidentiality is one of many professional challenges that you will face on your journey.

COLLABORATIVE LEARNING, PRACTICE, AND PROFESSIONAL DISCOURSE

You will evolve and get better, together with others. Remember the quotation at the beginning of this chapter—"it is through others that we develop into ourselves" (Vygotsky, 1981, p. 181). According to MacNaughton (2009), to think critically, dialogue is required, as "critical reflection is dialogic. It requires social connections with others, support from others, colleagues willing to spend time with you and a chance to share ideas and possibilities with others" (p. 5). Professional discourse can be your vehicle to create the culture of inquiry for professionals to discuss *big ideas*. **Discourse** is more than just talking. It "describes the ideas, feelings, words, images, practices, actions and looks that we use to build our social world" (MacNaughton, 2009, p. 81).

> **discourse** The ideas, feelings, words, images, practices, actions, and looks that define our social world.

In early learning environments, teaching cannot be separated from learning. That is the reason why we use the term *early learning professional*—because you are a teacher, a facilitator of play and learning experiences, a learning partner with children in their quest for learning, and a partner with families. It is an expansive role. Take a moment to reflect on what it means to be an early learning professional. As you engage in your practice, inquiry is necessary in order to keep the cycle of professional practice current. There is a constant need to ask questions and engage in a dialogue of inquiry with others who practise your profession.

Phillips and Hatch (2000) maintained that professional identities are based in part on the idealized images that early learning professionals have of what a good teacher is. These images may be influenced by discourse. Discourse is more than conversation; it is a way of constructing images as they relate to power dynamics in relationships. Foucault (1971, 2002) has been particularly influential in explaining discourse as a type of truth that becomes so pervasive that it produces culturally and historically significant meaning. This would suggest that as students, you may shift and change perspectives and practices depending on the discourse in which you are situated. Examining new models, approaches, or curriculum frameworks may evoke feelings of disequilibrium.

Disequilibrium as the intrinsic force behind development drives your professional journey. It provides the impetus to progress, to take the path that leads onwards to a new level of professional practice and self-image (Kashin, 2009). Through the process of examining the feelings of disequilibrium and power relations, the hope is that you may develop alternative ways of thinking and strengthen potential ideas or practices. As you expand your breadth of experience and knowledge, you may take up different positions, perspectives, or identities within different discourses (Davis, 2000; O'Brien, Novinger, & Leach-Bizari, 2007). As a result, you may gain a clearer perspective of your values and beliefs.

SOCIAL ALTRUISM

If you are wondering why discourse is important, when all you really want to do is "teach" children, you may not be seeing the big picture. Remember that part of what defines a profession is a commitment to providing a significant social value. We encourage you to reach the highest possible level of quality in your work. As you engage with children and their families during such a critical period in the life cycle, you will benefit from building your capacity for altruism—"a constant focus on the best interest of others rather than one's self" (Feeney, 2012, p. 81). Ideally, early learning professionals strive to make a significant difference in the lives of others. We would like to think that as you develop more knowledge, skills, and competence, you will seek to continuously demonstrate your commitment to making a difference in society.

Using your professional knowledge and experience to help you make decisions that show that you respect yourself as a professional and the people you work with is essential in the early learning profession. Every day, you bring to your work a body of knowledge that influences the children's learning, development, environment, and experiences. That body of knowledge needs to be current, rather than reflect the status quo. It will stand in contrast to long-held beliefs and practices that you may observe in some early learning settings. When you experience disequilibrium from new theories or practices observed, you may need to critically reflect and challenge practices. Such processes support early learning professionals in making changes to ideologies and practices to reflect a rapidly changing world, and breaking from the constraints of the past and being open to the possibilities of the future (Brookfield, 2006).

PROFESSIONAL SKILLS AND COMPETENCIES

Throughout your studies and eventually in your professional practice, you will be demonstrating skills and competencies related to early learning. What skills do you think are required in order to be an effective early learning professional? Think about Rachel and Sherene in the story at the beginning of the chapter. What if you were placed in this environment as an early learning student? What skills and competencies would you need to demonstrate? Would you need to be skilled at communication? Would you need to be skilled at problem solving and making quick decisions? How might you need to adjust your ideas of programming and flexibility in your practice? In this textbook, we look to help you develop your skills and competencies related to building relationships, developing curricula, and providing an effective learning environment for children. In order to do that, you need to continue to think deeply about professional big ideas.

Professional Big Ideas

big ideas Concepts that underpin the work of the early learning student and professional.

The concept of *big ideas* was formulated by sociologist and philosopher Jürgen Habermas (1952–2010). In early learning, **big ideas** refers to the concepts that underpin the work we do—for example, listening to the voices of children, professional collaboration, professional advocacy, and connecting with families all stimulate big ideas. MacNaughton (2009) explained that for Habermas, critical knowledge of big ideas was linked to possibilities for a better world. Big ideas help early learning professionals build deeper understandings and expand their knowledge to improve practice. Thinking about big ideas is thinking about possibilities to make the world better for children and their families. We encourage early learning students and professionals to aspire to rise to this utopian thinking.

Big ideas can help to extend learning for both children and adults. Early learning professionals use the concept of big ideas to collaboratively or individually support children's learning. Big ideas expand the depth and breadth of thinking among the play partners and facilitators. In addition, they support deep thinking. Deep thinking is a process of inquiry, and we encourage it in early learning programs because it requires children to use more areas of the brain, resulting in higher-order processing.

Let's practise deep thinking about early learning. There are some big ideas presented in the opening vignette. Think again about this story. Does the story of this learning experience sound hard to believe, or does it seem realistic? Does it seem like a futuristic account, or does it seem plausible today? Did you regard the play experience as unlikely because Rachel and Sherene supported the children in continuing their play even though they were "soaking wet"? Do you think they should have stopped the children and had them change into dry clothes? What about the references to Facebook, the classroom blog, and Twitter? Do you think this integration of technology in the learning environment is common or should even be part of the daily experience for children and staff? The narrative of Benjamin and his friends is a fictional account, purposely created to spark discussion that might lead to "light-bulb" or "aha" moments.

In this textbook, big ideas will be presented that link to how programming models, approaches, theories, and perspectives on early learning and programming emerge, evolve, and are influenced. People, culture, situations, philosophies, practices, and thinking influence big ideas and create the foundational attributes of early learning programs (Shulman & Shulman, 2004). Professional inquiry is not a simple process, but one that requires deep thinking and critical reflection on the complexities in the professional landscape of early learning.

THE PROFESSIONAL LANDSCAPE

Within a culture of inquiry, early learning professionals reflect on the professional landscape, or the big picture, and use big ideas. They visualize the context of the professional landscape and look for complex perspectives that will broaden their knowledge base and transfer knowledge to application and practice. Critical reflection is a core attribute of continuous learning. This textbook is based on the big picture/big idea approach because this allows us to conceptualize theories and concepts in broad terms. How you view the landscape will determine how dimensional it becomes. In this textbook, we use the lens of postmodernism to view the big picture. The postmodern perspective supports new directions in defining the early learning professional.

The modern era has given way to the postmodern era. In the modern era of the early learning profession, theories that focused on children's ages and stages were dominant. They contributed to the way we defined children and learning. Early learning programs planned experiences for children based on this very linear and developmentally based perspective. **Postmodernist** thought, on the other hand, promotes the idea that there are many different perspectives. It asks you as a student to challenge those modern views of development and learning. It is an evolving theory, as it is open to many different kinds of voices (Dietze & Kashin, 2012).

postmodernism A way of seeing the world from multiple perspectives.

Postmodern Perspectives

When examining through the lens of postmodernism the role of a student like you who is studying to launch a career with young children, these kinds of questions become important: How do students seek to figure out who they are and what their role is in working with children? How do their past experiences influence their future directions? How do we reconstruct thinking about the traditional roles and responsibilities associated with working with children to advance thinking and, in essence, cause discourse to create unconventional descriptions of what an educator of young children might look like? The way in which professionals and students identify their role and their profession also influences their professional practice. From a postmodern perspective, an early learning professional's "identity is never singular or stable, but instead multiple and constantly shifting" (O'Brien et al., 2007, p. 206). This reinforces the importance of constantly examining values, beliefs, and practices.

A postmodern perspective embraces a focus on the immediate and dynamic aspects of facilitating play and learning experiences for children, which in turn reinforces the complexity of working with children and their families (Carter & Curtis, 2010). This postmodern perspective requires the motivation to engage in visioning and seeking an understanding of discourse, practice, reflection, community, and networking. The success of adapting to a postmodern practice is highly influenced by how well adults preparing to work with children come to understand and internalize the theories that will guide their practice. Contemporary early childhood professionals not only "know" standards of practice, but they also recognize that the nature of working with children requires fluidity of ideas and notions, and that questioning and challenging present practices leads to evolving the practice.

THE EVOLUTION OF CURRICULUM FRAMEWORKS

Historically, from a Canadian perspective, early learning curricula have gone through iterations of philosophies, curriculum models, and approaches that were deemed the most appropriate for children's early learning. Research within the educational, medical, and psychology fields has advanced findings on the importance of child development and learning during the early years for later school success (Mustard, 2006). It is also widely accepted that children learn through play (Pascal, 2009). Early learning professionals understand how children learn through play and now, more than ever, how they are partners in supporting children's learning and will be held accountable for the experiences that are available to children. Advancements in research are requiring increased accountability for early learning professionals (MacNaughton, 2009). This is the world in which we now live. The future is now. Early learning professionals are not educating future citizens—all children are citizens of this world. The early learning experiences that children have are vital to the development of our society. As a result, the roles of early learning students and professionals continue to be complex, challenging, and difficult, but ultimately rewarding and personally satisfying. You will make a difference in the lives of others.

Since 1997, "an unprecedented number of provinces have developed early learning curriculum frameworks" (Langford, 2010, p. 3). A curriculum **framework** is an organized plan providing the components to shape and guide the design and development of early learning programs within particular jurisdictions. The development of curriculum frameworks in Canada has been influenced by the global movement to recognize the importance of early learning. These frameworks are intended to guide early learning students and professionals in developing professional practices that are responsive to the children and their areas of curiosity and interests. One of the major advantages of curriculum

framework A document early learning professionals can use to guide decisions about practice. It is an organized plan that can serve as a pedagogical tool. It is meant to be applied with flexibility.

Programming and curricula are documented in many ways.

Angela Brant and Fox Hollow Child Care Centre

frameworks is that they support and guide early learning professionals by making specialized professional knowledge accessible. This will solidify the professional image of those who devote their careers to children during the early years. Ultimately, you will need to be able to articulate the curriculum that defines your practice. Frameworks serve as a professional tool that will help you do this. Further information on curriculum frameworks will be presented in Chapter 5.

MODELS, APPROACHES, FRAMEWORKS, AND THEORIES

Programming models, approaches, and frameworks emerge in many ways and are influenced by culture, people, places, and policies. A **model** can be described as an idealized description of a program that can be copied or reproduced across practice and settings (Spodek, 1973). Models serve as conceptual frameworks for curriculum decisions. They offer those working with young children a structure for the curriculum that is offered; however, they vary in the amount of freedom available in implementing the model. For example, some models are flexible, whereas others strictly define what is expected from the early learning professional. The differences among the models suggest variations in values concerning what is more or less important for young children to learn (Goffin & Wilson, 2001).

model A specific design of experiences or environments that is copied from other sources.

Approaches are programs that prefer a title that reflects an emerging and flexible curriculum. In Reggio Emilia, Italy, a community of early learning programs has been capturing the attention of the world (Goffin, 2000). Thousands of educators visit these programs every year, and the Reggio Emilia approach is seen as a worthy choice to consider for professional practice (Moss, 2005). When on a "Reggio study tour," visitors have the opportunity to spend time within these inspired learning environments but are asked to refrain from taking photographs of the classroom interiors. The purpose is not only to protect children, but also to reinforce the concept of an approach rather than a model. In other words, visitors are not meant to try to replicate everything they see, but instead to allow the images to inspire their own evolving authentic curricula in connection with

approach Programming beliefs and strategies used to facilitate play experiences and support children and families in early learning programs.

their particular geography and demographics (Kashin, 2009). For these reasons, the curriculum inspired by the educators in Reggio Emilia is called an approach and not a model.

In Canada, while multiple provincial curriculum frameworks exist, there is no national plan for early learning. Early learning students and professionals should not feel limited in their use of frameworks. These are thinking tools, and we believe that students and professionals will benefit from examining, exploring, and critically reflecting on multiple frameworks in order to build an authentic curriculum. Frameworks are usually influenced by and constructed from **theories** related to a philosophy or worldview of education.

theory A set of principles that help to explain something.

Actual practice is often guided by one's own set of underlying principles, perhaps without a theoretical basis. We believe that early learning professionals must develop their practice based on a theoretical construct. Knowing the theoretical foundations of early learning is critical to providing quality programming (Carter & Curtis, 2010). Everyone can theorize, from children to adults. Early learning has been influenced by major theorists, but your own ability to formulate theories can be just as influential to your practice. Theory and practice need to go hand in hand. The Brazilian educator and theorist Paulo Freire described the unity between theory and practice as *praxis*. Linking what happens in practice to a theoretical framework is fundamental to teaching and learning (Freire, 1970).

curriculum A course of study.

Curriculum is the approach to learning that is used in the classroom and has come to signify a course of study (Ellis, 2004). It has an academic focus that is often associated with older students and concerned mostly with the cognitive domain (Dietze, 2006). When the term is used to describe younger learners, it can result in a very traditional, prescribed approach, with the teacher setting out a plan of activities to help children acquire a predetermined set of outcomes. We see a need to take a broader perspective to support a play-based program that is co-constructed by children and adults (Dietze & Kashin, 2012).

emergent curriculum Co-constructing curriculum based on the interests and thinking of the learners.

Emergent curriculum refers to an approach that emerges from the interests of the learner and is co-constructed with the teacher (Jones & Nimmo, 1994). However, emergent curriculum is more effective when it goes beyond interests to focus on children's thinking. An emergent curriculum can be limiting if it is based only on things or topics in which children show an interest. Deeper questions need to permeate the construction of what goes on in the learning environment. What are the children thinking? Are they building respectful relationships and learning skills necessary for the twenty-first century? These skills will include the ability to be critical thinkers. Emergent curriculum should be socially constructed, but it only brushes the surface if decisions are made purely from an observation of interest. Just because the children seem to be interested in a particular cartoon character, that doesn't mean the subject is worthy of investigation and inquiry. Emergent curriculum has also come to be defined by project investigation. We feel there is a place for project inquiry in the early learning environment, but we caution early learning students and professionals not to overlook the learning that is possible in the ordinary moments of the day.

programming In early environments, involves developing curriculum based on play and has an emergent quality.

Programming in the Canadian early learning sector is a term that has become interchangeable with *curriculum* (Crowther, 2003). To make a distinction between the traditional, action-focused view of curriculum and the transformational practices of emergent curriculum, we have adopted the term **programming**. This term offers an alternative that we feel is associated with learning in a play-based environment. By offering play options instead of a prescribed curriculum, a programming process approach evolves, which, by its very nature, becomes emergent. *Emergent* and *curriculum* might be contradictory terms in some situations. However, emergent programming combines the infinitely empowering possibilities of play with learning opportunities for children, their families, and early learning professionals (Dietze & Kashin, 2012).

Children take what they have learned in one situation and apply it to another.

Kelly McPherson

In this textbook, we incorporate the idea of an everyday emergent programming process that is inquiry based. It is not always planned, but rather evolves from the process of engaging with others in the early learning environment. When early learning professionals plan for programming, they take into account multiple perspectives and emerging possibilities for further learning. Being open to multiple perspectives allows early learning professionals to plan for play-based experiences based on developmental domains, learning questions, curriculum areas such as drama and music, or big ideas proposed during everyday happenings. The key is that early learning professionals observe, document, and interpret the experiences. They analyze documentation and facilitate day-to-day or project-based learning that is developmentally holistic. They engage in conversations with children and families, and they take a collective approach to seeking information and the meaning of experiences and interests. An emerging programming process involves multiple developmental domains and goes beyond the traditional view of programming and development to incorporate current knowledge and skills that include the interpersonal, intrapersonal, and cognitive domains (National Research Council, 2012).

Pedagogy is the way you promote children's development and learning (Epstein, 2007). It is an interactive process that involves adults and children in every aspect of the learning environment (Lindon, 2012). Pedagogy is how you approach your professional practice in relation to teaching and learning. The image of who you are or will be as a teacher, combined with a view of the child as learner, forms a pedagogical orientation. The image of the child and the image of the teacher merge to create a theory of teaching and learning that we know as pedagogy (Hill et al., 2005). Your pedagogy is your own; it is your approach to teaching and learning. It includes the curriculum or, in the case of this textbook, the program and the vision for what you do within the learning environment. In this textbook, through the use of discourse around professional big ideas, we look to you to engage in deep thinking about pedagogy. This exploration will enable a deeper understanding of your practice and the reasons why you work in certain ways (Lindon, 2012).

pedagogy An approach to teaching and learning.

FEATURED RESEARCH

To understand the early learning professional landscape, we look to south of the border to a twenty-year study examining the early learning workforce: http://1.usa.gov/1jGR4d1; http://bit.ly/15n5B2V. For a Canadian perspective, see http://bit.ly/195muXk.

PEDAGOGICAL TOOLS

In order for you to engage in pedagogical thinking, each chapter in this textbook will introduce you to pedagogical tools that will help you in your professional journey. The first tool is one that we encourage you to use throughout your practice. Keeping a journal will help you to engage in reflective thinking (Loughran, 2006). We recommend that you use a model for reflection that O'Connor and Diggins (2002) called the DATA method:

1. *Describe* in detail an incident related to your practice or your practicum experiences.
2. *Analyze* the incident, examining the underlying values, beliefs, and assumptions that help you make sense of the incident.
3. *Theorize* about additional sources of knowledge that would help you make sense of the incident. Think beyond your own perspectives in order to broaden your understanding.
4. *Act* by putting your new way of thinking into practice and trying to do something differently.

The following link provides three different formats for reflective journals that you may want to use: http://bit.ly/146tJY6. In the case study below, you will be introduced to an early learning professional who decided to begin recording her thoughts in a reflective journal after a particularly difficult day at work. What incident do you think she decided to write about, and how do you think her practice might change because she took the time to reflect in her journal?

PROFESSIONAL CASE STUDY

Gupal is an early learning professional working in a program that is housed in an elementary school in an urban neighbourhood. She has an early childhood education diploma and is currently taking courses to complete her degree at night. She has three children of her own and still manages to provide an exciting and stimulating play-based program for the five- and six-year-old children in her care. She works closely with Wendy, another early learning professional, and they take great pride in the projects in which the children are engaged. This is clearly evident from the documentation posted of the children's learnings. After finding numerous snails in the school's garden on Wednesday, Wendy, Gupal, and the children have begun a snail study. On Thursday, the children were invited to the school library to look at books about snails. They took turns on the computers to search for information about snails. On Friday, the children, Wendy, and Gupal had a meeting to discuss what they were going to learn about snails and how they were going to learn it. Everyone was excited when Monday came around, except for Gupal, who was tired from a busy weekend. With two children sick at home, she didn't get much sleep but still managed to visit a neighbouring store to buy garden gloves and shovels for the children to use in their investigation of snails. At least, Gupal thought, she had the later shift and didn't have to come into work until 9:30 a.m. When she arrived in the morning, the children were busy drawing snails and creating spiral patterns with loose parts. Gupal checked in with Wendy and asked how the morning arrival time went. Often when parents drop off their children for the day, they have important updates to provide to the early learning professionals. Wendy recounted that a couple of children were also away sick and she was keeping her eye on a few children who seemed particularly tired that morning, to make sure that they, too, were not coming down with something. She said the only problem she had during the morning drop-off was that the morning was so busy that even though she took attendance, she couldn't remember what she did with the form. Just as Wendy was telling Gupal this, a small argument broke out between two girls over some shiny rocks in the block area. Gupal and Wendy watched and were pleased to see that the children were able to resolve their own conflict. Gupal went to sit with them anyway. During the time she spent with the girls playing with the loose parts, Gupal noticed that Dory, who was five, seemed to have a difficult time sharing with the other children, as she continued to take rocks and disrupt the creations of others. Gupal told Dory that she wanted to talk to her later. Wendy went to sit with a group of children in the book area, as they had questions about snails. The morning seemed to fly by, and when the children asked Wendy if they could go and find some more snails in the garden, she motioned to Gupal that it was time to go out. The children tidied up, and as they finished putting away the toys and materials that they had been playing with, they went to the cubby area to get their jackets. There was lots of commotion as all the children were excited to get outside to look for snails. Gupal made sure that she had the shovels and garden gloves. Outside, after what seemed like only a few minutes but was actually about a half hour, Wendy noticed that Dory was missing. Did she come outside? Was she still inside? Did she walk off into the busy neighbourhood? Now would have been a good time to have the attendance sheet. Wendy used her cell phone to call the director of the program and ask her to send another staff member outside so that she could try to find Dory. She was quite concerned but tried to remain calm to avoid alarming the other children. She quietly explained to Gupal that Dory was missing and then Gupal remembered that she had told Dory that she needed to talk to her when she was playing in the block centre. Once Chris arrived outside to help supervise, Gupal ran into the classroom to find Dory sitting in the block centre crying. Gupal said, "Why didn't you come outside?" Dory replied, "You told me you needed to talk to me." Gupal gave Dory a big hug and told her that she had been worried about her.

REFLECTION QUESTIONS FOR SELF-LEARNING

Deep thinking should help you think critically about professional practice. It will not necessarily produce one right answer or answers that will be the same for everyone pondering the questions. Thinking about the case study presented, answer the following questions in your professional journal:

1. Do you think Gupal and Wendy demonstrated ethical behaviour in the course of the morning that they spent with the children? If so, in what ways?

2. Think about the case study. Were there any instances of questionable practice? If so, describe the instances and why you think they might be questionable.

3. How do you think Wendy and Gupal can improve their practice?

4. Do you think Gupal or Wendy should talk to Dory's parents about the situation that occurred? Why or why not?

BIG IDEAS FOR DIALOGIC LEARNING

Dialogic refers to dialogue. Dialogue involves a conversation between people. With others, share your interpretations of the following questions. Remember to follow a protocol when engaging in dialogic learning. A protocol is an established and agreed-upon set of procedures that will guide your conversation. We ask you to (1) be respectful of the ideas of others, (2) allow those you are conversing with to finish their thoughts without interruption, and (3) be open to change.

1. What is your interpretation of an ethical early learning professional?
2. Why are values and beliefs important to professional practice?
3. Who determines what constitutes ethical professional practice for the early learning profession?
4. Why should professionals be open to transforming their practice?

VISION

In striving to be transformational in our approach to teaching and learning, we need to examine the broader influences on early learning programming. The early years have not always been viewed as important, and early childhood education worldwide is still an evolving profession. Fromberg (1997) identified distinct characteristics of a profession, including ethical performance, a high level of expertise and skill, a body of knowledge and skills not possessed by lay people, considerable autonomy in practice and entry to the profession, commensurate compensation, and a professional organization. However, the landscape is changing, and it is our vision that the profession of early learning will embrace the changes that come from a new age.

Our vision is that early learning professionals will embrace accountability and be able to readily demonstrate their professional knowledge. We see the future as now. Even though the story that leads into this chapter seems futuristic, it is within the realm of possibility. We have moved from the industrial age of the twentieth century to the digital age of the twenty-first century, where increased availability of technology and information has changed the way we teach and learn. The way you played and the way you learned as a young child are no longer entirely applicable. The skills for success today require engagement and deeper learning. Deeper learning is the process through which a person becomes capable of taking what was learned in one situation and applying it to new situations.

We have a vision of a better world. We engage in utopian thinking, and we ask that you do the same. What is the best possible world for children, families, and early learning professionals? By imagining this world, we can strive for perfection while understanding that this utopian vision can never be realized. We embrace "the Utopian possibility, a possibility full of hope and excitement, a prize almost beyond measure" where early learning environments "become loci of ethical practices, and by doing so contribute to relationships, with each other as well as our environment, which are founded on a profound respect for otherness and a deep sense of responsibility to the Other" (Dahlberg & Moss, 2005, pp. 191–192). This vision permeates this text and is part of the Making Connections feature that appears at the end of each chapter.

MAKING CONNECTIONS

We recognize that we are now in a digital age. New technologies are becoming part of our daily lives and changing the way we teach, the way we learn, and the way we program for young children. Social media have heightened the opportunities to communicate and share with families and with one another. We believe in the infinite potential of social media and new technologies to support early learning students and professionals. However, it is vital to remember that the internet is public and images of children should not be posted without obtaining informed consent from parents or guardians. First and foremost, you need to demonstrate ethical practice. Capturing images of children has never been easier, but for the purposes of this textbook we will encourage students to use only environmental images in their work unless otherwise instructed by the institution in which they are studying or the early learning program in which they are practising. There are many ways to use new technologies and social media in your practice without compromising your ethics. We are going to introduce many ways throughout the textbook. One useful tool is word graphics, sometimes referred to as *wordles*. These graphics can be used to stimulate creative thinking and to promote deep reflection. The Key Terms section of each chapter will be depicted using a wordle. For more information on how you can create a wordle, see www.wordle.net.

KEY TERMS

Approach   17
Big ideas   14
Critical friend   9
Critical reflection   3
Curriculum   18
Discourse   13
Early learning professionals   2
Emergent curriculum   18
Framework   16
Model   17

Pedagogy   19
Postmodernism   15
Profession   6
Professional   6
Professional practice   7
Professionalization   6
Programming   18
Theoretical language   5
Theory   18

Figure 1.6 Key terms wordle

SUMMARY

This chapter reflects the landscape as a journey for early learning students and professionals. The authors of the textbook are guides for the journey ahead. This is a complex profession that requires deep thinking. In summary, we will discuss the most salient points made in this chapter by reflecting back on the learning outcomes.

1. Those involved in early learning can consider themselves professionals while the field is undergoing a process of professionalization. Critical to their professional role is continuous reflection on practice.

2. Early learning professionals are required to have a diverse background of core professional knowledge, as well as occupationally related skills and abilities. By using pedagogical tools such as a professional journal, early learning students and professionals can critically reflect and improve practice.

3. Theoretical language refers to the terms used by a profession. We introduced you to seven common theoretical language concepts of the early learning profession, including constructivism, professional images, professional habits of mind, critical thinking, professional knowledge, professional self, and professional responsibilities.

4. A framework is a document early learning professionals can use to guide decisions about practice; it is meant to be applied with flexibility. An approach is a set of beliefs that can guide programming. A model is an idealized program that can be copied or emulated in practice and across settings. It is important for students and professionals to embed theories or sets of principles into practice.

5. Big ideas help early learning professionals build deeper understandings and expand professional knowledge that will improve practice. By engaging in dialogue with others, students and professionals can think deeply about professional big ideas.

6. By envisioning a better world for children and exploring the potential of new technologies, early learning students and professionals can expand their understanding of professional practice.

For Further Thought

We recommend the following website to expand your thinking about philosophical big ideas. In considering how you would engage children to think big, you will learn about some fundamental philosophical principles that will also help you to think big: http://bit.ly/1oyJbuO.

Chapter 2
The Players

LEARNING OUTCOMES

After exploring this chapter, you should be able to

1. Describe and connect the relationship of children, parents, and early learning professionals to the well-being of families.

2. Discuss how Bronfenbrenner's ecological model may influence how early learning professionals view children in their practice.

3. Explain the value of play and particularly loose parts in children's learning.

4. Compare the core concepts of children as citizens and the seven essential skills that support children's life skills.

5. Describe how family engagement differs from family involvement and how these concepts relate to families as citizens and learners.

6. Outline why early learning professionals focus on their roles as learners and as citizens and how this benefits their professional practice and vision for the sector.

A CHILD'S STORY   Nikita

"The sky keeps changing," explains five-year-old Nikita to Katelyn. Katelyn is an early learning professional working in a program attached to the local small-town school. She was intrigued by Nikita's statement and responded to Nikita by asking her, "What do you mean by 'the sky keeps changing'?" "Well," said Nikita, "first, when I was painting at the easel, I looked out and there were big fluffy white clouds that looked just like the whipped cream Daddy put on the cake yesterday. When I went to look out the window at the fluffy, puffy clouds to see if they looked like the ones I made in my picture, they were all gone. I couldn't find them. Then, I looked at the sky and I saw great big lines across it. So, I went back to my picture and drew some lines, too. I wanted to figure out how big and how thick to draw my lines, but when I went back, those lines were all gone." Katelyn was

again intrigued by Nikita's observations of the sky. She asked Nikita, "Tell me more about the lines that you saw." Nikita said, "They were just like the ones I drew, long and squiggly and fluffy at the ends." Katelyn wanted to figure out if Nikita knew how those lines got into the sky, so she asked Nikita, "How do you suppose those lines got into the sky?" Nikita said, "Oh, the same way those fluffy, puffy clouds got there."

Katelyn needed to make some choices here in her role as Nikita's facilitator of learning. Should she extend the learning? Should she indicate to Nikita that the lines came from a jet? Should she extend the discussions on the fluffy, puffy clouds? Should she be getting books out about the sky? Should she bring Nikita's painting into the conversation? Or should she engage in some "nonsense language play" surrounding the fluffy, puffy clouds?

A child's perspective of clouds and condensation.

Peter Dietze

CHAPTER PREVIEW

Experiences in order to be educative must lead out into an expanding world of subject matter, a subject matter of facts or information and of ideas. This condition is satisfied only as the educator views teaching and learning as a continuous process of reconstruction of experience.

—John Dewey (1859–1952)

Working with children is a complex, multi-faceted process. As you can see in the child's story that leads the chapter, Katelyn had many questions about her role in extending learning with Nikita. Katelyn's primary role was to listen to Nikita. Katelyn gained the vital skills of listening and responding to Nikita by incorporating her knowledge and experience about how children learn into her practice. Katelyn used observation skills, communication skills, and planning skills to guide her in responding to Nikita. Katelyn has learned during her years of working with children that her best asset as an early learning professional is her ability to listen to children and reflect on their dialogue as a way to gain an understanding of how she can best support their experiences and, ultimately, their development. Katelyn has also learned that by truly listening to the children, she is better able to extend and share this skill with parents, families, and community partners. Listening gives her insight into families, cultures, traditions, and the people, places, and things in children's lives that positively or negatively affect their worlds.

The child is the primary focus of any early learning program. Early learning professionals are the pillars of the program. They work with children and their families to develop an

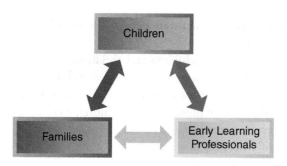

Figure 2.1 **A triad of players**

environment that offers a variety of opportunities and experiences that support children's learning, interests, and skills. In order to do so, early learning professionals listen to the children and create an environment where the voices of the children are heard and used to guide their daily play and learning experiences. As identified in Chapter 1, the images of children presented in this book reflect both a postmodern perspective and a constructivist approach, within a North American context. Working with children in other contexts may look different because of theoretical orientations for children's programming, cultural and family attributes, and government policies and programs related to children and families. Even within North America, a wide variety of approaches to working with children can be found.

The early learning landscape is complex, and differences abound depending on culture, education systems, and the public investment made in early childhood education. In this chapter, we will discuss who the players are within the context of early learning programs. We are influenced by the Reggio Emilia approach, in that we look to three key players of early learning: children, families, and early learning professionals. Children learn best when their well-being is honoured and is connected to the well-being of families and early learning professionals. The child is seen as having a right to high-quality care and education, and as an extension of that right, families are included and encouraged to be part of the learning experience (Kashin, 2009). Ultimately, understanding the United Nations Convention on the Rights of the Child (1991) and putting the rights of children and families first is one of the core commitments that early learning professionals make. In turn, to ensure this commitment can be carried out, the care and education extended to families and children must also be extended to the early learning professional. Professionals need to care for themselves. As an early learning student, it is important to think about the players you will meet in early learning environments. It may be helpful to visualize these players as a triad, as illustrated in Figure 2.1. We will structure this chapter by focusing first on children as the ultimate players.

FOCUSING ON CHILDREN

Many perspectives, influences, and contrasting theories are used to gain an understanding of children. For example, early learning professionals following a behaviourist approach would suggest that human traits are developed through responses to stimuli, experiences, and role modelling within the environment. Within the behaviourist approach, if, for example, a child was consistently hitting another child and redirection was unsuccessful, strategies such as a systematic reward system would be established to change that behaviour. Each time the child exhibited positive social behaviours, the adult would praise the child for the behaviour, while ignoring misbehaviour. Praise would be extended to other children nearby who exhibited positive social behaviours as a way to model the types of behaviour that were expected in the play environment (Parker & Neuharth-Pritchett, 2006).

From a sociology perspective, children and childhood are viewed from a social construct. A **social construct** is a concept that is created and developed by society; in early learning practice, this means that we collectively define what is meant by the child and childhood, and what the societal norms are for nurturing, educating, and parenting, based on influencers such as environments and culture. Children's experiences and social constructs may also be influenced by how society views their socio-economic class, race, and gender or the culture of families and communities (Shah, 2007).

Psychologists and biologists examine the constructs of child and childhood differently from educators and sociologists. Their focus, identified as a *psychological construct*, is on the biological and psychological needs of children. They are interested in ensuring that children achieve developmental milestones at prescribed times. This construct has led many early learning programs to create programming experiences that focus on specific developmental milestones at a particular age or stage of children's development (Parker & Neuharth-Pritchett, 2006).

Urie Bronfenbrenner (1979) developed the **ecological theory** of child development to focus on how the larger community influences development. Bronfenbrenner chose the word *ecology* to emphasize the importance of environmental influences, settings, and institutions in children's lived experiences. As illustrated in Figure 2.2, Bronfenbrenner maintained that there are multiple ecologies within the five major systems, with distinct layers that have the potential to affect children's development.

The first ecological layer, the *microsystem*, refers to the setting where children live, including home, the early learning environment or school, and the neighbourhood. The microsystem most directly affects development, as it encompasses the direct interactions, experiences, and influences within children's immediate environments, such as parents,

social construct A concept that is created and developed by society. It refers to a perception that an individual, group, or idea is constructed through social practice.

ecological theory The belief that development is affected by five environmental systems.

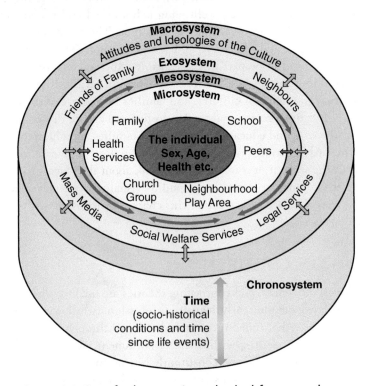

Figure 2.2 Bronfenbrenner's ecological framework

Source: Bronfenbrenner, 1979.

playmates, extended family, and early learning professionals. For example, a parent and early interventionist may provide information about a child to a speech and language pathologist; the speech and language pathologist may then share information with the early interventionist and the early learning professional, who collectively make recommendations to colleagues and parents. These interactions and relationships among the institutions become influencers for competence building, one-on-one communication skills, resiliency, and emotional wellness (Bronfenbrenner, 1979).

Bronfenbrenner (1979) suggested that the interconnection among the people in the microsystem creates the *mesosytem* ecological layer. In this layer, when there are positive interactions or connections among the people or organizations, further opportunities are afforded to positively influence children's strengths, interests, and cultural attributes, and greater options are provided for facilitating play and learning.

The exosystem and macrosystem have a more indirect influence on children's lives than the microsystem and mesosystem. The *exosystem* refers to the institutions or people who are not necessarily connected to the children but still influence their life experiences. For example, family friends may offer overall social and emotional support to the family or provide advice or comfort to the parents in time of need. Such contributions can promote a positive situation for the overall family, which, in turn, contributes to healthy child development opportunities (Bronfenbrenner, 1979).

The *macrosystem* focuses on the beliefs and ideologies of families, communities, cultures, local traditions, and country norms. Although not explicit, this layer has a significant influence on an individual child's development. For example, Berk (2006) has suggested that in cultures where physical punishment is used and accepted as a child guidance strategy, the incidence of child abuse is higher. In communities where respect for children is a core value, Berk determined that less abuse occurs.

Defining and understanding children and childhood is complex and reflects multiple perspectives. The definition is not clear-cut. How you define and understand children

Early learning professionals take different paths in learning and practice.

Peter Dietze

and childhood will depend on your knowledge; life experience; educational background; philosophy; community, including role models and mentors; and values. You will find similarities and differences in definitions among co-workers, families, and societal groups. The differences will contribute to how and why each early learning program is unique. This textbook offers support in developing your own perspectives and philosophies. You will also gain the experience required to be able to make professional judgments and ethical decisions about children and families. Let's begin to build your understanding by answering this fundamental question: How do children learn best?

Children as Learners

Understanding how children learn best is one of the most important questions that early learning professionals can ask themselves, as it will ultimately define how programming experiences are planned and facilitated. If you believe a child will learn best when receiving direct instruction from a more knowledgeable teacher, then your programming will reflect this. When you observe early learning professionals in practice, you will be able to interpret their view of children as learners. For example, if there is an abundance of materials for children to explore with, create with, and learn from, you can assume that a professional's understanding of how children learn is different from that of the early learning professional who has a more structured program plan involving direct instruction. Programming in every learning environment reflects the views of the early learning professionals working there.

play An experience that includes the ability to bend or invent reality and that has a strong internally based motivation.

Many early learning professionals believe that children learn best when they are allowed and encouraged to use all their senses (Hendrick & Weissman, 2006). Children's learning occurs using both active and passive mechanisms (Siegler, 2005). For example, through **play**, children will actively work toward constructing strategies to solve problems and will reflect upon their successes and failures. During play experiences where children are able to invent their reality, their minds are engaged. Although their level of reflection is different from adults', their "thinking-through" processes lead them to sort out other ways of reaching success in their play episodes. Children are thinkers. They think about the same type of problem or issue in multiple ways. The newer the experience for children, the more they will engage in different ways of thinking (Siegler, 2005). Children are also players. They use the process of play to discover and learn about their world in many ways (Dietze & Kashin, 2012). The complex process of play and learning is most beneficial to children when they initiate the play and have input into what they wish to learn and how they wish to learn it.

Contemporary and historical research about how children learn has identified play as the best medium for learning (Dietze & Kashin, 2012). In this textbook, we emphasize that children learn best when they have environments that support them in play because they are learning with their whole being. They are learning across multiple domains of development in authentic and meaningful ways related to knowledge, culture, and relationships. Play is a "vehicle in which cultural attributes are passed from one generation to another. Through play, children communicate their feelings and ideas to other children and adults. Children gain physical development and experimentation opportunities. In essence, the subject of child's play is complex as it formulates the foundation of child development" (Dietze & Kashin, 2012, p. 2). Play forms the foundation of learning; therefore, play is about children's learning and development. We are passionate about play-based learning and view loose parts as the ultimate materials that expand children's options for experimentation, creativity, problem solving, and making new learning connections. Figure 2.3 summarizes how children learn and should be referred to throughout your explorations and discussions of your readings in this text.

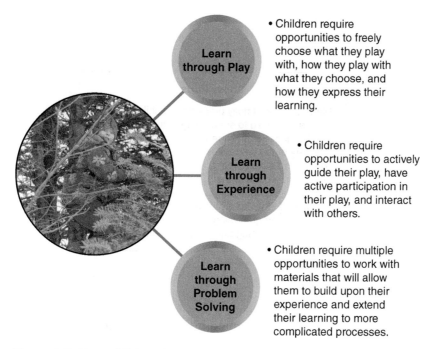

Figure 2.3 **How children learn**

Kelly McPherson

Learn through Play
- Children require opportunities to freely choose what they play with, how they play with what they choose, and how they express their learning.

Learn through Experience
- Children require opportunities to actively guide their play, have active participation in their play, and interact with others.

Learn through Problem Solving
- Children require multiple opportunities to work with materials that will allow them to build upon their experience and extend their learning to more complicated processes.

In the programming bubble in Figure 2.4 on the next page, we introduce you to a resource you have probably encountered previously; however, you may not have realized the potential of these materials. We have chosen a bubble format to present programming ideas throughout the textbook because it represents play and potential. Bubble play is a childhood favourite, and we imagine big ideas bubbling up when early learning professionals consider **loose parts**, or intelligent materials, in their programming (Thornton &

loose parts Materials thoughtfully presented to children of all ages and used to spark imaginative and creative play.

Intelligent materials create a sense of wonder with children—they explore, they think, and they incorporate new ideas into their play and learning.

Peter Dietze

Loose Parts

Materials thoughtfully presented to children of all ages can be used to spark imaginative and creative play. Consider the arrangement of the materials and the safety of the items presented (choose according to age and development), and observe children's interaction, recording their conversations and ideas. Think deeply about what you are seeing and hearing, as it will add to your professional knowledge about appropriate programming experiences for children's learning and development.

Figure 2.4 Programming bubble: loose parts

Burton, 2007). Early learning environments in Reggio Emilia are filled with materials labelled "intelligent" for their potential to enhance children's learning development. Beads, glass, bottles, paper, cardboard, tubing, fabric, plastic, rocks, cord, ribbon, and metal are all valuable materials with great potential. When they have access to baskets of everyday items with varying textures, purposes, colours, and properties, children create an understanding of the world around them by exploring the materials and forming ideas. Intelligent materials become the beautiful stuff of programming (Topal & Gandini, 1999).

Loose parts is a term coined by architect Simon Nicholson in 1971. The term is interchangeable with *intelligent material.* As long as materials can be moved, redesigned, put together, and taken apart in a variety of ways, they are classified as loose parts. In writing about these materials that allow for creativity and choice, Nicholson referred to the "theory of loose parts" (Nicholson, 1971). He said that in any environment, the degree of creativity and inventiveness is directly proportional to the numbers of variables in it. Loose parts provide the variables children require to create new options in their play. A beach is a good example of a loose-parts learning environment, with plenty of movable and adaptable materials, such as sand, water, rocks, and shells. Children can play for hours on the beach. Now, take the concept of the beach and think about how early learning programs can incorporate loose parts into their environment. What types of materials could be offered that would give children similar open-ended, flexible materials and add value to their play and their learning?

The perceptions that early learning professionals have about children and how they learn, guide their practice. Now that you have thought about how children learn, we are going to add another dimension to the discussion and for your reflections. How do early learning professionals view children as citizens?

Children as Citizens

citizenship Giving rights, privileges, and duties to citizens of a community.

What do you think of when you consider the concept of citizenship? Your concept of citizenship has been influenced by your life experience, including your culture, residency, and role models. **Citizenship** has the following four tenets:

Loose parts offer children flexibility in their thinking processes and allow them to make connections to their ideas and experiences.

Diane Kashin

1. As a citizen, you are part of a community.

2. As a citizen, you have rights.

3. As a citizen, you have a voice.

4. As a citizen, you have opportunities to be heard.

The concept of "voice" is fundamental to programming in the early years. We agree with Hall and Rudkin (2011), who proposed "that all children have the right to participate in the communities in which they reside, not as future citizens, but as citizens of the present" (p. 2). If early learning environments are seen as communities, an early learning professional's role is to help children give voice to their intent. Children who are supported in their lives by adults who help them make their ideas visible and encourage them to set their sights as high as their imagination will allow have limitless potential for learning. When teaching and learning experiences involve cognitive and symbolic expression, voice comes through in multiple ways—in one hundred languages (Gandini, 2004). Loris Malaguzzi (1998), considered the founder of the Reggio Emilia approach, speaks of the one hundred languages children use to discover their world in his famous poem (see www.innovativeteacherproject.org/reggio/poem.php). When school and culture try to take away the child's right to speak in a hundred languages, you can still make a difference. You have only to listen to the child who says, "No way. The hundred *is* there," and attend to the "many voices, languages, and abilities of children, parents, and teachers that are often lost in the teaching and learning process" (Fu, 2002, p. 25).

Attending to children's voices is important because children do not necessarily have a voice in their daily experiences, either in their homes or in early learning programs. There are many reasons for this—hurried lives, adults thinking they know what is best for the child, children exhibiting passive behaviours that imply they would prefer the

Honouring children's cultural heritage gives them a voice.

Peter Dietze

adult to make decisions, and so on. Since the United Nations Convention on the Rights of the Child was ratified by the Canadian government in 1991, children in this country have a right to have a voice and to have their opinions heard. For example, Articles 12 and 13 state

Article 12

States Parties shall assure to the child who is capable of forming his or her own views the right to express those views freely in all matters affecting the child, the views of the child being given due weight in accordance with the age and maturity of the child.

For this purpose, the child shall in particular be provided the opportunity to be heard in any judicial and administrative proceedings affecting the child, either directly, or through a representative or an appropriate body, in a manner consistent with the procedural rules of national law.

Article 13

The child shall have the right to freedom of expression; this right shall include freedom to seek, receive and impart information and ideas of all kinds, regardless of frontiers, either orally, in writing or in print, in the form of art, or through any other media of the child's choice.

Changing values, beliefs, and practices is a challenging process. As identified by Pascal and Bertram (2008), one of the first steps in changing the lens through which we look at and think about children is to view them as people rather than as subjects or objects. Children who are in environments where they are viewed as people have increased opportunities to live and play in a democratic environment and to have a voice. Early learning professionals who implement strategies that draw out and respond to children's opinions and perspectives about the events that occur in their programs give children voice. For example, how often do we ask children how they feel when other children are upset, crying, or noisy? How often do we ask them what they would like their environment to look like? How do we support children in undertaking new risk-taking experiences and ask them what they would like our role to be during that process? How do we empower children to be part of our participatory practice and allow them to have a voice and be actively involved in planning their days and their experiences? How often do adults put rules into place that cause children to find ways around them so that their needs can be met? Think of the rule that many early learning programs have that bans children from bringing personal objects to the program. Early learning professionals who have this rule suggest that it is in place so that children's possessions are protected from other children, and that it reduces disputes about sharing personal objects. Obviously, such rules demonstrate adult power over the children. But children figure out ways to get around the rule. How? They choose items that are small enough to fit in their pockets and then find ways to use the materials in their play with others. This example illustrates two important concerns. First, to give children voices in their environment, early learning professionals need to reflect on some of the rules that are imposed on children and determine how to give children input in deciding the rules. Second, before implementing rules, adults need to consider how their interactions with children reduce the opportunities for children to develop the confidence and competence to express their voice.

Early learning professionals benefit from stepping away from their current practice and reflecting upon how they are supporting children in having a voice and how they might want to change aspects of their practice to further assist children in finding their voice. Changing values and attitudes is required if early learning programs are going to clearly shift the power from the adults and consciously hear the voices of children. The younger the children, the easier it is for adults to silence them and exclude them from having input into decisions shaping their lives (Pascal & Bertram, 2008). Certain children may be more likely to feel voiceless in their environment, such as those from immigrant or refugee families because of the language barriers. What happens when early learning professionals or students adopt the notion that they know what is best for children? If adults believe that their role is to act on behalf of children, because they know what the children need, rather than empowering children, they may not provide the environment that is most conducive to learning and development. Early learning professionals who guide the play of children and allow them to determine the learning agenda are hearing the voices of children.

Seven Essential Skills for Children

When focusing on children's learning and development in your course of study, it is important to also include the concept of life skills. There are essential skills that children can learn. These skills are important for you to have, too. You, like children, need to learn facts, figures, concepts, insights, and understandings. Taken from a perspective that children have an amazing capacity for learning, Galinsky (2010) identified seven essential life skills that children can develop "that will serve them throughout their lives" (p. 5). Examine the skills listed in Table 2.1 on the next page. As you do, think about how these skills relate to your own life. Which of the skills do you think have been worthwhile to you?

Table 2.1 Seven Essential Skills for Children

Essential Skills	Why Essential?
1. Focus and self-control	This skill is necessary in order for children to achieve goals and to be able to focus in their world. Children need to gain skills in paying attention to the people and things in the environment, remembering rules, using flexible thinking, and being able to self-regulate their impulses and behaviours.
2. Perspective taking	This skill is necessary so that children can figure out what others think and feel and then consider how their behaviours may affect others.
3. Communication	This skill helps children to be able to understand language and communicate with others. They need to figure out if others received the message that they communicated in the way it was meant.
4. Making connections	Children require skills of making connections from their past learning and experiences with new discoveries. Being able to stretch the connections to wonder about new possibilities is core to creativity. This skill further demonstrates flexible thinking.
5. Critical thinking	Critical thinking is necessary for problem solving and advancing knowledge and skills. Effective decision making, actions, and beliefs are affected by one's ability to be a critical thinker.
6. Taking on challenges	Challenges are related to risk taking, curiosity, and problem solving. Children who are able to take on challenges are more flexible thinkers, which in turn advances new knowledge development.
7. Self-directed, engaged learning	Children who are able to participate in self-directed and engaged learning increase their ability to satisfy their curiosity and gain new learning. As technologies advance, children require the ability to determine what they need to know in order to achieve their big ideas.

Source: Adapted from Galinsky, 2010.

FOCUSING ON FAMILIES

Canadian families continue to change. As Table 2.2 shows, families living in Canada are diverse. What constitutes a family unit is influenced by experience, culture, diversity in thought among individuals and collective groups, and values and beliefs. It is clear that we can no longer assume that children in early learning programs come from or should come from a traditional nuclear family, consisting of a married couple with children. Every child and family is unique. Families come to early learning programs with their own values and aspirations for their children, family and community dynamics, and ways of being. As we outlined in Chapter 1, upon examining the roles of early learning professionals, it is important for you to process how you perceive a family and how you might respond to families whose structure differs from your values, beliefs, or experiences (Lyon, 2009). This type of reflection helps you to identify any potential prejudices and biases that you may have.

Table 2.2 Types of Family Units

Traditional nuclear family: A man and a woman who are legally married and have biological or adopted children.

Blended family: A man and a woman who are either legally married or live common law, where one or both adults have children from previous relationships and/or from this relationship.

Single-parent, shared parenting: Parents who have dissolved their relationship but share the responsibility of raising the children.

Foster family: An individual or couple who have been legally approved to assume responsibility for raising one or more children for a period of time.

Orphanage: An organization or group of adults who assume responsibility for raising children who are orphans.

Commune: A group of adults and children who live together in a single dwelling or property, where a mix of partnerships may exist. Parenting responsibilities may be shared among the adults.

Teen parents: A single or married teen mother and/or father who are under the age of eighteen and who take full responsibility for the care of their child or children.

Common-law family: A man and a woman who live together with their biological or adopted children.

Single-parent family: A family with one parent who has assumed the parenting of biological or adopted children on his or her own, either through divorce or separation, or has chosen to be a single parent through adoption, natural birth, or artificial insemination.

Grandparents or extended family: An extended family member or unit such as aunts, uncles, or grandparents who have assumed responsibility for raising the children.

Gay or lesbian families: Two gay or lesbian partners who parent their children from previous heterosexual relationships, adoption, or arranged births.

Group homes: An organization or group of adults who assume responsibility for creating a family unit with individuals who may require some health-related care or supervision that their biological or adopted families are unable to provide.

Homeless: A group of people who come together for support and who live on the streets.

Cross-cultural/religious families: A couple who bring different cultural or religious backgrounds into the union.

Focusing on the strengths of the child, and on how family processes and structures contribute to those strengths, helps early learning professionals make connections between human characteristics and environments. Bronfenbrenner's (1979) ecological framework supports this perspective. He suggested that the interconnections between the environments (i.e., the family and the early learning program) that children experience could be as decisive for development as the experiences and events that occur in those environments. A child's ability to learn specific skills such as climbing and hopping may be influenced not only by how the child is taught these skills, but also by the nature of the relationship between the early learning program and the home. For example, if the child comes from a family who fears their child may get hurt if she falls while trying to master climbing, the child may become afraid to try climbing. If she is in an early learning program that encourages climbing, the fear that the child's parents have may need to be addressed before the child will take the risk to pursue that opportunity. The family plays the most significant role in influencing the child's life, disposition, and zest for life, followed by extended relationships that may include the early learning professional and children in the program.

Although family structures and units are diverse, one thing they have in common is
the requirement that their basic needs be met, including the needs for nurturance, security, and connectedness to their world and to others (Maslow, 1987). Early learning professionals need to think about their beliefs and values regarding family structures and diversity
because if they have any biases toward different family groupings, they may cause pain or
stress in children and their families (Souto-Manning & Hermann-Wilmarth, 2008). Children flourish in early learning programs that exhibit inclusive practice toward all children
and families and that help children maintain their differences within the classroom setting
(Lyon, 2009).

Wilson (1991) made the following statement more than twenty years ago, yet it still
holds true for early learning professionals: Insensitive and inhumane teachers perpetuate a
"legacy of inhumanity" that they experience as "feelings of alienation, apathy, resignation,
fatalism, valuelessness, spiritual staleness, meaningless of life, indifference. . . . A lack of
human understanding breeds these and other pathologies that thwart our ability to BE and
that crush our caring" (Wilson, 1991, p. 183). Early learning students and professionals who
are able to identify and resolve their perspectives on topics that could negatively affect
families are not only better able to support children and families, but they are also modelling their ethical responsibilities and practices. We encourage you to engage in dialogue,
bring forth your questions and issues, debate them, and reflect upon the areas of concern
and questions. Your daily interactions with children and families are most valued when
they model acceptance of diversity and social justice. Children are not single entities. They
are embedded in a family and a community (Bronfenbrenner, 1979). This means that children and families in early learning programs are best served when their family beliefs and
concerns are embraced within the program. This view recognizes, celebrates, and honours
the individuality of the children's family structure, culture, religion, and parenting beliefs
(Fleer & Robbins, 2006).

We ask that you spend a few moments to reflect on your views on family types using
the questions identified in Figure 2.5 and then relate your views to the family-type descriptors in Table 2.2.

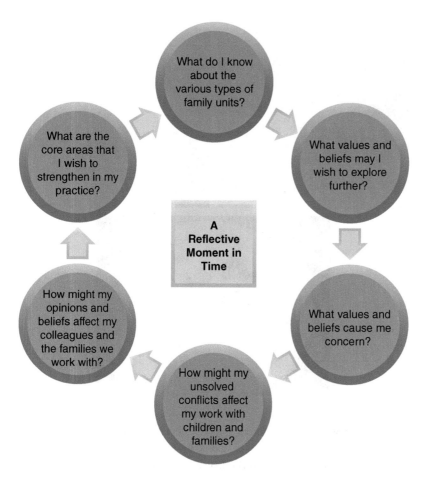

Figure 2.5 A reflective moment in time

Families as Learners

In building partnerships with families, you will have opportunities to share expertise in ways that are meaningful, authentic, and respectful. Early learning professionals have a professional responsibility to share knowledge with the families of the children they work with. How this is done will depend on the lens through which the professional views the families. If early learning professionals view families as partners, they will take time to hear the voices of the partners in order to engage families.

Early learning professionals can share knowledge about child development and parenting with families in a number of ways. Every day during morning drop-offs and evening pick-ups, professionals can engage parents in conversation. Realistically, these can be two of the most hectic times of the day, and so many programs will include other forms of parent education, including bulletin boards and newsletters. Many early learning programs use technology such as emails, Facebook pages, and blogs to share information that families will find helpful. Even this may not be enough. If you accept your professional responsibility to support children and their families, part of your role may include planning and delivering education programs for families. The families in your programs may request a particular topic that they would like you to address. The essential question then becomes, what makes an effective program for families to learn?

Early learning professionals would need to consider content and curriculum, program timing, program delivery, and teaching methodology (Samuelson, 2010). How families learn also requires consideration when deciding the teaching method. If you believe that children learn best when they are actively engaged, consider applying this principle to the

Family engagement includes field trips to family-owned businesses.

Susan Willis and Point Pleasant Child Care Centre

delivery of parenting workshops. In order to plan effective learning experiences for families, you need to be open to their perspectives. Consider ways in which you can engage families to hear their voices as your partners in the learning environment.

Families as Citizens

Children live their lives in a minimum of two worlds: that of their family and community, and that of their community within early learning environments. To accept children into a community is to accept and encourage their families. For families to feel that they are members of a community, they must feel engaged. **Family engagement** differs from family involvement. Pushor (2007b) differentiated the terms in the following way: "*Involvement* describes those activities in which parents are invited to serve the school's agenda, to do the things educators deem important. *Engagement*, differently, describes activities which are mutually determined by educators and parents to be important for children and are lived out in a respectful and reciprocal relationship" (p. 6). Family engagement requires dialogue and an examination of practices to view the connectedness of the family to the early learning program. According to Pushor (2007), this process requires educators to ask and analyze the following questions: What do we believe about the place and voice of parents in our school? How can we see our beliefs being lived out? Is there a match between what we say we believe and the practices we have in place? What unconscious or implicit assumptions may be at play in our practices? Family engagement is based on the assumptions outlined in Figure 2.6.

Family engagement has beneficial outcomes for the child, family, and early learning environment. For example, these relationships have a direct correlation to the types of experiences children will engage in and how they will be supported in their play and learning. Early learning environments that recognize family diversity and implement models of practice that involve parents in their children's programming have a richness of difference within the environment (Clarkin-Phillips & Carr, 2012). When differences within a community are looked upon as a positive feature of the environment, those families who may have previously felt marginalized become empowered to contribute to the early learning

family engagement Active engagement by families in a learning environment.

Figure 2.6 Key assumptions about a family engagement model of practice

community. This sense of worth and empowerment has a positive effect on the parents, children, and early learning professionals.

Clarkin-Phillips and Carr (2012) indicated that family engagement should include relational identity. Relational identity refers to "a set of dispositions [families have] towards themselves in relation to where they can enter, what they can say, what emotions they can have, and what they can do in a given situation" (Holland, Lachicotte, Skinner, & Cain, 1998, p. 21). Family engagement requires networking with families. Clarkin-Phillips and Carr suggested three levels of networking processes that would support opportunities for parent engagement, as outlined in Table 2.3 on the next page.

To practise principles of family engagement, early learning professionals need to work through the processes of "giving up some control, becoming vulnerable, and standing alongside parents instead of over them. It means being willing to accept that parents who have been welcomed into the school may have valuable suggestions educators and staff had not thought about, or that parents' perspectives may challenge staff's taken-for-granted assumptions and beliefs" (Pushor, 2007, p. 10). This process is not easy and may require early learning professionals to continuously check in with their feelings and beliefs. Rather than assuming that parents don't care, Pushor (2007) indicated there are benefits in early learning professionals looking inward to determine ways to extend different options to parents so that they gain comfort in becoming active in the environment.

A variety of strategies may be used to practise available, inviting, and personalizing models of practice that extend options of engagement to families. For example, Clarkin-Phillips and Carr (2012) indicated that when early learning professionals added a personalized invitation to families to be involved with their children's portfolios, those families embraced that opportunity. Every time the early learning professional added comments encouraging families to comment on the portfolios, the families did!

Table 2.3 Three Levels of Support Opportunities for Family Engagement

Opportunities are available	The opportunity is available. However, the opportunity that has been made available may not be recognized. Alternatively, it might be recognized but the families have not been positioned in such a way as to feel they are able or permitted to take it up.
Inviting	The opportunity is readily accessible and accorded attention in some way. It is insistent or inviting rather than just existing and available. This opportunity, of the many available, beckons, perhaps because someone has labelled its possibilities or the families in general have been in a climate of agency; they feel that they are able and permitted to take up this opportunity.
Personalizing	The opportunity is available, invited, and personalized. The possibilities have been personalized in one or two ways. First, a relationship has been forged with the invited person or family, and a personalized invitation has been made (perhaps with reference to specific interests). Second, a personalized opportunity refers to identity, to the way in which the person or family is recognized as having specific skills or qualities of value that could make a contribution.

Source: Adapted from Clarkin-Phillips & Carr, 2012.

Family engagement embraces openness and transparency about issues and topics that concern children. Its many benefits include the following:

- Changes to how early learning professionals view their roles and responsibilities with families, from that of a dominant role in decision making to the perspective that, collectively, the early learning professional, family, and children are interdependent in working to achieve a program that supports the interests of children in their play and learning.

- Stronger relationships with families, which leads to developing healthier relationships among families and the early learning program. This advances a shared accountability for the experiences of the children.

- With family participation in decision making, challenges to the status quo and resulting conversations and decisions that expand opportunities for children.

Creating approaches that support families in being active members of early learning programs requires significant planning, development, and understanding of family dynamics. For example, Hendrick and Weissman (2006) indicated that one of the best times to develop relationships and have core conversations with families is at the beginning of the day. They advocate that rather than being preoccupied with the children, it is a much better investment to view "this transition...as being the part of the daily curriculum intentionally devoted to 'family time'" (p. 23). Early learning professionals encourage parents to participate in small talk, which, as the trust and relationship builds, ultimately will advance to deeper conversations that help to bridge the home experience with the early learning environment.

Family engagement leads to parent self-development, which directly benefits children. For instance, over the past decade, a growing body of research has suggested that when parents are directly connected to the centre there is more support, encouragement, and reciprocal follow-through, leading to consistency for the child. In essence, family involvement in early learning programs is essential for collaborative processes.

As important as parents are to early learning programs, you may encounter some early learning professionals or centre philosophies that do not fully engage parents in their program. Many factors may contribute to this situation. One influencer is the power relationships between parents and early learning professionals. For example, assume that a mother is a single parent and lives in a low-income housing complex. At times, she is stressed wondering how she is going to make ends meet at the end of the month. She has feelings of distress and lower self-confidence than some of the parents she observes. Her level of self-esteem right now is contributing to her feeling that she has no power. She is so intimidated that it is hard for her to share much information. Another influencer is the knowledge deficit that families may feel in relation to early childhood education. If early learning professionals use theoretical language, some parents may feel that their knowledge deficit makes them unable to effectively contribute to the dialogue. The notion that knowledge equals power can dramatically affect relationships between families and early learning professionals.

The level of family collaboration is directly related to the structure of the environment and the people in the environment. To create an environment that supports active participation of families, intentional efforts need to be made to create a family engagement model that encourages and nurtures family involvement. This may require a paradigm shift, whereby parents and early learning professionals view each other as complementary facilitators of children's learning. By participating in dialogical conversations that shift the early learning professional from the expert to a partner with families, more shared experiences about children will occur, contributing to the development of trust, respect, and engagement and breaking down barriers to communication.

FOCUSING ON EARLY LEARNING PROFESSIONALS

Historically, early childhood education began as a social-welfare service. The role was custodial, aligned with substitute mothering or babysitting. Unquestionably, the early learning sector is composed predominantly of women. You can see that for yourself when you consider who your fellow students are or, if you are an early learning professional, who your colleagues are. Voice is a powerful tool for women's development, and silence is a developmental inhibitor (Belenky, Clinchy, Goldberger, & Traule, 1986). Development is seen as "constructive knowledge: integrating voices" (Belenky et al., 1986, p. 133) where "all knowledge is constructed, and the knower is an intimate part of the known" (p. 137). Recovering from a silent position of powerlessness and low status requires an integration of voices. Those voices include children, the families, and the early learning professional. If it is your professional responsibility to hear the voices of others, and, at the same time, your own voice must be heard. What are your learning and development requirements? How do you learn best? Take a little time to reflect by answering questions about your own learning in the Reflective Moment box.

≫ A Reflective Moment

How do you learn best? As an adult learner, do you agree or disagree with the principles of adult learning? Can you relate them to your own experience? Can you compare one learning experience to another and consider why your effectiveness as a student might be connected to the environment and the style of teaching presented? Think about two different courses that you have taken and compare and contrast.

Professionals as Learners

Many theories have contributed to understanding how adults learn. One of the most influential was put forth by Malcolm Knowles (1990), an adult education theorist. According to his theories, adults learn best when they

- are internally motivated and self-directed to learn;
- are able to bring life experiences and knowledge to learning experiences;
- are goal directed in their learning;
- find their learning relevant to their life experiences;
- have opportunities to engage in practical learning; and
- feel respected as a learner.

andragogy The art and science of helping adults learn.

These assumptions have been widely accepted by other adult learning theorists. Malcolm Knowles's theories are associated with the term **andragogy**, which he defined as the art and science of helping adults learn, similar to pedagogy, which is the way professionals promote children's development and learning. Historically, pedagogy has been seen as the way students are taught, with the emphasis on the teacher, who assumes a position of instructing. From an early learning perspective, pedagogy and andragogy are not in opposition; rather, the ways young children and adults learn are closely aligned.

Professionals as Citizens

By now you will have begun to see that you have responsibilities to children and families to help them feel part of a community. But how can you ensure that you too are viewed as a citizen with rights? If you take the view that you are part of a professional community and foster your professional relationships, do you think that will have an impact on your opportunities to have a voice? An integral part of being effective in planning and developing learning experiences and programs for families and children is being able to engage in dialogue with other professionals. You need to feel heard. You need to feel valued. You need to feel supported. Early learning professionals benefit from having designated reflective time to develop collegial relationships.

As citizens of a community of learners, early learning professionals benefit in supporting each other and to create environments that are conducive to learning. Colleagues show appreciation of each other and offer help and support so that everyone can reach their potential to learn and to teach. Professional, continuous learning can best be achieved when there is a shared vision of professional practice identified. To be a citizen of a community is to accept the responsibility to create a community of practice. Citizenship connects to the democracy. Democracy involves full participation of all members of the community requiring responsiveness to children, families, and each other (Wien, 2004).

PROFESSIONAL RESPONSIBILITY

As identified in Chapter 1, the early learning profession has undergone significant change over the past decade or so and will continue to evolve. We are in a time now of reimagining our views and perspectives on children. This reimagining requires early learning students and professionals to examine past perspectives about children and families and, in some cases, change the lens to become "multifocal when viewing the child, magnifying the child's strengths and interests and highlighting the child's perspective" (Burgess &

Fleet, 2009, p. 54). Changing the lens through which children are viewed also requires transforming the child–adult relationship from one where the adult has power and authority over the child to one in which the early learning professional has a democratic partnership with the child as a co-learner, a co–decision maker, a co-explorer, and a co-writer of learning and evaluation. This model of practice is aligned with Vygotsky's (1978) beliefs about how people and the environment are interconnected to children's well-being. This sharing of power occurs when the child is seen to have a more powerful role in the child–adult learning relationship, aligning with Vygotsky's (1978) facilitative, scaffolding relationship.

Drawing on principles from organizational theories, such as communities of practice (Wenger, 1998) and learning organizations, the movement toward partnerships between early learning programs and families requires environments that encourage and support open, two-way communication focused on children's experiences, learning, and shared power and decision making. How do early learning professionals work together to create a feeling of collective purpose or shared vision? Stephen (2010) has reinforced the perspective that children's learning varies with social and cultural experiences. The ways in which adults, other children, tools, and resources are available and incorporated in early learning environments contribute to children as active social agents in creating new ways of knowing (Stephen, 2010). If given the right environment to exercise their beliefs and values, they too contribute to cultural production and change. Nieto (2005) identified the need for a transformative process to occur. He further noted that "we must remember that many teachers have not had sustained contact with people of diverse backgrounds, nor have they learned about people different from themselves in other ways. As a result, it is no surprise that some teachers have negative perceptions, biases, and racist attitudes about students they teach, and about students' families, cultures, and communities" (p. 217). This possible scenario reinforces the importance of early learning professionals helping children find their own voices.

PEDAGOGY OF LISTENING

Rinaldi (2006) states that to truly listen to children, we need to be present. To be present means that we are focused on what is happening *right now*. Rinaldi (1998) referred to this search for meaning and understanding through active listening as the **pedagogy of listening**. More professionals need a mindful presence, a strong sense of justice, and the ability to observe and reflect in order to truly listen (Macfarlane & Cartmel, 2008). A professional resource from Scotland on listening to children can be found at http://bit.ly/ZHW89P. Viewing early learning and child care as a social constructivist paradigm reinforces why early learning professionals emphasize the importance of listening to children's voices: so that they are given opportunities to be active participants in their environment while they construct their own learning (Smith, 2007).

Children benefit greatly when adults view listening to them and sharing power and respect as important adult roles and responsibilities. Children who are empowered to be active citizens acquire skills that enable them to make choices, express their ideas and opinions, and develop a positive sense of self (Bruce, 2005; Roberts, 2002). Children are active citizens in the here and now as they gain experience in participating in a democratic life (Biesta, Lawy, & Kelly, 2008). When children are extended the full rights and responsibilities of a citizen, a learning democracy is present (Biesta et al., 2008). A learning democracy perspective, according to Dahlberg, Moss, and Pence (2006), acknowledges children as actors and stakeholders in their own lives and dispels the traditional notion that children are empty vessels who are incapable of acting with agency

pedagogy of listening Searching for meaning and understanding through listening.

and on their own behalf. Within this new paradigm, adults view children as powerful, competent individuals who are able to communicate their preferences, choices, and needs. For those who believe in this new paradigm, there is a need to recognize that the research that has been conducted and the advocates of this model have westernized views of what children's participation should be. Recognizing the diversity of our societies, children, and families requires their voices to be heard about how a democratic community that reflects their values and beliefs would look (Maybin & Woodhead, 2003). There may indeed be diverse perspectives on what this looks like for children and families within an early learning program.

Listening to children is a way of thinking. Rinaldi (2006) indicated that listening requires that we see ourselves in relation to others and the world. Therefore, early learning professionals need to empower and give voice to children. By bringing voice to their work and offering a forum for the voices of children and families, teachers become transparent in their practice, and collaboration can evolve. This can happen only if all involved are expressive instead of silent. As Malaguzzi (1998) has said, "teachers must leave behind an isolated, silent mode of working, which leaves no traces" (p. 69). A professional portfolio is a means to leave traces of professional practice.

FEATURED RESEARCH

Explicitly or implicitly, approaches to working with young children require environments that support them in exercising their senses of curiosity and wonderment, encourage their desire to experiment, and celebrate their discoveries, through active engagement with their physical and social environment. Families, community, and culture are influential in a child's learning and development. Children who participate in democratic societies experience the communication, participation, and associated living that gives them a voice and encourages them to be active contributors in their play and learning communities (Dewey, 1966). Our featured research is the **mosaic approach,** which has been widely used in the United Kingdom since 1999 and is spreading to other parts of the world as a way to ensure the voice of children is heard in their learning communities.

The approach encourages early learning professionals to give children a voice in the environment. Participatory tools such as the use of cameras, book making, tours, and map making support children in creating and documenting their perspectives (Clark, Kiorholt, & Moss, 2005). When children and adults reflect on the materials produced, children have an opportunity to share their thoughts. The mosaic approach employs a specific methodology for exploring practice and learning environments in order to understand the perspectives of others. It has multiple components, which we will outline further in Chapter 12 when we focus on the perspective of early learning professionals as researchers. For more information on the mosaic approach, go to http://bit.ly/ZopiIQ.

mosaic approach A method of research used by educators to access children's and their families' perspectives about their learning environment.

PEDAGOGICAL TOOLS

As a professional, you have access to an array of pedagogical tools that will help you learn about and reflect on your pedagogical orientation. A **professional portfolio** is a way to document your professional journey. It involves an intentional development process and leads to an end product that can be shared with others to make your professionalism visible. Portfolios can be

professional portfolio A document of early learning professionals' professional learning.

used in professional practice as a means to demonstrate standards. They are organized around specific components that can include program plans, observations, reflections, and professional entries. As you move forward on your journey, make sure to cultivate, collect, and curate evidence of your professionalism that can be put together into a portfolio when required. Jones and Shelton (2011) provided an in-depth definition that illustrates the potential benefits keeping a portfolio can have for your practice:

> Portfolios are rich, contextual, highly personalized documentaries of one's learning journey. They contain purposefully organized documentation that clearly demonstrates specific knowledge, skills, dispositions and accomplishments achieved over time. Portfolios represent connections made between actions and beliefs, thinking and doing, and evidence and criteria. They are a medium for reflection through which the builder constructs meaning, makes the learning process transparent and learning visible, crystallizes insights and anticipates future direction. (pp. 21–22)

There are essentially two parts to developing a portfolio. The first is the process of collecting, sorting, and organizing artifacts that represent your professional practice. The second is examining the examples to gain insight into how professional learning experiences align with your personal values, beliefs, and educational philosophies influencing your practice. The result of this learning process will be a product: a professional portfolio. *Process* and *product* are two common terms in early learning college and university classrooms and early learning environments. You may have heard the terms described as diametrically opposed, as in *product versus process*. We think that professional practice requires a less stringent view. In fact, we are opposed to using the term *versus* in connection to early learning practice. Portfolio development offers a unique opportunity to engage in a self-directed professional learning experience that is validating and professionally rewarding. A product enhances the process and is a rich, contextual documentary of professional learning.

PROFESSIONAL CASE STUDY

Fatima is an early learning professional who describes herself as Reggio inspired and passionate about nature-based learning. She works at a unique program for young children where the outdoor environment is considered as important as the indoor classroom. She has been to visit the programs in Reggio Emilia, Italy, where she participated in a study tour with other educators from Canada. She is a compulsive reader and enjoys finding new professional literature to study. She has applied and been accepted to a master's program to continue her passion to learn. She has just finished reading In Dialogue with Reggio Emilia: Listening, Researching, and Learning *by Carlina Rinaldi (2006), and while it was not an easy read, she stuck with it and feels profoundly affected by the book and its message about listening to children. Fatima sees every day as a gift from the children. She accepts the professional responsibility and challenge to be mindful of the learning environment and of what the children are truly saying. She incorporates, both indoors and outdoors, a commitment to democratic practices and to hearing everyone's voice. Lately, Fatima has felt frustrated when she comes to work. She feels a loss of joy and is always mindful of the words of Loris Malaguzzi: "Nothing without joy." She knows the source of her frustration is her new teaching partner. The director of the program, Samantha, told her that it had been difficult trying to hire someone to match her level of professionalism, but that Lindsay was impressive in her interview and was willing to learn. Lindsay is a very friendly early learning professional. She communicates with the parents, chatting easily about the weather, the traffic, and the local news. She often checks her cell phone for messages. She also loves social media, and sometimes when she is sitting with the children, she goes on her Facebook page and reads the newsfeed. Sometimes she shares postings with her friends, taking the time to write on their walls. Fatima is becoming irritated, as Lindsay does not seem to be truly present in her professional role. She is worried about Lindsay's ability to listen to the children.*

REFLECTION QUESTIONS FOR SELF-LEARNING

Interactions between the players within early learning programs are complex and not always perfect. We can have a utopian vision that illustrates a community where everyone is heard and everyone is valued, but in reality we will be faced with environments in which it is difficult to work. Fatima, the early learning professional in the case study, is an example. She has read an immense amount of professional literature, including research on organizational climate. She knows that the tension between her and Lindsay is creating an unhealthy work and learning environment. Fatima recently found a resource on the internet at http://bit.ly/1si3k7R that had many examples of questionnaires designed to address organizational climate. Fatima is concerned because when she filled out one of the questionnaires, she reflected on the staff morale and team spirit, and on whether her workplace was providing enough guidance to Lindsay so that she could learn new skills and competencies. She is concerned that Samantha does not spend enough time providing feedback to Lindsay and feels that action needs to be taken before others sense the tension between Fatima and Lindsay. Thinking about the case study presented, answer the following questions in your professional journal:

1. Do you think it is the responsibility of an early learning professional to address issues regarding colleagues' professional knowledge? Why or why not? Consider that this professional responsibility was addressed in the standards of practice that Fatima is required to adhere to as a member of a regulatory college. What would you do in this case if you were Fatima?

2. Do you think that Lindsay was listening to the children? If you were Fatima and the director of the program asked you to describe your concerns about Lindsay in a written statement, what would you write? In two paragraphs, write a professional report that could be given to a director of an early learning program.

3. What would you do to alleviate the problems within the organizational climate if you were the director? Come up with five strategies that you could employ to improve staff morale and team spirit.

BIG IDEAS FOR DIALOGIC LEARNING

In Chapter 1, we introduced you to the concept of big ideas as a way to extend learning for both children and adults. Helping children find their voice is a key role for early learning professionals. Dialogic learning involves creating early learning environments with children, families, and early learning professionals where the participants engage in conversation that encourages sharing, shaping, and bringing meaning to an idea, discovery, or area of wonderment. In Chapter 1, we posed some questions to help you engage in dialogic learning with other adult learners like you. Dialogic learning is not limited to adults. Children can be encouraged to converse on a deep level. Big ideas and dialogic learning require what Wells (2007) called "grand conversation" as a way to foster deep thinking in order to move one's thinking forward. Early learning professionals and parents encourage children to engage in dialogic learning through inquiry, development of ideas, and exploration of alternative solutions to set the stage for broadening their ways of thinking (Pantaleo, 2007; Wells, 2007). Conversations that support children in finding their voice, ideas, and experiences occur in environments where the adults do not dominate the dialogue. When adults dominate the dialogue, children view the adults as experts, which reduces their confidence in working out their own ideas. Big ideas and dialogic learning occur when adults facilitate children's responses without controlling the conversation. In essence, this means that when adults present children with comments and prompts, children can expand their thinking and move their thinking to new levels. Think about the opening vignette.

1. What types of questions or prompts might Katelyn have used to support Nikita in taking her ideas and explorations about the clouds and lines in deeper, new directions?

2. What types of materials could be offered to Nikita to help her expand the exploration of clouds and lines?

3. What types of outdoor experiences could be provided to Nikita to help her look closely at the clouds in the sky?

4. Do you believe that it is possible to ask a child too many questions?

Those children new to the dialogic process require time to internalize information, practise thinking aloud, and add to their ideas during the conversation or as they process new ideas. In essence, over a period of a day or days, Katelyn and Nikita may return to exploring the big ideas because as Nikita works through her knowledge building about the clouds and the lines, and makes new connections, she may need to test and retest her thoughts. By engaging in meaningful dialogue and providing materials to manipulate, in this case through art and loose parts that Nikita uses to make clouds and lines, the early learning professional expands the dialogue in ways that will spark big ideas and learning.

VISION

It is our vision that early learning professionals consider their practice as being shared and collaborative. We envision early learning professionals seeing their role as responsible for encouraging voice and participation, and for seeking out multiple perspectives. We embrace the evolution of thinking about children and childhood from a modern perspective with a romantic view of the child as innocent and needing protection to one that sees the child as capable and competent and as a theory builder. It is our vision that early learning programs will be democratic communities of learning. Democratic participation is an important criterion of citizenship; it is a means by which children and adults may participate with others in shaping decisions affecting themselves and their learning.

MAKING CONNECTIONS

Teaching and learning in the twenty-first century offers new technologies that can support family engagement, as well as collegiality among early learning professionals. Many early learning programs are using a number of technological tools, including regularly emailing families to share learning stories and programming updates. Early learning environments are realizing the benefits of Facebook as a platform to share with families. A search through Facebook will attest to the power of this social media tool. Remember that families must agree to the release of images through consent and that each child who is featured on a Facebook page should have an accompanying consent form. Facebook encourages interaction. Families can "like" postings or leave comments, offering their perspectives on the learning image. For a glimpse into how one early learning program uses social media, see http://on.fb.me/11mvFwJ. The early learning professional who posted the images of the children on this page did so with the written consent of the children's parents or guardians. You will note that the images of children are not connected to the children's names or tagged in any way with their names. The professionals are being mindful of the digital footprint of the children in their program.

KEY TERMS

Andragogy   44
Citizenship   32
Ecological theory   28
Family engagement   40
Loose parts   31

Mosaic approach   46
Pedagogy of listening   45
Play   30
Professional portfolio   46
Social construct   28

Figure 2.7 Key terms wordle

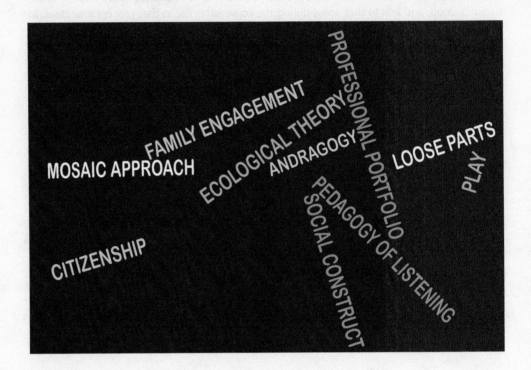

SUMMARY

In considering children's well-being in the learning environment, early learning students look to the concepts of citizenship, ecological theory, family engagement, and listening as ways to think deeply about practice.

1. Early learning students understand that the well-being of children is directly related to the well-being of families. The well-being of the early learning professional is essential to the triad of players in the early learning environment.

2. Bronfenbrenner's (1979) ecological model demonstrates an interrelated system of influences on children. Understanding ecological theory helps early learning professionals to have a more complete view of the children and families in their practice.

3. Recognizing that children learn in a social construct, early learning students and professionals can provide experiences that are play based and use loose parts to support children in their learning.

4. Children can be viewed as citizens with rights in the early learning environment. Essential to their well-being as citizens are the opportunities they have to develop seven essential life skills.

5. Family engagement differs from family involvement, as it is a much more inclusive process that values families as citizens and learners.
6. When early learning students and professionals see themselves as learners and citizens within the early learning environment, they create opportunities to critically reflect on their vision for their professional practice.

We would like you to continue the process of expanding your thinking about education philosophy. "Philosophy is a word that is frequently used in education, but infrequently explained" (Jones & Shelton, 2011, p. 66). We recommend the following site to give you an opportunity to think critically about professional practice by examining educational philosophy further: http://bit.ly/1oyJbuO.

For Further Thought

Chapter 3
Community, Culture, and Diversity

LEARNING OUTCOMES

After exploring this chapter, you should be able to

1. Describe the similarities and differences between the terms *diversity*, *culture*, and *cultural diversity*.

2. Outline the responsibilities of early learning professionals in creating a culturally diverse program with children and families.

3. Explain the types of programming processes that can create barriers for children and families such as Aboriginal, immigrant, and refugee families.

4. Describe how narrative learning, language, and literacy support can bring meaningful cultural experiences to early learning programs.

5. Explain how the concepts of community and community building contribute to the development of social, self-regulation, and cultural competencies.

6. Discuss how the concept of third space and environmental design influence community, culture, and diversity attributes.

A CHILD'S STORY   Ingrid

Things are so different now. I feel like I have big knots in my tummy every morning when I wake up. I know my Oma is going to tell me that preschool is good for me. But I don't want to go. I want to stay home, play with my Oma, and have her talk to me because I know what she is saying. Being in a place where all the other children speak English is hard. I know a few words in English now and I am figuring out more words, but it is so confusing. I don't use the words at preschool yet. Maybe soon.

Every day when I go to preschool, it is so loud. One teacher always puts her hand on my chin, turns me toward her, and speaks to me. Her voice is loud. Sometimes I think I understand what she is saying, and other times I just don't know. I think there might be other children who don't speak English there too because the teacher does the same thing to them but not to others. Sometimes I cry. I only want to be with my Oma. Oma tells me that it will get better.

Last week I tried to ask Sara if I could play with her. She said, "What you say?" I don't think she understood that I wanted to play. I couldn't say it again. I don't really know if I
said the words right. My Oma told me if there was something that I wanted to play with or someone I wanted to play with to go to the area. She told me to watch the other children and then gradually try to play alongside them. It all makes my head hurt. It is too much to think about when I just want to play!

Sometimes when the teacher wants me to do something, she takes my hand and walks to the area with me and then shows me what I am supposed to do. Like yesterday, she wanted me to paint a picture, so she took me to the easel and I think she said, "Would you like to paint a picture?" At the same time, she took a paintbrush and began to use it on the paper. I painted a picture. When I was finished, the teacher came back to the easel and talked to me, but I don't know what she said. Then, she pointed to the water and the cloth under the easel. I knew from watching other children that I needed to wash the paint and clean the brushes, so I did that. I wonder if that is what the teacher was saying to me. My head hurts. I feel alone and different from the other children.

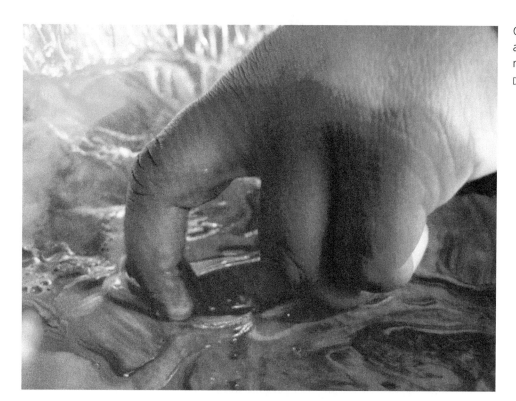

Children in new cultures
and environments learn in
many ways.
Diane Kashin

CHAPTER PREVIEW

*The soul takes nothing with her to the next world but her
education and her culture. At the beginning of the journey
to the next world, one's education and culture can either
provide the greatest assistance, or else act as the greatest
burden, to the person who has just died.*

—Plato (427–347 bc)

Early learning environments across Canada are increasingly diverse. Children, their families, and early learning professionals have various cultural backgrounds, mixed ethnic heritages, living environments and life experiences, and abilities. In 1971, with the adoption of a national multicultural policy, cultural pluralism was emphasized as a core element of Canadian identity (Asanova, 2008). Canada's changing cultural and ethnic landscape continues to underscore the importance of examining culture and diversity within early learning sector, and seeking ways to ensure that all children and families have access to inclusive programs. In urban areas, early learning programs may service newcomers, immigrants, refugees, visible minorities, and families with three or four generations living in Canada (Langford, 2007). In rural Canada, early learning programs are also beginning to service children and families new to the community who bring cultural diversity to the environment.

Early learning professionals require strategies that embrace diversity and support them in working competently with children, families, and colleagues who may have beliefs, values, and perspectives different from their own. The practices and beliefs that early learning professionals have about culture and diversity can either support and extend the richness of the experiences that children engage in or limit their exposure and learning options. Think about the story that begins this chapter. If you have not had experience working with children learning another language and you do not speak the child's mother tongue, how do you support the child? How do you comfort the child? How do you support the family? It is the responsibility of the professional to support all children, regardless of their backgrounds. This chapter will help you to explore your professional responsibility with regard to culture and diversity.

The concept of culture and cultural diversity is grounded in principles of social justice and equality. This means "certain cultural identities or communities should not be ignored just because they do not conform to the dominant cultural group" (Ang, 2010, p. 42). Ideally, early learning professionals create environments that clearly model the moral ideal that all children and families have a fair and equitable experience in the early learning environment.

Culture and cultural diversity are complex concepts, requiring early learning students and professionals to examine the terms and processes within their programs from multiple perspectives. Early learning professionals think about their position on diversity, which in broad terms may include cultural differences, family differences, and community values. They examine how their perspective can challenge or bring harmony to their practice. This may be difficult for you as an early learning student. It may be particularly challenging for students who are new to Canada or who have not had many life experiences with people from different cultures. It can be difficult to reconcile cultural differences with the homogeneous norms, or uniform customs, that are sometimes found in early learning programs. For example, assume that you are from a culture where infants are not necessarily responded to immediately when they begin to cry. Your family and your extended family have maintained this practice in your life in Canada. Now you learn, as you begin your studies in early childhood education, that from a child-centred pedagogy, the expectation is that you will respond right away when a baby cries, as professionals have suggested that this is how a child will develop a sense that the people in her life care for her. Or assume that you have grown up in a rural community where you have had limited exposure to different cultures, and you learn that a family at your centre has a custom to generally eat their food with their hands rather than utensils. How do you respond to such differences? How do you work through them? And how do these differences affect your current program? Reconstructing beliefs, values, and practices surrounding diversity and culture brings forth discourses at an ideological level, which in turn contributes to dialogue about how to achieve a standard of practice that models inclusion (Ang, 2010).

As identified by Langford (2007), there is a need to expand our conceptualization of the effective early learning professional in pedagogical discourses to include difference. By examining differences through the lenses of equality, fairness, and respect, early learning professionals are able to work out what an inclusive program would look like and consider types of experiences and options that would allow differences to be explored and celebrated. Examining difference requires early learning students and professionals to reflect on situations and deconstruct them, so that difference is examined beyond a narrow view in which children's cultural identities might be placed in polarized categories.

In this chapter, we introduce you to the concepts of community, diversity, and culture and discuss the responsibility of early learning professionals to create places of play and learning that support children and families. As in Chapters 1 and 2, at times we will encourage you to reflect upon your beliefs and practices as a way to help you bridge your perspectives within your professional practice. You may be required to think deeply about what you believe and to figure out the roots of those beliefs. You may need to think about how to reconfigure some of those core messages in your current belief system so that you embrace diversity and the learning community concept. Discussions on cultures, beliefs, and practices can bring out disequilibrium and discourse. By having conversations and being open to new ways of thinking, you'll find opportunities to reposition your thinking

and, ultimately, your practices. This leads to expanding upon the foundational skills necessary to launch big ideas within programming that will promote learning and development. Such discourse helps to stretch beyond the perspectives of the dominant culture and values to guide your practice so that programming is ultimately about social advocacy and respecting the uniqueness of all children and their families.

DIVERSITY

There is no one definition that describes **diversity**. The meaning of diversity depends on life experiences and beliefs. Broader definitions may include the examination of individual differences, such as culture, gender, learning styles, community, or religion. From an eco-cultural perspective, "diversity is a relational and context-embedded reality" (Barrera & Corso, 2003, p. 103). DuCette, Sewell, and Shapiro (1996) identified diversity as "encompassing the domain of human characteristics that affect an individual's capacity to learn from, respond to, or interact in a social environment" (p. 324). These definitions help us to examine the interconnectedness between the family structure and the social environment.

Viewing diversity as merely cultural is not enough. Diversity is more than cultural differences. Early learning students and professionals strive to support and respect all kinds of diversity among children and families by creating environments that will facilitate children in their personal, interpersonal, and community development (Harry, 2002). This is an encompassing professional responsibility.

The early learning environment is a social environment. In examining what connects the players in the environment, early learning students and professionals build upon the diversity among the children, families, and staff to create a community of learners. Early learning students and professionals understand that families are influenced by a multitude of factors (Lim & Able-Boone, 2005). By taking the approach of viewing the heterogeneity, or diversity, of everyone instead of examining their

diversity An examination of individual differences, such as gender, learning styles, community, or religion, going beyond cultural differences.

The feeling tone in the environment influences how children engage with one another.

Diane Kashin

race/ethnicity or class, professionals provide more opportunities to exhibit inclusive practice. In this type of space, it is more likely that the early learning environment will support the individual and group needs and rights of the players. This is a responsibility that needs to be a feature of professional practice, for it has far-reaching implications. Irwin, Siddiqui, and Herzman (2007) described the social environment as "the environmental conditions to which children are exposed including the quality of relationships and language environment [that] in the early years literally 'sculpt' the developing brain" (p. 7). The early learning environment's *feeling tone* significantly influences how children connect with others, explore new ideas, and develop the confidence to express their individuality and uniqueness. The feeling tone is created by the aesthetics of the environment and the interactions among the adults and children. One's body language, facial expressions, and tone of voice influence how comfortable children will be in the environment.

Canada has a diverse population. How diverse early learning programs are depends on where they are located. For example, an early learning program in Truro, Nova Scotia, will have different levels and types of culture and diversity from programs in Ottawa, Ontario, or Regina, Saskatchewan, do. The level of diversity and the breadth of experiences that early learning professionals have with diversity will also differ. The needs of the families may vary, as will professional practices and processes. In this chapter, we will examine diversity from the perspective of Aboriginal, immigrant, and refugee families. We acknowledge that other components of diversity are also important to early learning programs and encourage you to think about how the key elements presented here may be transferable to other situations.

Examining Diversity

As identified in Chapter 2, Canada's families are diverse in many ways, including family structure, ethnicity, culture, and abilities. Building a community within the early learning environment that respects, celebrates, and integrates diversity is a requirement for professional practice. With globalization and digitalization, the world is diversifying as never before. Would it not be ideal for the early learning environment to be one in which there is respect for differences? Cope, Kalantzis, and Lankshear (2005) referred to this environment as the **third space**. Our global environment is deeply multilingual, with various discourses and many differences. Working in this third space requires professionals to develop skills that model respect and communication across language, culture, and human differences. Thus, early learning students and professionals need to clearly examine the kinds of engagement and the kinds of human beings, sensibilities, and dispositions that should be built into early learning environments (Cope et al., 2005).

third space A metaphor for a space that respects differences through environmental design and programming.

A major aim for early learning programs is to create a third space that accommodates children's cultures, languages, and differences (Bhabha, 2004). When children have a sense of comfort within their environment and feel valued by the adults and others, they are better able to adjust to new situations and are more open to new exploration and learning. This means that when children from various cultures are in heterogeneous early learning programs, it is essential that experiences be culturally diverse and that many experiences or examples of different cultures be provided within the space. The resources and the experiences not only reflect the diversity of the children and families served, but extend to other cultures not necessarily represented in the learning community. Adopting an inclusive pedagogical approach goes beyond providing examples of what may happen or be practised in a particular culture. Children engage in experiences that will require them to be stretched beyond what they currently know or experience. For example, many of the physical materials are culturally relevant to some and new to others. Collectively, the children and early learning professionals explore these materials and seek assistance from children and families who are familiar with them so that shared learning and discovery occurs.

In early learning programs, children need to acquire experiences through interpersonal relationships and materials that will support them in understanding other ethnic groups. But if the learning environment ignores or denies children's home languages, this means that early learning professionals have not yet internalized the significance of inclusive pedagogy in their practice. Research continues to suggest that many "immigrant children enter a majority language vortex in the classroom where their home language socialization is at best ignored in curricular aims and teaching practices and at worst derided" (Lotherington, Holland, Sotoudeh, & Zentena, 2008, p. 139). This does little to create an inclusive practice that acknowledges and celebrates differences.

When early learning programs embrace a "community of learning" process, opportunities to develop knowledge of the languages and cultures of communities are enhanced. This approach changes the discourse, reflection, and dialogue—and it develops "habits of the mind that are questioning and critical" (Leach & Moon, 2008, p. 168). The discussions and changes to practice ultimately lead to positive thinking and the promotion of play and learning experiences from an individual to a family and a community perspective. Within communities of learners, differences are respected, and this provides the foundation for programming.

CULTURE

culture The values, beliefs, and traditions of a particular group of people.

Understanding culture and figuring out how it informs practice is a complicated process because cultures are constantly changing as they interact with other cultures. Similar to diversity, there is no single "correct" definition that describes culture. **Culture** can be defined as the values, beliefs, and traditions of a particular group of people. From these values, beliefs, and traditions, a set of rules evolves that are intended to guide the behaviour of individuals who are members of that group. Another definition suggests that culture refers to how a particular group can be defined in terms of national origin, racial experience, linguistic experience, religious background, and socio-economic status. Within any culture, differences may also exist in "age, gender, and sexual orientation" (Gonzalez-Mena & Bhavnagri, 2000, p. 31). On another level, Derman-Sparks and Edwards (2010) determined that culture is a set of unconscious rules that govern everything we do, including all that we learn early in life. Culture is deeper than what we see on the surface. Finally, culture can be viewed from the perspective that "lived practices and values of particular groups of individuals and communities is used more commonly today in the sociological paradigm to define the concept of culture in a more inclusive way" (Ang, 2010, p. 42). Seeing culture as lived practices and values of particular groups supports inclusionary practices.

cultures in-between The idea that cultures are viewed as heterogeneous or different among and within themselves.

Bhabha (2004) introduced the term **cultures in-between** as a way to emphasize the diverse and complex nature of cultural identities and communities. He determined that culture must not be viewed simply as a series of fixed or predetermined cultural norms or behaviours that define a particular group. Instead, culture includes diverse values and practices, as well as the social processes that contribute to the interactions and evolution of cultural norms. This means "cultures are not homogenous but heterogeneous, where diverse cultural communities can and should be differentiated both amongst and within themselves" (Ang, 2010, p. 43). Cultural identity is continually changing. Think about children who are second-generation Chinese Canadian. Their values, beliefs, and identity may vary from those of their parents, who are first-generation immigrants to Canada, simply because

All families make valuable contributions to early learning programs.

Diane Kashin

of their different life experiences in Canada. Ang (2010) drew attention to the term *global mélange* used by Pieterse (2004) "to describe the fluidity and hybridity of cultures and cultural identities, especially those of second-generation migrant families" (Ang, 2010, p. 48). Second-generation immigrants display mixed cultural traits—"a separation between and, next, a mix of a home culture and language (matching the culture of origin) and an outdoor culture (matching the culture of residence)" (Pieterse, 2004, p. 3). Therefore, early learning professionals need to be flexible in their practice and recognize that families will have different perspectives and requirements for their children.

Professional Responsibilities

The Child Care Human Resources Sector Council's (2010) *Occupational Standards for Early Childhood Educators* is a nationally compiled list of required skills, abilities, and core professional knowledge for those working in the early learning sector. This national set of standards has identified the valuing of cultural diversity as a fundamental occupational requirement. Constructing the knowledge and skills to value cultural diversity and difference occurs in a number of ways and at a variety of levels. One of the most significant strategies for early learning professionals is to partner with families and communities in their programs to ensure that the environment provides materials, experiences, and activities that reflect diversity and promote a positive attitude toward differences.

Early learning students and professionals respect the cultures of Canada and create programs that support and celebrate culture and diversity. This is a standard for the profession that informs the scope of their practice. A single framework or multiple frameworks can provide a guide to programming, including historical and contemporary frameworks such as Montessori, Waldorf, HighScope and the Reggio Emilia approach. Over the past fifteen years, many provincial and international curriculum frameworks for early learning programs have been developed to provide early learning students and professionals with examples of programming approaches that support cultural diversity. Although the use of these curriculum frameworks varies from optional to mandatory, effective early learning professionals will use them as a resource to support them in determining their philosophical beliefs and for programming support. Curriculum frameworks are open to interpretation.

By exploring various frameworks, early learning students can expand their knowledge and beliefs about culture and diversity. Then, through critical reflection and discourse, they may develop a way of thinking that gives options for many perspectives and understandings about cultural diversity. This process encourages early learning students and professionals to reach out, assess, and support children and families in gaining a sense of belonging in the early learning setting.

How Cultures Influence Early Learning Programming

Aboriginal Families   Aboriginal peoples in Canada include First Nations, Inuit, and Métis people. In this text, we will focus on First Nations families; however, Inuit and Métis people also experience many of the same issues as First Nations families and communities.

First Nations people live in many types of communities in urban and rural settings across Canada, either in communities known as reserves or off reserve. First Nations families today continue to be affected by the earlier policies and actions of the Canadian government, such as removing children from their families and placing them in federally run residential schools. Although the last residential school closed in 1996, the impacts of separating children from their family, language, community, and culture continue to play out in First Nations family relationships, languages, knowledge about their heritage and culture, and ways of life today. Many Aboriginal families are in need of healing and support to overcome the intergenerational impact of colonization, including the residential school system. Some of this healing and support begins with the types of experiences Aboriginal children are exposed to during their early years (Chakraborty, Patrick, & Lambri, 2013).

Current research on the importance of valuing cultural diversity has reinforced the need for early learning programs and professionals to gain new knowledge that will help them in designing culturally focused programs and experiences that support Aboriginal children. For example, in a report entitled *Creating Pathways: An Aboriginal Early Years Five Year Strategic Plan* compiled by Little Drum Consulting (Bolduc, Schneider, Gerlach, & Gray Smith, 2009), the authors noted that "aboriginal culture and language are currently an 'add-on' in many early years programs and models of service delivery" (p. 6). As a result, many Aboriginal children are in programs where their cultural heritage is absent from their daily experiences. The report further identified that the lack of cultural competency of non-Aboriginal service providers is a barrier for Aboriginal families and communities. The authors indicate, "Culture and language need to be imbedded in the curriculum because if it isn't, it lets people off the hook and becomes an 'add-on'" (p. 6).

Moomaw and Jones (2005) identified how insensitivities to culture can happen. Early learning students and professionals who lack a background in Aboriginal culture may suggest children participate in experiences that perpetuate stereotypes or provide misinformation about Aboriginal lifestyles and customs, as do many of the projects suggested in curriculum books. For example, some feathers are sacred to Native peoples, so if early learning professionals suggest that children make headdresses from feathers, they are showing a lack of respect for the sacred meaning of the feather and misinforming children about their use. Similarly, totem poles are important to many and often used in Native ceremonies. Having children create totem poles as a craft project shows an insensitivity to their deep meaning (Moomaw & Jones, 2005). Culturally appropriate programming in this instance would include community-based learning, elder involvement, environmental appreciation, language, and modelling of Aboriginal ways of life (Findlay & Kohen, 2010).

Immigrant and Refugee Families   The fabric of Canadian society continues to change as immigrant and refugee populations grow faster (13.6 percent between 2001 and 2006) than the Canadian-born population (5.4 percent; Statistics Canada, 2009). UNICEF (2009) defined an *immigrant* as "a person [or family] who has moved across international borders from their home country of origin and taken up residency in another country" (p. 4). Kirova (2010), using the definition set out in the United Nations Convention Related to the Status of Refugees (1951), described refugees as "persons in need of protection due to fear of persecution or . . . at risk of torture or cruel and unusual treatment or punishment" (p. 75). Immigrant families have opportunities to make informed decisions and choices about moving to a new country. Refugees generally come to a new country more quickly and without the same types of preparation, family, or financial resources that immigrants may come with. Refugees are seeking a safe place to live.

Immigrant and refugee families encounter a number of challenges and stressors as they establish their families in Canadian society. Some of the main stressors include parental underemployment or unemployment; language barriers; feelings of isolation from families, culture, and community; and cultural incompatibilities (Kirova, 2010). Kirova (2010) suggested that it is common for new families in Canada to experience different types of conflict from those they experienced in their home country. For example, immigrant families may experience conflict rooted in changing family dynamics, which is intensified by new living conditions and the rate at which each family member adjusts to new ways of living, including accessibility to familiar food and to people with similar beliefs and values, and the overall ability to adjust to change. Conflict affects family members in varying ways. Refugee families have stressors associated with the sudden and involuntary nature of leaving their home country and not knowing what even the short-term future holds (Kirova, 2010; Suárez-Orozco & Suárez-Orozco, 2001).

Immigrant and refugee families with young children may face additional challenges in having access to or finding early learning programs that are supportive of their needs. Kirova (2010) identified accessibility and responsiveness as key barriers for refugee families seeking culturally relevant early learning programs. As illustrated in Table 3.1, early learning professionals benefit from examining their established policies or practices in relation to refugee families. Think about the questions in Table 3.1 and determine how accessibility and responsiveness may contribute to refugee families either being able to establish feelings of comfort or feelings of barriers and discomfort in their new community.

Working in our multicultural society requires early learning students and professionals to clearly examine and learn about cultures; exhibit respect for diversity; and recognize that children's values, communication processes, and ways of being are highly influenced by their family's culture, beliefs, and support systems (Dietze, 2006). Kirova (2010) determined that in order to understand children and childhood, dialogue with children and their families is necessary so that their voices may be heard. This type of partnership creates a feeling of equal power among the players, who can advocate for and mobilize change.

Early learning students and professionals use conversation to broaden their understanding of immigrant and refugee children and families in their practice, and to explore a potential model of inclusive practice so that the needs of these children and their families are met fairly. A relationship exists between parental background characteristics

Table 3.1 How Early Learning Programs Support or Inhibit Refugee Families Gaining Comfort in Their New Communities

Accessibility

How might community and early learning programs transportation policies support or inhibit refugee families in having access to culturally relevant programs?

How might popular programs with waiting lists support or inhibit refugee families from gaining access to culturally relevant programs?

How might registration fees and program fees support or inhibit refugee families from gaining access to culturally relevant programs?

How might staffing policies in early learning programs support or inhibit refugee families from having access to individuals who understand their needs?

How might the income status of refugee parents inhibit accessibility to culturally relevant early learning programs?

Responsiveness

How might family involvement expectations of early learning programs positively or negatively influence refugee families?

How might the language and cultural practices of refugee families inhibit their involvement in early learning programs?

How might exposure to new cultural practices support or inhibit refugee families from feeling that they can fully participate in early learning programs?

How might the values, beliefs, and practices of early learning professionals influence refugee families feeling positive or vulnerable in understanding their needs?

How might the first visit and orientation to the early learning program influence how refugee parents feel about being members of the early learning community?

and children's life course that includes education, income, longevity, satisfaction with their life, and susceptibility to illnesses (Chakraborty et al., 2013). For example, immigrant parents who have been successful in creating a new life in Canada for themselves and their families are more likely to be able to offer their children educational options than immigrants who have struggled to adapt to living in their new country. Much research has found a relationship between parents' educational and cultural characteristics, as well as their behaviours, and their children's life course (Chakraborty et al., 2013; Jaeger & Holm, 2007; Jensen, 2009). This link between parents' experiences and their children's outcomes reinforces the need for early learning programs to partner with families and children in program design and implementation.

Peer Culture

Peer culture provides another way for early learning students and professionals to examine culture. **Peer culture** describes "a stable set of activities or routines, artifacts, values, and concerns that children produce and share in interaction with one another" (Corsaro, 2003, p. 37). Peers offer children opportunities for independence from adults and can help shape children's identities, both positively and negatively (Corsaro, 2003). Corsaro and Johannesen (2007) developed a theoretical approach termed *interpretive reproduction* to refer to the innovative and creative aspects of children's participation in society. For example, children produce and participate in their peer cultures by extracting information from the adult world to address their peer concerns. The process is *reproductive* because children do not simply internalize their living space, experiences, and culture, but instead actively contribute to cultural production and change. Peer culture is as active as other cultures in early learning environments.

Early learning students and professionals can reflect on what children do when they are learning and living in a social construct by observing children in their social interactions to see how the peer culture in the environment is establishing itself. Engaging in

peer culture Children doing things together, in the process creating a shared set of activities or routines, artifacts, values, and concerns.

Children learn about different cultures from their peers.
Diane Kashin

A Reflective Moment

What are three ways children might try to take control in the early learning environment?

What are three ways you might see children sharing control in the early learning environment?

How do these struggles for control affect children's development?

dialogue with all the players about peer culture will aid the professional in making ethical decisions about practice. According to Corsaro (2000), there are two basic themes in the peer culture of young children. The first is that children make persistent attempts to gain control over their lives, and the second is that they share that control with one another. How is this search for control observable in the early learning environment? It involves the give-and-take interactions that children engage in. Take some time with the accompanying Reflective Moment box to think about how children try to gain and share control.

Cultural Competency

Another essential skill for early learning professionals is **cultural competency**. A culturally competent professional is someone "who is able to facilitate mutually rewarding interactions and meaningful relationships in the delivery of services for children and families whose cultural heritage differs from his or her own" (Sareen, Visencio, Russ, & Halfon, 2005, p. 8). To be culturally competent, early learning professionals need to be aware of their own cultural beliefs and values. For early learning students, integrating self-awareness during your course of study can be an effective way to acquire cultural competency. A self-assessment checklist on cultural competency for those working in human services professions can be found at http://bit.ly/12YbWC1. It provides examples of the kinds of values and practices that foster cultural competency in settings such as early learning environments. The answers will help you to reflect on what you frequently, occasionally, or rarely practice with regard to cultural competency in the learning environment. If most of your answers are "rarely" or "never," the assessment provides examples that can help you improve your professional practice.

> **cultural competency** The ability to facilitate mutually rewarding interactions and meaningful relationships in the delivery of services for children and families whose cultural heritage differs from one's own.

Narrative Learning

Narrative learning is prevalent in early learning programs and is a way for children to learn about cultural diversity. Cortazzi and Jin (2007) defined narrative learning as "learning from, about and through stories, and learning through reflecting on the experience of narrating and the narrating of the experience" (p. 65). Narrative learning is a **scaffolding** experience, meaning that adults create a support structure to help children build new ideas upon their prior knowledge. First coined by Jerome Bruner (1978), scaffolding is similar to Vygotsky's concept of the zone of proximal development (ZPD), which describes "the distance between the actual developmental level as determined by independent problem-solving and the level of potential development as determined through problem-solving under adult guidance or in collaboration with more capable peers" (Vygotsky, 1978, p. 86). Bruner (2004), like Vygotsky, emphasized that learning takes place in a social construct and that other people can help children develop skills through the process of scaffolding.

Through storytelling, early learning professionals may embed authentic and consequential experiences for children to support their development in the cognitive, social, and linguistic domains. Storytelling occurs as a consequence of programming, so it is a natural,

> **narrative learning** Learning from, about, and through storytelling.

> **scaffolding** A support structure early learning professionals create to help children build upon prior knowledge.

Exposing children to literature and relevant materials supports them in gaining cultural awareness.

Rosalba Bortolotti

authentic extension of everyday lived experiences. As outlined by Bruner (2004), the stories that children learn to tell scaffold their perceptual experiences and organize their memory. "Narrative comprehension is a general feature of young children's thinking that is critical for cognitive development and early literacy" (Paris & Paris, 2007, p. 34). Using children's literature, early learning professionals support children in retelling stories, allowing them to incorporate meaning that is powerful for them, while incorporating cultural attributes into the story.

In preparing to work with children with diverse racial/ethnic, cultural, language, or socio-economic backgrounds, early learning students can practise using authentic materials and resources and understanding various cultures. In thinking about the core concepts of diversity, culture, and community covered in this chapter, big ideas for programming may bubble up (see Figure 3.1). Children's literature provides multiple opportunities to support children's learning in the areas of social responsibility and diversity.

Children's Literature

Having an extensive, attractively displayed, and accessible library of children's literature available to act as a prompt for programming can expand children's knowledge and experience with social responsibility and diversity. When multiple languages are represented, it can also support a variety of emerging literacies.

Figure 3.1 **Programming bubble: children's literature**

We have chosen an award-winning literary example to illustrate this programming bubble. In Canada, winter, including snow, is part of the common experience of most children. *Sadie and the Snowman*, by Allen Morgan and Brenda Clark (1987), is a timeless story that can be used to develop programming experiences and opportunities for children to learn the scientific attributes of snow. After reading the book with children, a number of ideas might bubble up. We suggest that providing an invitation in the form of various materials (including paper, glue, paint, and clay) can be provided for the children to make their own representations of the snowman in the story.

A storyboard is an artistic tool that includes a sequence of drawings, representing the unfolding of an artistic representation of a story that can be told in multiple ways. A storyboard can be made that sequences the time, temperature, and melting process of the snowman. Then the children can act out the melting of the snowman. The children can make a video retelling the story in their home languages. Children and their families may also decide which types of items might be used to dress Sadie based on their cultures and traditions. An outdoor dramatic centre could be created with similar props to those in the story, which would be another invitation for the children to explore the story. Such an experience is based on the principles of an *emergent curriculum*—taking the experience to the depth and breadth that children are interested in, and to the extent that children wish to draw upon their families to further develop the ideas. This illustrates the core principles of a learning community where children, families, and early learning professionals connect to bring their cultures into the environment for the purpose of advancing children's play and learning. All involved benefit from being encouraged to share popular stories from their cultures and to have children transfer the stories to their ways of knowing.

Children require visual representations and concrete materials that reflect different cultures and languages (Lotherington et al., 2008). Creating stories in different languages provides children with visual models of writing the same story as a culturally validating practice. Visual support is a necessary component that facilitates oral language development, metacognition, and writing skills (Cortazzi & Jin, 2007). Early learning students and professionals examine the materials extended to children to ensure that the materials are not contributing to misinformation or inaccurate portrayals about various cultures. For example, Moomaw and Jones (2005) indicate that if picture books, puzzles, and authentic materials that depict Native peoples in historical clothing and dwellings are offered rather than ones showing contemporary perspectives, this has the potential to perpetuate the belief that "Indians living today dress and live as they did hundreds of years ago" (p. 91). When children are not provided with accurate information about various cultures, they will form their ideals, perceptions, and beliefs based on life experiences, which may include what they hear from the adults who influence them, and what they see or hear on television or in other forms of media. Once those perceptions are formed, it takes time and relearning to change the misinformation.

Languages and Literacies

Early learning students and professionals may have a narrow view of what it means to be literate. Similarly, the concept of languages may be viewed in a limited way. The Reggio Emilia approach has underscored the idea that children can learn and express themselves in many languages, such as paint, sculpture, dance, and song (Kashin, 2009). Literacy is not just about language, reading, and writing. To be literate today, children are required to be multi-literate. This means that children need to be exposed to traditional print as well as digital print. "It is no longer appropriate to focus on literacy as a paper-based activity when children access text in a range of modes, e.g. on computers, television and mobile phones" (Marsh, 2004, p. 52). Just as children can express themselves in multiple languages, they can learn to become multi-literate.

multiple literacies An expanded view of literacy beyond reading, writing, and speaking to include multiple ways of being literate.

The theory of **multiple literacies** is influenced by the philosophical work of Gilles Deleuze and refers to an expanded view of literacy that goes beyond "reading, writing, speaking and listening practices" to include new terms such as "media literacy, information literacy, critical literacy, affective literacy, medical literacy, statistical literacy, technological literacy" (Masny & Cole, 2009, p. 1). For more information on multiple literacies theory, go to http://bit.ly/11x5wHt.

According to research, literacy learning should be developmental, constructivist, and incremental in nature, and it should be embedded within cultural and community practices (Gillen & Hall, 2003; Kennedy et al., 2012). Programs that make use of multiple literacies and languages are advancing children's learning and development in a variety of ways. Using the resources available through technology can support diversity in the early learning environment by facilitating opportunities for children's expressions in multiple languages, including their own.

There are many ways to encourage children to bring culture to the environment. For example, having children greet early learning professionals and their peers in their native language is a simple yet powerful way to promote the diversity and talents within the learning community. Bringing families into the learning environment is essential to cross-pollinating learning about other cultures. For example, as we described earlier in the chapter, this is what happens when you take a favourite children's story and have children and parents tell the story to other children in their languages. Such experiences have the potential to spark children's curiosity about languages and their desire to try speaking different languages. They allow early learning professionals, children, and families to explore cultural differences in a safe *third space*, while early learning professionals learn about new cultures so that they may provide accurate information to the children.

COMMUNITY

The *New Brunswick Curriculum Framework for Early Learning and Child Care—English* (Government of New Brunswick, 2008) is values-based. One of the core values the province has for its youngest learners is that children and families be respected and share responsibility for one another in order to enhance communities and cultures. The concept of community is a core value in other frameworks as well. These values follow the assumption that children are social beings and learning takes place in a social construct. If a **community** represents a group of people living in a common place, the early learning environment is a community. Early learning professionals support this community, as it creates a place where children and families are respected and valued.

community A group of people living in a common place.

Children are connected to a family, community, culture, and place (Millei, 2011). Children's learning is influenced by their familes, communities, and cultural experiences (Chakraborty et al., 2013). Through their daily living interactions and experiences within their family and community, children construct their identities and their beliefs about how the world works (Millei, 2011). The term *community* is multi-faceted. Millei (2011) described community as a "space of emotional relationships through which particular identities are constructed through their bonds to micro-cultures of meanings and values" (p. 47). In *Belonging, Being and Becoming: The Early Years Learning Framework for Australia*, published in 2009 by the Department of Education, Employment and Workplace Relations (DEEWR), community and identity are highlighted as important considerations in children's programming. Community is viewed as a place where children actively participate in multiple encounters with others and the broader society. Being a member of a community contributes to learning about social practices, culture, and empathy for others in the community. Active participation means that "children actively construct their own understandings and contribute to others' learning. They recognize their agency, capacity to initiate and lead learning, and their rights to participate in decisions that affect them, including their learning" (DEEWR, 2009, p. 9). Children contribute to peer experiences and their learning.

Children's identities reflect the experiences they have in their communities. It is the "children's evolving experiences and relationships [that] define the child's identity[;] an identity is not fixed" (Millei, 2011, p. 20). If we think of community and identity as they are described in *Belonging, Being and Becoming* (2009), this reinforces the importance of "recognizing the existence and legitimacy of distinct cultures, values, and socio cultural mores that shape continuously children's identities" (Millei, 2011, p. 47). Children and families develop a part of their identity, then, through their communities.

Early learning professionals intentionally and continuously acquire new information about the diversity among families, children, staff, and their communities so that the early learning program can offer appropriate and meaningful experiences and reach for what is possible. In his seminal work, *Life in a Crowded Place: Making a Learning Community*, Peterson (1992) focused on the older student, but his ideas can be applied to early learning environments as well. He said that it takes courage, intelligence, and heart to seek out and create an order that will support the growth and existence of learning communities. Early learning professionals have the capacity for courage, intelligence, and heart to model and formulate effective learning communities.

Imagine what it is like to be in an early learning environment every day with twenty-four children who spend their day from 7:30 a.m. to 6:00 p.m. with two to three adults trained as early learning professionals. Peterson (1992) compared a classroom to a *large living room*. When you arrange furniture and provide materials that support children's curiosity and interest in exploring new ideas, it can become a very crowded place. In that space, if children and adults don't feel validated and respected, it is unlikely that all will reach their fullest potential. Thinking about how it feels to enter an early learning environment is a helpful way to reflect on whether the space is metaphorically a *crowded space* or a *third space*.

When children cross the threshold that divides the learning environment from the rest of the world, they should feel welcomed, respected, valued, and validated. Their families should have the same experience and a similar feeling of comfort. Early learning students who enter a learning environment require a feeling of comfort and a sense of confidence that they can reach their fullest potential. Can you recall entering a classroom where you were too timid to respond to questions or speak out about what you observed or questioned? What were the conditions like in that learning space? Can you compare the feelings associated with being in such an environment with what it must feel like when you belong, are accepted, and are cared for? Can you imagine environments where you develop feelings that you are supported to learn with others? Peterson (1992) determined that "learning awakens a variety of internal processes that operate only when the child is interacting with others in his [or her] environment and in cooperation with his [or her] peers" (p. 3). Peterson also stated, "Even mainstream educators are beginning to recognize that education fails when it focuses solely on the accumulation of demonstrable facts and skill. An image is taking shape that acknowledges a more complex and irreducible phenomenon; the social person" (p. 3). When early learning professionals see the child as a social person, the sense of community becomes even more important to professional practice.

To be socially and emotionally competent is an aim for early learning programs so that children and their families develop a sense of respect for both the social and the emotional self. The early learning professional is responsible for building community—for bringing it into existence in a shared third space. Early learning professionals consider what makes a community in practice by examining the core concepts related to what it means to be part of a community.

Building a learning community includes the incorporation of ceremony, rituals, and rites (Peterson, 1992). Ceremonies are important features of communities, and when early learning professionals use ceremonies to start the day, to end the day, and to mark special occasions, this helps in "bringing shape and life to the learning community" (Peterson, 1992, p. 20). Rituals are ways of connecting to a larger community and constitute symbolic acts that ground family and community life. For example, when children sit together on a carpet every day to share information, this becomes known as a community ritual. Early learning professionals look for ways to enrich the community experience so that group time becomes something to celebrate, with children being active participants in the dialogue and the experience. As identified in Figure 3.2, Peterson (1992) outlined three daily rites occurring in learning communities: transition, incorporation, and separation.

Transition rites include the ways children and families enter the learning environment; incorporation rites involve those practices that help members of the community to feel that they belong; and separation rites involve the practices related to the end of the day.

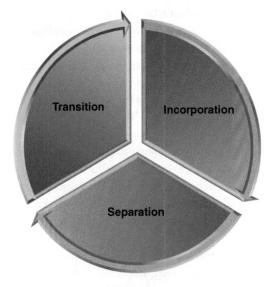

Figure 3.2 Daily rites in early learning environments

By understanding the meanings of ceremonies, rituals, and rites, early learning professionals use these principles to support them in creating a community of learners. For example, early learning professionals may wish to think about how children enter or leave a learning environment. Is it important for children under the age of five to line up? Why or why not? Should children be required to wait until all children are ready before going outdoors? Too often, these types of practices create chaos and competition to be first in line. Sometimes it creates a longer transition time than necessary, and then children are reprimanded for not staying in the line or for acting out as they wait for others. Early learning professionals can relate their practices to the concepts of community and look for ways to enhance children's development in the social and emotional realm.

Many provinces and countries are establishing curriculum frameworks that recognize the importance of children having opportunities for experiences that support the development of self-regulation skills. **Self-regulation** is "the ability to adapt one's emotions, behaviours, and attention to the demands of the situation" (Pascal, 2009, p. 1). People within children's communities influence how they develop self-regulation skills, such as exercising patience, persistence, flexibility, and curiosity in their environments. Some frameworks have documented explicit objectives that encourage children to participate in developing social attributes that will strengthen their sympathy and empathy toward other children and people in their communities. For example, Jenson (2009) described the objective of the Swedish National Agency for Education (Skolverket, 2006) that "no child should be subjected to discrimination at pre-school based on gender, ethnic belonging, religion or perception of other belief, or sexual orientation" (pp. 3–4). This position statement reinforces how the relationship between the children's family environment and the early learning centre influences lifelong learning, including children's societal understanding of others and democratic values (Jenson, 2009).

Democratic values are fundamental to community. Moss (2011) referred to John Dewey (1859–1952) in positioning democracy as a first practice in early learning environments: "This implies maximizing opportunities for sharing, exchanging and negotiating perspectives and opinions. It also implies that democracy is a way of relating to self and others; an ethical, political and educational relationship that can and should pervade all aspects of everyday life" (p. 1). The responsibility of the early learning professional is to place high value on democracy within a community of learners.

> **Self-regulation** refers to a child developing the ability to adjust to and calmly cope with situations by being able to have self-control over one's emotions and reactions to the people and the stimulation in their environment.

Professional Practices

In adhering to the standards of the profession, early learning professionals have a responsibility to all children in the early learning environment. Jensen and Mehlbye (2009) identified that early learning professionals need to pay particular attention to including the socially endangered child within the community. They defined *socially endangered children* as including "children from poor families" and "children from socially deprived families." The definition also includes "at-risk children," "deprived children," "children disadvantaged by poverty," or just "disadvantaged" children. The range of definitions can be related to the different views that adults take of the situation. "If the problem is considered an individual one, the term 'deprived children' is most likely to be used, while a contextual perspective employs terms like 'children at risk for marginalization'" (Jenson, 2009, p. 9). The term can also relate to children's vulnerability from a social context perspective as a result of the interaction between children and their surroundings. Children who do not exhibit the behaviours related to being part of the community can become marginalized or socially excluded.

Early learning professionals benefit from viewing practice from multiple perspectives. Bronfenbrenner's (1979) ecological model, as outlined in Chapter 2, reinforces the importance of acknowledging that family, cultural systems, and community significantly influence children's development. The learning community, the environment, and early learning practices demonstrate an emphasis on diversity that is visible and celebrated. Community partnerships play an important role in embracing differences in culture and language and in supporting early learning programs that effectively serve the diversity inherent in working with children and families. Bringing a community of learners into existence involves reaching out to others. When practising within a community of learners' framework, early learning professionals strive to work together to empower one another through dialogue about situations that may be new, different, or causing confusion because of differing opinions. Early learning professionals may find themselves in situations where they are out of their comfort zone. This will require the ethical professional to confront beliefs and values about diversity and cultural differences. Every early learning student brings specific beliefs about child raising, discipline, and healthy living practices. As a professional in training, it is essential to confront any biases so that embracing and exhibiting diversity competence becomes a professional practice. Confronting biases is an essential beginning.

Professional Challenges

Early learning professionals confront biases as part of professional practice. Early learning students will learn to identify, reflect on, and confront their own biases. Consider this example: a new family has joined an early learning program. During the orientation, Alfran's parents identify that adhering to religious beliefs, Alfran's diet does not include pork products. Although the families in the centre have various religious backgrounds, this is the first time in the three years since the centre opened that there has been a child with a restricted diet. Staff immediately begin conversations about how much extra work would be involved in ensuring that the food served contains no pork products. Then they look for solutions. They explore the idea that perhaps Alfran could bring his own food to ensure that it contains no pork products. As the staff think about that solution, they soon realize that this would single Alfran out from the others—this isn't a solution. They examine the typical menu to see how often pork could be an issue. They determine that pork is served at least once per week. As they think about the issue, Jamil reflects on her experience at a previous centre that was peanut-free owing to allergies. Using that experience, Jamil and her colleagues stretch their thinking on how they can incorporate Alfran's needs into their practice. As a staff group living in a largely white Anglo-Saxon rural community without much exposure to families with diverse needs, they have to explore options first and then extend the conversations to the family. This process helps them to think about ways in which family needs can be accommodated without marginalizing them or contributing to the children potentially feeling different from their peers. The experience requires the early learning professionals to confront their biases, values, and cultural beliefs.

Early learning students and professionals consistently reflect upon professional practice and compare their perspectives with those of the families with whom they are working. Reflective practice helps us understand how communication, body language, and established policies and processes may potentially affect interactions with families (Miller et al., 2003). Early learning environments benefit from having staff members with diverse backgrounds and experiences. These differences bring richness to the environment as long as early learning professionals work together to understand and develop an appreciation for differences. For example, assume that a colleague comes from a culture where children are bottle-fed and spoon-fed during infancy and toddlerhood. As she begins practice in an early learning program where the philosophy is based on supporting children in achieving autonomy and independence, the differences, if not discussed, could cause tension. Think about this. How might this situation cause tension? How might it be resolved? Who decides and how? By examining the similarities and differences in beliefs and practices, can a new discourse be found that will integrate practices from both perspectives? What are the benefits? What are the challenges?

According to Dillabough (1999), "differences sit at the centre of identity rather than lurking on the margins" (p. 389). She further articulated that

> identity is not simply recognition of difference as a part of oneself, that is, the authentic individual as expressed in liberal theory. It is recognition that teachers are embedded in a meaningful social and political context where multiple selves meet with a dialectical frame. It is at this moment of "meeting" that one can identify with difference as part of oneself and others. (p. 389)

Identifying and celebrating difference requires openness, communication, exploration, reflection, and an understanding of personal and professional philosophy.

A POSTMODERN PERSPECTIVE

A postmodern approach to diversity and culture would suggest that early learning professionals who use self-reflection as a strategy to think about their beliefs are able to embrace pedagogical discourses as they evolve. This process allows for the expansion of one's understanding about people's beliefs and practices, which in turn may also develop a deeper understanding of cultural knowledge and ways of knowing (Langford, 2007). Maher (2001) reinforced the importance of examining diversity. He said that simply treating diversity "as a matter of life-spicing variety" and viewing "inclusiveness as a panacea for difference" does not address how "differences of power lie behind all diversities" (p. 23). Early learning professionals do not try to neutralize others' ideas to create a common perspective. Rather, they work toward understanding the diverse thoughts and building a learning community that incorporates varying cultural, ethnic, and family identities so that individuals and families do not feel stripped of their "being and belonging" or put in marginalized situations. Engaging in reflective practice and analysis of what it means to be part of diverse cultures is necessary for developing a pedagogy that makes diversity an explicit part of the program and process. Early learning professionals assist children in observing and thinking critically about the richness of cultures and diversity in their own families and in the early learning program. They weave in cultural experiences so that diversity becomes part of social structures and practices within the environment. As identified in Figures 3.3 and 3.4, early learning programs and professionals model practices that are inclusive of children, families, staff, and communities.

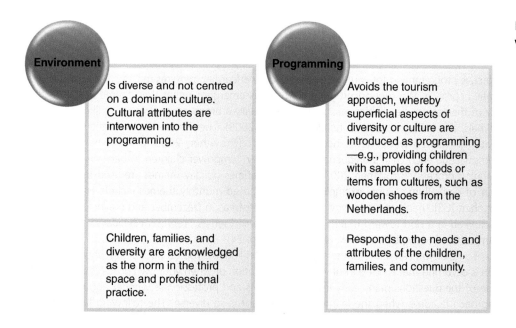

Figure 3.3 Postmodern view of cultural education

Environment

Is diverse and not centred on a dominant culture. Cultural attributes are interwoven into the programming.

Children, families, and diversity are acknowledged as the norm in the third space and professional practice.

Programming

Avoids the tourism approach, whereby superficial aspects of diversity or culture are introduced as programming —e.g., providing children with samples of foods or items from cultures, such as wooden shoes from the Netherlands.

Responds to the needs and attributes of the children, families, and community.

Confront one's values, beliefs, and biases. Develop a hybrid understanding of roles and responsibilities (Langford, 2007).

Build a community of practices to support new knowledge development and understanding of diversity in practice.

Develop collaborative practices to assess programs and strengthen culturally diverse practices.

Engage in discourses so that differences can be identified and shared understanding of discourses evolve.

Figure 3.4 **Postmodern professional practices for promoting culturally diverse environments**

UNIVERSAL DESIGN

How early learning professionals design the learning environment can influence the opportunities to cultivate and celebrate community, culture, and diversity. Creating spaces that allow for social interaction among children, as well as areas for a child to find solace in being alone, shows respect for the group and individual differences. A framework for supporting all learners in the environment is called **universal design**. Conn-Powers, Cross, Traub, and Hutter-Pishgahi (2006) suggested that this framework calls for early learning professionals to acknowledge

> the importance of planning learning environments and activities for a diverse population, by creating universally designed settings in which all children and their families can participate and learn. The principles of universal design for learning can guide professionals in designing programs in which all children and their families have full and equitable access to learning and social opportunities. (p. 1)

Further information on design will be presented in Chapter 8. Think about how the principles of universal design might be represented in an early learning environment.

universal design A framework of principles professionals can use to design programs that support include all children and their families.

FEATURED RESEARCH

Effective programming for young children's play and learning requires moving away from a thematic approach. We support programming that is emergent rather than theme-based, as the use of themes can be problematic. A theme is usually a broad concept or topic, like seasons or animals, and is often based on holidays (Kashin, 2009). Themes are based on the assumption that "all children will benefit and be interested" (Crowther, 2003, p. 40). Themes do not acknowledge each child's uniqueness, nor do they "empower children to become part of the planning process" (Crowther, 2003, p. 40). Sometimes holiday themes are used to plan a full year of curriculum. "Some examples of holiday-based monthly themes include Halloween in October, [US] Thanksgiving in November, and Christmas in December and maybe Kwanzaa or Hanukkah in a nod toward multiculturalism." These themes "represent holidays of the dominant culture" (Campbell, Jamsek, & Jolley, 2005, p. 24).

Some of you can relate to the experience of feeling like you do not belong when a celebration is occurring that is not part of your family tradition or when your own holidays are ignored. One of the questions many early learning students and professionals wonder about is how to approach holidays when the learning environment is so diverse. The following link provides useful resources to provide programming experiences that are inclusive of all children and their families: http://bit.ly/148EeMT. Campbell and colleagues (2005) suggested that developing "a holiday policy, like other program policies, requires a basis in knowledge and ethics" (p. 24). For more information on what would be involved in a holiday policy and more resources for programming, see http://bit.ly/12Y2rTp.

PEDAGOGICAL TOOLS

A useful pedagogical tool for students and professionals is the consideration of **ethical dilemmas**. An ethical dilemma is a complex situation where there is a moral conflict requiring resolution. Follow this link: http://bit.ly/11NxggR. It will take you to a site that features articles with opposing views. The first column presents a common ethical dilemma in early learning environments, and the second provides a response to the dilemma. Ethical dilemmas are pedagogical tools. When analyzing and thinking about what an ethical early learning professional would do, you are engaging in critical reflection that will support your understanding of working within a diverse learning environment.

ethical dilemmas Complex situations with moral conflicts requiring resolution. Can be used as a pedagogical tool to examine values and beliefs about culture, community, and diversity.

PROFESSIONAL CASE STUDY

Cheryl is an early learning professional working in a large program located just north of a big city. Many of the families bring their children to the program early so that they can begin the long commute to the city. Cheryl loves where she works. It is close to the city but has the features of country living with parks and forests. Cheryl has acute asthma, so she is particularly grateful to be away from the smog of the city.

Ever since little Victoria moved up into her group from the toddler program, Cheryl has been questioning her practice and her values. Victoria is a vibrant and talkative two-and-a-half-year-old. She has a mop of blond curly hair and loves wearing dresses. Most of her dresses seem like hand-me-downs, and some days they aren't even clean. Cheryl's biggest problem with Victoria is that she loves to be hugged and cuddled, but her hair and her clothes always smell like cigarette smoke. This disgusts Cheryl. She finds the smell a trigger for her asthma. She also is very much against smoking. Her grandparents owned the local tavern, and even though her grandmother never smoked a day in her life, she got lung cancer and passed away. Victoria always wants a hug in the morning. Cheryl will need to do something.

REFLECTION QUESTIONS FOR SELF-LEARNING

Coming to terms with diversity, cultural differences, and overall difference among the players within early learning programs can cause disequilibrium in one's belief systems and understanding of practice, and may require personal change. Think about the feelings that the child described in the opening story. If you were an early learning professional in that setting, how might you support the child in this new environment? Think about the child described in the case study. If you were Cheryl, what would you do? Considering both case studies, answer the following questions in your professional journal:

1. Do you think it is the responsibility of an early learning professional to support a child who does not speak English in the program? Why or why not? Would it be better for the child to learn English and then come to the program? How are you guided by the Canadian Occupational Standards for Early Childhood Educators in making your decision?

2. Do you think the early learning professional in the opening story understood how Ingrid perceived her practices as making her feel different? If you were the early learning professional, how might you use the family as a resource and source of learning?

3. What types of professional learning might you seek out if you were not familiar with strategies to embrace different cultures and needs of children and families?

4. How do you think early learning students and professionals can overcome biases that affect a child's experience in the early learning environment?

BIG IDEAS FOR DIALOGIC LEARNING

By engaging in dialogue with others, you can expand your professional knowledge and start thinking broadly and in more complex ways about culture, community, and diversity. We invite you to join in a group discussion and answer these questions:

1. If you were to bring to the group one item that represents your culture, what would it be and why?

2. Relating to your own experiences, what are ways that you have observed early learning environments positively supporting culture, community, and diversity?

3. Have you observed any negative practices that do not support culture, community, and diversity? Why were they negative?

4. Have you had any personal experience with discrimination or prejudice where you feel you were treated inequitably?

5. How do societal inequities play out in early learning programs? Give some examples. What is the impact of societal inequities on children and their families?

VISION

It is our vision that early learning professionals develop their practice to model a culturally relevant and inclusive community of practice. We see early learning professionals adapting pedagogy by using a lens that values and interacts with diversity, culture, and difference in ways that are meaningful and interwoven into daily practice. We embrace the learning community concept. Such a community offers children, families, and early learning professionals a collective space to develop cultural competency and consciousness, leading them to stop current oppressive or inappropriate practices and replace them with strategies that strengthen the acceptance of difference. For viable cultural competency to evolve, early learning professionals examine their biases and come up with meaningful ways to create the connections that illustrate the richness of experiences when children, families, and early learning professionals become partners in learning and play. The process of creating a culturally appropriate pedagogy begins with early learning professionals knowing their own identities and understanding that their identities may differ from those of the children and families they serve. Embracing difference is critical in creating an inclusive, universally acceptable place for children and families to establish feelings of comfortable and equitable learning.

MAKING CONNECTIONS

To celebrate diversity and create community, early learning professionals can look to multiple means of connecting with children and their families. Technology can increase the potential to reach and share with families. We support the use of technology in the learning environment. In the following article, Mitchell, Foulger, and Wetzel (2009) offer ten tips for using technology to support communication with families: http://bit.ly/15sZITF. If you were to create a blog or Facebook page for an early learning program, what could you post to support and demonstrate culture, community, and diversity?

KEY TERMS

Community 67
Cultural competency 63
Culture 58
Cultures in-between 58
Diversity 55
Ethical dilemmas 73
Multiple literacies 66
Narrative learning 63
Peer culture 62
Scaffolding 63
Self-regulation 69
Third space 57
Universal design 72

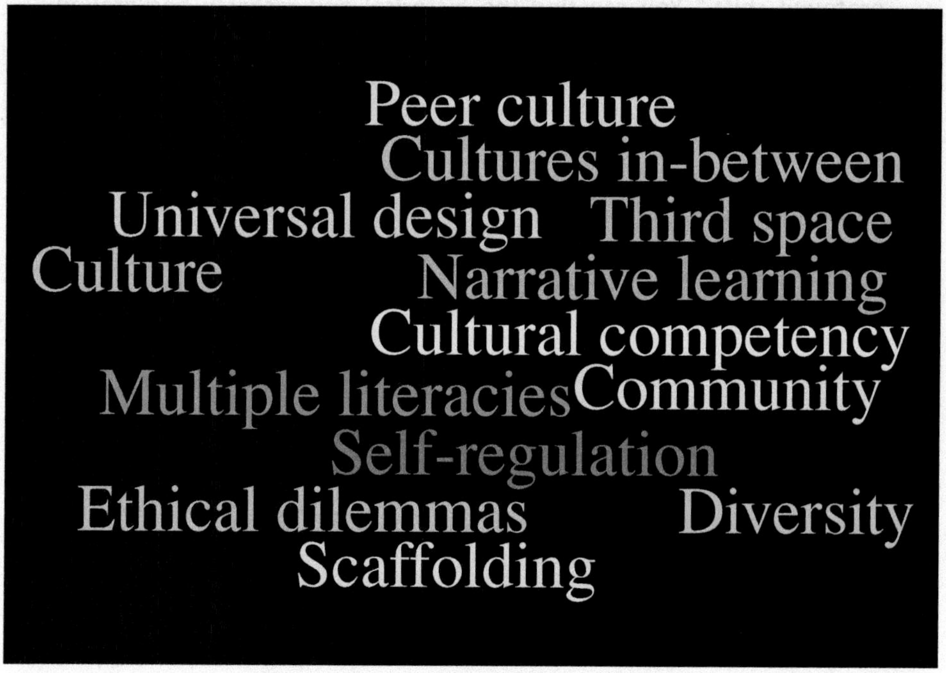

Figure 3.5 Key terms wordle

SUMMARY

Early learning professionals design and create spaces that include all children and support community, culture, and diversity, and incorporate the concepts of universal design and the third space. Using strategies such as scaffolding, narrative learning, and opportunities to be multiliterate, they can help children scaffold their development and learn to self-regulate. Ethical dilemmas will provide a means to critically reflect on values and beliefs as they relate to the core ideas of this chapter.

1. In examining the terms *diversity*, *culture*, and *cultural diversity*, early learning students can understand how to design and create spaces where all children and families are respected.
2. Early learning professionals have a responsibility to create a culturally diverse program for children and their families.
3. Programming processes can create barriers for some children and families. Early learning professionals can recognize and help others to overcome these barriers.
4. Early learning professionals can use strategies such as narrative learning to provide meaningful cultural experiences, thus creating opportunities to engage with multiple languages and literacies.

5. When early learning professionals engage in community building, they contribute to the development of social, self-regulation, and cultural competencies in children.

6. The way the environment is designed affects the building of a diverse community. Early learning students and professionals who understand the concepts of third space and universal design demonstrate a culturally diverse community.

For Further Thought	**In their article, "What if All the Children in My Class are White?" Derman-Sparks and Ramsey (2005) call for the dominant culture to "undergo a profound shift." You can find the historical and research background supporting this article at http://bit.ly/1ejhHPU. It will be helpful in thinking further about culture and diversity.**

Chapter 4
Programs and Approaches

LEARNING OUTCOMES

After exploring this chapter, you should be able to

1. Describe the historical, classical, modern, and postmodern traditions that influence early learning programming.
2. Examine the relationships between ideologies, philosophies, and theories.
3. Discuss the similarities and differences among a minimum of five early learning program models, approaches, and implementation processes.
4. Explain the professional responsibility that early learning professionals have in planning and implementing a program that aligns with an approach or model.
5. Discuss why and how theories, philosophies, and programming models or approaches may change over time.

A CHILD'S STORY   Aubree

My mom has been telling me for a long time that our family is going to have a new adventure. She says that we are moving to a new place. Tomorrow we are going on an airplane, and then when we get to our new place, we are going to find me a new playschool. I will be sad to leave Ramim, Kyle, Jake, and Jack. Like yesterday, we took big boards from the supply shed and got some sticks, and then our teacher Myra helped us find some blankets. We were having so much fun that Myra stayed outside with us until lunchtime.

The plane ride was long and we had to go up and go down and go up and down again. We went to visit two new playschools. The first one was big inside and there were lots of kind-of-different things there from my other school. The teacher showed me the pink tower and the brown stairs, and then she sat with me to show me how to use the pink tower on my very own carpet. Later, children who wanted to attend the talking circle could. I sat with my mummy there and the teacher said I was a visitor. After the conversational circle, my mummy and I left so we could go to another playschool.

When we were driving to this next school, my mummy said this one was different from any school I had ever been to. She said it is out in the forest. Oh, I thought to myself, I like being in the woods—is that where the school is? When we arrived, the teacher walked my mummy and me around the area. I just wanted to play. There were stumps to climb on, there were trees that we could climb, there was a hut to go in, there was a brook with rocks to jump on, and there were great big wooden blocks. As my mummy was talking to a teacher, Allie asked me to climb the tree with him to see what he could see. I turned to my mummy and said, "Oh Mummy, I want to play here!" My mummy said, "We will see." I hope my mummy chooses this playschool. I want to go up the tree again with Allie.

Children and their teacher on their way to the forest.

Rosalba Bortolotti

CHAPTER PREVIEW

*The child's own instincts and powers furnish the material
and give the starting point for all education.*

—John Dewey (1859–1952)

Your practice as an early learning professional occurs in a social context that is diverse. In any early learning setting, adults and children bring with them differing abilities, interests, cultures, values, languages, and experiences. The programming decisions that you make should reflect an understanding that relationships are at the heart of what you do. Decisions about which professional tools, materials, and methods you select can be complicated because there is an "astounding array of choices (technologies, ideologies, theories, materials)" (Follari, 2011, p. 1). To be successful in supporting children, families, and colleagues, it is important that you have a solid foundation of professional knowledge to draw upon in guiding and supporting the decisions you make about what programs or approach to follow (Follari, 2011).

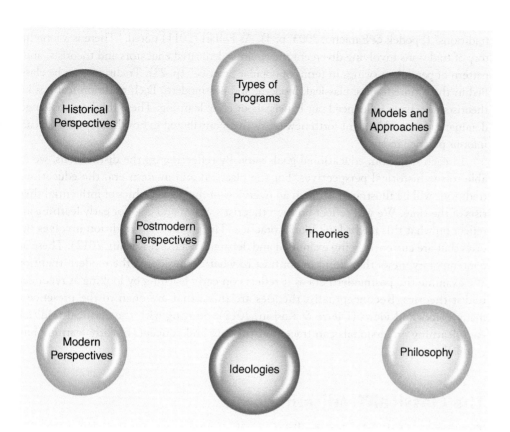

Figure 4.1 Influences on program models and approaches

Early learning professionals worldwide are being asked to make critical decisions about curriculum as public and professional interest in early learning increases globally. What children should be learning, how children should learn, and what teachers should be teaching are questions being asked by experts, teacher educators, professionals, and parents alike. Early learning is at a critical juncture because the distinction between teaching and learning is not clear—children can teach and teachers can learn. Programs that value relationships and promote participatory curricular decision making are expanding. Your values and beliefs are shaped by your understanding of the historical and current perspectives of the development of early learning as a distinct profession and curriculum. According to Hill (2005) and colleagues being aware of the history of early learning "positions us to better understand our approach to teaching and learning in the context of how teaching has developed and changed over time" (p. 13). As identified in Figure 4.1, to understand current programs and approaches, we need to examine the influence of past, present, and utopian perspectives.

HISTORICAL PERSPECTIVES

The study of early learning has changed significantly over time. Examining traditions will help early learning professionals or students understand how historical perspectives have influenced current curriculum models and programs. *Traditions* are long-standing customs and/or beliefs that influence professional practice and continue to evolve in the early learning sector (Spodek & Saracho, 2003). Traditions develop and then disappear or reappear in novel forms. "Oftentimes it seems that traditions swing back and forth like a pendulum, as contemporary tradition emerges and early childhood experts respond by creating alternative traditions" (Spodek & Saracho, 2003, p. 3). As Follari (2011) noted, "There is a long history of traditions involving divergent viewpoints, dedicated educators and theorists, and a pattern of pendulum swings in terms of popular practice" (p. 23). Traditions can be classified in three time frames: classical, modern, and postmodern. Each tradition features key theorists who have influenced our beliefs about early learning. These thinkers challenged dominant ideas and brought forth new ideals that contributed to how history unfolded and informs practice today.

In each tradition, educational goals vary. By reflecting on the distinctions, we are able to see historical perspectives. For the classical and modern era, the educational traditions will be illustrated through an overview of the philosophies of influential theorists of the time. We will reflect on each theorist's vision and goal for early learning and reflect on what this might look like in practice. The postmodern tradition involves theories that are currently being examined and debated (Dietze & Kashin, 2012). These are contemporary views that stand in contrast to what is considered the modern tradition. We examine the postmodern era as it reflects on early learning by looking at reconceptualist theories. Reconceptualist theories are those that are open to the presence of many voices and views (Dietze & Kashin, 2012). Starting with the classical tradition, early learning professionals can trace how theories and concepts of early learning have evolved over time.

The Classical Tradition

classical tradition In early learning, the theories that were common prior to the First World War.

The theories of the **classical tradition** are those that were prevalent before the First World War (Dietze & Kashin, 2012). Prior to the 1600s, children were generally treated as small adults, and thus early learning was considered unimportant. Childhood was not "necessarily valued as an important phase of life" (Follari, 2011, p. 24). Life was harsh for children, and if they did receive an education, it was often focused on religious learning and or trade skills that would be required as adults (Follari, 2011). The goal of education was piety and preparation for trade. In the classical period, thinkers such as Jean-Jacques Rousseau (1712–1778) emphasized that childhood was a distinct period of life and children were by nature "good." This view contradicted the commonly held belief that children were born evil, and, therefore, punishment was acceptable to drive out the evil from within (Hill et al., 2005). In Figure 4.2, we list classical theorists and their educational vision and goals. The classical era is also referred to as the *romantic* or *radical era* because in this period, early learning and education became more focused on the child, who was now seen as innocent and needing protection (Follari, 2011). These theories radically changed the way in which children were taught and greatly improved the conditions for learning.

The Modern Tradition

modern tradition In early learning, the theories that evolved after the First World War.

The **modern tradition** evolved after the First World War (Dietze & Kashin, 2012). During this time, many diverse types of programs for early learning evolved, which will be discussed later in the chapter. Many programs were influenced by the progressive ideas of the educational theorist John Dewey, who introduced to early learning the ideals of constructivism. At the same time, the progressive education movement, which lasted from the late 1800s to the mid-1900s, changed education at the elementary level. For example, "a new kind of school emerged from these ideals. Moveable furniture replaced rows of benches. Children's projects, some still under construction, were found everywhere" (Gordon & Browne, 2011, p. 10). The curriculum had a broader focus than just academics. The way in which early learning

John Amos Comenius (1592–1670)

His vision was that education should be for all children and will promote social harmony and religion. He believed that mothers are their children's best educators and that children require active learning rather than excessive academics (Dietze & Kashin, 2012; Follari, 2011).

John Locke (1632–1704)

His vision was that children are blank slates to be moulded by experiences that are favourable, free, and playful. Educational experiences should centre on children rather than religion. Children's behaviours should be guided with reasoning rather than punishment (Dietze & Kashin, 2012; Follari, 2011).

Jean-Jacques Rousseau (1712–1778)

His vision was that education should occur in a natural environment based on children's experiences and that childhood should be viewed differently from adulthood. Education supports the individual to learn within a social group and focuses on life experiences rather than academics. Parents' involvement is necessary but they are not sufficient educators of young children (Hill et al., 2005).

Johann Heinrich Pestalozzi (1756–1827)

His vision was of universal, democratic education where children naturally learn by doing through their encounters with real objects in their environments.

Friedrich Froebel (1782–1852)

His vision was that education should be considered as a protective garden. Educators need to make the connection between their philosophical beliefs and practical actions. Children learn through play experiences and the natural materials that are offered within their environment.

Figure 4.2 Classical theorists

unfolded in the modern era was influenced by societal, economic, and political forces. Sometimes the pendulum has swung in favour of models and approaches that are aligned with theorists such as Dewey, and at other times there has been a push toward a more academic focus. We encourage you to become familiar with the modern theorists as presented in Figure 4.3 on the next page. Take a reflective moment to become more familiar with how early learning has evolved over the years (see the accompanying box).

Aside from Howard Gardner, none of the theorists described in Figure 4.3 are still living. As a result, early learning professionals and students may question the relevancy of studying the theories of these philosophers. Examining the theorists can offer us insight into these pedagogical thinkers and their ideas for the time. We examine their thinking and have discourse on their theories and philosophies, as the process of discourse opens up opportunities for new ideas to be identified.

Theories of early learning are still being formulated today, and many great thinkers who are still alive are influencing early learning. One of the most influential is Howard Gardner (born in 1943), who devised the theory of **multiple intelligences** (MI theory), based on the concept that children learn from the different ways they interact with their environment. Gardner (1999) described eight intelligences within each person, as outlined

multiple intelligences A theory developed by Gardner (1999) that describes eight different intelligences influencing learning.

A Reflective Moment

Visit the link provided here to find a detailed history of early childhood education in Canada. After reading, reflect on this question: Where do you think the field of early learning is headed in the future?

http://bit.ly/15okz8V

John Dewey (1859–1952)

His vision was that experiences for children should be planned according to their needs, interests, and abilities. Children learn by doing in environments that support their whole development.

Rudolph Steiner (1861–1925)

He believed that curriculum and play experiences evolve from an individual child and groups of children in environments that are aesthetically pleasing and encourage social interaction among children and adults.

Maria Montessori (1870–1952)

Her vision was that children gain competence and responsibility in orderly and beautiful environments that are planned based on the observations of children's developmental stages and skills.

Lev Vygotsky (1896–1934)

His vision was that children learn when they play within a social context, and that social and cognitive development should work together. Children require opportunities to cross their zone of proximal development through more knowledgeable others, such as the teacher.

Jean Piaget (1896–1980)

His vision was that children learn through hands-on experiences within environments that offer them a variety of materials to support their play and advance their cognitive development. Children benefit from having teachers who facilitate opportunities for new experiences and learning.

Erik Erikson (1902–1994)

His vision was that children learn through their environment and from social relationships, diversity, culture, and real things. Through play, children take charge of their problems and figure out ways to resolve issues.

Loris Malaguzzi (1920–1994)

His vision was that schools are places for adults and children to experience a feeling of belonging in a world that is alive, welcoming, and authentic. The goal is that children and families experience "nothing without joy" and that children, parents, and teachers observe, document, and interpret, thereby making learning visible.

Howard Gardner (born 1943)

His vision was that children learn from the different ways they interact with their naturalistic environment, including family, culture, and those in their learning community. Through observation and documentation of how children solve problems and create new learning, adults gain insight into the children's strengths and interests.

Figure 4.3 Modern theorists

in Table 4.1. There has been discussion about adding more intelligences, such as a ninth spiritual intelligence. To see what Howard Gardner thinks about adding more to his list, go to http://bit.ly/17qudyO.

Howard Gardner's theory of multiple intelligences is evident in Reggio Emilia–inspired programs in many ways, including the principle that the environment is the "third teacher." This means that early learning professionals pay particular attention to the organization of the "space, relationships; aesthetics; promoting choices and decisions about how to execute projects; and partnerships among children, adults, and families" (Dietze, 2006, p. 104). Early learning programs that are influenced by Gardner's theory would further ensure that children have choices and options for exploration that further support cultural attributes such as music and art. Nature and environmental principles are also evident.

During the modern era, a number of theorists took a *behavioural approach*, including John B. Watson, Albert Bandura, B.F. Skinner, and Edward Thorndike. These theorists suggested that children's learning and behaviours occur as a result of how people respond to their behaviours and the consequences that occur. The frequency of positive or preferred behaviours is increased when positive reinforcement is provided immediately after the behaviour occurs. Gradually, the reinforcement is reduced as the behaviour becomes

Table 4.1 Gardner's Multiple Intelligences

Intelligence	What It Refers To
Bodily-kinaesthetic	The ability of children to use their bodies or parts of their bodies in various ways for personal expression.
Intrapersonal	The ability of children to understand their strengths/knowledge about a variety of topics and experiences and the areas that require further development.
Interpersonal	A child's abilities to work with peers and others to assume a leadership role and to communicate effectively with people in the learning community.
Linguistic	Children's ability to use language in multi-dimensional ways, including reading, writing, and conversing with others.
Logical-mathematical	Children's logic and ability to use numbers, understand patterns, and complete mathematical experiences.
Music	Children's ability to create, perform, or enjoy music.
Naturalistic	Children's ability to discriminate among living things, such as plants, animals, and people, as well as other naturalistic issues that affect daily living.
Spatial	Children's ability to create a visual image of an idea or a project and then produce a model or presentation of that idea.

Source: Adapted from Gardner, 1999.

established. Skinner suggested that adults can support or eliminate children's behaviours and reactions to situations through the environments they create. Follow the link in the Reflective Moment box and explore how the historic British Infant Schools used a behavioural approach to programming. Then think about this approach and how it relates to your values, beliefs, and ideas of how children play and learn.

For many early learning professionals, the behavioural approach may not be a preferred practice; however, as identified by Hendrick and Weissman (2006), before "blindly condemning such theory, why not become aware of how we often employ such strategies on an informal basis" (p. 14)? Think about early learning programs that choose to use a "time-out chair" with a child when a teacher believes that a child's behaviour is inappropriate. The child is required to sit on a chair for a specified period of time without contact with others. This strategy is a form of behaviour modification. From a behavioural perspective, this approach, by removing the child from the social setting, is intended to cause the child to reflect upon the unacceptable behaviour and realize why it was wrong. Many suggest that this approach reduces children's self-esteem and opportunities to internally build self-regulation skills (Dietze, 2006). Early learning professionals who believe in providing children with a voice and in not exhibiting power over them are strong advocates of examining the environment,

⟩ A Reflective Moment

The British Infant Schools (http://bit.ly/105Jr6O) and the Direct Instruction Model (http://bit.ly/1486cGp) are two examples of programs that followed the tenets of behaviourism. For a critique of these programs, see http://bit.ly/16QoiPL.

After reading the essay by Alfie Kohn, what is your position on the goals of behaviourist education?

the situation, and play experiences that may need to be adjusted to support the needs of children, rather than using a time-out chair. Child guidance techniques that support children in maintaining their self-esteem and reciprocal respect are most conducive to changing behaviours. Programs that fall within a behaviourist paradigm reflect a narrowing of goals for early learning from a developmental concern for the whole child (across developmental domains) to an academic focus.

After the 1970s, there was unparalleled expansion in early learning services based on a proliferation of program models and approaches (Spodek & Saracho, 2003). According to Spodek and Saracho (2003), the new programs that dominated the end of the twentieth century were "often based on or inspired by different theories of development—theories that provided a great deal of optimism" (p. 7) to early learning. The majority of programs that propagated the landscape after the 1970s fall into two categories: the child-centred, play-oriented, emerging curriculum model and the academic model. Leading into the twenty-first century the pendulum swung toward narrowly focused early learning as programs began to focus exclusively on "readiness" (Spodek & Saracho, 2003, p. 7). Today, the question of which way the pendulum will swing—and why—remains up for discussion. With the advent of the postmodern tradition, multiple perspectives and discourse about early learning will contribute to examining, critiquing, challenging, and bringing clarity and greater understanding to the complexity of early learning programming.

The Postmodern Tradition

postmodern tradition An approach that explores multiple theories and perspectives about early learning.

Looking back at the history of early learning, the pendulum seems to have swung back and forth several times from progressive positions, such as those espoused by John Dewey, to a narrow emphasis on academic priorities. The **postmodern tradition** challenges this as narrow focus. "Postmodernists consider that there are many different voices, and many styles, and take care not to value or privilege one set of values over another" (Penn, 2005, p. 28). The assumption is that teaching enacts power relations, making multiple voices necessary to prevent privilege (Ryan & Grieshaber, 2005), whereas the modern tradition fails to reflect the beliefs and experiences of everyone. Postmodernists ask that we question what we know and trust our own experiences and perspectives, in addition to the claims of experts. Currently, we can see the pendulum swinging as more challenges are being directed to theories that too often have been left unquestioned, such as the teacher-directed role rather than the social-constructivist teacher role. We see the evolution of the postmodern tradition allowing for the ebb and flow of ideas that will lead us to consider an array of possibilities for the future of early learning and the early learning profession.

Contemporary theories are also currently being examined and debated (Dietze & Kashin, 2012). Any theory from either the classical or the modern era can be viewed from a postmodern perspective. A postmodernist looks at theories critically. For example, one modern theory that is currently being debated from a postmodern perspective is *developmentally appropriate practice*, or DAP theory. DAP has been widely and enthusiastically embraced by some and disputed by others. When DAP became prominent in the 1980s, it represented a reform effort in early learning. At the time, Bredekamp (1987) suggested that the concept of developmental appropriateness has two dimensions. The first dimension is age appropriateness, which uses human development research to guide practice according to predictable sequences of growth and change. The second dimension is individual appropriateness, which encourages early learning professionals to plan and implement an inclusive curriculum because each child is considered "a unique person with an individual pattern and timing of growth, as well as individual personality, learning style, and family background" (Bredekamp, 1987, p. 3). In addition to emulating the early theories of Pestalozzi, DAP curriculum was influenced by the constructivist theories of Jean Piaget (Kashin, 2009).

Developmentally appropriate and developmentally inappropriate art experiences, both representing "trees."

Diane Kashin

DAP models value child-centred, experience-centred, and process-oriented practices. For proponents of DAP, learning occurs in developmental stages, with children able to understand, process, and construct knowledge at different levels and in different ways in successive stages (Raines, 1997). In spite of enthusiastic acceptance of DAP in the late 1980s and early 1990s, some critics have suggested that with adherence to developmental stages, the complexities of development are reduced to simplified and quantifiable representations (Dahlberg, Moss, & Pence, 1999). There is an assumption that this developmental theory is value free and focuses on the individual child's areas requiring development, rather than viewing the child in a social, cultural, political, and economic context (Kashin, 2009).

Reconceptualist scholars question the existence of a singular truth and, consequently, of universality. If there is no single truth, then early learning professionals need to recognize the importance of context and values when making programming decisions. **Reconceptualization** or "the reconceptualist movement postulates the validity of many truths relative to their contexts" (Pacini-Ketchabaw & Pence, 2005, p. 7). Critics of DAP have emphasized the ways in which relations of power, social and cultural reproduction, social constructions, and assumptions of universality are embedded within the theory and how it is applied in practice. Even though critique of the DAP discourse has been a central theme among reconceptualist thinkers in the United States, DAP has retained its dominant status in U.S. early learning programs. Canadian reconceptualists have taken a more active role in the area of cross-cultural research by examining the early learning experiences of immigrants and Aboriginals from multiple perspectives (Kirova, 2010; Pacini-Ketchabaw & Pence, 2005).

reconceptualization A movement that challenges the existence of a singular truth and instead believes in multiple perspectives.

IDEOLOGIES

The differences between various models or approaches to early learning are essentially a reflection of thought processes about **ideologies**. The concept of ideology refers largely to a "world-view, or collective mind-set, that characterizes a population" (Fiala, 2007, p. 18). Early learning systems reflect, and are influenced by, ideology and organizational processes at the individual, group, and societal level (Fiala, 2007).

ideologies Worldviews or collective mindsets of a population.

Examining the distinctions between particular ideology and total ideology, as inspired by Mannheim's (1936/1959) discussion of ideology and utopia, provides early learning professionals with a deeper understanding of the influence of ideology on early learning. *Particular ideology* refers to the psychology of early learning professionals that is "used to justify and legitimate action that is driven by self-interest" (Fiala, 2007, p. 19). *Total ideology*, on the other hand, refers to the "whole outlook of a social group" (p. 19). In essence, *ideology* is a system of ideas or ideals that form the basis of programming policies. Ideologies become the organizing principles for programming, and they push the notion of creative thought to create images of utopia. Utopian thinking occurs when individuals or groups break the cycle of familiar practices and establish a new reality (Mannheim, 1936/1959). Ideological systems may have aspects of utopian thinking built within them; then, through critiquing and reconstructing, change to the systems or processes occurs and these new systems become the social norm (Fiala, 2007).

More than forty years ago, Kohlberg and Mayer (1972) identified three distinct streams of educational ideology that continue to influence early learning programs today. They are the romantic stream, cultural transmission, and the progressive stream. The *romantic stream* is evident in developmental theories such as those of Arnold Gesell and Sigmund Freud. Early childhood programs with child-initiated and child-centred characteristics model this ideology. The *cultural transmission* ideology is exhibited within a program that focuses on passing down information from one generation to the next, through direct instruction or apprenticeship-type experiences. The *progressive stream* emphasizes the use of social life within the learning community as a source of knowledge. Early learning programs that support and encourage children in creating their knowledge through the human and environmental resources available to them would fall under the progressive ideological stream. These differing ideologies are examples of how the competencies of early learning professionals are expected to continuously be reconstructed as a result of the influences of a changing society and the shifting of values, beliefs, and intentions related to children, families, pedagogy, and programming models or approaches.

PHILOSOPHIES

The term *philosophy* is often used but not necessarily explained. Jones and Shelton (2011) define *philosophy* as "a personal clarification and articulation of your educational beliefs and values. You define yourself by it; your practice reflects it" (p. 66). Your philosophy is influenced by your life experiences and ideology, and by how you incorporate new information into your existing professional knowledge. This process requires some deep thinking that might produce disequilibrium. One way to think about philosophy is to imagine that over centuries, like-minded people constructed ways to explain life and the universe that resulted in the articulation of a variety of beliefs, ideals, and philosophies.

Early learning professionals adopt a philosophical approach to programming based on a set of assumptions that they have examined, reflected upon, and articulated. Early learning professionals' philosophical approach is influenced by

- their understanding of how children learn;
- their beliefs about the relationship of play to learning;
- their ideas about how environments affect children's levels of curiosity;
- their beliefs about their roles in programming and facilitating options for play and learning; and
- their interpretation of how theorists' perspectives view children and the role of the adult and the environment.

Metaphysics	**Espistemology**	**Axiology**
• What is the nature of reality?	• What is the nature of knowledge?	• What is the nature of values?

Figure 4.4 Contexts for philosophy

Source: Adapted from Jones & Shelton, 2011.

Having a theoretical perspective for programming guides the way in which the environment is prepared for children and their families, and the parameters that are for children executing play experiences. In the Pedagogical Tools section of this chapter, you will be guided through the process of creating your own philosophical statement. According to the Ontario Early Learning Framework (2006), the two most common philosophies that you will see in early learning environments are constructivism, which is part of progressivism, and instructivism. **Constructivism** refers to knowledge that is acquired through active involvement with content and experimentation (Kashin, 2009). Building on that, progressivism emphasizes learning by doing, experimenting, and using problem-solving and critical-thinking skills to create new knowledge and skills. **Instructivism** refers to learning that involves instruction imparted from the expert to the learner, with the learner taking on a passive role rather than being actively involved.

Instructivism in the discipline of philosophy relates most closely to behaviourism in the early learning field. Early learning professionals may find it helpful to relate their philosophical thinking about children to the three main contexts in the practice of early learning illustrated in Figure 4.4 (Jones & Shelton, 2011).

In Figure 4.5, the two common schools of thought in early learning are presented as they relate to the three contexts of philosophy, contrasting program goals, and what you might expect to see when each theory is applied to practice.

It is important to choose a workplace where your philosophy aligns with the program philosophy. Generally, the program philosophy statement originates from the board of directors or owner(s) of the early learning centre and is based on the decision makers' theories about how children play and learn. A philosophy statement should change over time as early learning professionals provide and new research and resources become available.

constructivism A theoretical perspective that refers to the gaining of knowledge through active involvement.

instructivism Learning that involves instruction delivered to the learner via an expert, with little active involvement.

Constructivism or Progressivism

Metaphysics

• Reality is experience derived from interactions between the individual and the environment.

Epistemology

• Knowledge comes to be known through experimentation using the scientific method. Truth is never fully known.

Axiology

• What is ethically or morally good is judged on the basis of what works for the larger community. It is relative and situational.

Goal and Practice

• To promote autonomy, problem solving, lifelong learning, and social responsibility by children being self-directed, intrinsically motivated, and actively engaged within an environment and with others. The teacher acts as a facilitator and guide, offering opportunities for children to participate in cooperative learning, problem setting and problem solving with open-ended activities.

Figure 4.5 Two common philosophies (*continued*)

> **Behaviourism or Instructivism**
>
> **Metaphysics**
> - There is no such thing as free will. Individuals are products of their external environment.
>
> **Epistemology**
> - Knowledge and learning are derived from external stimuli.
>
> **Axiology**
> - Values are environmentally formed.
>
> **Goal and Practice**
> - To promote conformity to authority and passivity by children following directions and engaging in a prescribed program of learning with skill and drill exercises, mastery of discrete bits of knowledge, use of worksheets, and receiving awards for desirable behaviours and performance.

Figure 4.5 Two common philosophies *(continued)*

Source: Adapted from Jones & Shelton, 2011.

THEORIES

Theories are the foundation for programming and practice. A *theory* refers to a "collection of ideas, concepts, terms and statements blended to illustrate behaviour" (Arce, 2000, p. 9). Early learning professionals combine theory and practice in evidence-based decision making—a process of integrating current research evidence with family and professional beliefs and values. In evidence-based decision making, participants in the learning community examine issues and ideas in broad terms so that different ways of knowing evolve (Buysse & Wesley, 2006). Evidence of practice can be found in the features, philosophy, and programming invitations provided for children.

Making theory a component of practice should be a desired goal for early learning professionals who are committed to personal and career development. Accepting theory into practice propels early learning professionals, as a group, to higher levels of professionalization and, as individuals, to higher planes of development (Kashin, 2009). We will begin by exploring the influence of theories on programs. As you will see in the next section, and as identified in Figure 4.6, a variety of programs are encompassed by the field of early childhood education.

PROGRAMS

Many types of formalized early learning programs exist, as identified in Figure 4.6. Formalized early learning programs have a history dating back to the nineteenth century when the "day nursery" was a place for women and children to seek assistance in times of need. At that time in Canada, there were only a handful of day nurseries, because demand was limited by a small population and low numbers of poor, wage-earning mothers. Growth of the field paralleled urban development, and six of the seven largest Canadian cities had

Figure 4.6 Formalized early learning programs

at least one nursery by 1912. The nurseries were a social-welfare product—a charitable response from philanthropists to help families in peril (Prochner, 2000). At the same time, the kindergarten movement, spurred by the work of Froebel, was gaining momentum, resulting in the emergence of nursery school programs.

Modest growth of child care continued, but the economic depression of the 1930s made it difficult for women to find work. Stagnation lasted until the outbreak of the Second World War. While wartime nurseries served relatively few families, for the first time, group child care was promoted as a normal support for families. However, many day nurseries closed after the war. Those that remained open functioned in a custodial mode. In the 1960s, there was again a movement to rejuvenate kindergarten education, especially in central Canada because of increasing concern for social inequities. This time, kindergarten was receiving attention under the umbrella of departments of education. At the same time, child care was also undergoing restructuring, but again as a social service (Prochner, 2000).

The main difference between nursery schools, kindergartens, and child care programs is that the first two are considered educational services, while the last is viewed as a social-welfare program. The half-day nursery school is usually privately funded, attracting children from middle class and affluent families, whereas child care most often has some public funding and is used by lower-income families. Nursery school is seen as a socialization play service for children, while child care is considered a service for parents, providing institutional, custodial care or babysitting (Caldwell, 2004). Over the last five years, increased professionalism of the workforce and the unparalleled expansion of child care programs, as well as the combining of child care and full-day publicly funded kindergarten, are blurring the lines across many jurisdictions in Canada. Although the distinctions are less visible, there are further complications with regard to the auspice of the programs.

Auspice refers to who runs the program. Some programs are run as businesses by owners and are often referred to as *for-profit* or *commercial*. Some of these programs are single entities, while others are part of larger corporations. Some programs are managed by large companies who offer *workplace* early learning/child care as a service to their employees. Not-for-profit or *nonprofit* programs are incorporated and licensed or approved by a designated provincial or territory department and overseen by a board of directors that includes parents and community members. They too can be single entities or part of a much larger nonprofit organization.

auspice The governing body of an early learning program. Auspice is considered a determinant of quality.

Some nursery school, child care, and specialized programs are attached to universities and colleges; these are often referred to as *lab schools*. The history of lab schools goes back to John Dewey, who established a lab school at the University of Chicago in the early 1900s that attracted attention from around the world. It was the "center of thought on progressive education, the movement toward more democratic and child-centered education" (Mooney, 2000, p. 2). Lab school programs are sites where early learning faculty, students, and professionals come together with children to apply theory to practice and, in some instances, undertake research on various aspects of early childhood education.

In some major hospitals, you will find another program type, often referred to as a *child life* program. The first formal child life program was started by Emma Plank in the early 1960s at the Cleveland Metropolitan Hospital in Ohio. The programs were established to support the physical and psychological care of children while recuperating from illness or injury. Child life professionals build relationships with children and their families and advocate for children's experiences in hospital settings to reflect normal daily living patterns of families, including play experiences and education. According to Robinson (2012), child life professionals draw upon attachment theory and Erikson's psychosocial development theory as a framework for their practice. Child life specialists observe children and draw upon their daily interactions with them to determine the types of experiences or programming that will be offered. Child life specialists focus on their daily interactions with children and families and on making the play and learning environment positive and supportive.

Seneca College's Newnham
Campus lab school.

Diane Kashin

Over the course of centuries, many well-known programs, such as Dewey's famous lab school, have garnered attention. In Table 4.2, we introduce you to five program exemplars and list the main features and the theorists or theories that influenced the program.

Table 4.2 Program Exemplars

Program	Features	Influential Theorists/Theories
Bank Street Founded by suffragette Lucy Sprague Mitchell in 1916. It began as an experimental nursery school and continues to offer teacher education and a lab school. See http://bit.ly/16Qp8fu.	• Child development principles inform practice. • Curriculum evolves from the child. • Early life experiences influence lifelong learning and living outcomes.	• Erik Erikson's psychodynamic theory
Creative Curriculum Developed over thirty years ago, creative curriculum is described as a content-rich, developmentally appropriate program supporting active learning in all developmental areas. See http://bit.ly/11BKGbt.	• Designed to meet children's basic needs, foster social/emotional development, and support cognition and brain development. • Secure attachments are important.	• Abraham Maslow's hierarchy of needs • Erik Erikson's psychodynamic theory • John Bowlby and Mary Ainsworth's attachment theory

Program	Features	Influential Theorists/Theories
Head Start The first Head Start pilot program started in 1965 in the United States. The primary goal is to alleviate risks to children living in poverty. It has become one of the largest providers of early learning in the United States (Follari, 2011). Head Start programs are prominent on many First Nations reserves across Canada. See http://1.usa.gov/181ha6b.	• Provide experiences to foster healthy development. • Provide early intervention. • Take a holistic view of child development. • Parental involvement is considered important.	• Jean Piaget's cognitive constructivism theory • Lev Vygotsky's social constructivism theory • Jerome Bruner's theory of readiness • Developmentally appropriate practice
City and Country Established in 1914 by Caroline Pratt, a follower of John Dewey. Pratt believed that children should have the opportunity to play and represent what they see in the world. She believed that observing children was essential in learning about them and from them. The wooden unit blocks Pratt developed to use in the City and Country School are still widely used today. See http://bit.ly/16QpHFX.	• Provide open-ended materials for children to recreate the world around them. • Children use dramatic play to recreate events.	• John Dewey's progressivism theories
Tools of the Mind For almost two decades, the program developed by Bodrova and Leong (1996) has been promoting children's intentional and regulated learning. Research indicates that interventions in the early years can have a positive influence on self-regulation and the development of executive function in the early years and beyond, which supports academic success. See http://bit.ly/123ywuU.	• Teachers systematically scaffold children's self-regulation skills. • Children gain control of their behaviours by learning to use a variety of mental tools. • Reflective thinking and cognition are emphasized. • Children practise self-regulation throughout the day by engaging in increasingly more complex imaginary play scenarios.	• Lev Vygotsky's social constructivism theories

Source: Adapted from Follari, 2012; Bodrova & Leong, 1996.

MODELS AND APPROACHES

The term *curriculum model* refers to a conceptual framework used for making decisions about education priorities, including policies and practices regarding instructional and evaluative methods (Goffin & Wilson, 2001). We use the term *approach* in addition to *model* because some of the programs we describe view the term *model* as less flexible. The articulation of a program model or an approach to programming is often a licensing requirement for early learning centres, depending on where the centre is located. Many early learning centres will proclaim their affinity to one model or approach in their *philosophy statement*.

Understanding theories, how theories inform practice as well as influence environmental designs and the programming model, is a complex process. Developing a programming model or approach that is inclusive of children's needs and aspirations, family values, and cultural diversity, and that is responsive to the children as a group and as individuals, adds to the complexity of the process. One of the first steps is to examine the various theories that guide program models and approaches. As you explore the theories and programming models and approaches, we encourage you to reflect upon your beliefs about children and your vision for what programs might look like in your practice.

This reflective process may bring forth some "aha!" moments, disequilibrium, or the need for discourse with colleagues and your critical friend as a way to support you in bringing further clarity to your vision. Expanding your understanding of how theories influence early learning programming is essential as background for you in defining your personal philosophy about early learning programming, children, play, and family engagement.

While you may already have an affinity with a certain philosophy or may have been inspired by a particular approach, we encourage you to expand your professional knowledge and to become articulate about the background, history, philosophy, and programming scope of each variation. The strategy we suggest for doing this is called *curation* and employs social media to share with colleagues, helping to create a social construct for professional learning.

The term *curate* is most often associated with museums and art galleries and refers to selecting and organizing information to be exhibited. The social media platform Pinterest (www.pinterest.com) lets you curate your own professional learning topic and share it with others who have similar professional interests. You can browse boards created by other people to discover and learn new things about your topic and how it relates to your professional practice. Pinterest gives you a forum to be inspired and to share your inspiration with others.

On Pinterest, you will be able to find many examples of images representing the various programming approaches described in this textbook. We encourage you to use the process of curation to collect and manage your own professional learning boards. With each model or approach described in this chapter, we will give you a number of links to pins that can serve as an illustration. For more information on Pinterest, early learning, and curation, visit http://bit.ly/1aRe9F7.

Each program model or approach has its own distinct features. If you walk into an early learning environment that builds its program upon a particular model or approach, this should be immediately observable. There should be clues in the design of the space, the furniture and equipment, the aesthetics of the environment, and what is posted on the walls. You should be able to see theories reflected in the environment and in the interactions between children and their teachers. In the next section, we will introduce you to models and approaches commonly used in programs today.

The Unit or Thematic Approach

Historically, the word *thematic* was used to mean a broad topic for a unit in a school curriculum model (Vartuli & Rohs, 2006). Robinson and Schwartz (1982) noted that "themes represent an effort to integrate curriculum and to retain the design of interest centre activity, which has been the traditional format for programs for young children" (p. 3). Themes are either teacher planned or teacher and child planned. The duration of a theme may be several days or longer. The theme is generally integrated across the curriculum and broken into meaningful activities or experiences. Goals, objectives, and outcomes are usually established prior to implementing the theme. Children may or may not engage in in-depth inquiry, depending on the way in which the theme is presented and the types of activities and materials that are made available. Having selected a theme, the teacher plans ahead for activities and materials to present information that will provide some interesting facts about the theme and, possibly, opportunities to practise specific mental ability skills, such as simple classification or letter recognition (Kashin, 2009).

When you walk into a program using themes, you will probably see the evidence on the classroom bulletin boards. "The teacher controls the agenda for action" and "there is a prescribed range of possible responses that the children are permitted; activity outside the range is corrected" (Wien, 1995, p. 8). In trying to duplicate a school model, early learning professionals may feel it provides an academic focus, especially with the use of worksheets. Programs may use instructional group experiences, construction paper cut-outs (e.g., turkeys at Thanksgiving, pumpkins at Halloween, and shamrocks for St. Patrick's Day), and worksheets to "teach" the children.

A number of criticisms have been made of thematic or unit program planning. For example, according to Hendrick (2004), curricular decisions around which theme to follow may occur when a teacher "may dredge something out of a box she has saved from last year and the year before that" (p. 43). Another major criticism of using themes is that they often involve a mimetic focus, with the children imitating an adult's conception and understanding of the theme rather than having the option to use their sense of curiosity and interests to guide their learning. If themes are used, from a constructivist perspective the topics would be chosen by the children and support active learning. Children's interests could also be used as a source for selecting a theme.

A third criticism is that often teachers are distracted by their obligations to follow the theme of the week and the strict timetable that corresponds with the implementation of a theme-based curriculum (Fleet, 2002). Time frames and transitions that accompany the day and the theme often ignore the possibilities of challenge and the time that children require to embark on active engagement. Taking the colour red as an example of a narrow theme, Fleet (2002, p. 21) challenged early learning professionals to ask, "Why focus on a primary colour and does it matter?". When themes are tightly scripted and dependent on teacher direction, they provide a predictable program sequence for the teacher. However, children's curricular needs are not so clear-cut or predictable. Other examples of theme topics could be water, spiders, transportation, and community helpers. If early learning professionals find themselves working in a program using themes, they may need to reconcile their own values and beliefs with the curriculum model. They can take responsibility as a professional to offer as many creative and open-ended experiences as possible within the restrictions of the theme program model.

Montessori

In 1907, Dr. Maria Montessori (1870–1952), Italy's first female doctor, founded Montessori education. Montessori believed that children can teach themselves in a "prepared environment" with self-correcting apparatus for learning (Daniels & Gamper, 2011, p. 62). In prepared environments, children are active explorers of their environment, learn at their own pace, and choose a variety of materials and activities that emphasize learning through the senses. Montessori felt that children learn best in environments where adults and children exhibit respect for each other (Daniels & Gamper, 2011). According to Montessori, during their development children pass through numerous "sensitive periods"—"genetically programmed blocks of time when young children are especially eager and able to master certain tasks" (Henninger, 2002, p. 102). For Montessori, one of the core roles of the adult is to conduct observations and use their findings to carefully prepare the environments with experiences that become more complex as the child gains new skills.

Montessori emphasized the importance of specialized training for early learning professionals that focuses on roles and strategies they can use to support children in their learning. She viewed the teacher's role as one of a guide for children, preparing the environment for learning and ensuring that there are neat and orderly classrooms, activities, and didactic materials in the environment so that children can easily access what they need.

Upon entering a Montessori school, you may expect to see children placed in three age groups. For example, children aged three to six are placed together, children aged six to nine are in the same group, and children aged nine to twelve are in a separate "community." Within each community, the older children "spontaneously share knowledge with the younger ones" (Daniels & Gamper, 2011, p. 62). You can expect to see child-sized furniture and many accessible materials (Howe, Jacobs, & Fiorentino, 2000), as Montessori crusaded for educational programs for young children to be more than just smaller versions of elementary education programs (Follari, 2011).

There have been some criticisms of the Montessori approach. One is that Montessori emphasized the importance of children having one-on-one experiences rather than group or teacher-led activities (Howe et al., 2000). The criticism is that this leads to limited interaction with peers and opportunities to learn within a learning community environment. The necessity to have trained teachers who introduce and model the didactic materials has also received criticism because of the perceived structure of how the children should use materials to acquire the right answer. A related criticism is the limited creative development through activities such as art, music, and outdoor play.

Montessori programs offer an alternative to the modern child care facility and are viewed as specialized programs that have become popular with middle-class families (Howe et al., 2000). They promote children's practical life skills such as doing chores, practising buttoning and unbuttoning, and pouring and stirring. In addition to practical life skills, the programs also include sensorial activities, cultural activities, language activities, and mathematics (Follari, 2011, p. 232).

HighScope

The programming framework of HighScope was originally known as the cognitively oriented curriculum and was developed by Weikart, Rogers, Adcock, and McClelland (1971). It is grounded in Piaget's cognitive development theory and constructivism and influenced by Vygotsky and Dewey. The program, heavily grounded in research, was designed to specifically support children living in poverty. It is most famous for the Perry Preschool Study, which concluded that there are positive lifetime effects when children are exposed to high-quality early learning environments.

When you walk into an early learning environment based on the HighScope model, you should see interest areas arranged for the children and a posted daily routine that permits children to plan, carry out, and reflect on their own activities. You should see the early learning professionals joining in the children's activities, engaging them in conversations that scaffold and extend the children's plans, and helping them think through their ideas and identify new potential areas of interest. Children are encouraged to make choices, solve

A practical life experience.
Diane Kashin

Pinterest Links

www.pinterest.com/pin/71142869087886342
www.pinterest.com/pin/71142869084655301
www.pinterest.com/pin/71142869086048729

problems, and otherwise engage in curriculum activities and experiences that contribute to their learning on key developmental indicators encompassing all areas of intellectual, social, emotional, and physical development (Schweinhart & Weikart, 2010).

Critics of the HighScope program object to its emphasis on cognitive development over social-emotional development and cite it as being developmentally inappropriate in its expectations of children. Teachers in HighScope programs have been criticized for not being accepting of children's incorrect answers and for interfering too frequently in play. Quebec was the first Canadian province to develop a curriculum framework using the HighScope model, but the framework has since been revised to address concerns about transferring an American-made curriculum to a French-Canadian setting. There was also concern that teacher training was not easily available for Canadians, and without extensive teacher training, the model might be implemented in a haphazard way (Howe et al., 2000).

The Project Approach

The project approach, while considered new and exciting, has a long history in early learning. "Projects to facilitate the education of young children have been part of the progressive tradition for over 80 years" (Spodek & Saracho, 2003, p. 3) despite being viewed by many as an innovation over the last twenty years (Kashin, 2009; Spodek & Saracho, 2003). The project approach "refers to a way of teaching and learning as well as to the content of what is taught and learned" (Katz & Chard, 1989, p. 3). It is a set of teaching strategies that enables, teachers to guide children through in-depth studies of real-world topics (Katz & Chard, 2000). Children are instrumental in deciding on topics, becoming the experts, and sharing accountability for learning with adults (Katz & Chard, 2000). Investigations may be undertaken by a small group of children within a class, sometimes by a whole class, and occasionally by an individual child (Katz, 1994). The promoters of the project approach, Sylvia Chard in Canada and Lillian Katz in the United States, based it on the work of Vygotsky, Piaget, and Dewey. In fact, projects were an important part of Dewey's Laboratory School at the University of Chicago at the beginning of the twentieth century (Tanner, 1997).

According to Katz and Chard (2000), the project approach is not referred to as a method or model; this suggests that investigative projects constitute only one element of an early childhood curriculum. As part of the curriculum for children aged about three to eight years, project work functions in tandem with other aspects of the curriculum. Since it is not a total teaching method or model, it does not require the abandonment of a wide variety of other pedagogical practices that support children's development and learning. Projects are part of other curriculum approaches or models.

The project approach can be considered a framework for emergent curriculum. As suggested by Katz and Chard (2000), projects are intended to be emergent as they develop from the ongoing interests of the children. In contrast, themes are usually not considered emergent (Kashin, 2009).

When you walk into a learning environment using the project approach, you should see highly engaged children and evidence of project work in what is displayed on the walls or at defined display areas. Children and the early learning professionals decide on a project topic. This can come from the expressed interest of the children or through observations of the children.

There are three phases to project work. During the first phase, it is the responsibility of the early learning professional to find out what the children *know*, what they *want* to know, and *how* they are going to find out what they want to know, and then to assess what the children have *learned*, which can be represented as KWHL. This should be a co-constructive process with the children. The process can be organized in a KWHL chart and/or a schematic map called a *curriculum web*. During the second phase of the project, the children investigate and research the topic, representing what they are learning in multiple ways (e.g., two- or three-dimensional methods). The final phase of the project involves concluding with a culminating event (Follari, 2011).

What you see displayed on the walls in an environment that is using the project approach will reflect the project topic under investigation. It includes the planning charts and webs, as well as the children's representations and the early learning professionals' written reflections. This is considered documentation. If the documentation is to become pedagogically focused, it needs to be interactive and open to interpretation. If documentation is static and is used for display purposes, it should still make the children's learning visible.

Pinterest Links

www.pinterest.com/pin/71142869085871736
www.pinterest.com/pin/71142869085871738
www.pinterest.com/pin/71142869085871732

Waldorf

During the early decades of the twentieth century, much of Europe was "struggling to cope with the devastation of the aftermath of World War I." Rudolf Steiner (1861–1925) envisioned a better world and "devoted his life to exploring human potential, spirituality, and growth and development" (Follari, 2011, p. 243). As a result, he developed a programming model that emphasized the importance of an arts-based curriculum that incorporated imagery, music, movement, drawing, painting, mixed media, drama, and rhythm as core program components. Arts-based programming encourages children to pay particular attention to their environments from both natural and aesthetic perspectives. He suggested that when children develop a sense of their environments, they develop inherent appreciation for their surroundings, including social environments and the people within those environments. The symbolic conditions are also essential to Steiner's beliefs and practices. The stories, poetry, and documentation of diverse experiences promote culture and a breadth of learning that expands beyond family principles and practices (Driscoll & Nagel, 2005).

While Steiner was influenced by John Dewey's perspective of children learning by doing, he developed his own form of spiritual science called *anthroposophy*: "a philosophy based on examining more deeply the three parts of the human being (body, mind, and spirit) and the connections that bond humanity together" (Follari, 2011, p. 243). One of Steiner's core principles was that all play experiences should come from the children and that this is necessary for their self-worth and sense of curiosity. Steiner pointed out that contrary to the thinking of many educators, teachers should not provide experiences for students. Rather, they should provide the conditions, such as the materials, space, and options. The children are given the power to lead the program design and the ways in which they create their learning (Driscoll & Nagel, 2005).

A Waldorf environment is very distinctive, from the colours to the furniture and materials that are provided. It is designed to be a place of harmony, beauty, and gentle guidance. The materials are natural and inspire creative play; the food is organic and nutritious and is often grown by students and their teachers. Outdoor play is encouraged so

Waldorf materials.

Diane Kashin

that children develop a connection to nature (Follari, 2011). Indoors, children are involved in creative play experiences where they are able to use their imagination through the manipulation of open-ended materials such as blocks, puppets, painting, drawing tools, clay, and items from nature. Children participate in gardening and playing musical instruments. They also express themselves through storytelling, chanting, and body movements known as *eurhythmy*. The approach uses the arts to enrich cognitive learning and help children become more fully human (Dietze & Kashin, 2012).

The Reggio Emilia Approach

Reggio Emilia is one of several small, wealthy cities in Emilia Romagna, a region in northern Italy with a history of collaboration and political activism (New, 2000). Shortly after the Second World War, during a time that also saw the end of the Fascist dictatorship in Italy, the first early learning program for young children was established. It was inspired by the parents of the community who had a shared desire to create a new, more just world, free from oppression (Gandini, 2004). In order to rebuild the war-ravaged economy, the parents needed to work and so required care for their children. They wanted an environment where children could acquire the critical-thinking and collaboration skills essential to rebuilding and ensuring a democratic society (Gandini, 2004). This strong sense of purpose inspired Loris Malaguzzi to join the collaborative effort (New, 2000). Malaguzzi, a young teacher influenced by Dewey, is credited as the guiding force behind the unique philosophy that emerged. His inspiration was those concerned parents who started the first preschools. In one of his interviews, speaking of the first school, Villa Cella, he said,

> They asked for nothing less than that these schools that they had built with their own hands be different kinds of schools, preschools that could educate their children in a way different from before. . . . These were parents' thoughts, expressing a universal aspiration, a declaration against the betrayal of children's potentials, and a warning that children first of all had to be taken seriously and believed in. (Malaguzzi, 1998, p. 58)

For Malaguzzi, the central notion for the philosophy of Reggio Emilia resides in the concept of images. The image of the child is one in which children are strong, competent, intellectual builders of theories. Stremmel (2002a) suggested that this image counters current perspectives of children as powerless, passive receptacles into which knowledge or skills are poured, and he advocated for the Reggio image as an alternative. He maintained that "instead of fixing children by teaching them to memorize and be obedient, we should be helping them to develop dispositions of caring, fairness, and justice, or how to engage in ethical reflection and live responsibly within a democratic society" (p. 43). Children flourish in programs where they have adults who support them in constructing environments that reflect their interests and options for expanding their experiences and levels of curiosity.

While the educators in Reggio Emilia acknowledge the influence of Dewey, as well as Piaget and Vygotsky, their emphasis on their own continuous research and analysis of practice. This approach allows them to formulate new theoretical interpretations, hypotheses, ideas, and strategies about teaching and learning (Stremmel, 2002a). If you were to walk

A Reggio-inspired toddler room.

Diane Kashin

into a Reggio-inspired program, you would find distinct guiding principles or fundamental ideas emanating from the research and analysis that provide the foundation of the Reggio Emilia approach. While presented separately for clarity and condensed for brevity, they "must be considered as a tightly connected, coherent philosophy in which each point influences, and is influenced by, all the others" (Gandini, 2002, p. 16). The principles, expanded upon in Table 4.3 on the next page, include

1. the image of the child;
2. the three subjects of education: children, parents, and teachers;
3. the image of the teacher;
4. pedagogical documentation;
5. environment as the third teacher; and
6. organization as fundamental.

These principles are used to guide practices, evaluate programming, and participate in utopian thinking with parents, educators, and the community.

At this time, the Reggio Emilia–inspired approach is highly recognized as one that is responsive to children and families. The attention given to placing an aesthetic value on children's efforts, such as their artwork and documentation of their projects and experiences, aligns with a high regard for respect of the child.

Table 4.3 Reggio Emilia Principles Reflected in Programming Features

Principle	Description	In Practice
The image of the child	All children have a right to be viewed as competent, capable, and able to build their own theories.	Children use many materials to discover and communicate what they know, understand, wonder about, question, feel, and imagine, making their learning visible through many languages (Cadwell, 2004).
The three subjects of education: children, parents, and teachers	In order for children to learn, their well-being has to be guaranteed. Such well-being is connected to the well-being of parents and teachers. Parents are a competent and active part of their children's learning experience (Gandini, 2004).	Families are actively engaged in the program. Families are seen not as a threat, but as an intrinsic element of collegiality, as well as the place of integration of different wisdoms (Gandini, 2004).
The image of the teacher	Reggio teachers have to question themselves and to change their interactions based on their reflections (Rankin, 2004). The teacher is seen as a researcher (Hewett, 2001).	Continual internal dialogues and discussions with others provide ongoing training and theoretical enrichment. Teachers see themselves as researchers, preparing documentation of their work with children (Fu, 2002).
Pedagogical documentation	During this process, teachers are learning how to "make learning visible"—their own and that of the children (New, 2003, p. 37). Careful consideration and attention are given to presenting the children's learning. The teacher's commentary on the purposes of the study and the children's learning process, transcriptions of children's verbal language, photographs of their activity, and representations of their thinking in many media are composed in carefully designed panels or books (Cadwell, 2003).	Documentation in this form is not just the display of a project's topic-related materials but is pedagogical. Pedagogical documentation as content refers to the materials that record what the children are saying and doing, "for example, hand-written notes of what is said and done, audio recordings and video camera recordings, still photographs, computer graphics, pieces of the children's work" (Dahlberg et al., 1999, p. 148). By having the documentation open for interpretation, it becomes pedagogical as it can lead the direction of the curriculum (Kashin, 2009).
Environment as the third teacher	Such care is taken in the preparation of the environment that it acts as a third teacher (Fraser, 2000). There is an underlying order and beauty in the design and organization. Every corner of every room has an identity and a purpose, is rich in potential to engage and to communicate, and is valued and cared for by children and adults (Cadwell, 2003).	The attention to detail is everywhere, from the colour of the walls to the shape of the furniture, and the arrangements of simple objects on shelves and tables. Lights, plants, and mirrors are used to help provide a pleasurable atmosphere while offering possibilities for reflection and exploration. The environment is filled with the essence of the children, as their paintings, drawings, and sculptures are everywhere. The remaining spaces are filled with the documentation (Gandini, 2004).
Organization as fundamental	The organization is organic instead of rigid. It serves a larger purpose. It is not neat and tidy; rather, it reflects the complexity and order of the universe. It evolves; it is flexible. It has a flow and movement, growing from a group working closely together (Wheatley & Kellner-Rogers, 1996).	Intricate and complex organization appears within every context—from the collections and arrangements on the shelf to the daily preparation and serving of meals eaten family style, to the thoughtful selection of small groups of children with multiple perspectives, to the layered agenda and inclusive dialogue of an evening meeting with parents (Cadwell, 2003).

Source: Adapted from Kashin, 2009.

Concerns have been expressed about ways to transfer this approach to communities in North America. For example, documentation is such an important part of the approach, yet when visiting the Reggio Emilia schools, photographs are forbidden not only to protect children, but also to reinforce the concept of an approach rather than a model. Visitors should not try to replicate everything they see but instead should allow the images to inspire their own evolving authentic curriculum as it connects to their particular geography, demographics, and beliefs about how children learn. Others suggest that this approach cannot be easily transferred to North America because of the cultural differences between the environments (Fraser & Gestwicki, 2012).

Outdoor Programs

The importance of outdoor play and learning was inspired by Froebel's belief that children's play in gardens offers richness to the development of the whole child. Montessori and Dewey also recognized that "children's learning and development were greatly enhanced through direct experiences of nature and natural materials" (Davis, 1998, p. 119). In the early part of the twentieth century, the McMillian sisters reinforced the importance of outdoor play and learning by creating an open-air nursery school in Britain. Like Froebel, the McMillians focused on carefully designing the outdoor garden to provide children with a wide range of resources, materials, and experiences within a natural setting (Bilton, 2002). At the same time, Steiner promoted the importance of children's environments providing the opportunity for "the wonder" to be present, and noted that the adult should become a guide to the children rather than the "teacher" or director of experiences. The garden space; the place; and opportunities to move freely, to explore, to create, and "to be" were essential to outdoor programming. Authentic materials such as those found in natural play spaces have long been recognized for their play value and learning options, and for the depth of learning that occurs when using them.

Currently, outdoor programming for the early years has gained momentum that could evolve to become a naturalistic movement. Forest schools, outdoor classrooms, and eco- or green schools are changing the landscape of programming in the early years. Since the turn of the twenty-first century, there has been growing interest in programs that use the outdoor environment as play and learning space. There are many reasons behind this pendulum swing, including increased obesity rates among children, the nature-deficit phenomenon, and the general decline in children's active play outdoors (Maynard, 2007).

Warden (2010) described nature kindergartens as "an approach of naturalistic, wild spaces that provide children with a landscape in which to play for very long blocks of time" (p. 7). She further suggested that children's natural play space encompasses aspects "from the landscape, to the food, to the materials and resources used and the sense of community within it" (p. 13). In addition to the space and materials, natural play spaces offer children the freedom to have their voices heard and to design their experiences based on their interests. There are many advantages to children having access to naturalistic programs, including the benefits identified in Figure 4.7 on the next page.

To support children in taking advantage of the many opportunities presented by outdoor play, early learning professionals benefit from doing less talking and more listening to the children. Ollin (2008) called this notion *silent pedagogy*. It is important for children to have opportunities to observe, to think, and to figure things out without ongoing questioning by or interactions with adults (Ollin, 2008). For example, assume the children are watching water and sticks flow over rocks. For some children, the sound of the water provides a moment in time of calmness and wonderment. When adults intrude in that moment, children are unlikely to be able to return to that same place. Warden (2010)

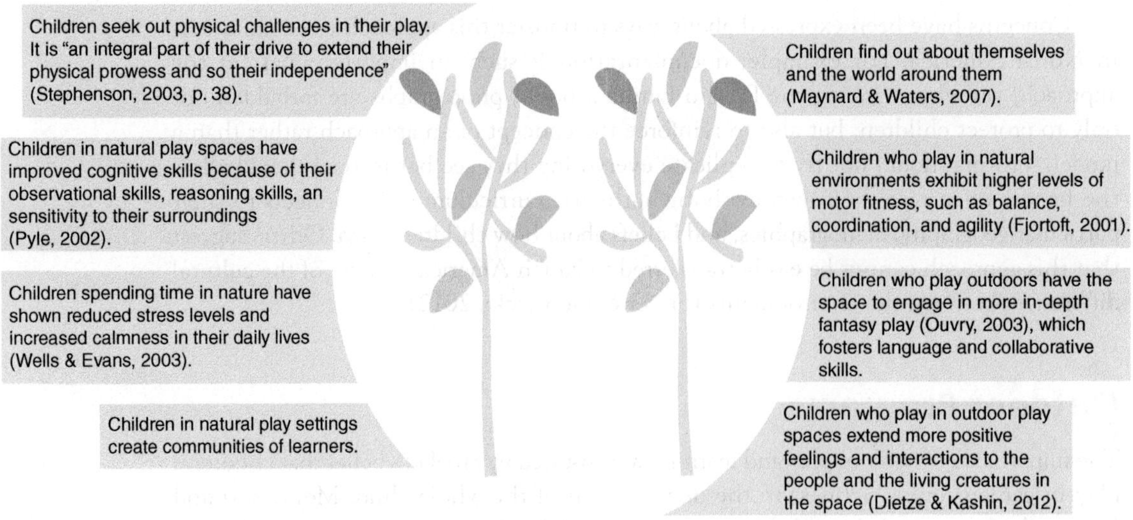

Children seek out physical challenges in their play. It is "an integral part of their drive to extend their physical prowess and so their independence" (Stephenson, 2003, p. 38).

Children in natural play spaces have improved cognitive skills because of their observational skills, reasoning skills, an sensitivity to their surroundings (Pyle, 2002).

Children spending time in nature have shown reduced stress levels and increased calmness in their daily lives (Wells & Evans, 2003).

Children in natural play settings create communities of learners.

Children find out about themselves and the world around them (Maynard & Waters, 2007).

Children who play in natural environments exhibit higher levels of motor fitness, such as balance, coordination, and agility (Fjortoft, 2001).

Children who play outdoors have the space to engage in more in-depth fantasy play (Ouvry, 2003), which fosters language and collaborative skills.

Children who play in outdoor play spaces extend more positive feelings and interactions to the people and the living creatures in the space (Dietze & Kashin, 2012).

Figure 4.7 Benefits of outdoor play

Source: Adapted from Dietze & Kashin, 2012.

Pinterest Links
www.pinterest.com/pin/71142869085804449
www.pinterest.com/pin/71142869085613078
www.pinterest.com/pin/434386326528833091

clearly advocated for quiet space because "in silence the brain can process, reflect, consider, assimilate or discard ideas and then store pertinent information" (p. 31).

If you found yourself in an outdoor program, you would see children playing freely and adults observing carefully and listening intently. The role of the early learning professional in nature play spaces reinforces the importance of learning evolving from the child. Children have more "retention when [learning] is intrinsically motivated, when it inspires and connects to them" (Warden, 2010, p. 30). Outdoor play environments offer many options for play and learning that are different from those in the indoor play space.

There are criticisms of this outdoor play movement. Some suggest that it is not a feasible model for the Canadian climate, even though it has been implemented in countries such as Norway, which has weather patterns similar to Canada's. Another critical issue is that early learning staff do not have the training or experience to implement a full-day outdoor program using the environmental attributes that can become the foundational elements in children's program planning.

PROFESSIONAL RESPONSIBILITY

Each program model or approach has its own history and is based on various theories that have influenced how children are invited to learn in the program. In your practice, whether you are currently a student or a professional, part of your responsibility will include setting up and providing materials for children to experience and use for learning. Regardless of the approach you follow, you are accountable for programming. This requires you to make complex decisions about your curricular choices, how they are aligned with the philosophy of the program, and how they support positive outcomes for children.

Engaging with children in professional practice.
Rosalba Bortolotti

Some curriculum frameworks identify the types of outcomes expected from children's learning at various stages of their development. To determine whether a child or a group of children have met the desired outcomes, you will need to think about assessment. We caution against using assessments that are too technical and that are not aligned with ethical practice or that focus on children's deficits rather than strengths. If early learning professionals complete children's assessments, from an ethical perspective, their assessments should be tied to observations, pedagogical documentations, and family and cultural backgrounds and experiences. Early learning professionals do not diagnose developmental delays or behavioural issues. Outcomes-based learning and assessment will be further explored in Chapter 11.

FEATURED RESEARCH

These links will take you to research that further explores programming approaches and models: http://bit.ly/13Wh8bF explores three traditions—Montessori, Waldorf, and Reggio Emilia. To research five program outlines, go to http://bit.ly/1sAKPM2.

PEDAGOGICAL TOOLS

When early learning professionals plan a program, they consider both the program's philosophy and their own philosophy. In this section, we provide you with a step-by-step guide for creating your own professional philosophy statement.

1. Identify your values and beliefs

You should have some notes about your values and beliefs in your professional journal. Start by reading those notes. Think about your

- beliefs about the way children develop;
- beliefs about the way children and adults learn; and
- personal motivations for choosing early childhood education as your profession.

2. Reflect

In order to have a coherent and congruent product (your statement), you need to go through a clarification process. Review your values and beliefs.

- Think about what you are "doing by default" (acting without thinking).
- Examine the "default action" in light of new experiences and knowledge gained from this module.
- Identify conscious, informed choices that will change behaviour, if necessary.

3. Develop content for your philosophy statement

Now document your draft philosophy statement. Think about

- the source of your motivation for learning;
- your belief about how people learn;
- your image of children;
- your image of yourself as a professional/your professional role; and
- your beliefs about learning environments.

4. Format your philosophy statement

Now review your draft statement and prepare it for presentation so that it

- is succinct (one page or shorter);
- focuses on highlights rather than a stream of consciousness; and
- is organized and well written.

5. Submit your statement

You may have the opportunity to submit your philosophy statement during your academic studies, or it may be something that you wish to include in a professional portfolio. You may be asked to share your philosophy in a job interview. Writing your statement now, however, should not deter you from revisiting it as you gain more experience and professional knowledge. You may find that your values and beliefs change over time.

PROFESSIONAL CASE STUDY

The not-for-profit Seeds of Learning Early Learning Centre opened eight years ago. Since its inception, the centre has adopted an eclectic approach to its philosophy and programming model. The board of directors chose to take an eclectic approach because they felt that there was more flexibility to programming if staff could take a "bit from this philosophy or approach and a bit from that philosophy." Although that model offered children and families interesting play experiences and was thought to be effective, the board has asked the executive director and his staff members to review the research on the benefits and challenges of eclectic programming models for children in comparison to programs that have a more clearly defined philosophical foundation, such as Froebel, Montessori, Reggio-inspired, or Waldorf programs. The staff are excited about doing this, as it is a way for them to take stock of their program and ensure that their practices are aligned with the latest thinking on early learning principles and practices. They have determined that in addition to conducting research, each staff member will visit various programs to see the approaches or models in action. They will then prepare a report on their findings for initial discussion as a group and then with the board of directors.

One staff member has become interested in a Waldorf program she visited. She feels the creative arts focus cultivates a sense of exploration and creative thought process that she'd like the children in her program to experience at the same level. Her enthusiasm for this approach leads her to read Cultivating Curious and Creative Minds *(Craig & Deretchin, 2010) to see if she can gain further insight into why the program "spoke to her." She knows that she had an "aha!" moment and that whatever the new direction for the centre is, she wants to ensure that creative arts opportunities and processes are explicitly available to the children.*

As staff members begin to present their research findings and documentation panels from their field visits, it becomes clear that each staff member has gained valuable information about how a program with a defined approach or model differs from their eclectic program. They all acknowledge that this is a turning point for them, but a new direction isn't apparent. Some members of the group have had their eclectic program philosophy endorsed, while others are in disequilibrium, thinking that a defined program approach has merit. One member of the team advocates that further research into a Reggio-inspired program be undertaken, while another suggests that there is merit in the Forest School approach. The director believes the discourse has been healthy for the centre staff because they have gained professional learning about new ways of programming and reflected on their values and beliefs about children, families, and programming as individuals and as a group. Determining how to move forward will be a challenge for the board, the executive director, and program team.

REFLECTION QUESTIONS FOR SELF-LEARNING

Interactions among staff, the executive director, and the board of directors are necessary when there are potential changes to programming direction and practices. Staff members have important roles in sharing with the board of directors the latest research on early learning programming and their observational findings without bias. In this case, once the staff have presented the information to the board of directors, they will collectively benefit from engaging in creative brainstorming and in articulating what their utopian vision might be for the centre. As a way to support staff in the process and to reinforce that revising a philosophy is a process, the executive director found the following resource online, http://bit.ly/12Yu2ZP, which discusses the process that one early childhood program went through when staff participated in a revision of their philosophy. Thinking about the case study presented, answer the following questions in your professional journal:

1. Why do you think the board of directors is exploring a potential new direction for the Seeds of Learning Early Learning Centre? Do you think that it is the role of the early learning staff to gather the research and visit particular programs? Do you think there should be a blueprint established for examining the programs?

2. What do you see as the benefits and potential challenges for the Seeds of Learning Early Learning Centre in changing its direction and programming approach? Do you think that there is some danger that staff may become fractured through this process? Why or why not? If there is some friction among staff, how might this become apparent in the children's program?

3.	What leadership practices would the executive director need to demonstrate throughout this process? What strategies might you suggest be used to determine if the philosophy should change? If there is a movement to change it, how would you suggest the board of directors and staff make that decision? Why?

4.	If the philosophy and approach to programming change, what do you believe are the top five priorities that must be addressed? How would you proceed?

BIG IDEAS FOR DIALOGIC LEARNING

Thinking deeply about big ideas with others requires time. Being an early learning professional is demanding. Imagine what a typical day might be and think about how you would incorporate opportunities for dialogic learning. Begin by thinking on your own about what would be required to allow for dialogic learning.

1.	What is required to provide early learning professionals with opportunities to come together in a community of learners?

2.	What are the obstacles preventing early learning professionals from engaging in big-idea group thinking?

3.	What is the number one reason early learning professionals would have for not engaging in dialogic learning?

4.	How could you advocate on the behalf of early learning professionals so that this issue is addressed?

VISION

It is our vision that every early learning professional, regardless of the constraints of a program, will find opportunities to build authentic and meaningful learning experiences for children. We accept that early learning professionals may find that their own values and philosophy do not align with the programming directions and expectations where they work. We envision a world where professionals do not compromise their ethics. Through critical reflection and support from others, we hope that curricular decisions will be based on a complex understanding of the big ideas of early learning programming.

MAKING CONNECTIONS

By being involved in a dialogic community, you can think deeply about programming in the early years. We recommend that you share your personal professional philosophy through the use of a social poster. The following link will take you to an example of a social poster that supports the theory of loose parts: http://checkthis.com/dpt4. Creating and sharing a social poster is not time-consuming, and it allows you to articulate your philosophy and make your professionalism visible.

KEY TERMS

Auspice 89

Classical tradition   80

Constructivism   87

Ideologies   85

Instructivism   87

Modern tradition   80

Multiple intelligences   81

Postmodern tradition   84

Reconceptualization   85

Modern tradition
Auspice
Ideologies
Multiple intelligences
Classical tradition
Instructivism
Constructivism
Reconceptualization
Postmodern tradition

Figure 4.8 **Key terms wordle**

SUMMARY

Programs and approaches in early learning are based on different traditions with varying ideologies, philosophies, and theories. In considering programming for children, early learning students and professionals have a wide range of choices to make, requiring deep thinking and reflection about a number of big ideas.

1. Early learning has historical roots influenced by classical, modern, and postmodern traditions. From Comenius in the 1500s to the current theories of Gardner, a broad range of influences are important to recognize, as they can become part of professional practice.

2. When the complex relationship between ideologies, philosophies, and theories is acknowledged, this will enhance understanding.

3. The similarities and differences among the early learning program models and approaches described in this chapter reflect philosophical influences and contextual factors. Comparing these to the context of practice will benefit the professional in making choices appropriate for the early learning space.

4. By articulating professional responsibility for planning and implementing a program that aligns with an approach or model, early learning professionals can become confident in their choices.

5. Theories, philosophies, and programming models and approaches are not stagnant—they change over time to reflect changes in contextual factors.

Think about how you could set up an invitation to play and learn for children based on any of the programs and approaches in this chapter. For more on the concept of invitations, see http://bit.ly/1lQkUyo.

For Further Thought

Chapter 5

A Pan-Canadian and Global Review of Curriculum Frameworks

LEARNING OUTCOMES

After exploring this chapter, you should be able to

1. Describe what is meant by the two broad types of curricula approaches—the social pedagogic approach and the pre-primary approach.

2. Discuss the concept of curriculum frameworks and their purpose in early learning programs.

3. Examine the similarities and differences among the seven Canadian curriculum frameworks presented and describe how international curriculum frameworks have influenced Canadian curriculum frameworks.

4. Discuss the guiding principles that should be evident in Aboriginal early learning programs.

5. Explain why and how theories, philosophies, and programming models or approaches may change over time.

6. Explain the roles and responsibilities of early learning professionals, educational institutions, and government departments in advancing the knowledge about and ability to use the context of curriculum frameworks in practice.

A CHILD'S STORY   Jacob

I am school-ager now! I get to play with the big kids. Last year I was still in kindergarten, but now I go to school all day and come to the school-age program in the afternoon. We get to play with board games, cards, and computers when we are inside, and when we go outside we play sports. I love being a school-ager! I like our new project on the Beatles. I love my new teachers too. They don't seem as stressed out as my teachers last year. Last year they were always talking about things I didn't understand. They kept talking about something they called ELECT. It confused me. They would say, "Is that in the ELECT?" or "Check the ELECT." They would even talk to my parents about ELECT. Now that I am *in the school-age program, I don't hear that word as much, but yesterday we had a class meeting and we were talking about our class community. We talked about making sure everyone in the class feels like they have a voice and are being heard. Our teacher Masooma told us that we should try to have a democratic classroom. She said our government is democratic. My friend Jeremy then suggested that we have an election for a class leader. When Masooma said that we could "elect" a leader, I got really confused. Today at our meeting I am going to ask her why we never had a class leader in kindergarten when the teachers were always talking about elections.*

A child's representation of a project topic.

Diane Kashin

CHAPTER PREVIEW

*It should be realized that genuine interest cannot be forced.
Therefore all methods of education based on centers of interest
which have been chosen by adults are wrong.*

—Maria Montessori (1870–1952)

Across Canada, the early years are increasingly subject to a variety of public policies associated with provincial and territorial initiatives. A current trend in the early learning sector in Canada is the adoption of either pedagogical curriculum frameworks or curricula to guide practice. Of the existing frameworks, some are mandatory and some considered optional. However, nowhere in the country is the same curriculum extended to both kindergarten and child care (Beach & Friendly, 2013). These emerging frameworks are most often designed for programs serving children before they enter the public education system, and they are seldom aligned with kindergarten or primary school curricula. School-operated kindergarten curricula, usually mandated under the provincial education jurisdictions, follow a more defined, educator-guided curriculum, with specific learning standards or expectations divided into subject areas. These curricula and learning standards provide the impetus for the program-planning process, as does the assessment or testing of children's skills (McCain, Mustard, & McCuaig, 2011). Pedagogical curriculum frameworks are being adopted as a way to guide practice and increase the quality of programming for young children in organized early learning environments. Bennett (2005) has determined that "in terms of content, frameworks generally identify the key goals of early childhood services and propose how early childhood centres should support children's learning" (p. 8). Early learning professionals benefit from a close examination of these documents, including the foundational principles upon which the curriculum frameworks are based.

Bennett (2005) noted from his review of early learning policies, practices, and curricula in more than twenty countries that two primary approaches are most common in curriculum design. The first is a **social pedagogical approach**. This model is based on Bronfenbrener's ecological model, with the contextual focus of children's learning opportunities evolving from their environment—the people, places, and things within their environment, and past and current experiences within that environment. The second approach, known as the **pre-primary approach**, focuses on teaching, child outputs, and preparation for entry to the school system. Table 5.1 provides a comparison of the two approaches. The curriculum frameworks presented in this chapter have common features—they all take a social pedagogical approach to curriculum planning and implementation and are based on the principles that relationships with families are paramount to supporting the development of children, children learn through play, and the early learning professional plays a significant role in how the environment is created for and with children.

Bennett (2005) noted that a quality curriculum framework should be a guiding document for early learning professionals and parents. For example, he suggested that a framework have a statement of principles and values to guide early learning professionals, as well as a summary of program standards that would be transparent to parents, children, and visitors entering early learning environments. Curriculum frameworks outline broad goals and pedagogical guidelines that the early learning centre will pursue, reflective of and responsive to the unique individual, social, and cultural experiences and needs of the

social pedagogical approach An approach to curriculum that uses the child's context as the focus of the learning opportunities offered.

pre-primary approach An approach to curriculum that focuses on teaching, meeting outcomes, and school readiness.

Table 5.1 Comparison of Pre-primary and Social Pedagogical Approaches

Pre-primary Approach	Social Pedagogical Approach
Has a core centralized curriculum with defined goals and outcomes.	Focuses on broad-based curriculum outcomes with a local curriculum to reflect diversity among children, families, cultures, and community.
Teacher–child relationships focus on the teacher providing instruction toward achieving defined knowledge or skills to meet curriculum goals and standards.	The teacher–child relationship is collaborative in exploring and learning about ideas that are derived from the children's interests or broad curriculum goals.
Evaluation processes are used to assess each child with respect to the defined goals and competencies achieved.	The teacher, child, and parents together determine goals and outcomes. Assessment strategies such as narrative stories, portfolios, or pedagogical documentation are used to facilitate children's learning and areas of interest.

Source: Adapted from Bennett, 2005.

children in the program (Bennett, 2005). Bennett summed up his perspective on curriculum frameworks by saying they "will be strong on guiding principles and structural requirements, but flexible enough to allow practitioners to experiment with different methodological and pedagogical approaches, and to adapt overall goals to special needs children, and to local needs and circumstances" (p. 19).

The use of curriculum frameworks in public and private school settings is mandatory in Canada. When available, a curriculum framework is highly recommended for other settings, such as licensed child care, although it is not required. This is the case in British Columbia, Saskatchewan, and Ontario (McCain et al., 2011). Whether frameworks are mandated or voluntary, they offer early learning professionals a view of the deeper ideas that come with their use and of the complexity of working with children in their formative years. Some people assume that curriculum frameworks will be embraced and become a voluntary approach for early learning professionals. Others suggest that if frameworks are mandatory, there will be automatic, but perhaps not enthusiastic, compliance. Burgess and Fleet (2009) maintained that mandated initiatives may produce only surface adoption. How do you mandate an early childhood professional's practice when it involves philosophies and beliefs (Fenech & Sumsion, 2007)? One of the disadvantages of frameworks not being mandated as part of the standard of practice is that early learning professionals may not be interested in adopting them, which could result in an attitude of maintaining the status quo in programming.

Ultimately, a framework is intended to bring change to practice that enhances opportunities for children to have optimal play and learning experiences in early learning programs. Burgess and Fleet (2009) suggested that when early learning professionals engage with a curriculum document, they will perceive a potential benefit from making changes to practice. They will be able to "successfully implement the change, which may involve transforming their beliefs" (p. 47). The question then becomes how to provide the impetus for early learning professionals to engage with frameworks and to participate in discourse with colleagues so that the meaning of the document and ways of using it to guide practice may be examined. We suggest reviewing the following survey of provincial and international frameworks as a first step in engagement.

THE PURPOSE OF FRAMEWORKS

Internationally and across Canada, a number of jurisdictions have invested in the creation of curriculum frameworks for early learning programs. The purpose of each framework is to provide a guiding document that supports early learning professionals in creating pedagogical, focused learning communities that value children's exploration, autonomy, and desire to take risks and seek new ideas and learning. According to McCain et al. (2011), the curriculum frameworks developed to support early learning tend to be holistic and child-centred in their approach and are constructed around learning and developmental goals.

THE RATIONALE FOR FRAMEWORKS

Recent developments in neurological research have reinforced the importance of experiences and relationships in the first three years of life (Frost, Wortham, & Reifel, 2005; McCain, Mustard, & Shanker, 2007). This research has reinforced what many early learning professionals have always known—that the growth and development of the brain is influenced by a child's experiences and the environment (Dietze & Kashin, 2012). With this evidence, advocates for early learning have recommended increased attention to the environments and experiences extended to children. Early learning lays the foundation for future learning.

In the 1980s and 1990s, the Head Start and Perry Preschool projects in the United States produced an abundance of data demonstrating that investing in early learning programs has long-term benefits not only for the child, but also for the broader society because the "children grow up and become productive, well-adjusted citizens" (Victorian Curriculum and Assessment Authority, 2008, p. 12). In addition to the developmental benefits that children acquire from environments that follow curriculum frameworks, there is an economic rationale for frameworks to be used to guide and support early learning programs.

SURVEY OF CANADIAN FRAMEWORKS

Seven of Canada's provinces and territories have developed or adopted a curriculum framework for early learning. Others are considering development or are in the process of developing a curriculum framework. Table 5.2 lists current framework documents in Canada and provides websites where they are discussed and/or reviewed in full. In the sections that follow, we also provide a brief introduction to each of the frameworks. The frameworks have not been developed in isolation; in the various frameworks, you will find summaries of other provincial frameworks. For instance, in the Ontario early years framework, you will find summaries and reviews of frameworks from other provinces and countries.

Table 5.2 Provincial Curriculum Frameworks

Province	Year	Title	Requirements	Website
British Columbia	2008	*British Columbia Early Learning Framework*	Optional	www2.gov.bc.ca/assets/gov/topic/57FDB4389CD0FB3F6EC9948B610A6BA9/earlylearning/early_learning_framework.pdf
Manitoba	2011	*Early Returns*	Mandatory in funded centres	www.gov.mb.ca/fs/childcare/pubs/early_returns_en.pdf
New Brunswick	2008	*New Brunswick Curriculum Framework for Early Learning and Child Care—English*	Mandatory	www.gnb.ca/0000/ECHDPE/curriculum-e.asp
Ontario	2007	*Early Learning for Every Child Today*	Optional	www.edu.gov.on.ca/childcare/oelf
Prince Edward Island	2011	*PEI Early Learning Framework: Relationships, Environments, Experiences*	Mandatory to implement in the province's early years centres	www.gov.pe.ca/eecd/earlychildhood
Quebec	1997 and 2007	*Meeting Early Childhood Needs*	Optional	www.mfa.gouv.qc.ca/fr/publication/Documents/programme_educatif_en.pdf
Saskatchewan	2008	*Play and Exploration: Early Learning Program Guide*	Optional	www.education.gov.sk.ca/ELCC/play-and-exploration-program-guide

British Columbia (2008)

The development of the *British Columbia Early Learning Framework* was led by the Ministry of Education, in partnership with the Ministry of Health and the Ministry of Children and Family Development. Although the document was influenced by early learning frameworks from other jurisdictions, including New Brunswick, the northern Italian city of Reggio Emilia, Italy, Ireland, Sweden, and New Zealand, input was also provided by British Columbia families, early learning professionals, researchers, and post-secondary institutions. The framework was developed to be "uniquely British Columbian" (Government of British Columbia, 2008, p. 2). The British Columbia curriculum framework is used voluntarily by programs and adults who work with children in a variety of settings (Beach & Friendly, 2013).

British Columbia "is home to almost 200 First Nations, speaking more than 30 ancestral languages and dialects, along with First Nations, Inuit, Metis and Aboriginal peoples from other parts of Canada and the world" (Government of British Columbia, 2008, p. 5). The *British Columbia Early Learning Framework* acknowledges the importance of every child having his or her unique identity as well as cultural identity.

Vision The vision for children and early learning in British Columbia,

> is based on the image of the child as capable and full of potential. Early learning is envisioned as a dynamic process, actively supported by families and other adults who care for and teach children in their homes and communities. Children, adults, and environments play distinct but interacting roles in promoting early learning. (Government of British Columbia, 2008, p. 14)

The framework outlines three core visions:

- the vision for children up to age five;
- the vision for families, communities, and governments; and
- the vision of children's environments.

These core visions are interwoven throughout the document and are intended to be evident in practice.

About the Document   The *British Columbia Early Learning Framework* document is intended to support adults working with children in creating environments and early learning experiences that reflect current research and practice. The document is designed to provide users such as early learning professionals with tools to use in reflecting on experiences and dialogue with children and their families. The framework is also designed to support adults who interact with children in strengthening "children's individual, social, cultural, and linguistic identities, and their respect and appreciation for other people's identities" (p. 3). The framework is based on the following principles:

- Children are born with the innate desire to learn.
- Families are the primary caregivers of children and have the most important role in promoting their children's well-being, learning, and development in the context of supportive communities.
- Play is vital to children's healthy development and learning.
- Consistent, responsive, and nurturing relationships are essential to the well-being and early learning of children.
- All aspects of children's development and learning—physical, social, emotional, cultural, linguistic, and intellectual—are interrelated and interdependent.
- Language plays a central role in connecting thought and learning.
- Children are active participants in their families and communities.
- The individual, cultural, and linguistic identities of children and families are respected and integrated into early learning settings, programs, and activities.
- The physical environment shapes children's learning and well-being.

The document is divided into three sections: the structure of the document, the background for the document (including the context for British Columbia), and the framework at a glance, including vision, principles, and areas of early learning. It provides learning goals and questions for readers to reflect upon and consider as part of their practice.

Manitoba (2011)

Early Returns: Manitoba's Early Learning and Child Care Curriculum Framework for Preschool Centres and Nursery Schools is designed to support and be used by all the funded centres in Manitoba (Beach & Friendly, 2013). The curriculum framework reflects current research and best practices. Throughout the document, the information is intended to support adults working with children to think about what they do in their practice, explain the reasons for their practice, and discover ways to evaluate and enhance curriculum choices.

Vision   Manitoba's vision for children is that they have access to early learning and child care programs that demonstrate quality and foster and support children's social, emotional, physical, and cognitive development. "Developmentally appropriate early learning and child care practice is child-centred, reflects family and community contexts and encourages meaningful partnerships between each child, his or her family and early learning and child care staff" (Government of Manitoba, 2011, p. 1).

About the Document   The *Early Returns* framework is divided into three sections: interactions and relationships, environments, and planned and spontaneous experiences. Throughout the document, the curriculum components presented are based on the perspective that children learn through play. The document provides contextual information on each topical issue, as well as examples of common comments and open-ended questions that may stimulate children's reasoning processes. There are also core questions that early learning professionals may ask themselves as part of their reflective practice. The *Early Returns* framework acknowledges that Manitoba's early learning programs use many different curriculum approaches and emphasizes the importance of early learning professionals having "well thought-out plans, systems, and processes—intention and purpose—for your curriculum" (Government of Manitoba, 2011, p. 20). The document suggests that the planning process for and with the children is as valuable as the particular program model used.

New Brunswick (2008)

In 2008, New Brunswick's Department of Social Development produced an English curriculum framework and one designed for the francophone population (Langford, 2010). For the purposes of this textbook we will focus on the English version. The curriculum framework, a requirement for use in licensed early learning programs (Beach & Friendly, 2013), "is firmly committed to a vision of all children developing to their fullest potential" (Government of New Brunswick, 2008, p. 1). The framework promotes the importance of focusing on the strengths that children bring to the environment through broad-based learning goals and the use of narrative assessment (Whitty, 2009).

Vision   The New Brunswick English curriculum framework states,

> Our vision is that all children will grow to their fullest potential with dignity, a sense of self-worth, and a zest for living and learning. It is a holistic vision that seeks to provide the environment and resources needed to support dynamic development in young children who are:
>
> - curious, courageous, and confident in their pursuit of knowledge and skills;
> - secure in their linguistic and cultural identities;
> - respectful of diversity, and
> - contributing to the development of a just and democratic society that nurtures connection and care for life on the earth. (Government of New Brunswick, 2008, p. 1)

The vision statements are illustrated in a variety of examples throughout the document.

About the Document   The curriculum framework, reflective of contemporary research and theory, and in keeping with the perspective that each child is unique, outlines a spectrum of approaches to support the diversity of children's abilities, strengths, and ensure that cultural and linguistic identities are honoured. The framework reinforces the importance of play and of children being viewed as confident and active learners, as well as their relationships with the people, places, and things in their environment.

The *New Brunswick Curriculum Framework for Early Learning and Child Care—English* values and promotes children's experience of:

- safe and caring environments where their emotional and physical health, positive self-identities, and sense of belonging are nurtured and protected;
- open and flexible environments where playful exploration, problem-solving, and creativity are encouraged and purposefully planned;
- intellectually, socially, and culturally engaging environments where their communicative practices, literacies, and literate identities are valued and supported;

■ socially inclusive and culturally sensitive environments in which consideration for others, inclusive, equitable, democratic, and sustainable practices are enacted, and social responsibility is nurtured. (Government of New Brunswick, 2008, p. 1)

Within the four sections of the framework, the following are outlined: a context and the requisite conditions for early learning and care; four goals for early learning and care; narratives and sample provisions and practices; and pedagogical issues and conditions for elaborating on the framework, including a literature review.

In addition to the early learning and child care curriculum framework, there are supporting documents that provide early learning professionals with ideas and examples for collaboration explorations. The supporting documents may be found at http://bit.ly/1ffAzzR.

Ontario (2007)

In 2007, the Ontario government published *Early Learning for Every Child Today*, a "curriculum and pedagogical framework for children from birth to age 8" (Langford, 2010, p. 3). Building on the Early Years Study (McCain & Mustard, 1999) and Ontario's Best Start Plan to support young children, the curriculum framework is intended to be part of the building-block process that will provide children with a best start (Best Start Panel on Early Learning, 2007).

The framework was developed based on extensive research and a review of early childhood curricula and pedagogy both in Canada and internationally, as well as on expertise from a variety of stakeholders, including early childhood professionals, teachers, directors, and post-secondary educators. It is often referred to as the ELECT or the OELF (Ontario Early Learning Framework), and sometimes the ELF (Early Learning Framework). The OELF is not a mandatory document; early learning professionals have the option to use it in their practice in Ontario (Beach & Friendly, 2013).

Vision   The Province of Ontario believes that "every child has the right to the best possible childhood. Ontario's vision is to make Ontario an international leader in achieving the social, intellectual, economic, physical, and emotional potential of all its children" (Best Start Panel on Early Learning, 2007, p. 3).

Early Learning for Every Child Today was developed based on the following principles:

■ Early child development sets the foundation for lifelong learning, behaviour, and health.

■ Partnerships with families and communities strengthen the ability of early childhood settings to meet the needs of young children.

■ Demonstration of respect for diversity, equity, and inclusion are prerequisites for optimal development and learning.

■ A planned curriculum supports early learning.

■ Play is a means to early learning that capitalizes on children's natural curiosity and exuberance.

■ Knowledgeable and responsive early childhood practitioners are essential in early childhood settings.

About the Document   The purpose of the practical guide is "to support curriculum and pedagogy in Ontario's early childhood settings, including child care centres, kindergarten classrooms, home child care, nursery schools, Ontario Early Years Centres and other family support programs and early intervention services" (Best Start Panel on Early Learning, 2007, p. 3). The document is intended to complement curricular and pedagogical approaches and regulated requirements, as well as provide support for programs that may not necessarily have a defined curriculum model or pedagogical approach.

Documentation in a toddler classroom featuring a project based on the book *Red Is Best*
Diane Kashin

The guide is organized into the following five sections: "Statement of Principles"; "Understanding Children's Development"; "Into Practice"; "Assessment, Evaluation and Monitoring"; and "Glossary." It provides comprehensive information on the developmental domains and skills, indicators of the skill, and interactions that support children in each phase of development. These developmental domains and skills are featured in a continuum that is designed to be applied to practice. The guidelines for the practice section provide an overview of the principles and understanding of development, along with examples of programming that would support practice guidelines. Appendix 2 of the document, entitled "Best Start: Parent Involvement," acknowledges that parents play a significant role in children's learning and care. It provides an overview of the research on parent involvement and gives strategies for early learning staff to support and encourage parent involvement.

The province also offers a website that supports the early learning framework by providing information on observation, documentation, and interpretation as a means to put the framework into action or practice. You can also find information on learning environments and the continuum of development, as well as questions and considerations for further discussion, at http://bit.ly/11Qm0vy.

Prince Edward Island (2011)

The Prince Edward Island Department of Education and Early Childhood Development created the *PEI Early Learning Framework: Relationships, Environments, Experiences* to focus on children from infancy to school entry. The framework was written for directors and educators in all of the province's early years centres (Beach & Friendly, 2013). The *PEI Early Learning Framework* "is specifically designed to provide consistency in methodological approaches and structure to the scope of learning in Early Years Centres" (Flanagan, 2011, p. 5). The framework recognizes the importance of having early childhood educators design and implement programs and experiences that are "relevant to their communities, respectful of PEI's different cultures and languages, and that are appropriate for children with a wide range of abilities" (Flanagan, 2011, p. 5). Within the document, Flanagan (2011) acknowledged the need for early childhood educators to have a strong background in early childhood education and child development. She also pointed out that directors have a key role in exhibiting strong pedagogical leadership.

Vision   As part of the province's Preschool Excellence Initiative, a Vision for Children was created and underpins the framework. The vision statement is intended to support and facilitate the reciprocal relationship between the early childhood educator and children. The Vision for Children statement is,

> Children in PEI are healthy and happy, curious and creative, playful and joyous. They are loved and respected, and are safe and secure in their families, homes and communities. Children are our collective responsibility. They are valued for who they are today, and as the future parents and leaders of tomorrow. (Flanagan, 2011, p. 6)

About the Document   The document provides the reader with an overview of the theoretical perspective at the beginning of each of its sections. The eight sections of the document are the introduction, which includes theory; "Learning through Play"; "Role of the Early Childhood Educator"; "Inclusion"; "Learning Principles," examining relationships, environments, and experiences; "Learning Goals"; "Strategies and Reflections"; and "Documentation and Assessment."

Quebec (1997 and 2007)

In 1997, Quebec was the first province in Canada to develop an early learning framework. It drew upon the HighScope curriculum approach. In 2007, the framework was revised and updated (Government of Quebec, 2007; Langford, 2010). Quebec's framework is not mandatory (Beach & Friendly, 2013).

Vision   The Quebec early learning framework aims to foster the full and harmonious development of children so that they can realize their full potential in every dimension of their being. As quoted in the Ontario early years framework, the Quebec framework emphasizes the child's development process and refers to the social-emotional, moral, linguistic, cognitive, and psychomotor domains, "rather than the acquisition of specific skills or the potential product of a child's action." What is seen as important is "the children's ability to interact constructively with the environment" (Best Start Panel on Early Learning, 2007, p. 105).

About the Document   The document is divided into two parts. The first provides the objectives of the framework and other important references, including the theoretical influences and principles. The second part discusses application to practice, including observations, planning, and materials. Quebec's document links the goals of the early learning frameworks with kindergarten learning outcomes (McCain et al., 2011). The theoretical foundations of the document are aligned with an ecological approach and attachment theory (Langford, 2010) and support adapting the American HighScope approach to focusing on the development of the whole child.

As identified in the Ontario framework (Best Start Expert Panel on Early Learning, 2007), Quebec's framework is based on viewing each child as unique and on pedagogical principles that

- focus on play as the venue for children's learning and development;
- see educators, parents, and children contributing to creating environments; and
- focus on experiences and opportunities that support the harmonious development of each child.

Saskatchewan (2008)

In 2008, Saskatchewan launched *Play and Exploration: Early Learning Program Guide* (Langford, 2010). The program guide is designed to promote high-quality play-based programming for three-, four- and five-year-old children in a variety of early learning programs. Although implementation of the curriculum framework is considered optional (Beach & Friendly, 2013), "the intention is that all programs will reflect the vision, principles and quality elements described in the Guide" (Government of Saskatchewan, 2008, p. 1). A number of examples are presented in the document that would be helpful for early learning professionals to consider in their practice.

Vision   The guide outlines the vision for early learning programs that are holistic, responsive, and developmentally appropriate. They focus on the healthy development of the whole child, including social, emotional, physical, intellectual, and spiritual development. Children, family members, and early childhood educators collaborate in enriching children's learning and growth (Government of Saskatchewan, 2008). Early learning professionals are therefore encouraged to think about the following:

- children and their learning experiences;
- children and their relationships; and
- children and their environments.

About the Document   The guide was developed based on "early childhood education research, examples from successful practice of early childhood educators and understandings passed on through community culture, values and beliefs" (Government of Saskatchewan, 2008, p. 1). The guide presents the user with information on children as competent learners, the changing role for educators, how young children learn, observation and reflection, and high-quality programming. Each section provides an overview of the theoretical context, as well as prompts for early learning professionals to use to engage in reflection and in decision-making processes that include reflection, action, and evaluation. The final section of the document provides a comparison of selected early program approaches and key recommended references. In addition to the guide, there are supplementary *Into Practice* booklets and companion guides, including *Play and Exploration for Infants and Toddlers*, which can be found at http://bit.ly/105uKAt.

Curriculum Frameworks under Development

At the time of writing, the Newfoundland and Labrador government had made a commitment to develop an early childhood learning curriculum framework. The framework is intended to outline a pedagogical approach that emphasizes play-based learning, the role of adults in creating environments that model a holistic approach to children's development and learning, and inclusion of children with exceptionalities. In addition, as identified on the Newfoundland and Labrador Department of Education website, the framework will include

- a priority focus on parent–child interaction in relation to emergent literacy skills and child development, targeting infant and children from birth to age eight; and
- a curriculum with guiding principles for the early learning of children across all settings, such as regulated child care, family resource programs, early intervention programs (e.g., Direct Home Services Program), schools, early literacy programming, and homes.

Go to http://bit.ly/13pRZZ1 to learn more about the development of the curriculum framework in Newfoundland and Labrador.

In Alberta, a discussion paper was released in 2010 that calls for the establishment of a provincial curriculum framework for the early years. At the time of writing, it was thought that a group of Alberta provincial ministries would work together to develop a framework to be used in all regulated early learning settings. The framework will outline learning principles for different-aged children and identify key learning areas for programs to include in their service. "In developing the framework the ministries will be seeking a wide range of input internally and from other jurisdictions with early learning frameworks or curricula" (Muttart Foundation, 2010, p. 24). The paper, *In the Best Interests of Children and Families: A Discussion of Early Childhood Education and Care in Alberta*, can be found at http://bit.ly/16PQ2UH.

Other Guiding Practices: Nova Scotia

In Nova Scotia, licensed child care facilities are required to have a documented daily program plan. The actual approach to curriculum will vary from centre to centre. The daily program standards, established by the Nova Scotia Department of Community Services in accordance with the Day Care Act and Regulations, are necessary so that play-based and child-centred programs are delivered.

Promising Practices for Aboriginal Early Childhood Curriculum Frameworks

In the mid-1990s, Canadian royal commissions on Aboriginal people and education highlighted the need to improve Aboriginal education, beginning with early childhood experiences. This led to First Nations communities prioritizing early childhood care and education as an important strategy to promote the optimal development of their children, while maintaining and building on their traditional culture, their language, and the overall prosperity of their communities and societies. This resulted in Aboriginal Head Start initiatives being expanded in off-reserve and on-reserve communities. The curriculum framework for Head Start programs is based on six component areas: culture and language, education and school readiness, health promotion, nutrition, social support, and parental and family involvement (Health Canada, 2004). According to Nguyen (2011), the first two components—culture and language, and education and school readiness—are viewed as the most important guidelines. The culture and language component is designed to provide children with experiences that will revive and retain their culture and language, and support them in learning their languages and participating in their communities' culture. The education component is designed to

> support and encourage each Aboriginal child to enjoy life-long learning. More specifically, the projects will encourage each child to take initiatives in learning and provide each child with enjoyable opportunities to learn. This will be done in a manner which is appropriate to both the age and stage of development of the child. The ultimate goal is to engage children in the possibility of learning so that they carry forth the enthusiasm, self-esteem, and initiative to learn in the future. (Public Health Agency of Canada, 2004, p. 13)

In addition to the principles outlined above, the Aboriginal Head Start programs have adopted the HighScope curriculum and a generative curriculum model inspired by the Italian Reggio Emilia approach.

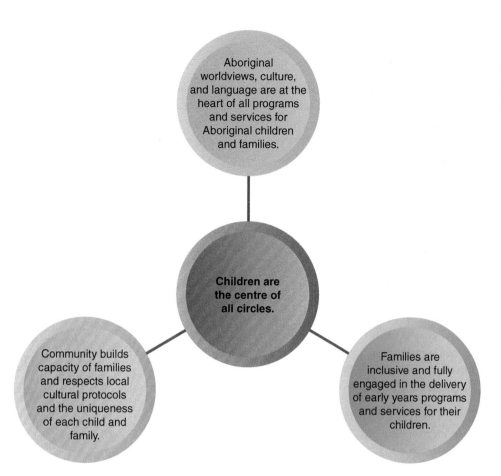

Figure 5.1 Guiding principles for Aboriginal early years programs

Source: Adapted from Bolduc et al., 2009.

Bolduc, Schneider, Gerlach, and Gray Smith (2009), in their document *Creating Pathways—an Aboriginal Early Years Five Year Strategic Plan*, identified that the guiding principles illustrated in Figure 5.1 are the ideal foundation on which to build early childhood programs and must be transparent to families and communities.

SURVEY OF INTERNATIONAL FRAMEWORKS

Early learning and child care curriculum frameworks have been developed relatively recently in many provinces across Canada; however, in other countries they have been in prior to or since the turn of this century. Although each jurisdiction has created a framework that is intended to reflect its vision and views of children, early learning professionals in Canada may see themes or positions that support aspects of their own frameworks, while other aspects remain distinct. Below, we provide summaries of six international frameworks.

Australia

Australia's *Belonging, Being and Becoming: The Early Years Learning Framework* was designed to provide high-quality early childhood education and care for children from infancy through to five years of age throughout Australia. The Australian government has a goal that all children will begin school as healthy and confident learners. The following five principles are embedded in the framework:

- secure, respectful, and reciprocal relationships;
- partnerships;
- high expectations and equity;

- respect for diversity; and
- outgoing learning and reflective practice.

The framework emphasizes that children require environments that are play based and contain appropriate stimuli that will support optimal brain development. The framework also outlines the need for early learning programs to be rich in communication and language, early literacy, and social and emotional developmental experiences—and for such experiences to be clearly present throughout the program. The framework can be found at http://bit.ly/1qm1gHW.

New Zealand (*Te Whariki*)

The *Te Whariki* curriculum was developed based on the following aspirations for children: "to grow up as competent and confident learners and communicators, healthy in mind, body, and spirit, secure in their sense of belonging and in the knowledge that they make a valued contribution to society" (Ministry of Education, 1996, p. 9). The curriculum has a contemporary focus on the critical role that socially and culturally mediated learning has for children. As well, this framework emphasizes the importance of the individual child, and the reciprocal and responsive relationships that children and their families should be exposed to with people, places, and things in their environment.

The guiding principles of *Te Whariki* are that

- the curriculum is to support the holistic development of children;
- empowering children is an essential role of adults and the environment (Maori principle);
- family and community are partners with children and are continuously strengthened; and
- children learn and thrive through responsive and reciprocal relationships.

Some of the key attributes of this framework are the emphasis on the interactions and the role of the adult with children and continuity. The document also reinforces the importance of celebrating bicultural values and diversity. For further information, go to http://bit.ly/14MCqJO.

Sweden

The Swedish curriculum framework emphasizes a social pedagogical, constructivist approach to curriculum and the importance of children learning through play and meaning making. The framework suggests that children's knowledge is created by the relationships they have with other children and adults in their lives. Play, social interaction, creativity, observations, discussions, reflective practice, and language are viewed as the essential attributes of early learning environments to support children in bringing meaning to their experiences. The curriculum, which was updated in 2010, can be found at http://bit.ly/19lpN9v.

England

The current curriculum document for England incorporates goals from the *Early Learning Goals* document released in 1999, with a specific focus on the early years. The document has a strong focus on thirteen principles for early years education. Within these principles, the knowledge, skills, abilities, and roles of early learning professionals in partnering with children and families to create inclusive environments are addressed. The framework, which was updated in 2013, can be found at http://bit.ly/19VKLyD.

What do you think the purpose is of early learning professionals and government departments examining curriculum frameworks from international jurisdictions? How might this knowledge strengthen our work with children in Canada? How might examining curriculum frameworks support us in working with children who are new immigrants to Canada?

Scotland

Curriculum for Excellence is Scotland's curriculum for children and young people aged 3 to 18. It replaces A Curriculum Framework for Children 3 to 5 and the 5-14 curriculum.

Scotland's framework promotes active, experiential and holistic learning through play. Mulit-media support to facilitate the implementation of the new curriculum can be found in Curriculum for Excellence: Supporting the early level http://bit.ly/Zw2QBa.

Internationally and provincially, frameworks are gathering momentum and driving policy directions for early learning. While we can supply only an overview of provincial and international frameworks, we encourage early learning professionals to think critically about overarching principles and applications to practice from as wide a perspective as possible. We ask you to read the Reflective Moment box above and consider international and provincial frameworks and their possible implications for practice.

PROFESSIONAL RESPONSIBILITY

Implementing curriculum frameworks requires a collaborative approach among professionals in the early learning setting and within government departments.

One of the first strategies for early learning professionals is to clearly distinguish between the terms *curriculum* and *curriculum frameworks*, as "a curriculum framework is not the same thing as a curriculum" (Office of Childcare, 2004, p. 20). As identified in Chapter 1, *curriculum* refers to how early learning professionals organize the overall programs, experiences, and environments for children that align with the centre's goals and philosophy. According to the New South Wales Office of Childcare (2004), a *curriculum framework* is "a sieve through which the professional 'sifts' thinking as a means of reflecting critically on practice" (p. 20). The curriculum framework is a "thinking" document that becomes a guide or tool to support early learning professionals in determining their values, principles, and perspectives related to pedagogy, how children learn, and how programs and environments can be designed to reflect their pedagogy (Langford, 2010).

Early learning students and professionals benefit from examining the curriculum frameworks and using them to support children in their play and learning. All the frameworks we've presented suggest that high-quality early learning programs are ones where children's play and experiences are co-constructed by the children and adults, and are reflective of principles and practices that are consistent with curriculum models and curriculum frameworks. What this means is that early learning students and professionals can and do use curriculum frameworks to support their practice and ensure that the indoor and outdoor environments offer children rich play experiences; that the communication among children, teachers, parents, and visitors is respectful and inviting; and that the children and early learning educators are involved and engaged in the process of intentional play and learning.

The curriculum frameworks we've presented clearly articulate the importance of the role of early learning professionals in working with children and their families. Bennett and

Leonarduzzi (2004) suggested that early learning professionals' roles and responsibilities are changing from being primarily required "to provide a secure and stimulating environment for young children who would then ensure their own development" (p. 16) to understanding that "human development and learning is an exercise in co-construction, in which children, parents and educators all have a role to play" (p. 16). Similarly, as outlined in the Saskatchewan framework, early learning professionals are encouraged to take on several roles, including observer, researcher, co-constructor of play and knowledge creation, communicator, and guide.

As various curriculum frameworks suggest, early learning professionals determine "where the child is at" by considering ways to assess and document children's interests, learning, and ways of knowing (Best Start Panel on Early Learning, 2007). The curriculum frameworks we've presented offer a variety of assessment strategies for early learning students and professionals to use in their work with children. These strategies include pedagogical narration, learning stories, anecdotal records, portfolios, observations, albums of learning events, project webs, and various samples of children's creations and work (Langford, 2010).

IMPLICATIONS FOR PRACTICE

Curriculum frameworks offer early learning students and professionals pedagogical tools that will support them in thinking about their philosophy, perspectives, and ways of creating environments that will offer children rich places to use their sense of curiosity, wonderment, and discoveries for learning. Each of the frameworks introduced offers a theoretical and application context that, if explored and reflected upon, provides professionals with suggestions for discourse among colleagues and guidance in areas that may be new to the individual or trigger more in-depth examination of practice.

Bennett (2005) noted that in order for curriculum frameworks to be successfully implemented, the following three conditions must be present:

1. well-qualified, motivated staff who have been trained to understand the framework and ways to effectively implement curriculum;

2. adequate investment in buildings, outdoor play environments, and human resources, including adequate ratios of qualified educators to children and an array of materials that support children's interests; and

3. monitoring processes and support systems that offer early learning staff information about, and opportunities to continuously improve, program quality and accountability.

Kagan and Kauerz (2012) maintained that one of the problems in implementing and understanding the effectiveness of curricula and frameworks "is the lack of clarity about the distinctions between curriculum and pedagogy" (p. 2) among early learning professionals. Bennett (2005) also identified a concern that early learning professionals might not have adequate pedagogical theory and practice. He suggested that within early learning environments there are many examples of

insufficient or inadequate interaction with children; little appreciation of horizontal learning for other children; a lack of training in managing groups and classrooms effectively; failure to provide or renew stimulating learning environments; insufficient team-working and reflection on practice; too great a focus on academic goals, or on the other hand, excessive suspicion of "schoolification" and reluctance to orient children toward learning goals valued by parents, schools and society. (pp. 14–15)

Bennett (2005) pointed out that early learning professionals using frameworks benefit from referring to what the research and observations tell us about children. Children have

a tremendous capacity to learn, and their learning and behaviours are grounded in the affective and social domains to which they are exposed.

Langford (2010) suggested that without professional development, it may be difficult to sustain staff motivation and commitment "to put into practice a framework's vision and principles"(p. 27). In addition to the need for ongoing professional development, provincial governments and territories with curriculum frameworks must ensure that the correct resources and educational opportunities are made available in college and university early childhood programs, so that upcoming professionals will have a thorough understanding of how curriculum frameworks inform practice and are interwoven into practice, evaluation, and professional learning plans.

FEATURED RESEARCH

In *Innovations in Provincial Early Learning Curriculum Frameworks*, Rachel Langford (2010) examined the possible incentives for the recent emergence of frameworks, either as policy or regulation in Canada. The research base was established by 2004, when most of the Organisation for Economic Co-operation and Development (OECD) countries had developed either pedagogical frameworks or curricula for children aged three to six. When the OECD evaluated early learning programming in Canada, it recommended a national framework. Some provinces began working on framework development, encouraged by the federal government's move toward a national, universal, and regulated early learning system. They continued that work in spite of the cancellation of the plan after the election of a new Conservative federal government in 2006. According to Langford (2010), the key purpose of frameworks is to stimulate discussion among early learning professionals and offer pedagogical tools for providing "rich early learning experiences for young children that reflect a framework's vision and principles" (p. 11). Taken together, all the frameworks focus on children as competent learners and agents of their own development. In addition, the British Columbia, Saskatchewan, and New Brunswick documents highlight the importance of early learning professionals examining their image of the child, as well as children's rights. All the frameworks focus on relationships with families and reaffirm the importance of play as central to early learning. As a whole, the frameworks also reveal four tools for practice: learning goals; reflection questions; educator–child interactions; and assessment and documentation of learning. There are differences among the provinces in terms of implementation strategies; Langford (2010) concluded that while early learning professionals "across Canada may be aware of their provincial early learning frameworks, the extent to which they are using them is quite uncertain" (p. 27). Langford suggested that what is needed are opportunities for input from early learning professionals in "identifying at a national level a body of agreed-upon values, principles and objectives for early learning" (p. 30).

PEDAGOGICAL TOOLS

Creating metaphors of practice and reflecting on images can be pedagogical tools for early learning students and professionals. A **metaphor** involves using a word or phrase in order to suggest comparison to another object or concept. An **image** is an idea or mental representation (Kashin, 2009). Images are one of the ways we make sense of the world. Metaphors and images can be used to capture the essence of what you do in a creative, expressive manner that challenges you to "be imaginative, to think, to reflect, and to find deeper meanings and understanding" (Hill et al., 2005, p. 31). Becoming conscious of images activated by practice can lead to professional growth. You can use metaphors as a catalyst for thinking deeply about your professional practice in many ways. Thinking about the work you do with children, do you see yourself as a farmer, a mountain climber, a conductor, or a zookeeper? You can see why metaphors can reflect who you are, including your values and beliefs. What is a metaphor that you could use to describe your professional responsibility in adopting curriculum frameworks in your practice? Write it down, and create a visual to represent your metaphor.

PROFESSIONAL CASE STUDY

After three years of working in a province that did not use a curriculum framework, my family has relocated to a province that has developed a curriculum framework as part of an early childhood education initiative. I have heard about curriculum frameworks but haven't invested time in examining them in relation to my practice. As I prepare to review curriculum frameworks in relation to my practice, I am trying to figure out answers to so many questions, such as where to begin in understanding how curriculum frameworks inform practice, how the framework will be visible in early learning programs, and how the framework will be used at staff meetings and for my performance review. I also wonder how curriculum frameworks align with my beliefs about how children learn and develop. If my beliefs and practices differ from the framework, how do I proceed in my practice? What will the discourse with my colleagues focus on in relation to the framework? How and where will I get the ongoing professional development I need to use curriculum frameworks as part of my practice?

Although I am excited to begin a new journey of incorporating my new province's curriculum framework into my practice, I am also scared. I keep asking myself why I feel scared. Maybe it is because this is a new journey for me in early childhood education, and with any new journey that I have embarked on in my career, I have always had mixed emotions until I have found colleagues with whom I can engage in discourse. I know that once this happens, I will be able to bring clarity to how the curriculum framework can enhance my practice and ultimately the environments I create for and with children and their families.

REFLECTION QUESTIONS FOR SELF-LEARNING

Exploring the context of frameworks, reflecting on the context and how that transfers to practice, and having discourse about how curriculum frameworks inform practice are necessary components in figuring out how curriculum frameworks can guide the co-construction of early learning experiences with children and families. Working together groups of early learning professionals have important roles in sharing their perspectives of how curriculum frameworks apply to their practice and more broadly to the program experiences and learning opportunities offered to the children. When early learning professionals work through questions in discussion with fellow staff members, and then reflect upon practice using each section of the curriculum framework, over time comfort will be gained to use the framework as a support tool in practice. Early learning professionals may want to begin by examining YouTube clips that discuss curriculum frameworks, such as the following: http://bit.ly/147Hjuv. Thinking about the case study presented, answer the following questions in your professional journal:

1. Why do you think this early learning professional is feeling scared about incorporating curriculum frameworks into her practice? Does her experience working with children put her at an advantage or disadvantage in adapting her practice to include a curriculum framework?

2. Do you think individuals moving to a province that has a curriculum framework should be required to have specific training in it before being eligible for employment? Why or why not?

3. What roles should executive directors play in ensuring that their staff members are using the curriculum framework in their practice? What types of observations would executive directors make to determine how well staff members are using the framework?

4. How might staff and the executive director use the curriculum framework to support their program philosophy and approach to programming? What do you believe are the top five priorities that must be addressed? How would you proceed?

BIG IDEAS FOR DIALOGIC LEARNING

In the previous section on pedagogical tools, we asked you to explore the concept of metaphors as tools to examine professional practice related to curriculum frameworks. To encourage dialogue and to open your learning to multiple perspectives, we recommend a metaphor exchange. Draw your metaphor on a piece a paper and display your drawings as a group. Use the metaphors as an impetus for discussion about the values and uses of curriculum frameworks, in addition to exploring images and perceptions of early learning and early learning professionals. You may also wish to discuss and compare your answers to the following questions:

1. Do frameworks limit autonomy?

2. What would you do if you disagreed with your provincial framework in some way?

3. How would you use a framework in your program development and implementation?

VISION

In a perfect world, every early learning professional would have the supports and resources they need to examine curriculum frameworks within a community of other professionals. Given the enormity of the documents and the reality of practice, without these supports, implementation may be unrealistic. We envision a world where early learning professionals are provided with training at both the pre-service and in-service level to support their understanding and use of frameworks. We see the possibilities of using technology to encourage dialogue among these professionals and look to the example of Australia for inspiration in the hopes that one day, Canada will have a national framework with similar resources and supports. For more information on the Australian framework, go to http://bit.ly/1IJMZVE.

MAKING CONNECTIONS

Advances in technology, in particular the widespread use of social media platforms, are globalizing the early learning profession, with many opportunities to make connections with others from all over the world. Your technological challenge is to get a glimpse into the early learning sector outside of your own context, whether in another province or another country. If you start with a Twitter account, you can search for early learning professionals practising in other places. Can you get a glimpse of what it would be like to practise as an early learning professional in other parts of the world, using social media as your vehicle? For an idea of how to use this social media platform to connect with like-minded educators from around the world, go to https://twitter.com/DianeKashin1 and check out the followers' profiles. Read the tweets of these individuals to see what they find interesting to discuss.

KEY TERMS

Image 126
Metaphor 126

Pre-primary approach 110
Social pedagogical approach 110

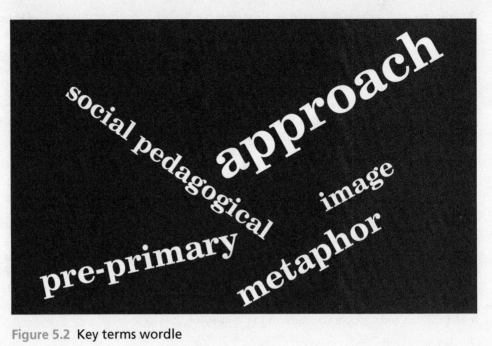

Figure 5.2 Key terms wordle

SUMMARY

By examining curriculum frameworks from around the world, early learning students and professionals acquire guidelines for pedagogical practice.

1. Early learning students and professionals can consider the two broad types of curricula approaches in use globally—the social pedagogical approach and the pre-primary approach—and relate these to their own practice.

2. There are multiple benefits to using curriculum frameworks as part of professional practice, as they increase knowledge, offer theoretical perspectives, and offer practical suggestions.

3. An examination of the similarities and differences among the seven Canadian curriculum frameworks shows the influence of international curriculum frameworks.

4. As Aboriginal frameworks are developed, early learning students and professionals will understand the guiding principles that should be in place for Aboriginal early learning programs.

5. Theories, philosophies, and programming models or approaches are influenced by the passage of time. Early learning students and professionals can reflect on these changes to understand historical perspectives and their relationships to future trends.

6. Early learning professionals, educational institutions, and government departments have a responsibility and role in advancing the knowledge about and ability to use the context of curriculum frameworks in practice.

For Further Thought

The OECD has a helpful resource to delve further into the concepts of curriculum frameworks that looks at strategies to tackle challenges in designing and implementing curriculum features from a wide range of countries. You can find it at http://bit.ly/14hLp9P.

Chapter 6

Building Relationships and Rapport in Children's Communities of Play

LEARNING OUTCOMES

After exploring this chapter, you should be able to

1. Explain the concepts of relationships and rapport and their connection to working with children and families in early learning programs.

2. Describe what is meant by self-regulation and how self-regulation influences children's behaviours.

3. Highlight how environments and program designs influence children's play, learning, and ability to develop relationships and rapport with others in their play and learning community.

4. Outline the roles and responsibilities of early learning professionals in establishing and promoting quality relationship and rapport building in early learning programs.

5. Describe how dramatic play can support children in developing self-regulation skills, rapport, and relationships with other children and adults.

A CHILD'S STORY   Kayah

Last night, Mommy told me that we would have to get up early in the morning because it will be the first day for me to go to my new playschool. I know Mommy will be coming into my room soon to tell me to get up. I hear her with my baby brother. She is singing to him. Mommy is happy. I am sad. I wish I could stay home today with Mommy and she would sing to me. I don't want to go to a "big girl's school"! That's what Daddy calls it. I wish Daddy was here. He works at night. When he comes home, I won't be here. Daddy says it's better because I wake him up too much. He says I will have fun at my new playschool. Here comes Mommy. She tells me I have to hurry up now because Mommy let me lie in bed too long and now we are going to be late. She helps me with my shoes and tells me to eat quickly because we have to leave. She doesn't see that I am sad. Mommy puts me in my car seat beside my baby brother and I am still sad. I want to cry but Mommy told me that big girls don't cry. When Mommy says, "We are here," I see a gigantic

building, and Mommy says our entrance is by the playground. I don't want to go in, even though I have been for a few visits with Mommy before. Mommy is pulling me. I can't help it; tears are coming out of my eyes. When we get to the door, Mommy talks to a lady and the lady named Roya smiles at me and takes my hand. Mommy comes in with me, helps me take my coat off, watches for a minute, and then says goodbye. I hear her singing to my brother as she leaves but soon I don't hear her at all. Roya tells me to put my tears away. But I don't know where to put them! She tells me to go and play but I am scared. There are so many children in the room. I don't want to play. It is so noisy. I want my mommy. I am going to cry and I am going to shout so Roya knows that I want my mommy. Maybe I can cry loud enough so Mommy hears me. I am not going to play. I am going to stand here and cry and scream so my mommy comes back. Through my tears, I can see that Roya isn't smiling at me anymore.

Children's cubby area in the morning.
Diane Kashin

ing and promoting quality relationship and rapport building in early learning

CHAPTER PREVIEW

*Learning awakens a variety of internal developmental
processes that are able to operate only when the child
is interacting with people in his environment and in
cooperation with his peers.*

—LEV VYGOTSKY (1896–1934)

relationships The way two or more people are connected.

In the first five chapters of the text, you were introduced to theories, concepts, and perspectives that have influenced the evolution of early childhood education and are guiding the direction of early learning today. In this chapter, we ask that you think big and reflect on the importance of establishing and maintaining meaningful and authentic **relationships**, or connections with all the players in the early learning environment. Think about Kayah in the opening vignette. What do you hear this child expressing? What are your feelings when you read Kayah's story? What do you envision your role to be with Kayah? Why? Remember that thinking big is thinking critically about what early learning professionals do and why they do it. We ask you to think about the professional skills required to create a play and learning community that is shared with all the players—the children, the families, and the early learning professionals—and where everyone feels valued and supported and makes a contribution.

Early learning professionals create rapport and reach out to families and children, thereby building on the strength and diversity of the community's members. This is part of professional practice. In this chapter and in the upcoming six chapters, you will note a new feature asking you to *claim a particular aspect of professional practice* as related to the chapter content. In Box 6.1, we ask you to think about the image that you wish to exhibit as an early learning student.

Chepko Danil/Fotolia

CLAIM YOUR IMAGE as an early learning student who is competent and capable of being part of a community of learners together with others.

Early learning professionals nurture relationships and build rapport so that there is an understanding of the other players' perspectives. Remember that the players include children, their families, your colleagues, and you. Thinking of children as active citizens with a voice may be a new concept for you. Reflect on how viewing children with a voice could counter the perspective that sees children only as "entities on their way to adulthood" (Steinberg, 2011, p. 5). If we reconceptualize children as *being* rather than just on their way to becoming adults, we can begin to examine ideas and concepts from their perspective. Children have the right to a voice. They have a right to be involved and to have input into early learning programs.

Adults work toward giving children a voice in early learning programs for many reasons. When children feel safe and valued, learning and optimal development are more likely. This can be the outcome of establishing community. In Chapter 5, we introduced you to curriculum frameworks from across the globe. A common concept among the frameworks is that of relationship building as the foundation for programming and child development. Early learning professionals work in spaces that are designed for children and their families. As identified in Figure 6.1 on the next page, environments influence how children develop relationships and build rapport with those in their learning community.

We envision that early learning professionals are critically engaged with colleagues, parents, and children to widen their view and to see multiple perspectives, thus increasing their understanding of the players' rights within the play and learning community.

Figure 6.1 Environmental conditions that support children's feelings of worth

Rosalba Bortolotti

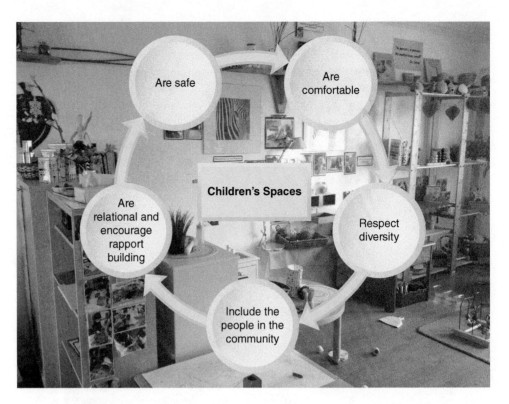

THE IMPORTANCE OF RELATIONSHIPS AND RAPPORT

Children's families influence relationships, rapport, and communication strategies with others in their community. The interactions among adults, family values, the support that children give to and receive from their parents, and their perception of reciprocity influence how children build other relationships. As you read in Chapter 5, the various curriculum frameworks that have been developed across Canada and internationally all identify the relational component as a key attribute in high-quality early learning programs.

Erikson's (1963) psychosocial theory is one framework that early learning students and professionals can use as a guide when developing rapport and relationships with children and families. Erikson's theoretical framework suggests that children flourish in environments that promote opportunities to meet their needs for autonomy, initiative, and identity; these rich environments encourage interactive play, exploration, and connections with other children, the program, and families. For example, early learning professionals and families think about what an effective transition model may be for children and families when children are starting new early learning programs. The objective is to have a model where the children and parents experience the least amount of stress in moving into the playschool environment for the first time. In this way, the foundation for healthy relationships is established at the onset of the children entering the environment. Take a moment to think about what behaviours and experiences children might bring with them when entering a new environment (see the accompanying Reflective Moment box). Early learning professionals observe children in their individual and group play experiences and use their findings to support them in promoting positive pathways in rapport and relationship building.

The quality of the early learning professionals' relational pedagogy contributes to the level of engagement children have in their play and learning experiences (Gurland & Grolnick, 2008). Post-developmental perspectives in early learning emphasize "ethical issues, cultural contexts, and the struggle for equity" when considering relational pedagogy

Building a relationship with the environment.
Rosalba Bortolotti

(Edwards & Nuttall, 2009, p. 3). Advocates for children recognize that what works with one child or one family may not work for another—there is no single "best practice," since that concept is value-laden and relative. One of the key roles of early learning professionals is to build relationships with children and families that are based on ethical choices (Moss & Petrie, 2002). This requires early learning students to engage in **deep thinking**, or moving from a literal understanding to a deeper, more abstract level, as a way to assimilate and practise these core processes. The predominant worldviews or paradigms in our early learning sector have shifted. Today, children and adults are partners in play and learning.

deep thinking A process of moving from a literal understanding to a deeper, more abstract level.

As early learning students and professionals, we stand on the shoulders of giants. Although we are moving toward a new era for our profession, it is still important to consider the past. Spodek and Saracho (2003) helped to remind us that "in understanding the past and the contribution of those before us, we are able to know the saga of early childhood education and are able to become better, more reflective, more understanding, and more professional in the field" (p. 4). Researchers, philosophers, and theorists alike have thought deeply about relationships. Lev Vygotsky's theory of social constructivism, which was presented in Chapter 3, guides the perspectives presented in this chapter. Vygotsky (1981) suggested that "it is through others that we develop into ourselves" (p. 161). This statement reinforces the importance of rapport and relationships, and of establishing early learning communities of play and learning. Connecting with others within a caring community will contribute to a program that respects relationships and provides children with a comfortable environment away from their family.

⟫ A Reflective Moment

Think about children entering new spaces and places such as an early learning environment. What might children bring to their first-time encounters with unfamiliar children or adults? What styles and behaviours might early learning professionals use in their attempts to build rapport with children and families in order to be more successful in developing a positive relationship?

ATTACHMENT THEORY

If we focus too much on learning within a structured curriculum, we may fail to pay enough attention to children's social and emotional development. On Kayah's first day at her new playschool, she will benefit from her early learning professional's attention to relationship building and rapport. Bowlby (1973) reinforced the importance of examining the emotional and behavioural reactions of children who experience separation from their primary caregivers. He recognized human intimacy as a primary component of human life and believed that relationships, starting with rapport, contribute to the healthy psychological development of children (Alsop-Shields & Mohay, 2001). Bowlby's attachment theory emphasized the importance of the quality of the parent–child relationship. In his view, children's confidence in managing in an environment reflects their perceptions of their primary caregivers responding to their needs (Bowlby, 1973). The quality of children's prior attachments is extended to their relationships with early learning professionals and children.

Mary Ainsworth (1979) was inspired by Bowlby's work. She created the *strange situation* theory to assess children's attachment type, based on observation of children as they respond to their caregivers' behaviour. The strange situation is a form of natural observation over a twenty-five-minute continuum of planned separations and reunions. Based on the child's observed behaviour, a type of attachment is determined. This important research has led to the development of prevention, early identification, early intervention, and treatment of attachment disorders. However, Ainsworth's research is not without criticism. As with the theories and perspectives presented in previous chapters, we encourage you to think critically about theories, research, models, and approaches to determine their strengths and weaknesses and how the theories align with or are controversial in relation to your current philosophy.

CRITICAL PEDAGOGY

Early learning professionals are taking on the role of *critical pedagogue* (Giroux, 1988). A critical pedagogue thinks of oneself as capable of intellectualizing the concepts and thinking big about their meaning and how they might be actualized in practice.

critical pedagogy An approach to teaching and learning that involves critique.

Critical pedagogy provides early learning professionals with a language of critique that they can used to view and analyze their practice. The language of critique has a further purpose: by critically examining practice, new intellectual spaces are opened up to rethink theoretical frameworks and pedagogical practice (Kilderry, 2004). With this in mind, we suggest that you consider some of the criticisms of Ainsworth's research, such as the possibility that it may lead to the labelling of young children, and these labels may follow them throughout their life. The strange situation is also criticized for its time frame, as children who are being assessed have not yet developed a sense of time, and this is stressful for them. The children Ainsworth studied in Uganda and Baltimore had different cultural ideologies, and the children in her study were suspected of having "insecure" attachment types. This type of labelling brings up the issue of **ethical practice**. Rather than label children for their strengths and weaknesses, early learning professionals must consider the ethics involved in everyday encounters so that children such as Kayah feel that their relationship needs and rights are met in a kind and caring manner.

ethical practice Practising the rules and standards governing the conduct of members of a profession.

Having an understanding of the important work that has been done on attachment contributes to your professional knowledge. Knowing how to apply this knowledge in everyday encounters with children and their families contributes to your ethical practice. Dahlberg and Moss (2005) suggested that early learning environments should be locations of ethical practice and that in every encounter, early learning professionals need to consider the *Other* whom they cannot grasp. This would be deemed the ethics of an encounter. In Kayah's first encounter in her new playschool, we noticed that she was crying loudly and asking for her mother—she was heard but not listened to. The early learning professional in the room modelled that she could not grasp the complexity of Kayah's thought processes and her prior experience. Ethical practice involves listening beyond what is heard in the moment.

THE CONCEPT OF RELATIONSHIP RAPPORT

Relationship rapport is a complex construct that guides early learning professionals. The need to have positive relationships with others is essential to human development (McCelland, 1987), and such relationships are the foundation for rapport. **Rapport** refers to the interactions and the depth of the caring and concern expressed between two people. Early learning professionals build rapport with children and families by establishing environments that provide a sense of comfort, by exhibiting support and acceptance within the space, and by encouraging reciprocal interpersonal communication (Gurland & Grolnick, 2008; Robinson, 2012). When the environmental space and the people in the space foster reciprocal, respectful exchange, children and adults exhibit attributes that show caring characteristics, as outlined in Figure 6.2.

rapport The interaction and depth of caring and concern expressed between two people.

As ethical practitioners, early learning professionals adjust and restructure their attention to relationship rapport so that they are consistently responding positively to changing family dynamics. They ensure that the feeling tone in early learning programs meets the needs of children, families, and early learning professionals.

DEVELOPING RELATIONSHIPS AND RAPPORT

Early learning professionals play many important roles in the lives of children, one of which is as someone who helps them to establish meaningful relationships. Meaningful relationships influence and are foundational to children's play, their levels of exploration

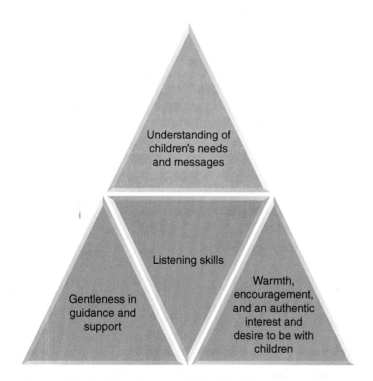

Figure 6.2 Caring characteristics that are present in environments of relationship rapport

and curiosity, and their development. Through observation, early learning professionals can determine strategies that will contribute to establishing a positive rapport with children. The program design is built upon the rapport established with children and families. For example, an early learning professional would acquire information about Kayah's interests from her parents prior to her coming to the centre. Then, the early learning professional would ensure that materials reflecting Kayah's interests were available. If there were other children who had a similar interest, the early learning professional might begin a play episode as a way to draw the children together. This process supports and focuses on the children's psychosocial needs so that relationship development occurs through play (Pond, Wojtasik, & White, 2009). Take a moment to consider how you can develop meaningful relationships (see the accompanying Reflective Moment box).

Early learning professionals become specialists in building relationships with children and their families by taking into account the perspectives of all who are a part of the environment. The level of rapport established among early learning professionals and children contributes to how valued children and their families feel as citizens with rights in their own community.

The needs of children and families may differ as a result of such factors as their experiences with early learning programs, their culture, and what parents and early learning professionals believe is best for children. Building on the ethical practice process, early learning professionals and parents develop partnerships so that they can collectively figure out the comforts children require to feel safe, secure, and confident in their daily environments.

Establishing Rapport

Early learning students and professionals draw upon their knowledge of a variety of theories, perspectives, and approaches to figure out their approach to children and how to support them in new experiences with people and things in their environment. As children enter early learning programs, they are dealing with a new environment, meaning that they must adjust to new adults, other children, routines, expectations, and the loss of their previous daily routines. As children become comfortable in the environment, they establish themselves. At this point, early learning professionals can offer them new challenges in their play. Challenges in play help children to take risks; problem solve; and advance their sense of wonderment, exploration, and experimentation. Children who do not establish a foundational sense of rapport within their play community engage less readily in the "what ifs" offered by that community.

Consider the story of Kayah coming to the early learning program during her first day, first week, and first month. She is faced with meeting at least fifteen other children, four adults, and a new routine. She may be challenged by the noise of others, she may be confined to spending more time indoors than before coming to the program, and she may be required to sit in group discussions about things that she is not interested in. Fortunately for Kayah, a number of early learning professionals check in with her throughout her first week as a way to support her adjustment to the environment. They stay in contact with Kayah's parents throughout the week via email and daily conversations during the drop-off and pick-up times. They listen carefully to the comments and questions that are asked. These actions are fundamental to establishing rapport with her family, which in turn helps Kayah to gradually build rapport with the people in her play community. By the end of the week, Kayah begins to show signs of comfort and confidence in her learning environment. She is exploring more of the environment, she is participating in more conversations with other children, and she requires less time and reassurance from the early learning professionals. For children entering new communities of play, the amount of time required to establish feelings of comfort and respect varies because of life experiences, temperaments, parent–child relationships, the early learning environments, and the strategies early learning professionals use to make connections with children.

Children's behaviours, experiences, relationships, and ability to build relationships are affected by their caregivers and environments. Similar to adults, young children react to change in their life experiences and routines. Children explore and learn in new environments only when they have developed the sense that the adults in their environment will respond to their needs, especially when they become upset. New experiences may elicit attachment behaviours such as clinginess, listlessness, or shyness (Robinson, 2012).

CHILDREN AND SELF-REGULATION

Self-regulation is a deep, internal mechanism that allows children and adults to perform mindful, intentional, and thoughtful behaviours (Bodrova & Leong, 2008). Pascal (2009) described self-regulation as "the ability to adapt one's emotions, behaviours, and attention to the demands of the situation" (p. 4). He further suggested that self-regulation is "about establishing one's own internal motivation for adapting to, and understanding emotional and social demands. In fact for many children, requiring compliance undermines their own abilities to self-regulate" (p. 4). Self-regulation includes children's abilities to manage their emotions, focus their attention, and restrain themselves from performing some activities or behaviours while carrying out others (Rimm-Kaufman, Nathanson, Brock, Curby, & Grimm, 2009).

> **self-regulation** An internal process used to manage emotions, focus attention, and restrain oneself from performing some activities or behaviours while carrying out others.

Developing self-regulation skills is important to children, as it contributes to their self-confidence and emotional wellness. Children are born with some ability for self-regulation (Gillespie & Seibel, 2006), but they often find it difficult to control their strong emotions. Early learning professionals play a key role in creating environments that will allow children to express their emotions and develop the self-regulation skills necessary to function in a variety of situations. Gaining the skills and abilities to self-regulate is "interconnected to attention skills, memory, cognitive flexibility, and interpretation of behaviour and social skills" (Dietze & Kashin, 2012, p. 38). Children's play and their roles in communities of play and learning correlate to their level of self-regulation. Boyer (2009) identified that children's level of self-regulation is visible in their behaviours, as outlined in Figure 6.3.

There are two sides to self-regulation. One side is being able to control impulses to stop doing something (Bodrova & Leong, 2008). For example, a child may get off a swing to allow another child a turn, even if he does not want to. The other side is the capacity to do something even if there is no desire to do so (Bodrova & Leong, 2008). For example, a group of children will participate in tidying up the playroom, even though they do not want to stop playing and they want to come back to their play episode later.

From infancy, the human brain is capable of being motivated to "organize stimulation from the environment and to develop executive self-regulatory functions" (Bronson, 2000, p. 167).

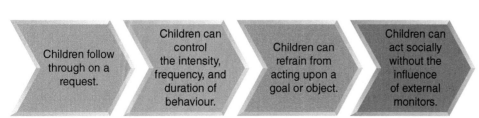

Figure 6.3 Children's level of self-regulation expressed in behaviours

Source: Adapted from Boyer, 2009.

Children follow through on a request.

Children can control the intensity, frequency, and duration of behaviour.

Children can refrain from acting upon a goal or object.

Children can act socially without the influence of external monitors.

Regulating the self means a child knows what behaviours are expected and will "search for, discover, and impose order and meaning on experience" (Bronson, 2000, p. 167). Part of this cognitive thinking involves children classifying information in ways that they can understand. For example, when infants begin to think and organize their environment, they are rewarded by "finding patterns, categories and predictable cause-effect sequences" (Bronson, 2000, p. 167). Predictable cause-and-effect relationships are rewarding to children because when they gain an understanding of what is going to happen, they can figure out how to act in those situations. For example, infants cry when they are hungry. They learn that this behaviour will result in an adult feeding them. They have learned a cause-and-effect sequence. When children have difficulty identifying patterns, they may exhibit signs of disequilibrium and agitation or restlessness.

As children establish a feeling of comfort, they are motivated to take more risks and to branch out to explore new options and experiences. Such experiences support children's problem-solving, critical-thinking, and creativity skills, which become lifelong patterns of practice.

For young children, the social, emotional, and physical environments provide a platform and the internal motivation to explore strategies that will ultimately contribute to self-regulation (Bronson, 2000). If children's play is restricted, their physical development is influenced, which can potentially restrict and limit their brain development. A child's brain function, combined with her physical abilities, develops to support self-regulatory functions (Bodrova & Leong, 2008; Bronson, 2000).

Children with self-regulation skills exhibit characteristics of patience, persistence, and flexibility. They also are more likely to exhibit a higher level of curiosity, to engage in more exploratory play, and to approach new experiences with a sense of intrigue and risk both in their individual play and as a member of a play community. Children with less confidence exhibit greater difficulty in forming relationships, sharing, and expressing their needs and perspectives.

Early learning professionals design play spaces and create an atmosphere that offers children opportunities to learn how to self-regulate behaviourally and emotionally. They role-model and offer play experiences such as dramatic play options that will allow children to practise self-regulation and apply the rules in new situations. Some children benefit from having visual and tangible reminders about self-regulation. In essence, the people, place,

When children participate socially they are exhibiting self-regulation.
Rosalba Bortolotti

and atmosphere of the space contribute to how children develop their sense and level of self-regulation (Rimm-Kaufman et al., 2009).

Three skills are required to achieve mature self-regulation: forethought, performance, and self-reflection (Schunk & Zimmerman, 1998). Forethought is questioning what is going to happen if you do something and what you have to do to reach a goal. Performance is engaging and observing yourself during the performance. If you don't observe or pay attention, you will be unable to self-reflect on the performance. Self-reflection refers to being able to think about the performance and assess whether or not it was satisfying and effective. Achieving self-regulation requires caring environments, motivation, and opportunities to engage in trial and error and problem solving (Bronson, 2000).

Early learning professionals support parents and families in understanding the process of self-regulation and emotional regulation. They partner with families to examine children's behaviours and offer support, guidance, and observations through this process (Boyer, 2009).

PROGRAM DESIGN FOR CHILDREN

A 2011 study on competence requirements in early childhood education and care (CoRe), financed by the European Commission Directorate-General for Education and Culture, highlighted quality as a multi-dimensional and generic construct. Quality in early learning is a process that "unfolds—and has to be proactively developed—in at least five dimensions" (University of East London, Cass School of Education, & University of Ghent, Department for Social Welfare Studies, 2011, p. 24). Table 6.1 lists these dimensions and gives examples that have been adapted from the CoRe report.

The first dimension, which focuses on experiences of and outcomes for children, is an excellent foundation for practice. Early learning professionals may work with children ranging in age from infancy to middle childhood. Each stage requires early learning professionals to be knowledgeable about child development and about program design principles and processes that will guide the types of experiences and play spaces that are created to complement and build upon children's sense of belonging within their community. Now consider the first dimension in relationship to the third: interactions. The everyday interactions that

Table 6.1 Five Dimensions of Quality

Dimension	Example
1. Experiences of and outcomes for children	Experiences of belonging, engagement, well-being, meaning-making, and achievement
2. Experiences of families and professionals	Experiences of belonging, engagement, well-being, and meaning-making
3. Interactions	Interactions between all those who belong in the early learning environment
4. Structural conditions	Ratios, group size, space, environment, play materials as well as "non-contact" time, continuous professional learning, support for research, and critical reflective practice
5. Systems of evaluation, monitoring, and quality improvement	Ways of systematically including the views and perspectives of those within the community.

Source: Adapted from University of East London, Cass School of Education, & University of Ghent, Department for Social Welfare Studies. (2011). *CoRe: Competence requirements in early childhood education and care: A study for the European Commission Directorate-General for Education and Culture. Final report.* Ghent, Belgium: Centre for Innovation in the Early Years, pp. 24–25.

take place in the learning environment support the healthy development and well-being of children. Considering interactions and reflecting upon them will support the professional, whose role is to ensure that desired outcomes, whether internally or externally set, are met. Early learning professionals provide opportunities for an experience to evolve from children and then assess by multiple means what the outcome of that experience was. Table 6.2

Table 6.2 Experiences and Outcomes for Children

INFANCY

Program Example	Values	Experience	Outcome
Caregiver Curriculum The approach to caregiving focuses on the concept of respect and responding to each child warmly and sensitively through planned and unplanned experiences that promote the child's development (Gonzales-Mena & Eyer, 2012).	Responsiveness Respect Care Learning Development	Lucy, who is fourteen months old, is sitting at the highchair awaiting lunch. When a bowl of avocado is placed in front of her she throws it and begins to cry. The early learning professional acknowledges Lucy's emotions and verbalizes the appropriate response, "No thank you," with a warm smile. The early learning professional later asks Lucy's caregiver if she eats avocado at home.	The child will feel safe to express herself and begin to learn appropriate responses. The caregiver also feels respected when consulted regarding diet and food preferences.

EARLY CHILDHOOD

Program Example	Values	Experience	Outcome
Reggio-Inspired These are programs that seek inspiration from the pre-primary schools in Reggio Emilia, Italy. The child is seen as competent and capable, and the three subjects of education are teachers, parents, and children (Kashin, 2009).	Creativity Curiosity Trust Competence	Jake discovers a new way to use paints—he uses his hands rather than the paintbrushes provided. The early learning professional acknowledges and encourages his curiosity by commenting positively on his method and suggesting that he demonstrate his innovation to his peers.	The child is reassured by the trust instilled in him and will henceforth continue to express his creativity and explore his curiosity. He is comfortable sharing with his peers and feels valued as a member of the learning community.

MIDDLE CHILDHOOD

Program Example	Values	Experience	Outcome
Tribes This process of Tribes involves teachers, administrators, children, and families working together to create a learning community dedicated to caring and support, active participation, and positive expectations for all (Gibbs, 2006).	A caring culture Communities of learners Responsiveness Collaboration	A group of ten children attending a before- and after-school program meet together weekly to develop and maintain their daily pledge to listen attentively, respect one another, be appreciative of others, avoid put-downs, and feel safe and comfortable in interactions.	Children feel a sense of ownership in their own environment, and that they are able to voice their concerns but also have the "right to pass" (Gibbs, 2006), which allows them the option of not participating if they are not comfortable. The early learning professionals feel that there is a lessening of behavioural issues as the children become more capable of problem solving.

Source: Adapted from Gibbs, 2006; Gonzales-Mena & Eyer, 2012; Kashin, 2009.

features programming examples that value relationships, the possible experiences children might have through the implementation of this program, and the potential outcomes for children.

PROGRAM DESIGN FOR FAMILIES

Early learning professionals take into account the experiences, cultures, and values of families in program design and philosophy. Incorporating these elements into the program design requires early learning professionals to engage parents in dialogue while listening intently for cues that provide insight into the strengths that parents can bring to the children's play community. Reaching out to parents, empowering them to be contributors to the play program, and sharing key stories of how their contributions have influenced children in the program build rapport and encourage relationship building between families and early learning programs. Professionals who do not embrace parental involvement may find designing programs that support families every day challenging, time-consuming, and in conflict with their beliefs about being in partnership with families. Programs without parental involvement often exhibit predetermined structured activities, experiences, and routines, which children are required to conform to.

Early learning professionals who focus on the needs of children and families seek out children's and parents' involvement in their programs. Once you have considered involvement, reflect on the concept of engagement. Involvement and engagement are terms that are sometimes thought to mean the same thing. However, Pushor (2007a) suggested that the term **engagement** is more fitting for a program that values parents and involves family-centred practice. Early learning professionals reflect deeply on terminology, as they recognize that the use of terms and language can influence image. For example, consider how much of an impact terminology might have and connect it to the words of Lev Vygotsky (1981): "The conception of word meaning as a unit of both generalizing thought and social interchange is of incalculable value for the study of thought and language" (p. 9). What does this statement mean to you? How might you see this in your future practice?

engagement Including families in early learning programs in ways that go beyond involvement.

THE ENVIRONMENT AND PROGRAM DESIGN

Quality early learning environments offer children places to be curious, places to wonder, and places to discover. Such environments encourage children to be stimulated and to experiment, which leads to new discoveries, knowledge, and skills. This approach supports the natural wonderment of children. Ideally, early learning professionals create play spaces that offer children the freedom to explore and to use materials and the environment in ways that support their interests and are authentic for their play. When children develop a comfort zone within their play spaces, they gradually develop the self-confidence needed to participate in advanced exploration and risk taking. Children flourish in environments that have meaningful, authentic materials and with adults who respond to their needs. In these environments, children will develop a sense of acceptance and calmness, and they will become desensitized to discomforts or anxiety that they may have previously experienced (Goldberger, Luebering Mohl, & Thompson, 2009).

Children's environments correlate to their ability to develop self-regulation. For example, when an early learning professional observes a child's interest in building towers, having a block centre that supports tower building can help the child to overcome a sense of aloneness and anxiety because of the absence of parents and create connectedness between the early learning professional and the child. This helps the child to reduce fears and contributes to advancing skills in rapport, relationship building, and self-regulation.

ROLES AND RESPONSIBILITIES OF EARLY LEARNING PROFESSIONALS

Early learning students and professionals build relationships among children, their families, and the early learning team. As children and families enter an early learning environment, the process of building relationships begins. Early learning professionals greet children during the initial introductions and speak with the children and families about their roles. They continue to give a warm reception and authentic greeting daily, as this interaction and conversational exchange contributes to developing a rapport with children and their families. Early learning professionals strengthen the two-way relationship by expanding opportunities for dialogue, extending play experiences, and offering comfort and reassurance when required. Young children learn and practise their coping skills and strategies as they create bonds and comfort with new adults and children in their community of play.

Children's play has many purposes. Creating environments that support children in establishing meaningful play is one of the most important strategies that adults use to connect children with others and to help them form relationships that support them in their development. Through play, children also release their stress or tension and work out their feelings of disequilibrium. Early learning professionals continuously try to create comfort experiences and places within the play space that support children in feeling accepted, safe, and emotionally comfortable (Jessee & Gaynard, 2009).

BUILDING PROFESSIONAL CAPACITY FOR DEVELOPING RELATIONSHIPS

Developing meaningful learning experiences and constructing positive adult–child relationships with all the children in the play environment is a challenging process, especially for the "many teachers [who] have never participated—as teachers or as children in families and classrooms—in the kinds of adult–child interactions that [are] expected of effective teachers" (Howes & Tsao, 2012, p. 3). Building capacity for developing relationships begins with how early learning professionals extend respect to and for the children, nurture relationships, and view children. For example, do you view children as partners in learning who have a right to be involved and engaged in the decision-making processes within the learning environment? What skills do you need in order to build relationships and rapport? The early learning and development framework in the state of Victoria, Australia, published by the Department of Education and Early Childhood Development (DEECD, 2009) makes eight suggestions for practice principles, which are divided into three categories (see Figure 6.4).

Figure 6.4 Practice principles for early learning professionals

Source: Adapted from DEECD, 2009.

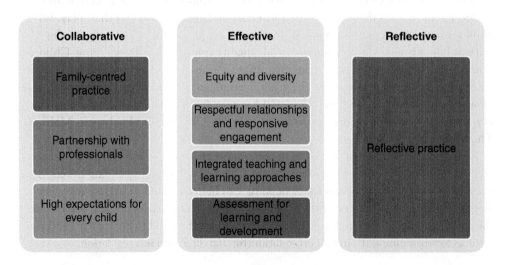

Collaborative, effective, and reflective early learning professionals build relationships and rapport. They do so by being family focused, working with other professionals, having high expectations for children, and being connected to each child. Early learning professionals are effective at what they do because they are respectful and responsive and celebrate the diversity within early learning environments. The Victorian early learning framework in Australia refers to equity, rather than equality (DEECD, 2009). Saffigna, Franklin, Church, and Taylor (2011), the authors of an accompanying evidence paper to support the framework, explained the difference between the two terms:

> *Equality* refers to the same conduct in communication and contact, quantity or values for all individuals. *Equity* refers to ideas of fairness and social justice, which may require challenging the dominant culture in order to provide different treatment, or special measures, for individuals or groups to ensure that they experience equal opportunities to succeed. (p. 8)

According to Marbina, Church, and Taylor (2011), the authors of the evidence paper for Practice Principle 6, "integrated teaching and learning approaches focus on the interweaving of child-directed play and learning, guided play and learning, and adult-led learning" (p. 6). Early learning professionals apply their professional judgment and assessments of children's learning and development to make programming decisions with the children and their families that are meaningful, balanced, and authentic. In the programming bubble in Figure 6.5, we highlight how children use dramatic play to support them in figuring out areas of concern, distress, and joy.

Dramatic play offers children a place to make many social and emotional connections (Bergen, 2002). The dramatic play centre is a venue for children to work through some of their feelings in ways that meet their needs. Although children experience similar feelings to adults', they generally do not express them in the same way—adults verbalize them, while children express their feelings through their play. Dramatic centres can assist children in playing out scenarios that are new to them or causing them anxiety. For example, when children first come to an early learning program, they may use the dramatic centre, which has dolls and a homelike setting, to play out their feelings. The children have the dolls take on the role of the child going to a new early learning program. This type of play helps children to reduce anxiety, understand traumatic experiences, and recreate pleasant or unpleasant experiences. Through dramatic play, children play and replay the situation as a

Children's Dramatic Play

The dramatic play centre offers children a place to try out interactions with other children, express feelings, and extend support and feelings of belonging to others, which can lead to friendships and group membership. Having a variety of props available for a dramatic play centre sparks connectedness to peers and their play. ▶

Figure 6.5 **Programming bubble: children's dramatic play**

Children becoming engaged in food preparation to share with others recreates positive social experiences.

Rosalba Bortolotti

way to assimilate it and to reduce the intensity of their feelings (Dietze & Kashin, 2012). Similarly, they use dramatic play to create and recreate positive feelings.

The dramatic play centre offers children the right environment to learn to be the regulator and the object of regulation. For example, Vygotskian theory proposes that children must learn to regulate the behaviours of others before they are able to regulate themselves (Bodrova & Leong, 2008). As children design play and play creatively in dramatic centres, they learn to take on roles and responsibilities, they negotiate, they follow rules, and they push one another to follow rules or collectively change rules. Vygotsky suggested that these types of play experiences are needed for children to develop the habits of self-control (Tough, 2009). Depending on the types of props that children have access to, their dramatic play experiences help them to bring meaning to the birth of a new brother or sister; to new situations, such as starting at a new early learning centre; or to new people in their lives, such as early learning professionals or family members. Children require real-life items in dramatic play centres, such as telephones, pots, pans, and dress-up clothing, as well as the freedom to express their feelings within their play. Early learning professionals assist children when necessary, but generally encourage children to use the dramatic play centre in a way that meets their needs. This requires children to determine the rules, work out a play plan, and figure out how to resolve potential issues with playmates.

FEATURED RESEARCH

Robyn Dolby (2007) is a psychologist specializing in infant mental health, with an interest in using attachment theory to inform reflective practice. She designed the Circle of Security early intervention program for parents and children, with a focus on building relationships and supporting children's emotional health. Central to the program is a map that helps parents follow the child's relationship needs. Early learning professionals may also find the program and the map helpful. It can be used with children of all ages and goes beyond the immediate behaviour of the child, encouraging adults to think about how to meet the child's relationship needs. The tool suggested to do this is "seeing and guessing" conversations between adults. In these conversations, adults first focusing on seeing what the child does and then guess how they might be able to meet the child's needs. By responding to the message beneath the behaviour, rather than trying to shape or control the behaviour, adults can meet the relationship needs of the child. These conversations are not value free. Consider what that means. For more information on this program, see http://bit.ly/1523mVZ.

PEDAGOGICAL TOOLS: CHILDREN'S PORTFOLIOS

In Chapter 1, pedagogy was defined as your approach to teaching and learning. As these two concepts cannot exist in isolation, early learning professionals apply strategic teaching tools to support children's learning. In previous chapters, we have considered pedagogical tools as they apply to the practice of early learning professionals, focusing on outcomes for early learning professionals. In this chapter, we reintroduce the idea of pedagogical tools as they apply to experiences for children, featuring the tool of children's portfolios. A portfolio is a purposeful collection of children's work that records the process of their play and learning. Grace (1992) suggested that the portfolio be a record of "what the child has learned and how she has gone about the learning; how she thinks, questions, analyzes, synthesizes, produces, creates; and how she interacts—intellectually, emotionally and socially—with others" (p. 1). Making learning visible is often associated with the pre-primary schools of Reggio Emilia and can be applied to the portfolio-assessment movement. A portfolio is a useful way to connect with families. It provides the professional with a form of authentic assessment that makes the child's learning visible and can be shared with the family as well as the child. Above all, the portfolio should be seen as a celebration of the child. By including samples of children's conversations, artwork, attempts to print, and photographic images of their play with others, as well as representations of their own achievements and accomplishments, early learning professionals create a valuable tool that shows respect for children's rights as citizens of their environment.

PROFESSIONAL CASE STUDY

This is a very exciting time in my career. I have been at a new early learning centre in an urban community for three months now. During my interview, the director emphasized that one of the centre's core values is promoting respect and dignity for all children, families, and staff. She identified that this should be a core value in any centre, but it is particularly important at this centre because of the diverse family backgrounds and experiences. This makes so much sense to me when I think of Bronfenbrenner's ecological model, which helps us to understand the interrelationship of children's families and their community in their development. He reminds us of how children develop self-esteem and how adults can influence that process. There is a link to how we exhibit respect for children and families. It becomes an ethical practice that requires a great deal of consideration and reflection.

Mistrella has just started to work with me and the children who are three years of age. I love this age group 'because when they are comfortable and safe in their environment, not only are their language skills, their need for activity, and the overall ways in which they express themselves heartwarming, but their connections to people and the environment guide our practice. One of our newer children, Hannah, has taken several weeks to begin to express her ideas to us. I have consistently greeted her when she arrives, reassured her, and acknowledged her at various times during the day, and I frequently write her a note that I put in her backpack for her to read with her parents during their evening time together. I do this to build rapport and extend the feelings of rapport and respect to the family. I was so excited yesterday because as she entered the locker room she started speaking with Rosia. This was the first time since Hannah came here that she exhibited spontaneous dialogue with an adult other than me. I felt so great! Finally, Hannah was comfortable. But not for long! As she started to enter our playroom, she did so swinging a rain stick and saying that she was magical because she could make it rain in the room. As I was about to respond to Hannah, Mistrella responded by saying, "Don't be silly—you can't make it rain." As soon as Mistrella said this, Hannah began to cry. Then Mistrella said, "This is nothing to cry about." Hannah ran to me sobbing. I picked her up to give her comfort. As I did so, I saw an expression on Mistrella's face that made me uncomfortable. I thought for a moment about the situation. Maybe I should not have picked her up; maybe I should have tried to change the subject. Maybe I was becoming too attached to Hannah and the other children. Or maybe I was reading too much into the situation. After a few minutes, Hannah got down and began playing at the water table. Later in the morning, she was in the dramatic centre with her rain stick. She said to Joey the doll, "I can make it rain. My mommy told me that when I use that stick, it sounds just like rain, so I can make rain." She repeated this over and over to the dolls.

At the end of the day when Hannah's mother came to pick her up, Hannah said upon seeing her, "I can make it rain." Hannah's mother responded, "I know, you are my magical girl."

I have been bothered by this situation all day. I decided that I would ask if Mistrella and I could talk about the situation with Hannah, because as an ethical professional, such issues need to be resolved so that we continue to create an environment that is harmonious for us and the children. I approached Mistrella and she agreed that it would be helpful to do so and we set up a meeting for the next day prior to the children arriving. I am glad that we are going to have time this evening to reflect upon the situation and have a discussion tomorrow. I am confident that this discourse will help us to think about how each child has different needs and how our responses to children can influence their play, learning, self-regulation skills, and overall feelings toward the other children and adults in their environment. I know that we collectively want the best for the children.

REFLECTION QUESTIONS FOR SELF-LEARNING

Professional partnerships with colleagues and professionalism in early learning programs are closely connected to the commitment that individuals make to engage in reflective practice and to their interpretation of what professionalism means (Day, 2000). The meaning of *professionalism* is culture-specific, and the term can be defined in different ways by individuals depending on their values and beliefs. Helsby, Knight, McCulloch, Saunders, and Warburton (1997) indicated the importance of distinguishing between *being* and *behaving* as a professional. They described behaving as a professional as involving "displaying . . . degrees of dedication and commitment . . . accepting the open-ended nature of the task involved . . . maximum effort to 'do the best you possibly can' and a constant quest for improved performance" (pp. 9–10).

Professionals who are lifelong reflective educators can influence quality in various types of programs and schools. The process of reflection and discourse among early learning professionals helps to develop and maintain critical-thinking skills and synthesize feelings and perspectives about the daily experiences that occur in the early learning space. Thinking about the case study presented, answer the following questions in your professional journal:

1. Do you think that the early learning professional should have approached her colleague, Mistrella, to discuss the situation with Hannah? Why or why not? Is this the role of a colleague, or should the early learning professional take the situation to the director to handle? Why or why not?

2. Do you think that Mistrella's comments were suitable? Why or why not? Would they have been more suitable in a different situation? Why?

3. What type of information would the early learning professionals gain from observing Hannah in the dramatic play centre? What might you take from the play episode and share with the parents? Why? What kind of note might you put in Hannah's backpack today? Why?

4. After reflecting on the situation, how would you begin the conversation with Mistrella, and what key points would you like to bring forth in your conversation?

BIG IDEAS FOR DIALOGIC LEARNING

According to MacNaughton (2009, p. 5), "critical reflection is dialogic." The following questions should be posed to a group in order to encourage conversations with others. Consider these questions collaboratively:

1. Do emotions and relationships influence children's learning and development? What sort of relationships do children need to support their learning and development? Can you share an example of a situation from your own experience that illustrates the importance of relationship for learning and development? Compare and contrast the examples given—are they positive or negative?

2. How are relationships affected by the opportunities children have to play? If your dialogue contains the word *free* as in *free play*, reflect as a group on this statement: "Free play is an impossibility to produce. Most play in early childhood centres is deeply linked to power relations between children" (MacNaughton, 2009, p. 58). Can you think of and share some examples of when play can be hurtful and even dangerous?

3. The words and images we use to express our ideas are part of learning in discourse, which implies a dialogue. Discourse in early learning should involve conversations about the impact of words (terminology) on our images as professionals. *Free play* is one example of a term we may use without thinking of its implications. Can you think of any other words or terms that may affect images? Consider images of the child, the family, and the professional.

VISION

Exercising utopian thinking (Dahlberg & Moss, 2005), we envision children's early learning communities to be play-based (Dietze & Kashin, 2012). Utopian early learning communities would be ones where relationships are nurtured by professionals who understand the ethics of communication, caring, and support involved in everyday encounters. Every time early learning professionals are with children, their goal is to work toward supporting and developing meaningful relationships where community members experience the feelings of being loved and being worthy of that love. Early learning professionals who believe that their role is to ensure the rights of children within the learning environment are ethical practitioners. With this in mind, we focus not on best practice but on ethical practice. We support the image of the professional as one who is capable of "complex ways of thinking about teaching young children" (Edwards & Nuttall, 2009, p. 4). We envision early learning professionals as empowered ethical practitioners whose professional knowledge informs their practice. We defer to early learning professionals as being the source of their own best practice, rather than seeking advice about what constitutes best practice from outside their own learning community.

MAKING CONNECTIONS

Technological tools can help early learning professionals make and strengthen relationships with families. According to the National Association for the Education of Young Children's (NAEYC) position statement on the use of technology, technology gives opportunities to "build stronger relationships with parents and enhance family engagement (2012, p. 7). There are accessibility issues, as not all families have access to computers and the internet, but these types of technology are becoming more and more prevalent. For many families, it is convenient to receive information about their children either via Twitter or Facebook or through video-conferencing when face-to-face meetings are not possible. Technology offers the early learning professional a way to exchange information and share online resources. It gives parents and families opportunities to ask questions, seek advice, and share information about their child (NAEYC, 2012). We suggest that early learning professionals collect email addresses and begin to use the technology that has become so much a part of our lives.

Email is now entrenched in the everyday lives of early learning professionals, families, and children. It provides an opportunity to connect to knowledge being disseminated worldwide. Numerous blogs have been created by parents to support other parents. Early learning students and professionals can access these blogs through social media, opening up a world of information. Even search engines can lead professionals to information that will enrich the lives of the families they support. Search engines such as Google have alert functions that offer daily updates on the latest information on specific topics. It is easy to create alerts; typing "parent education" as your search query will yield plenty of results, which can be shared with families. When a parent approaches the professional for advice, information is often only clicks away.

Your challenge is to use environmental images or, with consent, images of children to create a slideshow that can be embedded into a PowerPoint presentation. The objective of this challenge is for you to provide the parents with information on their children's learning and development. For this challenge, you should focus on social and emotional development. Consider this question: How does the environment support children's learning about relationships? Begin your presentation by outlining your objectives, followed by multiple images. End your presentation with a conclusion. Once you have completed this part of the challenge, compose an email for parents. Ethics requires this challenge to be a simulation of an email that you would send as a practising early learning professional. You would attach the PowerPoint for personal viewing or you could invite the families to a screening. At this point in your journey, we recommend that this be a practice exercise.

KEY TERMS

Critical pedagogy   134
Deep thinking   133
Engagement   141
Ethical practice   134

Rapport   135
Relationships   130
Self-regulation   137

Figure 6.6 Key terms wordle

SUMMARY

In summary, establishing relationships with children is a vital responsibility of early learning students and professionals. By thinking deeply about the learning outcomes of this chapter, students can understand why relationship building is core to early learning programs.

1. How you connect with children and their families will influence the sense of belonging for everyone in the learning environment.

2. Early learning students and professionals know that self-regulation is an important skill for children to develop for relationship building and overall success in life. Knowing the importance of self-regulation helps early learning students and professionals support children in developing this skill.

3. Relationships are influenced by environmental conditions and by how the program is designed to support children's play, learning, and abilities. Knowing this, students become familiar with the roles and responsibilities involved in promoting quality relationship building and rapport building in early learning programs.

4. Incorporating dramatic play in early learning programs offers children ways of practising and developing self-regulation skills, rapport, and relationships with other children and adults.

Early learning professionals support families in understanding the importance of rapport building, relationships, and self-regulation skills to children's development. One strategy that is gaining merit in family support programs is to provide parents with a link to a source on the internet, such as the two YouTube clips below. We recommend you examine these clips and search for two others, and then design four core questions that you would send to the parents with the clips. Think about the note that you would attach to the email for parents. How would you introduce this important topic and when would you do so? Are there specific times in the year when you might bring up this topic? Are there parent/child observations that may trigger you to promote this topic? Why or why not? Here are the links to the video clips: www.youtube.com/watch?v=GoftPC-eBxA http://bit.ly/1hEJbWp and www.youtube.com/watch?v=8Bas3pr6AXM http://bit.ly/10mWDB6.

For Further Thought

Chapter 7

Examining How Beliefs about Politics and Ethics Influence Professional Practice

LEARNING OUTCOMES

After exploring this chapter, you should be able to

1. Discuss differing perspectives on politics and ethics and explain how these beliefs can influence early learning programs and professional practice.

2. Describe the relationship between visioning, discourse, and ethics and how these relate to one's pedagogy of practice.

3. Explain what is meant by ethics and ethics of an encounter and how these influence planning and programming with and for children.

4. Explain how beliefs; philosophy; voice; rights; democracy; and the pedagogy of listening, social justice, and ecological education influence program-planning processes.

5. Outline ways in which program design strategies and processes used by early learning professionals can support and empower children and families.

A CHILD'S STORY   Rosemary

I have been playing with Alyssa all morning. We are both four years old and I am going to invite her to my birthday party. I like playing with Alyssa. When our teacher, Marc, told us the story of Little Red Riding Hood, we decided to go right to the dramatic play area as soon as we could because we had some ideas that we wanted to try out! We both put on red scarves and pretended to walk in the woods. We tried to use our tippy toes, but that was hard. We giggled when we couldn't do it. We thought our giggles would make the pretend wolf scare us. When we had our red scarves on, we were brave, strong, and smart. The wolf couldn't hurt us. Marc was watching us a lot. He was taking photos and writing words on little pieces of paper. We got a great big surprise when we woke up from our nap. Marc showed us our pictures and our words that he had written down when we were playing with the wolf. He had these pictures and words on a board. He called it something like a docu-board and told us we could share the story with our mommies and daddies when they pick us up. Then, he asked us more questions and wrote our answers on that docu-board. We looked at all the pictures and we told Marc our story about the wolf. He said it was a nontraditional story of female bravery. I am not sure what that means, but I can be brave. I think I want to make a picture. Maybe I will draw a wolf and print the word brave near it. I can't wait for Mommy and Daddy to see my story.

A child's drawing.
Rosalba Bortolotti

CHAPTER PREVIEW

Nature has given us two ears, two eyes, and but one tongue to
the end that we should hear and see more than we speak.

—SOCRATES (469–399 BCE)

In Canada, the federal, provincial, territorial, and municipal governments are involved in different aspects of early learning programs, such as funding models, standards and regulations, and availability of subsidized spaces. Although each level of government has a particular philosophical orientation toward early learning and child care, as a field of practice, according to Moss (2006), the ideology is dominated by an Anglo-American narrative and located in a liberal political and economic context. Moss (2006) suggested that because the field of early learning is further dominated by the psychology, management, and economics domains, particular expectations of what early childhood programming should demonstrate become articulated as best practice or the "norm." For example, across Canada, many advocates, including the Honourable Margaret McCain and Dr. Charles Pascal, have suggested the need for governments to develop policies that support universal early learning programs. The respect that they have gained for their contributions to the early childhood field and their influence among politicians and policy makers have led to their perspectives being adopted where possible.

Moss (2006) determined the need for early childhood professionals to question what we think is right and what we think is the norm. For example, he cautioned governments about developing universal programming as a way to promote social stability and economic success because it will most likely lead to public policies that emphasize "control, regulation and surveillance" (p. 128). Moss contended that by creating discourse among the critical thinkers in early childhood, the political landscape can be changed to focus on the image of the

Box 7.1 **Claim Your Knowledge**

Chepko Danil/Fotolia

CLAIM YOUR KNOWLEDGE as you begin to develop your roots and become a powerful, contributing member of your early learning community.

child rather than on political agendas and on practices that impede children from guiding their childhood experiences and meeting their needs for exploration, play, and learning. To move in this direction, early learning professionals have a role to play in understanding governments, politics, and the ethics and politics within the early learning field.

There are varying thoughts on the roles, definitions, and aspects of how ethics and politics influence professionalism and practice. We will be presenting differing views as a way to introduce you to the importance of examining such issues and working through what you believe and why you take the stance that you do. Examining these perspectives will influence your roots and your direction in identifying the type of teacher, leader, and advocate you wish to be for children.

EARLY LEARNING PROFESSIONALS AND POLITICS

politics A process by which groups of people make decisions.

Early learning students may not see themselves as political. The word **politics** has different meanings for individuals based on their experiences. For example, some may align the term with government parties. Others may view the word *politics* in relation to the tension that they may feel among colleagues in the workplace or learning environment. Students preparing to enter the early learning profession can gain a deeper understanding of their practice by engaging in thinking and dialogue about politics and how ideologies can be empowering or contribute to complacency. To be knowledgeable about politics as they relate to your practice is to have power. When using the term *power*, we are not referring to power over others; power is the combination of the process and the strategies used to empower others and yourself. With knowledge comes power. To gain knowledge about politics requires acknowledging the definition and the application of healthy power processes to your practice. Think about Rosemary story at the beginning of this chapter. What

Including the participation of children is empowering.

Rosalba Bortolotti

does it tell you about power? What does it tell you about the power of the children? How does this relate to power and politics in early learning programs?

Aligning the concepts of power, politics, and early learning can be challenging, and they may initially be viewed as concepts that should not mix (Fagan, 2011; Moss, 2006). Fagan (2011) defined *politics* as a process by which groups of people make decisions, an indication that politics permeates daily living and education. The bottom line is that "all acts of group decision-making in the education system are political" (p. 1). Politics revolve around three entities, as indicated on the next page in Figure 7.1. Each of these entities is multi-faceted. For example, resources include knowledge creation and experiences. People include the influencers in place and space. In early learning programs, people may include children, families, extended families, community partners, colleagues, and community professionals. Values focus on how beliefs, visions, principles, and ethical perspectives are modelled and embraced within one's practice.

Fagan (2011) suggested that in this context, resources include knowledge. The term **knowledge** has different meanings for individuals. What is knowledge in early learning? Whose truth about knowledge do we believe? In early learning, people seek truth. What is the truth about how children learn best? These core questions do not have one answer or necessarily a correct answer because what we see as truth depends on the politics of our time, experiences, and culture. MacNaughton (2009) suggested that early learning, politics, and truths be viewed in the following way:

> If truths of the child are articulated and circulated by those with institutional power, such as professors in esteemed universities, then they are more likely to gain the position of "truth" in Western early childhood textbooks. If those truths also link with political imperatives of the time, then they gain more power from being articulated by politicians and policy makers. Conversely if truths of the child are articulated and circulated by a young child in a remote and isolated village in the majority world, they are less likely to gain the position of "the" truth in Western early childhood textbooks. The theories that gain the position of "the" truth often serve the interests of the powerful and elite groups within a particular society at a particular point in time. (p. 75)

knowledge What is known about a subject, including the theoretical and practical understanding of that subject.

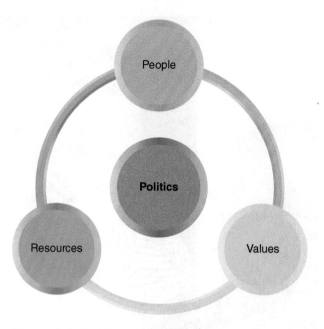

Figure 7.1 **Entities of politics**

Over the past several decades, early learning programs have been dominated by one particular story or narrative (MacNaughton, 2009; Moss, 2006). For example, the Anglo-American narrative currently dominates the early learning landscape, presenting a distinct vocabulary "in which terms such as 'development,' 'quality' and 'outcomes' are prominent" and "early childhood institutions are understood, first and foremost, as places of technical practice" (Moss, 2006, p. 128). When these vocabularies become part of practice, they tend to dominate thinking, program direction, professional practice, and focus areas for early learning programs. This leads to what Moss (2006) described as adults viewing children as "redemptive agents to be programmed" (p. 128). Early learning professionals have choices to make and can take a position of conformity, choose to reform common discourse, or transform. Taggart (2011) is an advocate of early learning professionals taking "a feminist notion of an 'ethic of care'... in which actions are seen as ethical in expressing and maintaining caring relationships rather than in being morally correct in an objective sense" (p. 86). He further argued that if early learning professionals drew upon a feminist thought process instead of a political ethic of care perspective, community and social justice would become embedded in practice. Transformation of practice requires a combination of politics and ethics as first practice in early learning.

If we think of early learning environments as spaces where the players can think for themselves and create knowledge, identities, and values by challenging the dominant discourses, it is possible to move away from the technical practice that conforms to measures of quality set by others and views children only in terms of their development. Technical practice is still a professional responsibility that is recognized as never neutral or absolute and is always permeated with values (Moss, 2006). We view technical practice as fluid. As new knowledge is gained, new observations are made, new ideas of practice are brought forth, and discourse occurs that leads to adjusting ways of knowing about, with, and by children.

If we accept that there is no universal truth and that the dominant discourse is not a necessity but a choice, then practice can evolve to newer heights and go beyond the technical perspective. Moving beyond the technical possibilities opens up many new avenues for

When documentation is shared, it helps in the examination of pedagogical work.

Diane Kashin

children and early learning professionals (Moss, 2006). Big ideas flow, possibilities emerge, and new ideals are conceptualized. Challenging the dominant discourse is

> to show that things are not as self-evident as one believed, to see that which is accepted as self-evident will no longer be accepted as such…since as soon as one can no longer think things as one formerly thought them, transformation becomes very urgent, very difficult and quite possible. (Foucault, 1988, p. 15)

When early learning professionals engage in thinking that evolves from how things are to what is possible, new possibilities are more likely to surface. Moss (2006) suggested that in order to bring new ideas forward, early learning professionals need to take risks and step out of their comfort zones and be open to examining other ways of practising pedagogical work.

Avis and Bathmaker (2007) argued that the current practices used to stimulate creative thought and innovation can provide the basis for transformative practices if participants are willing to "question existing structural relationships and interrupt the economic logic that drives the competiveness agenda" (p. 304). They further suggested that slogans such as "raising standards and changing structures" or "learning is at the heart of all we do" can reduce thinking options and discourse because such statements become viewed as essential guidelines to inform practice.

There is a relationship between discourse and visioning. Carter and Curtis (2010) remind us of the importance of figuring out what our personal **vision** looks like, because it

vision Our ideas about how we would like things to be and the ways we can make that happen.

⟫ A Reflective Moment

Think about being on an elevator with a parent who asks you what your vision is for today's preschool children. What would your two-minute message be?

Think about being on that same elevator with a government official. What would your two-minute message be? Would it be the same as or different from the one you gave to the parent? Why?

Now think about being on a playground with four-year-old children. What would your two-minute message be? Would the information be the same as or different from the previous two messages? Why?

describes how we would like things to be and ways in which we can make that happen. When we have a clear vision about early learning, the depth and breadth of our discourse is enhanced. Visions change as discourse occurs and new knowledge or experiences are added to our repertoire. According to Block (1987),

> a vision exists within each of us, even if we have not made it explicit or put it into words. Our reluctance to articulate our vision is a measure of our despair and a reluctance to take responsibility for our own lives.... A vision statement is an expression of hope, and if we have no hope, it is hard to create a vision. (p. 107)

By sharing their visions and having discourse about them, early learning professionals can clearly bring to life their pedagogy of practice in their work with children, families, communities, and spaces. Authentic pedagogies of practice have values and principles that place the children at the centre. Think about your vision for young children by taking a reflective moment to respond to the questions in the accompanying box (see the previous page).

ETHICS

Ethics are embedded in the field of philosophy, which focuses on posing questions about how morality is applied in various situations. Ethics are commonly examined by descriptors of ideal behaviour, such as those found in organizations' codes of ethics, and propose that human beings base their actions on reason (Taggart, 2011). Within the early learning sector, being ethical means observing principles and behaviours, illustrating behaviours that are concurrent with ethical principles, and being able to justify one's actions based on a code of ethics. Ethics and codes of ethics provide benchmarks from which actions may be measured through reflective practice (Taggart, 2011). Yet, Taggart (2011) suggested that if defined ethical behaviours and codes of ethics are viewed as absolute truths, the flexibility to examine the complexity of real-life situations is reduced. People will judge their behaviours against a list of values rather than ethical qualities such as "patience, courage, persistence or care in a flexible way" (p. 86). Having discourse about the meaning of ethics, ethical behaviours, and practice will help articulate how early learning professionals can adopt flexible practices that empower children and families.

Ethics of an Encounter

By making ethics and politics first practice, it is possible to reconceptualize professional practice (Dahlberg & Moss, 2005). Ethics are always present in your professional practice, even if they are not recognized (Dahlberg & Moss, 2005). Ethics, according to Dahlberg and Moss (2005), should be present and transparent in every encounter between players in early learning programs. They noted that we all have a responsibility to respect others. Dahlberg and Moss used the philosophical term **alterity** to refer to the "otherness" that needs to be respected in early learning environments. French philosopher Levinas (1906–1995) capitalized the term *Other* to illustrate that as students and professionals, we have a responsibility to think about the "unknowability" of the Other, whom we "cannot seek to understand through the imposition" of our own framework of thought (Moss, 2006, p. 130). Dahlberg (2003) expressed it this way:

alterity A philosophical term meaning "otherness."

> To think of an other whom I cannot grasp is an important shift and it challenges the whole scene of pedagogy.... From this perspective, teaching and learning have to start with ethics—with receiving and welcoming—and it is the receiving from the Other beyond the capacity of the I which constructs the discourse of teaching, a teaching that interrupts the philosophical tradition of making ourselves the master over the child. (p. 273)

Early learning professionals offer children and their families environments that give them multiple options and potential possibilities. This requires early learning professionals to be open to the "otherness" of the Other and not conform to ways of knowing that limit potential. Think back to the story of Rosemary at the beginning of the chapter. Marc, the early learning professional, created documentation that portrayed young girls as powerful. For many, this documentation showed a deep understanding of the "otherness" of the two young girls. By listening to Rosemary and Alyssa and providing an environment where they could enact power as they portrayed characters who overcame the threat of the wolf, Marc honoured the children while illustrating the importance of offering them alternative experiences to the view of girls as docile and obedient. Advancing the tenets of the political concept, early learning professionals can reconceptualize their practice to give children transformative experiences that are political in nature. "Girls need not always take on the role of the stay-at-home mother during enactments" (Dietze & Kashin, 2012, p. 107), nor do boys need to take on the role of the protector.

IMAGES AND POSSIBILITIES

Moss (2006) offered another discourse that values possibilities in programming, but cautioned against replacing one narrative with another. Building on the image of the child as discourse and understanding the role of politics and ethics, he determined that when the child is seen as "an active subject, a multi-lingual creator of knowledge and identity from birth, connected in relations of interdependency with other children and adults, a citizen

The child is seen as "rich" and competent.

Rosalba Bortolotti

image A view of others that can be positive, giving a person confidence in his or her thoughts and actions, or negative, making a person doubtful of his or her capabilities and ideas. Self-image is the idea, conception, or mental picture one has of oneself.

with rights," then the child is seen, to use Loris Malaguzzi's term, as a "rich child" (Moss, 2006, p. 129). The image of the child as a rich citizen is based on the child's potential to flourish in environments where such principles are evident (Moss, 2006). The image of the child connects closely to our professional or self-image. **Images** of how we view children and ourselves can have a profound influence on professional practice.

Images, possibilities, and visioning are further enhanced when we think of preparing to enter the early learning field as a "learner, a researcher, a critical thinker, and a reflexive as well as a dialogic practitioner" (Moss, 2006, p. 129). Children and early learning professionals come together in spaces designed for children where many possibilities, ideas, and experiments can flow and discourse can take place. Ideally, the environments model values of collective responsibility and voice; when the public space is rich with opportunity, it becomes a place for encounters, interactions, and connections among citizens in a community (Rinaldi, 2006). A children's place can be many things—a construction site, a workshop, or a permanent laboratory (Moss, 2006).

Two Programming Examples

Early learning professionals seek clarity on the image of the child, as this guides their practice. They also consider the meaning of knowledge in their work. Building on the Reggio-inspired framework, knowledge can be seen as a rhizome. Malaguzzi suggested visualizing knowledge as a tangle of spaghetti. A rhizome "shoots in all directions with no beginning and no end, but always with an *in between,* and with openings towards other directions and places" (Moss, 2006, p. 131). By pondering the meaning of knowledge, Reggio-inspired early learning professionals view a tangle of spaghetti as something that needs to be constructed, rather than as something that is given or delivered to children. How each child and adult construct the tangle of spaghetti will vary according to place, space, experiences, and the influence of other people. Research from various fields of study, such as early childhood, education, and psychology, has determined that there is no one "right way" that children learn. Learning is a messy process rather than a linear progression (Moss, 2006). Previous assumptions that all children must pass through a lock-step progression, meaning that you have to take the first step in order to get to the next, are changing. For example, when you start from an encounter with a child, you cannot accurately predict where it will lead. If more than one child is involved in the encounter, the process may be similar or very different for each child. This perspective reinforces the importance of challenging the dominant perception of knowledge as something that is acquired in a particular way (Moss, 2006). Moss (2006) used a tree metaphor to describe this mainstream image of a hierarchy containing a root, a trunk, and branches, which you don't have in a tangle of spaghetti. If you visualize a tree and then imagine a tangle of spaghetti and represent these on paper, you can take a reflective moment to consider how these metaphors influence practice (see the accompanying box). Knowledge as spaghetti produces the concept and practice of *progettazione.*

Progettazione, a term used by educators in Reggio and Reggio-inspired programs, emphasizes making flexible plans for the further investigation of ideas and devising the means for carrying them out in collaboration with the children, parents, and the larger community (Fraser, 2011). The search for *progettazione* is more than following the children's lead (Fu, 2002). The daily practice of observation-interpretation-documentation, as well as listening to the

⟩ A Reflective Moment

Visualize a tree and visualize a tangle of spaghetti. It might help you to draw both images. Now reflect on which image best represents how you learn in partnership with others.

children and their families, guides the programming or curriculum decisions. The process is flexible and subject to modifications and changes as the project inquiry proceeds. It is not linear and is open to the unexpected new thoughts of both children and adults (Moss, 2005).

In Chapter 10, we will expand on a programming process, including the Reggio Emilia concept of *progettazione*, which involves offering playful learning challenges to children, leading to joyful learning that they express in many languages. We liken the experience to a dance between and among many partners. We visualize a community engaged in a playful dance with bubbles and balloons. The back-and-forth process of programming is a dance among trial balloons set free in the learning environment, which leads to the bubbling up of the programming process. Programming in early learning environments involves learning in a social construct. Early learning students benefit from understanding the tenets of social constructivism as they prepare to engage in the dance.

THE INFLUENCE OF SOCIAL CONSTRUCTIVISM

As identified in earlier chapters, this text is focused on **social constructivism**, the theory that knowledge is constructed within a social context. Although there are other frameworks that may be considered, social constructivism supports experiential learning, communities of practice, sharing knowledge, and building upon individual and group learning, all of which are core components and skills necessary to function today. Traditionally, deep thinkers in early learning have been influenced by developmental approaches, but historically, scholars such as Cannella (1997) have suggested that these approaches view the child as "becoming adult," which then privileges adults and oppresses children (MacNaughton, 2009). According to Cannella (1997), "Child development is an imperialist notion that justifies categorising children and diverse cultures as backward, needing help from those who are more advanced" (p. 64). MacNaughton (2009) put forth the argument that "our perspectives on the child have contributed to their oppression and exploitation in different ways, because we are in a process of judging their differences from us as adults as inadequacies or weaknesses rather than alternative ways of knowing" (p. 75).

social constructivism From an epistemological perspective, a theory of the nature of knowledge. Based on the theories of Lev Vygotsky, it maintains that knowledge is constructed within a social context.

Sharing interests with children.

Diane Kashin

Figure 7.2
MacNaughton's
fundamental aspects
of social constructivism

Source: Adapted from
MacNaughton, 2009.

Fundamental Aspects of Social Constructivism

Children use their interactions with and observations of people and the environment to construct meanings.

Children are influenced by and construct their ideas about relations of power such as "race," gender, and class power by their experiences.

Children present multiple alternative ways of knowing, not inferior ways of knowing.

Children use their peers' knowledge and ways of knowing to expand personal possibilities.

Children offer a new lens for examining social justice and equality.

Postmodern approaches to early learning are more focused on programming that takes a social constructivist approach, as social constructivism suggests that there are multiple ways of living and being in the world. It opens up possibilities for everyone, including children, to examine their worlds and investigate areas of interest that intrigue them. Social constructivism purports that learning should take place in a social construct because it is possible that we "do transform each other through our interactions" (MacNaughton, 2009, p. 76). Learning is a social process.

As outlined in Figure 7.2, MacNaughton (2009) suggested that early learning professionals view social constructivism in ways that acknowledge the strengths and talents that children bring to any interaction and space. Early learning professionals can view social constructivist learning as occurring through intense participation and recognize it as a powerful form of learning (Rogoff, Paradise, Arauz, Correa-Chavez, & Angelillo, 2003). When children's strengths and talents are acknowledged, full engagement is more likely to occur, especially when their interests are stimulated by how they are embraced within their family, culture, and society. Children's ways of expressing their interests and their sources of creating knowledge about their world vary. When adults engage with them, children's interest in their surroundings and their motivation are strengthened (Dewey, 1913).

PHILOSOPHY AND THEORY

There are many perspectives on philosophies and theories and how they guide practice. As noted in Chapters 4 and 5, program models have been influenced by historical, contemporary, and postmodern views of children, families, and learning.

As part of the process of determining your philosophical beliefs about, and approaches toward, children and working with children, it is necessary to clarify your own beliefs and values. Early learning professionals may take the stance that conforming to a particular philosophical orientation limits children's potential to build on their interests and experiences. They may choose to take a reforming or transformative philosophical approach (MacNaughton, 2009). A reforming approach "sits most comfortably with what is described as a practical approach to curriculum" (MacNaughton, 2009, p. 160). The reforming approach is viewed as a liberal education process in which goals are derived from an organic process of reflection and interaction with children. In early learning programs, a reforming approach is often described as emergent and holistic, as the programming experience and approach focus on the whole child. Programming outcomes are based on creating spaces, places, and experiences that are generated from meaningful interactions with children.

The transformative approach evolved from the work of social theorists and social activists. It is based on the assumption that education is a political activity that emphasizes the benefits of empowering the adults and children in early learning programs. This approach calls for a reconstruction of early learning to address issues of inequity based on gender, class, race, and socio-economic levels, and requires early learning professionals to view programming goals as always political. Similar to the practical approach, as outlined in models of practice such as Waldorf pedagogy, the early learning environment focuses on providing practical, hands-on activities and naturalistic environments that encourage children to engage in play that supports their values, interests, and skills, rather than how and what teachers wish the children to know, do, and use. Taking both a practical and a social constructivist approach is intended to support children in experiencing and developing a high degree of social competence. Early learning professionals bring meaning to their programming goals by reflecting critically on their beliefs, values, ways of interacting with children, and approach to teaching and learning (MacNaughton, 2009). As in the practical approach, content is meaningful and generated from interaction with the children. One of the distinctions in the transformative approach is that the content is organized around current social issues, such as racism, classism, and sexism. A transformational approach to programming may include having daily meeting times with children so that they can voice their ideas and concerns related to a specific topic, or creating stories and documenting them in journals or with pictures (MacNaughton, 2009).

In both the reforming and transformative approach, it is understood that programming decisions are not value-free. They are political in nature. Although early learning professionals determine their orientation based on a number of factors, the concepts and ideas presented in this and other chapters are not aligned with a behaviourist approach because in programs based on this approach, programming goals become prescriptive and are designed to be met by all children. Programming decisions that are based on meaningful interactions with children and that are aligned with core concepts such as wisdom, voice, rights, democracy, the pedagogy of listening, and social justice, reflect postmodernist and transformative approaches.

WISDOM

Wisdom, a term often associated with life experience, is increasingly being considered in professional practice. An important feature of wisdom is that it's a process mediated by values supporting achieving the common good. From an early learning programming perspective, wisdom is about balancing various self-interests (intrapersonal) with the interests of others (interpersonal) and adapting to existing environments in the context in which one lives (extrapersonal) (Sternberg, 2004). Bassett (2005) created an *emergent wisdom* model that is composed of four major components: discerning, respecting, engaging, and transforming. As identified on the next page in Figure 7.3, each of the

wisdom Knowledge gained from life experience and a professional's ability to apply it to professional practice.

Discerning

The ability to distinguish between different qualities and characteristics of others.

Engaging

Pushing ourselves to action, changing past practice, doing things that we never thought we would or could do.

Respecting

Being able to express caring for others or feel empathy for others. Gratitude and consideration are evident.

Transforming

The reflective process where we think more deeply about people, relationships, and actions associated with the common good.

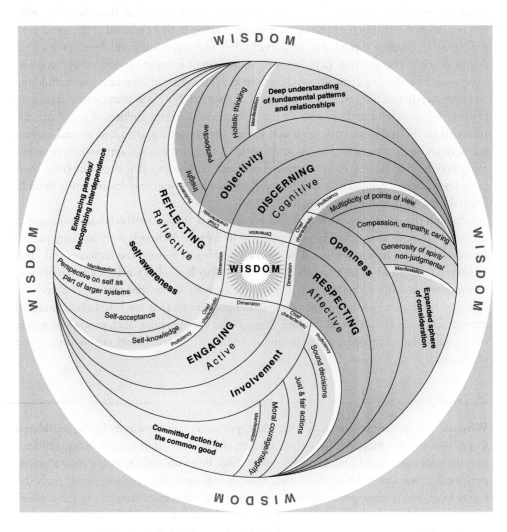

Figure 7.4 Bassett's wisdom model

Source: Bassett, 2005. Reprinted with permission.

Table 7.1 Emergent Wisdom

Dimension	WISDOM			
	Discerning (Cognitive)	Respecting (Affective)	Engaging (Active)	Reflecting/ Transforming (Reflective)
Chief Characteristic	Objectivity	Openness	Involvement	Integrity
Proficiency	Insight	Multiple perspective-taking	Sound judgment & adept decision-making	Self-knowledge
	Holistic thinking, systemic seeing into complexity	Compassion & caring/ empathy/love	Actions based on determinations of fairness & justice	Self-acceptance
	Balanced interests	Generosity of spirit/ non-judgmental	Moral courage	Perspective on self as part of systems
Manifestation	Deep understanding of fundamental patterns and relationships	Sense of gratitude/ Expanded sphere of consideration	Committed actions for the common good	Embracing of paradox & uncertainty/Ability to see beyond the self/ Growing recognition of interdependence
Developmental Stimulus/Learning Prompt	What's really going on? What's true?	Whose point of view am I taking? How does someone else understand reality?	What guides my actions? To what ends are my actions directed?	What are my values? How do I live them? Who or what is the "I" that I think I am? What am I part of?
	What's important? What's right?	How can I relate to them with magnanimity?	What means do I use?	

Emergent Wisdom © 2005 Caroline Bassett.

Source: Bassett, 2005. Reprinted with permission.

components has merit for early learning professionals when working with children, families, colleagues, and community.

There are many different paths to developing wisdom and acting upon it (Bassett, 2005). Early learning professionals who develop and maintain positive self-images, and who make professionalism visible in the process by observing, documenting, and interpreting children's learning, bring voice and wisdom to their professional practice.

Figure 7.4 and Table 7.1 further describe the emergent wisdom model. As you examine the model, think about how each of its elements can be integrated into your professional practice with children and families.

VOICE

Teaching in the early years can bring about power relations; thus, it is important to hear multiple voices in order to prevent privilege (Ryan & Grieshaber, 2005). To hear children's voices, it is imperative to listen. **Voice** can be defined as giving expression. It is more than the sound produced by the vocal cords. Children can express themselves in multiple ways, in words and beyond.

voice Giving expression and being heard.

Giving voice to children's interests and wonder requires adults to be comfortable with themselves and their wisdom. The process of pedagogical documentation gives children a voice. These visual, artistic representations—often referred to as "panels"—reveal children's thinking and theory building and, as identified in Reggio Emilia, allow for a hundred languages to be spoken, often without an audible word.

> Documentation provides an extraordinary opportunity for parents, as it gives them the possibility to know not only what their child is doing but also how and why, to see not only the products but also the processes. Therefore, parents become aware of the meaning that the child gives to what he or she does, and the shared meanings that children have with other children. It is an opportunity for parents to see that part of the life of their child that is often invisible. (Rinaldi, 1998, p. 122)

Documentation in this form is more than the display of a project's topic-related materials—it is pedagogical. Pedagogical documentation is a "vital tool for the creation of a reflective and democratic pedagogical practice" (Dahlberg et al., 1999, p. 145). Many of the provincial frameworks recommend the process of documentation as a way to put into practice and make visible conceptual frameworks of children's interests and knowledge. The word "display" is not used to describe the process. More information on pedagogical documentation will be presented later in this chapter.

RIGHTS

rights Human rights of children. According to the United Nations, all children have a right to survival, development, protection, and participation.

To see children as protagonists of their own experiences of learning is to support them in having the **right** to express their understanding of the world through many languages. In Reggio Emilia, this concept is visualized through the idea of the child as capable of speaking one hundred languages. According to Malaguzzi (2001), these languages already exist within each child and are a powerful force for learning if children's right to their hundred languages is honoured. For more information on the ideas behind the many languages of children, see http://bit.ly/1a7o46h.

DEMOCRACY

democracy A multi-dimensional concept that is usually associated with a form of government, but that also may refer to involving people directly in matters that affect them. Democracy can be understood as a mode of being in the world, as a form of living together.

Democracy, as the term relates to the concepts presented in this chapter, is more than a way in which government is formed and led. From an early learning perspective, **democracy** refers to a way of life that maximizes "opportunities for sharing, exchanging and negotiating perspectives and opinions" (Moss, 2011, p. 2). Democracy "is a way of relating to self and others; an ethical, political and educational relationship that can and should pervade all aspects of everyday life" (Moss, 2011, p. 2). Further information on how democracy relates to early learning and the profession can be found at http://bit.ly/1a7qMZz.

Democratic practice requires intention, supportive conditions, and thinking differently about daily practices—and it requires democratic professionalism (Oberhuemer, 2005). This means that early learning professionals "bring an important perspective and a relevant local knowledge to the democratic forum; they also recognise that they do not have *the* truth nor privileged access to knowledge" (Moss, 2007, p. 13).

Moss (2007) suggested that democratic practice flourishes in learning communities that exhibit the four elements outlined in Figure 7.5. Democratic practice requires thoughtful perspectives. Critical friends, as we noted in Chapter 1, help early learning professionals to include supportive and critical discourse in their professional practice. Democratic practice takes a commitment among professionals and democratic space for respecting diversity, bringing forth multiple perspectives, and using critical thinking in ways that are open and promote exploring curiosity, uncertainty, and subjectivity of options and opportunities.

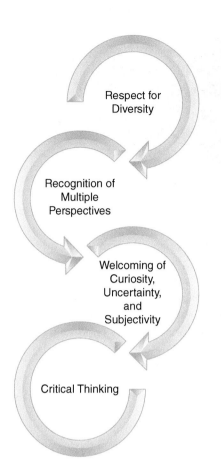

Respect for
Diversity

Recognition of
Multiple
Perspectives

Welcoming of
Curiosity,
Uncertainty,
and
Subjectivity

Critical Thinking

LISTENING AND INTRA-ACTIVE PEDAGOGIES

Two pedagogies guide early learning professionals in creating and maintaining social and physical environments that support children. The first, the *pedagogy of listening*, is a term coined by Carla Rinaldi, pedagogical adviser to the Reggio Children Foundation. This approach relates to learning and teaching and involves the search by children and adults for meaning and understanding through listening. The second is *intra-active pedagogy*, as described by Hillevi Lenz Taguchi (2010). It refers to the relationship between all living organisms and the materials found within the environment, such as artifacts, spaces, and places that are used on a daily basis. She further described materials as "performative agents," noting that these agents contribute to children's processes of learning, knowing, and inter-acting. For example, when children are in play spaces containing benches, trees, and twigs, these become performative agents. These agents, combined with the people in the environment, contribute to the intra actions and inter-actions that are encouraged or that occur. They also influence the depth and breadth of the sense of being within the space that emerges—that sense of being may be either empowering, where new thought processes are generated, or disempowering, depending on the interactivity and connectivity that occurs.

Early learning professionals ensure that when they are with the children, that they are fully present in that moment (Rinaldi, 2006). To be present means to be focused on what is happening right now, and to be open to and see the possibilities among the people, the spaces, and the materials within the environment. This requires "the openness and sensitivity to listen and be listened to—listening not just with our ears, but with all of our senses (sight, touch, smell, taste, orientation)" (Rinaldi, 2006, p. 65). **Listening** means paying attention to others. This needs time—time to be silent, to pause, and to listen to ourselves.

listening Giving attention to others that goes beyond hearing sound.

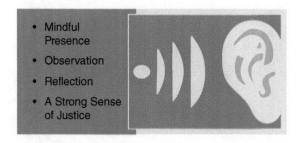

- Mindful Presence
- Observation
- Reflection
- A Strong Sense of Justice

Figure 7.6 Professional skills for listening

Listening to children's theories enhances possibilities and productivity of thought (Lenz Taguchi, 2010). These possibilities help early learning professionals to discover how children think and how they both question and develop a relationship with reality. This process of learning is magnified when it occurs within a group context that allows for the experience of others to be shared and debated. Early learning professionals are continuously developing, maintaining, and improving on the listening skills depicted in Figure 7.6.

SOCIAL JUSTICE AND ECOLOGICAL EDUCATION

In "Embracing a Vision of Social Justice in Early Childhood Education," Pelo (2008) recalled how the Reggio approach began. When the Second World War ended, the people of Reggio Emilia were determined to create a new culture in which the "fascism that had taken hold of Italy in the decades leading up to the war would find no foothold. The citizens of Reggio Emilia were clear about how to begin this work of culture-building: they would create schools for young children" (p. 2). Parents occupied an abandoned building and demanded that the government make it available for their first school. They and the teachers didn't want to create private schools available to only a few; instead, they wanted publicly funded schools open to all families in the community and organized around critical thinking and collaboration. For Pelo (2008), this was a reminder that "early childhood education is a political act, and that it necessarily involves values and vision" (p. 2). One of the core goals in becoming an early learning professional is to develop the skills to constantly reflect on how politics and ethics can influence early learning policies and program quality indicators. This requires an openness to rethink beliefs and values and to change some practices to reflect new growth.

social justice A concern for justice in all aspects of society.

ecological learning Studying the relationships that living organisms have with each other and with their environment.

The importance of engaging children and families in **social justice** and **ecological learning** is regaining attention among early learning professionals. These two areas of learning support children in cultivating lifelong dispositions of caring for others and for the environment (Barratt Hacking, Barratt, & Scott, 2007). Emphasizing the importance of social justice, Pelo (2008) suggested that programs include

- prioritizing anti-bias and culturally sensitive teaching and learning;
- organizing around play and ample time for exploration;
- using curriculum approaches that are responsive to children's developmental and intellectual growth;
- cultivating a sense of place—of belonging;
- emphasizing children's social-emotional and dispositional learning;
- learning from and standing with children's families; and
- advocating for children, families, and early learning professionals.

A social justice perspective assumes a transformative position. Early learning professionals who choose to take this perspective are conscious of politics and the importance of their responsibility to the Other. Early learning professionals who assume this orientation advocate for play as the foundation for all learning, and that play is the right of children as they learn. Learning to appreciate the ecological attributes of environments, children require opportunities to care for all life on earth (Duhn, 2012). To gain environmental ways of knowing, children require adults and spaces that foster ethics of care "by enabling children to participate and contribute to the issues that affect their lives now, and in the future" (Duhn, 2012, p. 21). Duhn (2012) suggested the need for rethinking childhood experiences so that eco-focused pedagogies are transparent in early learning programs. This will require listening to children's thoughts and experiences within their environment.

Listening to and documenting children's thoughts and ideas.

Diane Kashin

PROGRAM DESIGN FOR CHILDREN

Creating a daily program to facilitate play options for children is one of the key responsibilities of early learning professionals. By observing children in their play, staff see the incredible germinating processes and learning opportunities that are occurring (Carter &

Figure 7.7 Teacher scripts

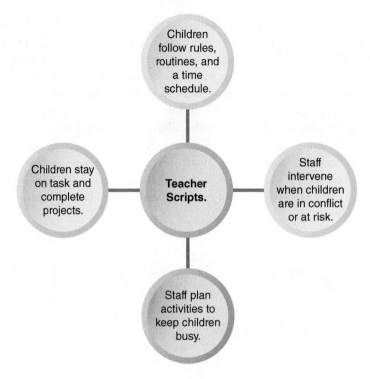

Curtis, 2007). Early learning professionals who "claim the power" in their daily work with children—meaning they have developed a vision and philosophy that guide their practice with both children and families—become a "powerful mediator of children's learning" (Carter & Curtis, 2007, p. 87). Sometimes, early learning staff benefit from slowing down or changing the routine, as this provides a place to pause and become alert to the ordinary moments that are unfolding, which can lead to meaningful experiences for children. Pausing helps to determine where and how to extend experiences that may lead to a collaborative process with the children where new inventions, questions, and creativity may occur. Here is where you can think about the trial balloons you will launch as a way to challenge children's thinking in a playful way. In designing a program that is empowering for children, early learning professionals avoid preconceived "teacher scripts" that may impede the programming process.

Carter and Curtis (2007) articulated the importance of early learning professionals knowing their teacher scripts—the repeated routines that are embedded in their actions (Wein, 1995). By reflecting on practice, early learning professionals gain the practical knowledge that defines their role in ensuring that children's voices are heard. The day-to-day practice of an early learning professional requires thinking on your feet and making multiple decisions that are ethical and supportive of children and families. Without reflection, you may respond to these scripts rather than to the children. Carter and Curtis (2007) outlined four typical teacher scripts, as illustrated in Figure 7.7.

By knowing yourself and recognizing your typical script, you can reflect on and change your practice so that it is consistently responsive to children. Based on the work of Carter and Curtis (2007), we have created three scenarios in Table 7.2 that illustrate teacher scripts. Read the Reflective Moment box, and then consider each of these examples and think of alternative ways that the early learning professionals in these scenarios could have behaved more responsively.

Table 7.2 Teacher Scripts in Ordinary Moment Programming

INFANCY

An Ordinary Moment	Initial Response	Listening for Scripts
A sixteen-month-old child is playing at a sensory table, when the early learning professional begins clearing toys from the carpet and singing the "clean-up" song. The child begins to try to lift the lid of the sensory table in response but has difficulty getting it into place.	The early learning professional's initial response is to thank the child for trying to help and to take the lid from the child and direct her to the cubby area so she can get her dressed to go outside and play.	The early learning professional feels a need to stay on schedule and to intervene, as the child may hurt herself while trying to put the lid on the sensory bin.

EARLY CHILDHOOD

An Ordinary Moment	Initial Response	Listening for Scripts
Two three-year-old children arrive early before the activities of the day are available and begin to build block structures embellished by loose parts they have taken from a bin at the math centre. Just when the construction appears to be nearing completion, they are asked to dismantle the blocks and meet at the carpet to discuss the activities available for the day.	The early learning professional's initial response is to ask the children to put the blocks away so that the children do not miss the rest of the activities planned for the day.	The early learning professional feels a need to plan activities based on keeping children busy and is not recognizing that the children need to have time for playing, as she tries to stick with the busy schedule.

MIDDLE CHILDHOOD

An Ordinary Moment	Initial Response	Listening for Scripts
In an after-school program, an argument erupts between two sets of children ranging in age from six to nine years old. The children had been working collaboratively to build a house from tables turned upside down, fabric, and other assorted materials. They had worked out a plan with the early learning professional to construct and enact a scene about a family. Three children decided that they wanted to leave and not follow through with the enactment. They wanted to go outside and play. The other children argued to say that they must finish. There was a lot of yelling back and forth.	The early learning professional's initial response is to intervene and tell the children to stop yelling. Once they are quiet, she asks the children what was going on. When she finds out that some of the children were not going to follow through to complete a project, she tells them they are not allowed to go outside to play until they are finished.	The early learning professional feels strongly that children should stay on task to complete projects. She also feels uncomfortable when children are in conflict and quickly intervenes to resolve their issues. She is not recognizing the need for children to learn to regulate their own behaviour and to make their own decisions.

❯ A Reflective Moment

Think of an alternative response to these ordinary moments. How might your alternative response affect the child? How might it affect the schedule? How might your response affect the early learning professional?

PROGRAM DESIGN FOR FAMILIES

In what ways can you design a program that invites the involvement of children's families? How can you use the diversity inherent in your program to integrate the point of view of others and enrich your programming possibilities? How does the examination of documentation help to involve families?

To guide your planning, you will analyze the results of documentation processes, such as photos of children playing with challenging learning materials you've provided, transcriptions of the words children use during their play, and children's representations of their play and learning. This is a critical juncture in the programming process, because if you allow your agenda to take over, you will overlook the different viewpoints and contributions families can offer.

learning stories Documenting, through narratives, what children can do and what they are learning.

Learning stories help connect children's experiences in early learning programs with their families. Learning stories are "a particular form of documented and structured observations that take a storied approach and a non-deficit (credit) approach, and an underlying agenda of protecting and developing children's identities as learners in accordance with the national early childhood curriculum" (Carr, Cowie, Gerrity, Jones, & Pohio, 2001, p. 29). Learning stories are by their nature democratic. Early learning professionals can make learning stories a feature of their program by sharing the narratives of individual children in aesthetically meaningful ways enhanced by digital media. This is a pedagogically relevant way to allow different perspectives to inform the planning process. Learning stories provide a means to include everyone's voice and to make the environment richer, and will reflect a community of learning environment for the children and their families. For more information on learning stories, go to http://bit.ly/1amnQN6.

THE ENVIRONMENT AND PROGRAM DESIGN

Early learning environment spaces, materials, and aesthetics influence the effectiveness of the program and the experiences in which children engage. Early learning professionals who are conscious of politics, pedagogies, social justice, and ecological education pay particular attention to environmental designs because they influence children's options for play, learning, self-regulation, and socialization. Understanding of the influence of environmental design on program design is enhanced when early learning professionals evaluate environments and make the necessary adjustments so that children are comfortable within them. Deviney, Duncan, Harris, Rody, and Rosenberry (2010b) created the Rating Observation Scale for Inspiring Environments (ROSIE), which professionals can use to evaluate learning environments. It is one example of an evaluative tool that can provide early learning professionals with an opportunity to reflect, have dialogues, and improve learning. Information about ROSIE can be found at http://bit.ly/1i9D8I6. A form for evaluating environments based on ROSIE can be found at http://bit.ly/11bvZdn.

The rating scale provides a way to examine current strengths and opportunities for change to the environment so that early learning programs reach their fullest potential as inspiring spaces for children and adults. Such tools help early learning professionals listen to the voices of others as expressed in multiple ways and in a hundred languages.

THE ROLES AND RESPONSIBILITIES OF EARLY LEARNING PROFESSIONALS

For professional practice in early learning programs, the primary focus is on the children and their play, and on engaging in listening deeply to children. Figure 7.8 summarizes ideas that support developing rich practices among teams in the programming process.

In the programming bubble in Figure 7.9, we focus on play to illustrate the possibilities inherent in this childhood right. Play is essential to programming.

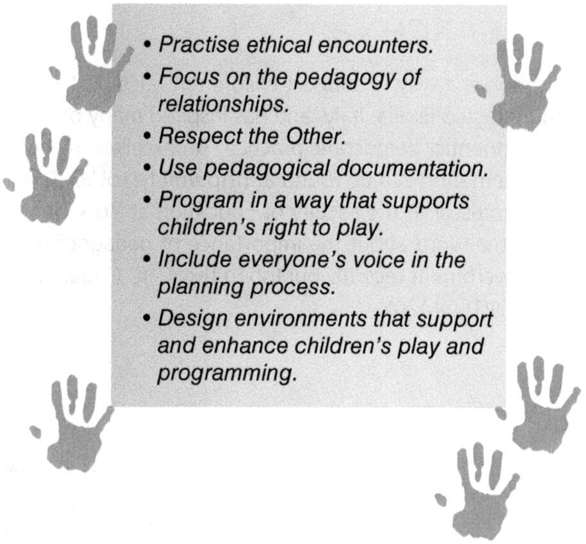

- *Practise ethical encounters.*
- *Focus on the pedagogy of relationships.*
- *Respect the Other.*
- *Use pedagogical documentation.*
- *Program in a way that supports children's right to play.*
- *Include everyone's voice in the planning process.*
- *Design environments that support and enhance children's play and programming.*

Figure 7.8 Ideas that support developing rich practices in the programming process

Figure 7.9 Programming bubble: play

Play

Play is a self-chosen activity that offers children opportunities to engage in a process of experimentation, exploration, and discovery. It is not meant for achieving or creating a defined outcome or product. Through play, children gain understanding and competence to interact with people and things in their social, communal, and cultural world.

Research suggests that children's play is linked to brain development. During the early years, "a child's brain is exquisitely primed to receive sensory input and develop more advanced neural systems, through the wiring and sculpting process" (McCain & Mustard, 1999, p. 29). Building on the importance of the experiences that children have during their early years, the Canadian Association for Young Children (2006) created a position statement on play for young children that reinforced the importance of early learning professionals viewing play as an integral part of a child's being, as identified in Figure 7.10. Go to www.cayc.ca/node/140 to view the position statement.

Figure 7.10 The importance of play in the lives of children

Play is fun, exciting, adventurous, and open-ended.

Play is creative, spontaneous, magical, complex, rewarding, and stimulating.

Play is non-judgmental, child directed, and full of choices.

FEATURED RESEARCH

Pedagogical documentation is a way to support children in building their capacity for learning. The process originated in Reggio Emilia, Italy, and has inspired many others around the world as an important aspect of authentic, democratic practice. An excellent resource for learning more about pedagogical documentation can be found at http://bit.ly/1oUIGeG.

Carol Ann Wien, a professor in the Faculty of Education at York University in Toronto, has contributed to spreading the word about the importance of pedagogical documentation to all educators. The Ontario government recently published the K–12 Capacity Building Series, which can be found at http://bit.ly/16OM2pY.

PEDAGOGICAL TOOLS

Observation–documentation–interpretation is the trio of words that defines professional practice. Pedagogical documentation is the ultimate pedagogical tool. Figure 7.11 illustrates the process involved in documentation. Early learning professionals observe children, listening in the everyday moments for how children are expressing themselves in multiple ways. As early learning professionals record and document the voices of children, they make their learning visible. Documentation is then shared so as to encourage and invite the interpretation of others. By critically reflecting and analyzing interpretations, early learning professionals can move the program forward in ways that reflect democracy and voice.

PROFESSIONAL CASE STUDY

For ten years, Georgina has been employed by a large, privately owned company that oversees sixty different programs for children from ages eighteen months to eight years. Until recently, Georgina loved going to work every morning. She couldn't wait to get home to tell her husband about her day and to share the joy she got from working with children. Her husband loved hearing her stories; it was a time to take a break from thinking about being a small business owner. Georgina's contributions brought in a steady income for the family unit, allowing luxuries such as cruises and a vacation home in the country. Now, the family was thinking about the implications if Georgina quit her job.

In the last five years, the company that owned the centre where she worked had not provided raises to their employees, had extended the work day, and had reduced some benefits, such as paid sick days and professional development funds. The owners explained

Figure 7.11 The documentation process

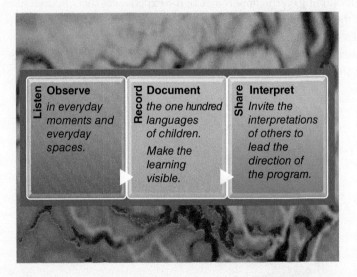

*in a company-wide memo that the changes needed to be made because of declining enrol-
ment. This made Georgina sad, not for herself but for her colleagues, some of whom were
single parents. With the unrest came discussions about unionizing, and this scared Georgina.
Her husband had always been vocal about his anti-union views, and she wasn't sure whether
she wanted to be a union member. There was much whispering at work, and all the staff
seemed caught up in what Georgina called "politics." What worried Georgina more than
anything was how the children were being affected. For example, yesterday Kris and Sandu
were so busy talking about a meeting they were going to organize with staff from the other
centres, that they weren't supervising the children properly in the playground. Georgina
was very uncomfortable being the only adult actually watching the children when they were
playing outside and was appalled when she heard Kris tell three children, "Leave me alone.
Can't you see that I am talking?" It was at that moment that Georgina realized the current
workplace was not supportive of her beliefs and practices. She needed to reflect upon her
ideals and utopia and determine what would be best for her.*

REFLECTION QUESTIONS FOR SELF-LEARNING

The case study describes a scenario where politics have entered an early environment in a negative way. Ask yourself the following questions to aid your ability to think deeply about the
impact of politics and the pedagogy of listening on professional practice:

1. Georgina had a big decision to make. How many different perspectives was she consider-
    ing before deciding whether or not to leave her current position? Describe each of these
    perspectives.

2. Was there anyone's voice that Georgina had not yet heard?

3. In what ways were politics influencing Georgina's decision? Describe these.

4. How does this case study connect to the concept of professionalism?

BIG IDEAS FOR DIALOGIC LEARNING

In most early learning environments, you will find documentation. There will be photos of children
displayed and bulletin boards with children's artwork. This may be what you visualize when you
think back to your own experiences in early learning environments. A distinction needs to be made
between displaying documentation and pedagogical documentation. When you read about documentation when perusing the internet and social media sites, you may see the term *display* used in
association with the process of documentation. When the educators from Reggio Emilia speak
about the process of observation and documentation, they don't use the word *display* but instead
refer to *interpretation*. Think about professional language. If you consider the process as one
word, *observation–documentation–interpretation*, where does the term *display* fit in? Why do you
think Reggio educators don't use the term *display* when referring to the process of documentation? Do you think early learning professionals should use the word *display* when speaking of
documentation? Why or why not? Can you think of other examples of words that early learning
professionals should avoid using? Do you think terminology influences professional practice? Think
of words common to the profession—do some have more positive connotations than others? To
practise social constructivism, all of these questions should be discussed with others.

Consider the following protocol to encourage consideration of the big idea of professional
language in a social construct:

1. In small groups of three or four individuals, consider the questions presented.

2. Each person in turn speaks to his or her perceptions of what the answers could be, mindful
    that there is no single absolute truth.

3. While each person speaks, the others practise pedagogical listening and are silent until it is
    their turn to speak.

4. After everyone has been heard, each person says one sentence that describes this dialogic
    experience.

VISION

Dahlberg and Moss (2005) have tried to imagine a different possibility for early learning environments, where they are used "first and foremost as a public space for ethical and democratic political practice, where education takes the form of a pedagogy of listening related to the ethics of an encounter, and minor politics confronts dominant discourses and injustice" (p. 178). What happens when you imagine such possibilities? What happens when you imagine possibilities as a community? Do you think there would be benefits to the players—children, families, and early learning professionals—if time was taken to engage in utopian thinking? Would it contribute to change?

Utopian thinking by itself is not enough to bring about radical change. "It needs spaces which enable thought to take place and a willingness to act, spaces where there is an openness to experimentation, research and continuous reflection, critique and argumentation—and to crossing boundaries" (Dahlberg & Moss, 2005, p. 15). In Chapter 12, we will explore the concept of utopia and how it relates to learning, development, and play in the early years, as well as to your professionalism and effectiveness as you expand your image to become a researcher of teaching and learning.

MAKING CONNECTIONS

If your only sense of the social media platform Twitter is from popular culture, you may be overlooking the power of Twitter for educators. It offers a way to reach out to others and to socially construct. Twitter is a democratic platform, in that it allows for the voices of others. Check out this ten-minute video that can help early learning students and professionals get started on Twitter: http://bit.ly/16OMiW3. You can also connect to these links to see more about how Twitter can be used to promote professional learning: http://bit.ly/168YMZ2 and http://bit.ly/10MhNb1.

KEY TERMS

Alterity 156	Politics 152
Democracy 164	Rights 164
Ecological learning 166	Social constructivism 159
Image 158	Social justice 166
Knowledge 153	Vision 155
Learning stories 170	Voice 163
Listening 165	Wisdom 161

Figure 7.12 Key terms wordle

SUMMARY

This chapter reflects the reality that early learning environments are political places. By thinking deeply about the learning outcomes of this chapter, students can reflect on the following:

1. Power and politics affect your role as a future early learning professional. It is important to create democratic communities where everyone has a voice.

2. Visioning, discourse, and consideration of ethics can support your pedagogy of practice.

3. Your philosophy and understanding of theory will influence program planning. Early learning students and professionals who reflect on social constructivism will be able to see the relationship between theory and practice.

4. Methods such as pedagogical documentation can be used to plan programming that is guided by the concepts of voice, rights, and democracy, and by the pedagogy of listening, social justice, and ecological education.

5. When early learning professionals take a collaborative approach to their practice, it opens up the possibilities of empowerment for children and their families.

Early learning professionals have a lot of programming choice. Moss (2005) offers a choice that is political and ethical, based on the answers to such questions as, What is our image of the child? How do we understand knowledge and learning? The choices that the educators of Reggio Emilia have made are clear. Early learning professionals have a professional responsibility to make a choice. To think further about this, read the two-page article written by Peter Moss for *Nursery World* **magazine at http://bit.ly/10mWDB6.**

For Further Thought

Chapter 8

The Environment

LEARNING OUTCOMES

After exploring this chapter, you should be able to

1. Explain how physical space and aesthetics influence children's development and play options.

2. Outline types of environmental conditions that influence children's conversations, socialization, behaviours, motivations, and connections to people and things.

3. Explain what is meant by the phrase "the environment as a third teacher."

4. Discuss the types of design elements that are considered when planning for indoor and outdoor spaces.

5. Explain why early learning professionals incorporate risk-taking, self-regulation, and environmental design principles in early learning environments.

6. Describe environmental design principles from the perspective of children in the environment.

A CHILD'S STORY Sophia

Grandma is taking me to school today. She has never been to my school and she wants to see where I play. I tell her all the time about the stuff I get to play with. We have a real sunflower that is so big and full of seeds that we are looking at it with a magnifying glass. We have our own garden that we started from seeds right in our classroom, and we are going to put the plants in the garden outside today! I want to introduce Grandma to our pet hamster, Charlie, and show her the portrait that I made of him on the wall. She will be able to find it because I wrote a big S like a snake on my picture. S is for Sophia. I am so excited because it is my turn to feed Charlie and Grandma said she would stay and watch. She is going to stay all morning and sit on the couch to wait for me, and then she is taking me out to lunch. I think she is going to want to talk to Rosanna because they both are artists. Rosanna loves to paint and my grandma is a sculptor. I am sad that Grandma has to go back to Montreal where she lives, but it is so great that she can stay with me in school today.

Sunflower representations.

Rosalba Bortolotti

*Modern life means democracy, democracy means freeing
intelligence for independent effectiveness—the emancipation of
the mind to do its own work.*

—JOHN DEWEY (1859–1952)

Never before have environments for children's play and learning been so important. Because environments have such an influence on learning, researchers and practitioners in a wide range of disciplines, from early childhood education to psychology and architecture, are identifying the need for professionals to clearly examine environments to ensure that they respond to the children's ways of learning today. Both the physical and the social space should be examined to determine their effectiveness (Fraser, 2011) because the learning environment influences children's sense of wonderment and mystery and their ability to engage in meaningful learning. Recognizing the relationship of the environment to learning has led to the phrase "the environment as a third teacher" becoming prevalent in the literature related to children's learning.

THE ENVIRONMENT AS A THIRD TEACHER

Gandini (1998) identified that children require environments that are flexible and adaptable so that they may be changed or reconfigured to respond to children's needs as they create new knowledge. Fraser (2011) further noted that spaces that function successfully as a third teacher "will be responsive to the children's interests, provide opportunities for children to make their thinking visible and will foster further learning and engagement" (p. 67). Gandini and Fraser clearly identified that the environment is directly correlated to the depth of learning that children will experience.

In Reggio Emilia early learning environments, the use of space encourages encounters, communication, and relationships (Gandini, 2004). Much care is taken in preparing the environment because according to the educators, it acts as a third teacher (Fraser, 2011). There is an underlying order and beauty in the design and organization. Every corner of every room has an identity and purpose, is rich in potential to engage and communicate, and is valued and cared for by children and adults (Cadwell, 2003).

With such attention to detail everywhere, from the colour of the walls to the shape of the furniture and the arrangements of simple objects on shelves and tables, children are easily engaged. They are experimenting with and manipulating the objects. There is so much to explore in these environments, which are built upon the theories of Piagetian and Vygotskian constructivism. Children are actively engaged, lessening the need for adult supervision (Isbell & Raines, 2003). A significant part of Reggio Emilia learning environments is the physical space devoted to specialized atelier learning, reflecting and embedding the constructivist philosophy of education.

Environments that are third teachers invite children to exercise their curiosity, exploration, discovery, and collaborative connections with other children, adults, and their natural environment. Creating a responsive environment that supports children's play, learning, and being is an important role for early learning students and professionals. The indoor and outdoor environmental surroundings influence how children exercise their curiosity. It is in the environment that children exhibit positive behavioural attributes and develop relationships with their peers and with adults. The learning environment is where children develop competency (Gorman, Lackney, Rollings, & Huang, 2007; Greenman, 2005). Adults and children can collectively create early learning spaces that express the children's personalities, values, cultures, and ways of knowing, while offering them challenges (Greenman, 2006). Greenman (2006) suggested that we think of children in their environment as trying to make sense of their world and attempting

> to construct or discover the properties, patterns, relationships that exist in the material world of people and things and to figure out where he or she might fit in. The path of learning and development is more like a butterfly than that of a bullet. Our job is to provide a setting where a group of energetic, idiosyncratic [children] seeks to go about this task and where all—adults and children—thrive amidst the daily rigors of group living. (p. 53)

People in a wide variety of disciplines are examining how physical space influences child development. Within environmental psychology, *proxemics* addresses how physical space influences social interactions (Gorman et al., 2007). The concept of proxemics, identified by Edward T. Hall (1966), suggests that the distance and space available between two or more people strongly influence social behaviours. For example, early learning spaces that have defined reading and science areas or *nooks* improve children's interest in exploring literacy and science (Gorman et al., 2007). Consider the definition of a nook as a corner of the room, offering seclusion or security. Do you remember as a child spending time in a nook? What did it look like? How did it make you feel?

The people, the space, and the materials within the environment contribute to early learning programs' effectiveness in offering children the opportunity to express their individuality. According to Evans (2006), a number of studies have concluded that young children socially withdraw when they are exposed to crowded and noisy spaces. A lack of space, in addition to crowding and noise in early learning programs can lead to attention deficits and children not being able to concentrate or stay on task (Evans, 2006). More recent research looks at how the design of physical space in programs for children can maximize their movement, because moving their bodies in various ways is a strategy that could reduce childhood obesity rates (Gorman et al., 2007). Other research focuses on how natural and outdoor play spaces contribute to children's self-regulation skills and mental wellness (Warden, 2007). Environmental designs, then, have a correlation to children's social, emotional, cognitive, and physical development. Think back to the opening story of Sophia. What do you know about the environment from this short descriptor? What does it tell you about the space and the things within the space? How does the environment support Sophia in connecting her knowledge about Rosanna with her grandma?

PHYSICAL SPACE

Creating an orderly, functional, healthy, and inviting environment for young children is an ongoing and challenging role for early learning professionals and the children (Roskos & Neuman, 2011). Aligning the **physical space** with the options that children require to explore, experiment, and discover requires early learning students to think about the space as fluid. In what ways can it be transformed to meet the children's play aspirations? In most spaces, early learning professionals try to look at constraints, such as the amount of space available, the configuration of the space and its pathways, the flexibility within the space, and accessibility of materials and resources. They then begin to consider ways that the space can be reconfigured. There is a constant need to balance what is possible and what is not possible within the space (Roskos & Neuman, 2011). Children's play is enriched when space and materials accommodate their ideas and images of what they need in order to execute play episodes. In Box 8.1, we ask you to think about how you can bring your creativity and aesthetic appreciation to the children and the play environment.

physical space The indoor or outdoor environment in which early learning programs take place.

Roskos and Neuman (2011) emphasized the need to focus on **design** principles in early learning spaces, as opposed to decorating the space. This requires adults to consider design principles related to space, colour, and order, and how the space may be used in ways that promote play and learning. Space design influences how children play, socialize, and experiment. One of the challenges for teachers is that there is no well-formulated body of knowledge

design Applying elements such as colour, space, scale, size, and order to the early learning environment.

on creating effective spaces to support children's play (Roskos & Neuman, 2011). Although the literature defines best practice, rather than following a defined model of practice, early learning students and professionals benefit from creating space for and with children by listening to the children and by thinking about how the people, materials, colours, and opportunities available within the environment support children's play. As a way to think about space for young children, we will introduce you to some environmental concepts that influence children's spaces and play.

One of the first considerations when designing space for children is to link the environment with purpose, as "the amount, arrangement, and organization of physical space influences human behavior" (Roskos & Neuman, 2011, p. 111). This fundamental principle was noted by Kounin and Sherman (1979) more than thirty years ago when they suggested that "what people do is markedly influenced by where they are" (p. 145). Early learning professionals strive to create spaces that are flexible so that children may actively engage in experimentation and exploration, either individually or in small groups, and so that the space may be used for various types of play.

A beautifully designed dramatic centre created to provide a sense of aesthetics and space.

Angela Brant and Fox Hollow Child Care Centre

AESTHETICS

Aesthetics have long been an important part of early learning environments. For example, John Dewey (1934) identified a relationship between the aesthetic experience and children's learning. He suggested that to understand the aesthetics of one's environment, you must first examine the events and scenes of daily life. Children need to shape their environment so that both the indoor and outdoor play spaces contain materials and organization that support them in carrying out their current areas of interests and focus. This is particularly important in children's outdoor play spaces, where they will find materials that they can manipulate, such as sand, water, and loose parts.

Early learning students and professionals focus on the aesthetics of the early learning space for many reasons. One of the major reasons is that aesthetics influence how children interact with the people and things in their environment. Children and adults are more engaged in their activities and experiences when they are in pleasant spaces (Greenman, 2005). Another reason to examine aesthetics is that "designers of child development centers are typically using colors and materials that are aesthetically pleasing to adults" (Read & Upington, 2009, p. 491), rather than designing space from the children's perspectives. Aesthetics are concerned with the nature and appreciation of beauty, especially in art. From a philosophy perspective, aesthetics focus on dealing with the principles of beauty and artistic impression. Epistemology is also a branch of philosophy and is concerned with the nature and scope of knowledge. Vecchi (2010) quoted Mauro Ceruti, a professor of philosophy in Reggio Emilia, who stated that "epistemology and aesthetics are synonymous" (p. 14). Does it make a difference to the learning environment if it is aesthetically pleasing? If environments are stale, pale, or stagnant places—for example, with damaged tables and chairs—do you think that learning would be enhanced or diminished? The photo here depicts a Reggio-inspired learning environment. Think of this when reflecting on the connection between aesthetics and epistemology.

If we draw a connection between aesthetics and epistemology, will it mean, as Vea Vecchi (2010) suggested, that art is no longer left to the walls of the gallery and museum but

aesthetics A set of principles related to the examination of beauty and the artistic aspects of environments.

A Reggio-inspired toddler room at Acorn School.

Diane Kashin

is brought to the environment because it will enhance learning for children? If we don't consider the "marriage of epistemology and aesthetics" according to Vecchi, we will be deprived of "a deeper understanding of things." Vecchi quoted Gregory Bateson, who said, "I hold to the presupposition that our loss of the sense of aesthetic unity was, quite simply, an epistemological mistake" (p. 19). Take a look at the Reflective Moment box to think deeply about this quotation. What does this mean to you? How might this influence the materials and environmental design that you think about for children?

We all may have different visions of what constitutes an aesthetically pleasant environment because we are each unique, with our own experiences and lenses that help us determine what we deem beautiful. What constitutes pleasant space differs among early learning programs also because of the uniqueness of the children, the families, the community culture, programming philosophy, and personal preferences about beauty and aesthetics. Differing approaches to aesthetics are part of diversity.

No two early learning programs will offer the same aesthetics or physical space arrangements. Greenman (2005) suggested examining early learning spaces to determine what the environment "says" to children and adults. He encouraged early learning professionals to stand back and look at the environment from an adult perspective and then consider what children might see, stating that

> most would likely reduce the psychedelic kaleidoscope of every wall and window covered with riotous color and huge amounts of information; the too-lush rain forest of hanging materials from the ceiling; and the proliferation of cute, commercial images, permanent murals, and cheesy décor. (p. 4)

There is a difference between the psychedelic kaleidoscope and the untidiness that comes from children's need to create props and ideas for their play episodes. As you begin to interact in environments with children, think about what works and what doesn't. Then try to determine what could be adjusted to make a difference in the aesthetic presentation. Think about the types of questions that you might pose to children when seeking to understand what they might like to see in their environment. Think about how you could incorporate their ideas into the environment.

In addition to hearing the children's perspectives, examine the wall colour(s), the amount of **white space** that is available, and how the wall space is used and organized. Each of these elements is linked to human learning (Lackney, 2005; Roskos & Neuman, 2011). Wall space either becomes an important place of learning or an area that detracts from learning. When the displays are more aesthetically pleasing, more interaction will occur among the children, early learning professionals, and families. When the wall space is more cluttered, children are less likely to explore the displays, thus reducing opportunities for learning. Early learning professionals are role models to children. As aesthetics and the appreciation of beauty begin to develop early in life, the time invested to create pleasant environments, such as in preparing pedagogical documentation that adorns the walls and captures children's experiences, helps them to develop their personal sense of aesthetics.

white space Empty spaces, such as walls, in an early learning centre. White space is used to separate or mark transitions between displays. White space is not always "white"—it is the empty parts of the walls or display areas.

A Reflective Moment

Gregory Bateson (1904–1980) was an anthropologist and social scientist whose work has been very influential. What do you think Bateson meant in the quotation on this page about the connection between aesthetics and epistemology? For more information about his work, go to http://bit.ly/10VaHr5.

Bateson was married to the famous anthropologist Margaret Mead (1901–1978). Their daughter, Mary Catherine Bateson, continues the work of her parents. An internet search for any of these great thinkers will give you other quotations that will help you think more deeply about your professional practice.

Children absorb visual stimuli from the colours, textures, and materials that are found throughout the centre (Read & Upington, 2009). The types of colours found within an environment influence how children feel about their space and how they navigate their surroundings. The tone of the environment has a direct correlation to how children find their way in the surroundings (Helvacioglu & Olgunturk, 2011). **Wayfinding** is the process that children use to reach a destination in familiar or unfamiliar environments. Helvacioglu and Olgunturk (2011) defined it as "the organization and communication of our dynamic relationship to space and the environment" (p. 410). From a young child's perspective, the space and place must offer them the comfort to be involved in the environment. They try to understand the setting they are in, how the environmental conditions speak to them, and the types of information that they obtain from the aesthetics and overall presentation of the environment.

wayfinding The process children use to find their way in familiar and unfamiliar environments.

Colours within early learning environments create environmental information that supports the hierarchy of spaces and expectations, as well as clarifying prominent features within designated spaces. Children require their environments to be interesting. Because children make associations with colours and shapes rather than form, they benefit from environments that provide visual interest through the use of warm hues and accent colours throughout the space (Helvacioglu & Olgunturk, 2011). The softer and more subtle the environment, the more likely children are to find comfort in that space. This influences their play options and the depth of their play experiences.

Children's play is challenged by the barriers and the feelings of transparency within the space. Space that does not have clear visual sight lines and barriers lessens children's feeling of comfort within the space, thus reducing the amount of time and the level of exploration that will occur in the space (Stankovic, 2011). Children require space for uninterrupted play. When space is broken into spatial units, the types of partitions and degree of transparency correlate to how children will use the space. Aesthetically appropriate environments support children in being able to see their friends, teachers, and materials that will support them in their exploration and engagement within the environment. The transparency in the environment should ease supervision while providing children with spaces to be alone. In order to achieve transparency in environments, early learning professionals benefit from analyzing the space to determine the materials that children are using at a particular moment and removing those materials that haven't been used for several days as a way to reduce feelings of clutter and promote minimalism in both the indoor and outdoor space.

ORDER AND SPACE

Messy, disorganized space detracts from children's play. Organization is fundamental. Children gain comfort in early learning programs where there is a sense of order and the space is pleasant. Children require space that is organized but not rigid, giving them the flexibility to use the space in ways necessary to execute their play episodes. When children have space where they have the option for it to be "right-sized" or reconstructed depending on the play, the types and levels of play that they engage in will be deeper and more intense. Gorman and colleagues (2007) advocate for programs to examine space and to create small, resource-rich activity pockets within the larger space that will accommodate active, small-group, and large-group play.

Children in early learning programs appear to function more comfortably in spaces that have defined boundaries and provide access to a variety of materials that will enhance their play (Roskos & Neuman, 2011). If the play space design is not balanced in presentation and overall space allocation, children may find more comfort using some spaces rather than others. For example, if there are large areas of unused space that appear to have no defined use, young children often will avoid that space and choose to use smaller spaces, even though they may feel cramped together; this reduces the types of active play in which they will engage (Evans, 2006).

The organization of the environment should be organic instead of rigid to allow for changes. In Reggio-inspired practice, the environment serves a larger purpose. The spaces are not neat and tidy; instead, they reflect the complexity and order of the universe. The universe evolves and is flexible, and so is the learning environment. It has a flow and movement, growing from a group working and learning closely together (Kashin, 2009). From the collections, arrangements, and care of materials on a shelf, to the daily preparation and serving of nutritious meals for children and adults, to the thoughtful selection of experiences and perspectives, to the layered agenda and inclusive dialogue of an evening meeting with parents (Cadwell, 2003), the environment must speak to the children in a way that does not add stress to their lives.

ENVIRONMENTAL CONDITIONS

Environmental conditions can either support children's play or cause stress for an individual child or among children. These conditions can influence a group's experience of working and learning together. Conditions such as light, temperature, air quality, and noise influence the children's conversations, socialization processes, behaviours, motivation, and connectedness to the people and things within the learning environment (Graetz & Goliber, 2003; Nixon, 2011).

Climate control, acoustics, crowding, ergonomics, and lighting directly influence children's activity patterns, levels of and abilities to handle stress, and appetite (Gorman et al., 2007). For example, Gorman and colleagues (2007) and Evans (2006) suggested that exposure to high levels of noise affects various aspects of children's learning, such as their attention to experiences and the peers with whom they choose to socialize. Noise levels may also affect early learning professionals, which may in turn influence the types of experiences and options they are able to extend to children (Gorman et al., 2007). Ideally, early learning professionals and children work together to create and promote an environment that encourages conversation and play that is respectful of the needs of individuals within the play setting.

For some children, new environmental arrangements can increase their stress levels. For example, when major changes are made to the play space, or the play space becomes disorganized in ways that are different from what children have experienced, they must adjust to how the space may now be used. Adapting to new environmental designs can take several days—or weeks—depending on the types of changes and the involvement that children have had in redefining the space (Boyle, 2006). Children may also react to environments where there is conflicting information or an abrupt shift in design elements, such as colour, texture, types of materials, and overall stimulation. Using more natural products in early learning environments, such as seed pods, leaves, and sticks for collages and sorting, and even bark, twigs, and rocks, connects children with items from their environment. The natural attributes of these items enhance creativity and appreciation of their environment (Boyle, 2006). These materials lead children to make connections between nature, the items in their environments, and their play and learning.

SPECIALIZED SPACES

Many early learning programs develop specialized spaces within their environments. These specialized spaces may reflect their program philosophy and the interests of the children. Specialized spaces are usually defined spaces designated for particular types of exploration and discovery. Although the spaces are constant, the materials and experiences that children engage with vary depending on the children's interests and the materials that are made available to stimulate curiosity and interest. One of the most famous specialized spaces designated in early learning programs is the atelier that is a feature of the Reggio Emilia approach. Other specialized spaces that are becoming common in outdoor play spaces are discovery and edible gardens. Each will be introduced below.

Atelier Learning

In Reggio Emilia early learning programs, an *atelier* and an *atelierista* are included in every site. The atelier is a common space in the learning environment where adults and children can explore, create, and express themselves; it is similar to an art studio. The atelierista is the studio teacher who supports the children's experiences in the atelier. In the atelier, children express themselves in many languages or through different avenues, including the arts, technology, science, and math.

Fundamental to the role of the atelier are the materials that are available to the children. Schwall (2005) described the atelier as "a workshop for children's ideas that manifest through the use of many materials" (p. 17). By examining the ideas from Italy, early learning students and professionals can think of ways of designing environments and choosing types of materials that will support children's freedom of expression wherever they congregate.

Piazzas

The *piazza* is a specialized indoor space in early learning programs, especially those in Reggio Emilia. These spaces echo the piazzas of the city, which are the traditional Italian town squares. Piazzas are the gathering spaces for the community, whether it be the citizens of the town or the citizens of an early learning environment. This is the central space where children can get together for social encounters in small or large groups. All rooms, including the kitchen, open directly off the piazza. The piazza is "the place of encounters, friendships, games, and other activities that complete those of the classroom" (Edwards, Gandini, & Forman, 1998, p. 64).

Discovery Gardens

In response to the ongoing concern that young children are losing their connections to nature and not acquiring an appreciation for their outdoor environment, interest is growing in establishing discovery gardens in early learning programs. Discovery gardens have many learning features. For example, they have the potential to provide children with new social skills and knowledge about ecological perspectives (Wake, 2004). Discovery gardens provide children with a venue of interactive exhibits that have been created by early learning professionals, children, and the community, in space specifically designed to intrigue children and encourage them to explore (Wake, 2004). Wake (2004) determined that discovery gardens "allow children to direct their own learning while in a secure and receptive environment of 'having fun, at play.' The resulting strong sense of 'ownership of place' that is engendered sets learners up well for gaining knowledge, independence and feeling empowered" (p. 222).

Discovery gardens follow the constructivist approach, as they are intended to offer children places to discover new knowledge and integrate it into previous perspectives. Similar to other aspects of their role, early learning professionals coach and support children in their discoveries in the garden. They prod, they offer open-ended questions, they research with children, and they collectively learn and discover things about their external environment.

Edible Landscapes

edible landscaping Using food-producing plants, trees, and vines for landscaping rather than traditional trees and plants. It involves growing food within one's living environment.

In some jurisdictions, **edible landscapes** in early learning programs are gaining consideration. Edible landscapes date back hundreds of years, when gardens were filled with fruits and vegetables. As farming became more associated with peasantry and gardening with upper classes in society, edible landscapes were replaced with more prestigious plants. With the resurgence of the desire to help children connect with nature and their environments, edible gardens offer a new environmental feature for children to explore. For example, rather than planting ivy vines along a fence or wall, grape vines could be used. Not only do grape vines offer interesting aesthetics to the environment, but children benefit from the process of caring for the grapes as they grow and harvesting the grapes. Children may care for herbs, peppers, or tomatoes in pots that are strategically placed within their play spaces. Think about the learning that children would acquire from caring for herbs or tomatoes. What might they learn about the bugs that these vegetables attract? What will they learn about blossoms and why tomato blossoms are "tickled"? What might they discover about harvesting tomatoes and using the combination of tomatoes, peppers, and herbs to produce edible food?

Discovery gardens and edible landscapes offer children many options for exploration. For example, the sensory spaces and experiences of discovery gardens and edible landscapes differ from those they would have exposure to in indoor environments. These spaces also provide options for children to explore the relationship of plants to habitat spaces. Such environments offer many alternatives for children to learn about their environment. To think deeply about these types of specialized spaces, take a moment to answer the questions in the Reflective Moment box.

Children pick green beans from their play environment.

Angela Brant and Fox Hollow Child Care Centre

Think about specialized spaces in early learning programs and then respond to the following questions:

1. Why might early learning programs wish to establish specialized spaces?

2. What types of knowledge about specialized spaces would you require in order to support children in their exploration of these spaces?

INDOOR AND OUTDOOR ENVIRONMENTS

There are many debates about which environment is more important—indoors or outdoors. Experts in the fields of geography, psychology, and landscape architecture are joining forces with early learning professionals to gain an understanding of how children use and experience space. Such interdisciplinary teams are also examining how the design of space can create barriers and constraints on children's use of space and their play options (Woolley, 2008). A major issue in the debate is the overwhelming change in the nature of childhood and the loss of outdoor play in the lives of children (Waller, Sandseter, Wyver, Arlemalm-Hagser, & Maynard, 2010). Waller and colleagues (2010) suggested that the loss of outdoor play and of space available for outdoor play have been influenced by legislation, social perspectives on what children need, and urban design, as well as technological and pedagogical factors. These combined changes have led to a "new type of childhood" that correlates with many early learning programs focusing their programming on experiences and opportunities in the indoor environment, rather than viewing the indoor and outdoor environments as having equal importance (Karsten, 2005).

In this book we view the indoor and outdoor environments as equally important and suggest that programming should move between the two spaces as children execute their play. We view early learning environments as the children's laboratories, where they should feel empowered to engage in action and where they explore and discover things. These laboratories are found within the indoor and outdoor spaces, where unique, open-ended materials are placed as a way to attract children to exploring.

Indoor and outdoor spaces are intended to support the various types of play in which children may engage. Figure 8.1 outlines fifteen categories of children's play

1. Symbolic play
2. Rough-and-tumble play
3. Social-dramatic play
4. Social play
5. Communication play
6. Dramatic play
7. Deep play
8. Exploratory play
9. Fantasy play
10. Creative play
11. Imaginative play
12. Loco-motor play
13. Mastery play
14. Object play
15. Role play

Figure 8.1 Fifteen categories of children's play

(National Playing Fields Association, 2000), each of which requires different kinds of space and materials. To effectively support these types of play, indoor and outdoor play spaces should be designed in ways that allow changes to the space to be made with ease in order to accommodate children's choices, experiences, or identified interests.

Woolley (2008) expanded the typology of play. She is an advocate for designing space that accommodates active movement and play, rather than more sedentary options such as sitting, talking, and watching. By building on Woolley's play perspectives, outlined in Figure 8.2, early learning students and professionals can examine the play space to determine which space best accommodates the high levels of verbal, imaginative, and physical play contents and to design the environment accordingly.

A common issue highlighted in the research is that space design and children's use of the space are influenced by the control that adults have over children's experiences (Woolley, 2008). Adults generally exercise control over what can be done in the space, how children may use it, and what materials are appropriate for the space (Woolley, 2008). In addition, adults may express their social fears related to the potential play options within the space. This is particularly evident during children's active outdoor play experiences.

Whether children are playing indoors or outdoors, Woolley (2008) has suggested that the following four elements are necessary when thinking about creating a child's play space: "a place to play, a time to play, friends to play with and what the child actually does" (p. 498). These four elements reinforce the need for children's play spaces to be flexible and diverse. There are many perspectives on how to assess the physical play space for children. Drawing on recommendations from the seminal work of Coffin and Williams (1989), many early learning professionals design play spaces for children so that they offer

- space to meet and socialize;
- opportunities for climbing, jumping, and balancing;
- places to explore and take risks;
- a place to pause and be alone;
- places to participate in fantasy and imaginative play;
- landscaping that supports various types of play; and
- different types of materials, textures, heights, and experiences.

Stine (1997); Frost, Brown, Suttenby, and Thorton (2004); and Woolley (2008) offered additional perspectives on ideals that support creating complex spaces for play. For example, more than fifteen years ago, Stine determined that outdoor play space should support a series of dichotomous relations, such as being accessible and inaccessible, natural and people-designed and built, private and public, simple and complex, active and passive, permanent and fluid. These considerations continue to guide the study of outdoor play space (Dietze, 2013). Accessible and usable space will be discussed further

Figure 8.2 Expanded play typology

Source: Adapted from Woolley, 2008.

in the upcoming section on universal design. Frost and colleagues (2004) identified the importance of thinking about design by examining a sense of place/uniqueness, stimulus shelters, variety, and complexity. Woolley (2008) reminds early learning professionals of how changes to landforms can support children with opportunities for movement, such as climbing and sliding, while mounds can offer barriers and wind shields for children in their active play. Moving or loose parts (Nicholson, 1971) increase the depth of play from an imaginative and language perspective. The levels of problem solving and creativity are also enhanced. Early learning play space should be examined for its "playful spaces" (Gill, 2006) and for the inspiration that the space extends to children. Deviney, Duncan, Harris, Rody, and Rosenberry (2010a) advocate for examining children's classroom space because how and what is presented in the indoor environment reflects on the depth and breadth of learning in which children will engage. They encourage us to view spaces to determine what level of inspiration is found within them. Attention to nature, furnishings, texture, displays, and focal points is essential in early learning programs because each influences children's conversations, their level of interest in wanting to explore in new ways, and their desire to embrace their space. See http://bit.ly/11O2ct7 for principles of creating inspiring spaces.

RISK-TAKING ENVIRONMENTS

Children require environments that allow them to engage in risk-taking play. Risky play helps children learn about their world; test out what is and is not possible; learn about making mistakes; and discover new things about their space, place, and environment (Pye, 2013). Risk-taking contributes to children's in-depth problem-solving and critical-thinking skills. Children in over-regulated environments have significantly fewer opportunities to master the challenges in active play spaces (Frost, Wortham, & Reifel, 2012).

Early learning professionals benefit from understanding the differences between risk and hazard. Crossley and Dietze (2002) defined **safe risk-taking** as "the opportunity for the active child to carry out an action involving risk in an environment that decreases potential for harm" (p. 141). Similarly, Frost and colleagues (2012) described risk as "an action chosen by an individual that poses a chance of injury. The level of the risk may vary widely, depending on the nature of the hazard, the abilities of the individual, and related factors such as weather, adult supervision, and maintenance" (p. 409). A hazard is an act or experience that children do not visualize or predict (Greenfield, 2003). The child makes the choice about if and how to pursue the experience.

As identified in Table 8.1, Frost and colleagues (2012) determined that there are generally three hazard levels considered within the environmental design and **risk management** plans that early learning professionals use to support children's risk-taking options. Early learning professionals examine their environments to determine how they can provide children with risk-taking opportunities that can be scaffolded so that they gradually increase the level of risk they can safely undertake as they acquire more experience, confidence, and success. The outdoor play space should be designed to provide a variety of graduated experiences that require children to use new skills, while building their confidence from the types of risk that they take in their play.

safe risk-taking "The opportunity for the active child to carry out an action involving risk in an environment that decreases potential for harm" (Crossley & Dietze, 2002, p. 141).

risk management A planning process used by early learning professionals to reduce potential hazards within children's play environments.

Table 8.1   Hazard Levels

Level I—Limited Hazard	Level II—Moderate Hazard	Level III—Extreme Hazard
Conditions that lead to minor injuries, such as scraped knees.	Conditions that cause serious injury, such as a broken leg.	Conditions that cause permanent disability or loss of life.

Source: Adapted from Frost et al., 2012.

Kelly McPherson   Kelly McPherson   Kelly McPherson   Kelly McPherson   Diane Kashin   Kelly McPherson

Figure 8.3 **Six categories of risky play**

Source: Adapted from Sandseter, 2007.

Children require environments created by early learning professionals who understand the importance of children being challenged within their environment. Sandseter (2007) identified six categories of risky play, as outlined in Figure 8.3.

These categories further support early learning professionals in viewing spaces where children play. Think about why it is important to accommodate each of these risky play types into children's environments. How might they look? Why are they important in the lives of children?

Risk-taking in the playground.

Kelly McPherson

SELF-REGULATING ENVIRONMENTS

Many aspects of learning occur during children's time in early learning programs. As identified in Chapter 6, children develop the foundational skills for self-regulation in the first five years of life (Galinsky, 2010). Children have different needs and they flourish in their environments in different ways. For example, some children are comfortable in places that are messy—the messier the environment, the more they explore and seek out innovative materials and ideas for their play. Others require a place where there is neatness, order, and structure (Greenman, 2006). Children's environments influence their self-regulation skills.

Florez (2011) noted that as we think about self-regulation and environment, we need to consider the relationship between the two. She suggested that there are "several complicated processes that allow children to appropriately respond to their environment" (p. 46). Early learning professionals focus on creating environments that support children's ability to self-regulate because there is a relationship between self-regulation and being able to master skills, concepts, and experiences that require more complex thinking and problem-solving skills. Similarly, each time children experience something new within their environment, they need to learn how to evaluate their feelings in addition to what they see, hear, and smell, and then compare these experiences to previous ones (Florez, 2011).

Table 8.2 How Environmental Conditions Can Influence Children's Behaviour

Response to Environmental Conditions	How Environmental Conditions Can Influence Children's Behaviours
Apprehension and nervousness	• Children's brain functions try to accommodate the feeling of anxiety which changes the normal functioning of the processing mechanisms, coding processes, and memory function. • Apprehension, nervousness, and anxiety contribute to children being distracted, reducing their ability to fully concentrate on particular activities, or fully engage in tasks or play experiences. • Children's stress levels reduce their desire or ability to be creative or take risks. • Children who feel anxious or nervous have more challenges participating in social networking skills and pro-social behaviour.
Feeling overwhelmed	• Feeling overwhelmed may contribute to children having reduced attention span in their play or their ability to take risks that support engaging in discovery learning and expanding learning in new areas. • Feeling overwhelmed interferes with children's use of imagery in play and learning, which is necessary for language, literacy, and creative thinking. • Distractions and lack of focus leads children to exhibit higher levels of agitation and negative behaviour, such as biting, hitting, and kicking.
Psychological discomfort	• When children feel discomfort in environments, this impedes their spontaneity to verbally interact with peers and adults, reducing language acquisition and vocabulary expansion. • Children's abilities to engage in social interaction and social networking are reduced in environments that cause them discomfort. This contributes to them having limited self-regulation skills needed to adapt to environmental conditions, including tolerance for cultural, gender, family, or atypical-development differences.

Source: Adapted from Dietze, 2006, with permission.

As Table 8.2 on the previous page illustrates, children's self-regulation is affected by the environmental conditions within their play space. The environmental conditions are reflected in the feeling tone that is created among children and adults. "Children and adults tell us how the room should be by their behavior" (Greenman, 1988, p. 136). When the environment is not right for children, they may become anxious, feel overwhelmed, or experience psychological discomfort. Think about a three-year-old child who is high energy with an interest in climbing, running, and playing ball. If this child is required to be indoors in small experience centres for long periods of time, it is likely that this child will react with behaviours that do not support a harmonious play environment. The opportunity for children in this situation to develop self-regulation skills is generally more challenging because of their need to invest great amounts of energy in controlling the various emotions they feel within the environment. When children exhibit behaviours such as aggression or anxiety, early learning students and professionals examine their environments and observe children within them to determine if specific elements of the environmental design may be triggering or contributing to the behaviours.

ENVIRONMENTAL DESIGN

Applying design thinking to reflections on learning environments helps early learning students and professionals understand the relationship of environments to educational philosophy. When you engage in design thinking, you recognize that the learning environment is the most visible symbol of your philosophy. According to Nair, Fielding, and Lackney (2009), sometimes what is being made visible is a philosophy that assumes that a predetermined number of children will learn the same thing at the same time, in the same way, and in the same place for hours a day.

As pointed out by Nair and colleagues (2009), during the early twentieth century, the standard for designing a classroom or learning environment was based on automotive factory design. The following website provides an extensive array of resources to help educators consider the design of the learning environment: http://bit.ly/125xX0H. Today, design thinking is being used in elementary and secondary schools. Early learning students and professionals can easily apply this type of thinking to the early learning environment.

Particularly intriguing when thinking about design are the archetypal ideas of the campfire, watering hole, and cave space. Archetypes are original models that have been around for thousands of years. According to Thornburg (2001), thinking about the campfires, watering holes, and caves as archetypal learning spaces helps educators think of ways to incorporate these ideas in to the environment. These are metaphors; obviously, inside a learning environment you would not see an actual campfire, but you can design spaces where children have opportunities to experience what our ancestors did when sitting by campfires. Campfires are places where stories are told and wisdom is shared with the younger generation, who, in turn, become storytellers for the next generation. Watering holes are places where we learn from our peers; each person at the watering hole is both learner and teacher at the same time. The cave is a place where you can find solitary solace in order to gain personal insights. Later in the chapter, we will present design thinking as a pedagogical tool and offer you opportunities to think about how you could add campfires, watering holes, and caves to the early learning environment.

UNIVERSAL DESIGN

Inclusive practice is intended to offer all children access to programs and services. Ronald Mace, founder of the Center for Universal Design at North Carolina State University, coined the term *universal design* to describe a thinking and action process that began with the architectural and design fields proactively considering human diversity and inclusiveness in the design of public spaces (Welch, 1995; Wilkoff & Abed, 1994). Universal design evolved from a concept in 1998 to a scientifically validated framework in 2008 (Edyburn, 2010). The Center for Universal Design website defines universal design as follows:

> Universal design is the design of products and environments to be usable by all people, to the greatest extent possible, without the need for adaptation or specialized design. The intent of universal design is to simplify life for everyone by making products, communications, and the built environment more usable by as many people as possible at little or no extra cost. Universal design benefits people of all ages and abilities. (Center for Universal Design, 2008)

Early learning programs that embrace universal design principles focus on how products, materials, and the overall environment may be designed to be accessible for all children and family members. Scott, McGuire, and Foley (2003) used the example of the integration of a ramp into building design. Although initially the ramp may be viewed as a necessary entry and exit point for children or adults using a wheelchair, it also is beneficial for adults with children in strollers. This approach requires staff and children to discuss the characteristics of the space, the potential use of the space, and how the space may need to be reconfigured to accommodate the idea for the space. Accessibility and usability principles are consistently examined when discussing potential space designs and ways that children may use the space.

Table 8.3 outlines three essential qualities of universal design that have merit in early learning programming.

A relationship clearly exists between early learning environments and children's sense of worth. Universal design principles reinforce the importance of early learning professionals designing spaces, creating policies, and implementing practices that are welcoming and inclusive. As we discussed in Chapter 6, early learning professionals create a climate of respect for and among all children and families within the program. Think about how conversations with children and families might change the use and the design of environments. What guidelines from the universal design concepts are relevant to early learning programs? Who are the core stakeholders who should be trained in universal design, and what would universal design look like in early learning programs? Who are the producers of early learning products and materials that embrace universal design principles? By answering these core questions, early learning students and professionals think about the users of space and the importance of space accommodating their diverse needs.

Table 8.3 Three Essential Qualities of Universal Design for Learning

Essential Quality of Universal Design	Implications in Early Learning Environments
Curriculum provides multiple means of representation	The experiences of children are displayed in a variety of ways, such as through pedagogical documentation, video clips, portfolios, displays, and children's stories.
Curriculum provides multiple means of expression	The environment, materials, and people within the environment support diverse expression of self through a variety of experiences, such as art, literacy, construction, dramatic play, and technology.
Curriculum provides multiple means of engagement	The environment and the experiences encourage children, teachers, family, and the community to be partners in learning.

Source: Adapted from Center for Applied Special Technology, 2002.

ENVIRONMENTAL DESIGN FROM A CHILD'S PERSPECTIVE

Carter and Curtis (2003) offered a list of ten statements written from a child's perspective to help early learning professionals assess the effectiveness of the environment. They suggested that "instead of evaluating your space from a set of standards, regulations, or curriculum models" (p. 12), early learning professionals reconsider the environment from a child's point of view. Think of Sophia's story when reading the statements that follow:

1. I can see who I am in the space and what I like to do here and at home.

2. There are places that are comfortable for Mommy, Daddy, Grandma, or Auntie to sit and talk with my teacher or me.

3. I play with and learn from lots of things from the natural world, including objects and animals.

4. There are magical things here that are sparkly, shadowy, and wondrous.

5. There are special objects that I can play with to try to figure out more about them and how they work.

6. There are materials here that I can use to make representations of what I understand or imagine.

7. I feel powerful when I play here, and I can be active.

8. I learn to see things from the perspectives of others when I play, especially when I take on roles in dramatic play.

9. I get to see my name written and I get to write my name and other words in this space.

10. In this space, I get to know my teachers—what they like, what they do when they are not here, and what people and things are special to them.

From Sophia's story, what ways can you see that the early learning professionals have set up the environment to reflect the child's perspective?

ARCHITECTURE AND EARLY LEARNING

What can early learning students and professionals learn from architects? Every time a new early learning space is created from a blueprint, architects are involved. The principles that architects use in planning new learning environments can be applied to thinking about spaces already in use. The Architecture of Early Childhood blog (http://bit.ly/125CJep) provides information about a study designed to raise awareness of the significance of architecture on early learning. These architects hope to instigate discussion about making environments conducive to learning and children's well-being by bringing together designers, architects, and early learning professionals.

How would you design a space for young children—from scratch—that is conducive to learning and well-being? Take a blank piece of paper and begin to sketch your ideas. Next time you are in a space for early learning, compare and contrast your sketch with the physical space you see. Look for ways in which the children use the space, and then think of ways you might make changes that build on the principles that architects use in design. For inspiration, you can find out more about the architecture of early learning on Pinterest: http://pinterest.com/archofec. Table 8.4 provides examples of program designs used to support children's environments.

Table 8.4 Program Design and the Environment

INFANCY

Program Example	Description	For More Information
A Landscape for Learning	A Landscape for Learning is a process for planning that can be built into the design or renovation of any environment for infants and toddlers. Through the use of platforms, lofts, recessed areas, low walls, and canopies, all placed along the periphery of the space, the room is sculpted to provide a variety of age-appropriate activity areas, including private spaces for rest.	http://bit.ly/1aQi0SX

EARLY CHILDHOOD

Program Example	Description	For More Information
Boulder Journey School	In Boulder, Colorado, young children were given extensive and meaningful opportunities to be included in a design process for a local civic area. The project lent credibility to the assumption that children have a great deal to offer about possibilities for planning and design. The website offers information about the time, space, and resources given to children and their families to include them in the design process.	http://bit.ly/1aQkdOa

MIDDLE CHILDHOOD

Program Example	Description	For More Information
School Age Care Environment Rating Scale (SACERS)	SACERS is part of a series of program assessment instruments that originated with the Early Childhood Environment Rating Scale (ECERS) and includes a scale for infants and toddlers as well. These scales are used to assess the effectiveness of environments for children. They focus on space, furnishing, health, safety, activities, and interactions.	http://bit.ly/15J4L0F

ROLES AND RESPONSIBILITIES OF EARLY LEARNING PROFESSIONALS

Inspiring, intriguing, well-organized environments that are carefully created by early learning professionals and children open up many possibilities for children to play differently, think differently, and use different approaches in their social and environmental interactions.

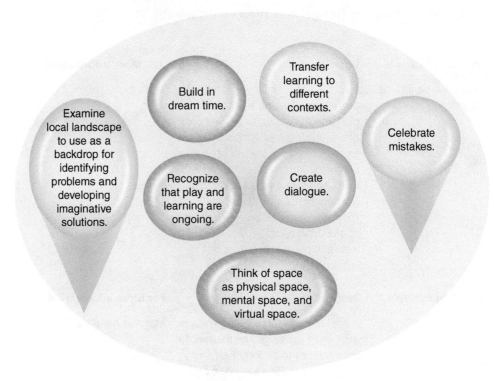

Figure 8.4 Preconditions that support creative, inspirational environments

In Figure 8.4, we outline Burke's (2007) environmental preconditions that support children in having access to creative and inspirational environments.

In the programming bubble in Figure 8.5, we examine the relationship of art and creativity to aesthetics, environments, and learning by focusing on programming that brings the art of famous artists to children.

Investigating Great Artists

Investigating the elements of art—
lines, shapes, colours, textures, forms,
patterns—through observation of and
interaction with great works of art
supports children to make meaning of
their experiences in their creations of
swirls, lines, colour, and material
combinations, reflecting who the
children are at any moment in time.

Figure 8.5 Programming bubble: great artists

When inspired by the art of the great masters, deeper connections are possible. Exposing children to world-famous masterpieces offers them an opportunity to explore aesthetics in their own learning environments. This photo illustrates what a four-year-old is capable of after a long-term investigation of the work of Vincent Van Gogh, focusing specifically on his masterpiece *Starry Night.*

FEATURED RESEARCH

In this section, we feature the work of an Ontario kindergarten teacher, Joanne Babalis, who has transformed her learning environment to become a place of wonder and discovery. Children have the right to reside in a space that is both functional and inspiring; that stimulates their learning and exploration; and that welcomes beauty, awe, and inquiry into their lives (Babalis, 2013). The question that acted as a springboard to the transformation was, How does one create a space that honours children, educators, and the curriculum? This became the foundation for an inquiry into kindergarten learning and environmental design. Joanne is a teacher in a full-day kindergarten program. In Ontario, provincially funded kindergarten programs are staffed by both a designated early childhood educator (DECE) and a certified kindergarten teacher. As early learning professionals, they work together to create transformative learning environments. Joanne and her colleague had several conversations about the learning environment. They shared the view that if they wanted children to thrive in their new school setting, it needed to meet their physical and developmental needs. It also had to be an environment that provided security, respect, and nurturing (Best Start Expert Panel on Early Learning, 2007).

Joanne and her partner discussed bringing beauty into the classroom—for example, fresh flowers or mirrors, and whether or not it would change the way that the children used the space and ultimately learned. Slowly, intentional changes were made to each learning area. Eventually, the classroom transformed from a traditional brightly coloured kindergarten classroom to a

inquiry-based learning practices Practices that involve the learner in the learning process by creating an atmosphere for wonder and investigation of the learner's questions, ideas, and theories. Inquiry-based practices can be used with learners of any age.

neutral-toned home-like environment centred on **inquiry-based learning practices**. The evolution took into consideration time, space, materials, listening, planning, and documenting student feedback, in order to create the ideal space for learning (Babalis, 2013). All areas of the program were slowly transformed together, rather than following a particular order or formula. When the transformation was complete, it became easier to engage with small groups and form research teams. This paved the way for the blog, Transforming Our Learning Environment into a Space of Possibilities (www.myclassroomtransformation.blogspot.com), where this transformative journey is documented and you can see the images of change for yourself. Designing an inspiring place for young children to engage in inquiry-based learning is possible when time, space, materials, listening, planning, and documenting work together in complete harmony (Babalis, 2013).

PEDAGOGICAL TOOLS

A pedagogical tool that early learning students and professionals may consider when critically reflecting on the effectiveness of the learning environment is *design thinking*. Design thinking helps learners develop creative confidence as they employ their imagination. Educators can provide experiences where learners apply design thinking in their daily lives, and they can use the tool to benefit their professional practice. By applying this creative approach to developing an effective learning environment, possibilities are enhanced. For more information on design thinking and how you might use it, see http://stanford.io/14cwVDf.

PROFESSIONAL CASE STUDY

For seven years, Mickala had been employed at a private early learning program working with children between the ages of three and four years. When beginning at the facility, Mickala was enthusiastic about considering what types of experiences would be triggers for children's imagination and sense of wonderment. She and her colleagues appeared to have freedom and encouragement from their director to offer children experiences in their environments that supported children in their play and learning. She was particularly excited to listen to the children today, because late last evening she and a parent from the centre placed a large fallen tree at the back of the yard for the children to explore.

When Mickala arrived at work, she was surprised by her colleagues' reactions to the tree. Two colleagues in particular were concerned that the children may not have the skills to climb on the tree, and they felt that the sharp branches may cause children to get scratched or cut. Mickala was pulled between knowing the importance of children having the freedom to explore and needing to consider the comments and concerns expressed by her colleagues. What if a child got hurt? What was the worst-case scenario?

Mickala and her colleagues determined that they needed to have discussions with the children before they actually began exploring the tree. The staff and the children gathered as a group to look at the tree and discuss the potential risks of playing on the tree. The children determined ways that they could use the tree in their play that would be safe. They determined that six children would play first around the tree and then others could join them.

As the children began to play, one of Mickala's colleagues began using language such as "Be careful," "Are you sure that you want to go there?" "Make sure you hold on," and "Watch your eyes." Mickala was concerned that the constraints and messages that children were receiving from her colleague would inhibit the children's play experience. She realized the importance of colleagues thinking about risk-taking and how different colleagues react to children's play. Mickala wondered why a tree was causing such discomfort for her colleagues, and yet it was such a rich learning experience for the children.

REFLECTION QUESTIONS FOR SELF-LEARNING

The case study in this chapter outlines a scenario where comfort levels toward risk-taking, active play, and approaches to new experiences differ among colleagues. Reflect on the following questions as a way to consider your perspective on the situation and how you might react if you were one of Mickala's colleagues. Why do you think the tree caused such discomfort for Mickala's colleagues? How might Mickala and her colleagues have benefited from a discussion prior to bringing the tree into the play space?

1. Since there was such discomfort with the colleagues, would it have been better for the colleagues and the children to avoid stress by not bringing the tree to the play space?

2. In what ways did personal philosophies influence how this situation played out?

3. How does this scenario connect with children's need for new experiences, risk-taking, and exploration to create new knowledge? Could the same objectives have been met with a different experience? Why or why not?

4. How does your philosophy fit with this experience? Would you pursue having the tree in the play space? Why or why not?

BIG IDEAS FOR DIALOGIC LEARNING

Blogs are online spaces that can be used for sharing and learning. Many early learning professionals, like Joanne in the Featured Research section, use blogs. Blogs can serve as a vehicle to share ideas among professionals or to include contributions from children and families. Blogs can easily incorporate text, images, audio, and video. Readers of the blog can leave comments. There are numerous sites that can help you as you learn to maintain a blog. This site from New Zealand provides guidance to early learning professionals interested in creating a platform for dialogic learning: http://bit.ly/11LhgLC. Consider the following as it relates to using blogging as a way to support your learning:

1. What do you think about blogging as a way of learning?

2. In discussions with others, what do you collectively think are the pros and cons of early learning professionals having a blog?

3. How might blogging contribute to the building of relationships in early learning environments?

4. How might you begin the process of blogging? What would you need to do to prepare for the process of blogging?

VISION

In a perfect world, every early learning environment would have the spaces, resources, and structures in place to offer children and early learning professionals environments that are intriguing, experiential, active, engaging, and inspirational. The environment would reflect the voices of the children and the diversity of children's interests, cultures, families, and community. Given the ongoing research that connects environmental conditions to children's learning and self-regulation, we envision a world where early learning professionals are provided with pre-service and in-service training that looks at early learning environments for their strengths and the ways in which they can be reconfigured to support the needs and interests of the children and their play. We see the possibilities of combining creative spaces with active spaces, active spaces with quiet spaces, natural spaces with children-generated spaces, and specialized spaces with new spaces. We see children and early learning professionals having dialogue about their spaces, and having the resources to design the spaces that represent their areas of exploration. We see using technology as a resource tool to imagine and explore the "what-ifs" and the possibilities of creating vibrant children's environments.

MAKING CONNECTIONS

One interesting way early learning professionals from around the globe are making connections and supporting children's creativity is through International Dot Day, which takes place on September 15 every year. Launched by a teacher who introduced his class to Peter H. Reynolds's book *The Dot*, the day has been celebrated since 2009. *The Dot* tells the story of a teacher who is able to encourage a reluctant student to trust in her own abilities by being brave enough to "make her mark." According to the International Dot Day website at http://bit.ly/1aiFOjC, "What begins with a small dot on a piece of paper becomes a breakthrough in confidence and courage, igniting a journey of self-discovery and sharing, which has gone on to inspire countless children and adults around the globe." The website also features resources and examples for Dot Day celebrations.

Dot Day documentation at Acorn School.

Diane Kashin

KEY TERMS

Figure 8.6 Key terms wordle

SUMMARY

This chapter illustrates the importance of the early learning environment as it relates to programming. To summarize, we will discuss the most salient points made by reflecting back on the chapter's learning outcomes.

1. Early learning students and professionals reflect on research to understand that physical space and aesthetics influence children's development and play options.

2. Environmental conditions influence children's conversations, socialization, behaviours, motivations, and connections to people and things. It is the responsibility of the early learning professional to be aware of these conditions and to facilitate creating environments that support children's needs.

3. "The environment as a third teacher" is a phrase that originated in Reggio Emilia and refers to creating and maintaining a learning space that is organized to maximize learning.

4. Many design elements can be considered when planning for indoor and outdoor play spaces.

5. Early learning professionals incorporate risk-taking, self-regulation, and environmental design principles in early learning environments to support children's learning and well-being in the physical space.

6. By reflecting on design principles from the perspective of children in the environment, early learning students and professionals broaden their understanding of how to create an effective environment in practice.

An article that offers early learning professionals support in making their environment a "third teacher" can be found at http://bit.ly/1grL7xY. Read the article and think about the advice given. Do you think this is possible in every early learning environment?

For Further Thought

Chapter 9

Materials for Sparking Children's Curiosity and Play

LEARNING OUTCOMES

After exploring this chapter, you should be able to

1. Describe what is meant by curiosity, the characteristics of curiosity, and the role of curiosity in children's play and learning.
2. Explain the theory of loose parts and open-ended materials in relation to the thinking lens framework.
3. Discuss the concepts of intelligent materials, materials with language, and materials as thinking tools in early learning programs.
4. Explain the Hawkins theory of messing about.
5. Document strategies for enhancing children's curiosity with materials and spaces in indoor and outdoor environments.

A CHILD'S STORY   Maddie and Bailey

As our daddy brought us up to the entrance of our play-school, I thought I saw something amazing in the play garden. From what I could see, it had a long stick and something on it that looked just like a lollipop. I said to Bailey, "I see lollipops in the garden." She said, "Lollipops in the garden. Are you kidding?" Then I said to my daddy, "I think I do. I think I do see a great big lollipop in the garden." Daddy said, "Lollipops in the garden? Great big lollipops in the garden. How would great big lollipops get into the garden? Shall we go look at the lollipops in the garden, because I have never, ever, ever seen great big lollipops in a garden!" Together we said, "Let's go see the lollipops!" As we entered the garden, we saw the most incredible thing in the garden. Bailey said, "Oh, it is far more beautiful than I had imagined! Look at the colours . . . look at the shapes!" Daddy said, "It is beautiful! Do you still think that it is a lollipop, or does it just look like a lollipop?" "Oh, Daddy, it is just too big to be a lollipop!" Then Daddy said, "Girls, why don't you think about this today and let's come back here when I come to pick you up and then we can discuss what our thoughts are about what this might be." Bailey said, "I am going to ask my teacher if I can take a picture of this, because I want to show Shawn when we get home." I said to Daddy and Bailey, "I think I know what it is . . . but I am not telling you until after playschool."

A children's play garden.

Peter Dietze

*Hold childhood in reverence, and do not be in any hurry
to judge it for good or ill. Leave exceptional cases to show
themselves, let their qualities be tested and confirmed, before
special methods are adopted. Give nature time to work before
you take over her business, lest you interfere with her dealings.
You assert that you know the value of time and are afraid to
waste it. You fail to perceive that it is a greater waste of time to
use it ill than to do nothing, and that a child ill taught is further
from virtue than a child who has learnt nothing at all. You are
afraid to see him spending his early years doing nothing. What!
Is it nothing to be happy, nothing to run and jump all day? He
will never be so busy again all his life long.*

—JEAN-JACQUES ROUSSEAU (1712–1778)

Environments that offer children opportunities to explore and learn are places of play
where early learning students and professionals provide rich learning experiences that
reflect the interests, rights, and needs of children and adults. These environments don't just
offer children similar experiences and materials on a daily basis; instead, they are places
that intrigue children with unique materials and resources that foster wonderment and curiosity and motivate them to explore and seek answers to their questions. Children's curiosity
and wonderment influence their social, emotional, cognitive, and physical development by
helping them bring meaning to people, places, and things in their world (Driscoll &
Lownds, 2007). In this chapter, we explore the big idea of curiosity and encourage early
learning students to claim their own, as depicted in Box 9.1 on the next page.

> Box 9.1 **Claim Your Curiosity**

Chepko Danil/Fotolia

CLAIM YOUR CURIOSITY as an early learning student who likes to explore ideas and create questions that will trigger children's sense of wonderment and intrigue when exposed to materials.

According to Heick (n.d.), before children become curious they need to have a sense of ambition. This means that before children will attempt to seek out answers to their questions, they first need to be in a psychological space and place where they want to advance their thinking. Without a sense of ambition, "curiosity is simply a biological and neurological reaction to stimulus" (Heick, n.d., p. 8). Early learning students' and professionals' values, attitudes, and sense of curiosity and wonderment can shape how children explore their environments and the materials available to them.

A variety of strategies are used to support children in fostering their sense of wonder and curiosity. Creating environments that have interesting materials, places for exploration, and adults who support their quest for answers to their questions all trigger children's curiosity, which leads them to "construct knowledge and go on constructing it" (Kamii & Devries, 1993, p. 54). When early learning students and professionals take a constructivist view of learning, children are more likely to have a greater number of opportunities for the wonder, exploration, and discovery that are part of the curiosity process. Think about the early learning environments that you have been in or observed. Is every child curious? Is every adult curious? Reflect on the opening story of Bailey and Maddie. Did they exhibit curiosity about what might be a lollipop in the play garden? How did their father stretch their potential learning opportunities? How might early learning professionals complement the children's curiosity?

WHAT IS CURIOSITY?

curiosity A multi-dimensional concept involving a motivation to explore, discover, question, and seek wonderment.

Defining **curiosity** is challenging because its meaning varies among disciplines and individuals, depending on one's theoretical framework and perspective of how children grow and develop. In reviewing the literature, evidence suggests that curiosity plays an important role in the lives of children and is strongly influenced by the adults and the environments to which children are exposed. Curiosity can be a powerful motivator of behaviour that stimulates children to initiate actions, make social connections, or access resources to explore and make sense of their world (Arnone, Small, Shauncey, & McKenna, 2011). Early learning students and professionals benefit from thinking about big ideas that could influence children's options for and levels of curiosity.

Curiosity and the process of being curious have been studied in a number of disciplines since the 1950s. For example, Piaget (1936/1952) examined curiosity from the perspective of children needing to make sense of their world through their innate "interest in novelty." He suggested that children's interest in novelty and the act of seeking answers to the things that trigger their interest is a cognitive process linked to the development of intelligence. Berlyne (1954/1960) examined curiosity from neurophysiological perspective. He viewed curiosity as a state of arousal influenced by changes to an environment or uncertainty within an environment (Arnone et al., 2011). Berlyne (1978) identified four forms of curiosity that could be used to analyze children's play behaviour: perceptual curiosity, epistemic curiosity, specific curiosity, and diverse curiosity. *Perceptual curiosity* relates to interest in and attention to novel perceptual stimulation, which is rewarding to the child and can lead the child to engage in further visual and sensory exploration. *Epistemic curiosity* refers to a quest for knowledge and is influenced by the materials and experiences offered within early learning environments to support children's play. *Specific curiosity* refers to having a desire to seek out specific information or knowledge on a topic, such as when children become interested in building bridges or wondering about monsters. *Diverse curiosity* is similar to being bored and seeking stimulation to bring a sense of excitement into the environment. For example, if early learning programming becomes stagnant, children might try behaviours that normally would not occur, such as throwing rocks at the fence as a way to seek stimulation.

Curiosity can also be examined from a multi-dimensional perspective. For example, Reio, Petrosko, Wiswell, and Thongsukmag (2006) suggested that curiosity be viewed as cognitive curiosity plus physical and social thrill-seeking. Children express differences in their preferences and depth of curiosity, thrill-seeking, or novelty, depending on life experiences (Chak, 2007). Some children may try to satisfy their curiosity by using their minds, while others will wish to explore using a more hands-on approach (Dietze, 2006).

Hands-on gardening with children—growing plants from seeds.

Bora Kim

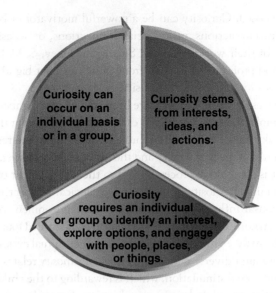

Figure 9.1 **Triggering curiosity is multi-faceted**

As identified in Figure 9.1, curiosity is multi-faceted and can be triggered by more than one stimulus in the environment. Early learning students and professionals facilitate opportunities for children to use new materials and have new experiences as a way to transform an expressed short-term interest or attraction into more in-depth, long-term exploration (Chak, 2007; Driscoll & Lownds, 2007). This can be achieved when early learning professionals and students adopt practices that focus on understanding children and their interests so that the resources provided are intriguing and spark curiosity.

When children are attracted to a stimulus, it is generally thought that they are seeking new information or trying to figure out how they can apply what they know about some topic to other situations. Children explore the stimulus and attempt to answer various epistemic questions, such as, What happens if . . .? Why does that happen? Would my idea of . . . work? Children have higher levels of exploration, discovery, and learning when they are in environments with unique resources and experiences that trigger curiosity and where curiosity is honoured (Perry, 2001).

Children may express their curiosity and levels of curiosity in a number of ways. Think about and watch children who are exhibiting a sense of wonderment when they first use a new loose part or intelligent materials. Examine the questions in Table 9.1 and think what you might observe when children become curious about new materials or experiences. Note how children increase their active play, their motivation to seek answers, their language skills, and connections to their playmates and adults when their curiosity has been aroused (Chak, 2007).

Drawing on practices of Reggio-inspired programs, another strategy that is used in programs today to spark children's curiosity is the use of provocations or invitations in the environment. *Provocations* are the deliberate and thoughtful actions taken by adults, or in some cases children, to provoke or extend children's sense of wonder and thinking, such as by adding displays or materials that may attract children to areas of the environment. Provocations, such as intelligent materials as outlined in Chapter 2, are placed in areas where children will discover and then explore them. Think about what might happen if a bouquet of flowers is placed near some paint and paper. How might that trigger children's sense of creativity and observations of the flowers, colours, and beauty within their environment? How might these lead children to explore mixing paint colours or using different paint brushes to create lines and texture in their artwork? Provocations are intended to entice children to expand their sense of wonderment and appreciation of how their environments can be intriguing and mysterious.

Table 9.1 How Children Exhibit their Curiosity

Observing How Children Express Their Curiosity	Examples of Children's Curiosity Behaviours
When children see new materials in their environments, how do they take initiative to explore the materials?	Children immediately are drawn to the area where the new materials are placed. Children ask questions of the early learning professional about the materials.
How do children explore the materials?	Children touch the materials and try to manipulate them, e.g., by bending or stacking them, or lining them up. Children ask questions of their playmates and adults. Children listen to conversations about the materials and observe how their playmates or adults use the materials before trying them.
What qualities do children exhibit when their curiosity has been aroused?	Children increase their activity level with the materials that they are curious about. Children use new language to include the materials, the attributes of the materials, and what they can do with the materials. Children may connect with other playmates, who can support them in gaining new knowledge needed to understand ways and try new possibilities in which the materials may be used.
What behaviours do children express when their level of curiosity has been fulfilled with the new materials?	Children quickly or gradually move from the materials. Children pose fewer questions to playmates or adults. Children's need for information and answers becomes less immediate. They move from exploring materials to incorporating materials into play episodes.

HOW CHILDREN'S SPACES INFLUENCE CURIOSITY

Many factors may trigger curiosity among children in early learning programs, one of which is the environment. The adults in an environment and environmental conditions can either facilitate children's desire to be curious and the depth to which they will explore their space or create barriers that reduce the desire to act upon their sense of wonder (Chak, 2007). Chak (2007) suggested that we think of a *psychological region* as the child's cognitive structure, including the do's and don'ts or rules and regulations within different environments. The *physical region* refers to the early learning floor space, outdoor space, and materials within those spaces. The *social region* refers to the children and adults in the early learning environment, as well as parents and extended family members. Each of these regions supports the concept of fluidity, movement, and change in early learning programs. For example, think about a child who is building a structure in a block centre. How does each region change for this child as other children are invited and join in on the building project? How might these regional changes alter the depth and breadth of the play and level of intensity of each child's curiosity?

Jenkins, Clinton, Purushotma, Robinson, and Weigel (2006) proposed using **affinity spaces** to promote informal learning cultures and participatory learning opportunities as a way to support children in using curiosity in their play. Affinity spaces are described as

affinity spaces Places in the indoor and outdoor environments where children can experiment, be innovative, and "mess about" with materials and ideas.

"experimental, innovative, having provisional rather than institutional structures, adaptable to short-term and temporary interests, *ad hoc* and localized, easy to enter and exit on demand and very generative" (p. 184). Affinity spaces in early learning programs could be places where children play, perform, put things together, take things apart, network with other children and adults, or work with a peer or group of peers to explore an idea. These spaces differ from the other spaces because children come to the affinity space when they have a clearly defined idea that they wish to pursue over the short or long term. The materials and resources are maintained as children work on them. Further information on materials will be discussed later in the chapter.

THE RELATIONSHIP OF CURIOSITY TO PLAY AND INQUIRY

Children's levels of curiosity and exploration are affected by multiple competing factors, such as the psychological, physical, and social regions within their life space (Lewin, 1951/1997). A child's life space takes on many characteristics owing in part to the people, the place, and the resources within that space. As early learning students and professionals think about the relationship of curiosity to play and inquiry, observations and pedagogical documentation will offer insight and guidance into how children use materials and resources as part of their learning agenda.

Renninger, Sansone, and Smith (2004) suggested that how children choose to engage in a learning activity or play episode is correlated with curiosity. They outlined three levels of engagement that children use in their play, as shown in Figure 9.2.

The first level is *participative engagement*. This refers to children engaging in the activity because of an imposed requirement by a parent or teacher. For example, if children are required to complete an art activity at a specific time using specified materials, the level of intrinsic desire to engage in messy play or muck about is greatly reduced. *Affective engagement* occurs when children participate in an experience for pure enjoyment. For example, if children are given the freedom to take a train and books outdoors, having choices of space and place contributes to the novelty and the level of enjoyment. Affective engagement may stimulate interest in new experiences, thus sparking curiosity, which could lead them to engage in the third level—*cognitive engagement*. This level of engagement occurs when children are intrinsically motivated and their curiosity is triggered to explore an interest either on their own or with others. Thinking about the connection between curiosity and learning, take a look at the Reflective Moment box to consider what would happen if the relationship was not acknowledged. As shown in Figure 9.3, when children are in environments that support curiosity, once they have acquired an answer to one question, new exploration and discoveries can trigger the process to begin all over again.

Children with a sense of curiosity display enthusiasm, ambition, and motivation, which lead them to explore and develop confidence. Children who are highly curious ask more questions of adults who are responsive and engaged with them than adults who are

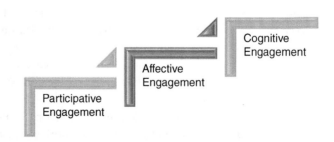

Figure 9.2 **Children's level of engagement in play**

If the relationship between curiosity and learning is not acknowledged or understood, how will you know when curiosity has the potential to enhance a child's experience? Take a reflective moment to think about your answer.

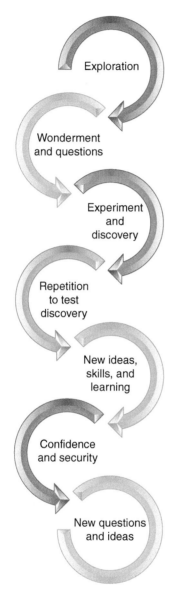

Figure 9.3 **Cycle of curiosity**

unresponsive or have limited connections to the children (Arnone et al., 2011). Adults who observe children and engage with them are better able to understand children's questions or pose questions that will support the children in taking their exploration to the next level. Children require adults who will listen to them and extend opportunities for them to be introduced to new ideas, resources, or experiences. Early learning professionals examine strategies and processes that will lead children to explore their ideas in new ways and offer various types of support if they become overwhelmed or frustrated or state that they can't do something.

There are many barriers to curiosity and play, one of which is the rules that are imposed on children. Barriers reduce movement and a child's natural instinct to explore. Often, such barriers are deemed to be put in place for safety reasons, but as you will recall in Chapter 8, curiosity is closely associated with risk taking. If children's sense of curiosity and risk taking is influenced by barriers, their sense of wonderment is reduced. Perry (2004) cautioned early learning professionals in constraining curiosity. He determined that for children, "curiosity dimmed is a future denied. Our potential—emotional, social, physical and cognitive—is expressed through the quantity and quality of our experiences. And less-curious children will make fewer new friends, join fewer social groups, read fewer books, and take fewer hikes" (p. 1).

Children are thinkers in their play. They require environments that offer them interesting materials, supports, and opportunities to take risks that will lead them to apply knowledge, try out new ideas, and develop new ways of thinking. When children are in stimulating environments, they will actively work toward constructing strategies to gain answers to their questions. They think about the same type of problem or issue in multiple ways. The newer the experience, the more ways of thinking children use to seek answers to the experience. Children need environments with materials or ideas that will trigger their curiosity.

Early learning students and professionals using big ideas with children can support what children know, as well as what they can learn. The experience of exploring deeply together can direct future experiences, such as how children will design and execute other play options. The collaborative pondering of ideas that can be explored in depth is intended to extend children's thinking and provide the impetus for more inquiry. Inquiry can provide the vehicle for learning every day during everyday moments. Inquiry can also lead to in-depth investigations through long-term projects. For professionals, big ideas are useful tools to support professional learning, curriculum development, and the creation of professional knowledge to guide practice.

STRATEGIES FOR TRIGGERING CURIOSITY

Children may be born curious, but environmental factors, such as available resources and the ways in which adults encourage their play, will influence how they continue to use curiosity in their learning. Early learning students and professionals play a significant role in promoting children's curiosity and their desire to explore their ideas and areas of wonderment.

Promoting wonder, exploration, and curiosity can take many forms with children and the materials in the environment. Early learning students and professionals consistently seek out information from children that will give them insight into how the children view ideas and situations. They use observations, discussions, and questions with the children to ascertain certain types of information that will give them insight into their mode of exploration and curiosity and the level of their thinking and conceptual understanding (Driscoll & Lownds, 2007). These adults can differentiate between how they view a situation and how children may view the situation (Lewin, 1951/1997). Children are encouraged to ask questions and form a hypothesis as a way to help them bring meaning and understanding to their experience. If the environment is rich with options, this will trigger children's questions and the sense of curiosity that comes from their own inquisitive nature and events in their environments (Church, 2007). There are many ways to trigger curiosity. We introduce you to three strategies that can be used as **investigative triggers** for children—ideas that surface from the "wonder-type" comments, conversations, or interests that children express during their play.

investigative triggers Ideas that surface from the "wonder-type" comments, conversations, or interests that children express during their play.

Wonder Walls

Wonder walls offer children and adults a visual, engaging space to record questions, ideas, or observations that are intended to spark conversation and lead them to explore materials or ideas further. They are places for children to gain basic knowledge about materials and their uses. When other children and adults pose further questions, wonder can be

A wonder wall visual used to trigger curiosity.

Peter Dietze

ignited. Wonder walls are places where children's curiosity may be sparked, leading them to take the idea in new directions. Such walls begin with children's or adult's questions. Examine the accompanying photo. What might be some of the questions that children posed? What types of questions might adults have posed to the children? How might materials on wonder walls, such as in the photo trigger further exploration and creativity?

Trial Balloons

Trial balloons is a new concept that the authors have used as a process of extending provocations to children. We view trial balloons as idea floaters. The purpose of trial balloons is to float an idea to children as a way to trigger their sense of curiosity and potentially expand their play experiences. These ideas may be curriculum based, such as, "How could we make an ice castle?" or a schedule idea, such as, "What would you do and what would you need to play outdoors from 9:00 a.m. to 11:00 a.m.?" Floating trial balloons is similar to planting seeds—the intent is to trigger children's thinking and actions and add new experiences or dimensions for exploration that children have not necessarily encountered before. Early learning professionals may use trial balloons as a way to incorporate the concept of big ideas into children's programming and their practice.

When early learning students and professionals are considering floating a trial balloon, there are benefits to having discussions with peers and critical friends to explore the various ideas, angles, and processes that may help them prepare to launch the trial balloon. Critical dialogue with critical friends provides early learning professionals with a plan of action and the confidence to launch the trial balloon. Collaboratively, the early learning students, professionals, and children explore, wonder, experiment, and create new options for learning. Telling the story of how trial balloons influence children's play and professionals' practice adds to knowledge for the early learning sector.

A Thinking Lens Framework

Carter and Curtis (2007) introduced a thinking lens framework that helps early learning students and professionals to think deeply and reflect on practice in a way that makes it meaningful and responsive to children's curiosity, learning, and development. You can find a handout with a full description of the thinking lens at http://bit.ly/12oz7Uh. Figure 9.4 lists six steps to take in order to see your practice through a thinking lens.

In the thinking lens framework, the first course of action involves knowing yourself. Let's think about materials. Think back to your own childhood and your most vivid memory of playing with materials. How would you describe the materials and the experience? You may have had many opportunities to play with materials, or you may have had more experience with traditional toys such as dolls and figurines. Some of you may recall experiences messing about with materials, where you had a chance to manipulate, create, and transform within a wide range of media. You may remember this as being messy. How do you feel about messy experiences for children? Think deeply about how your own experiences may influence what you would provide for children.

How does the environment need to be set up to give children easy access to materials? If the experience is messy, what does the early learning professional need to consider? How can spaces be designed so that children can create with materials? How can the day be scheduled so that there is ample time for children to play with intelligent materials?

From a child's point of view, what do you think would be preferable: open-ended, transformative materials, or closed-ended toys that can be used only one way? A child can

Figure 9.4 A thinking lens for early learning professionals

Source: Adapted from Carter & Curtis, 2007.

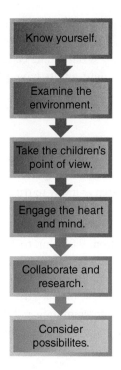

Know yourself.

Examine the environment.

Take the children's point of view.

Engage the heart and mind.

Collaborate and research.

Consider possibilites.

put together an airport from assorted blocks, boxes, paper airplanes, and other materials. A child might instead be given a toy airport to play with. From the perspective of the child, which do you think would be more fun to play with? Which experience would be more engaging and give the child a chance to play with others? Which perspective would support a child's sense of curiosity?

What do you need to think about during the children's experiences with materials? Are you thinking about skills, development, and learning? Are you thinking about how you can increase the value and potential of the experience? Are you considering how you can document the experience? What is pulling at your heartstrings? According to Carter and Curtis (2007), thinking about what is touching your heart and engaging your mind about the children's experience will help you apply a thinking lens to your practice.

Think about materials you could bring to early learning environments that are easy to find, inexpensive, and have plenty of play and learning potential. Do you think if you collaborated with others, your list of intelligent materials would expand? What if you did research? Collaborating with others and researching theoretical perspectives and development principles will increase your ability to apply a thinking lens. Applying a thinking lens will help to illuminate possibilities and opportunities for next steps.

THE THEORY OF LOOSE PARTS

When early learning professionals apply a thinking lens, they consider theoretical perspectives. Nicholson (1971) coined the term **loose parts theory** to describe the idea that children should be given open-ended materials to be used alone or with other materials, without specific direction, to spark their creativity. If you go to http://bit.ly/1aVM8xU, you will find a document that was created to support standards for "playwork" in the United Kingdom; it provides background on the theory as it relates to those standards, and provides a list of suggested items that can be used for loose parts. Thinking deeply about the theory of loose parts will bring to light the complexities of these often simple materials as the basis for learning and development in the early years. To begin your thinking, consider this quotation from a book about John Dewey's educational theories, which describes what can happen when such materials are brought into the learning environment:

> The materials we choose to bring into our classrooms reveal the choices we have made about knowledge and what we think is important to know. How children are invited to use the materials indicates the role they shall have in their learning. Materials are the text of early childhood classrooms. Unlike books filled with facts and printed with words, materials are more like outlines. They offer openings and pathways by and through which children may enter the world of knowledge. Materials become the tools with which children give form to and express their understanding of the world and the meanings they have constructed. (Cuffaro, 1995, p. 33)

Early learning students and professionals embed theory into practice. When loose parts are offered to children, they provide many opportunities, provocations, and invitations to use, transport, combine, and transform them. Making connections to theory in practice requires a thinking lens. Imagine seeing the learning environment through a lens that helps you envision the theory behind the practice. Viewing materials as intelligent is a perspective that brings theory to life.

INTELLIGENT MATERIALS

Intelligent materials are open-ended materials that are full of potential to spark children's creativity. The more a material can do, the more intelligent it can become with children, because what a material can do determines the potential for learning. In early learning environments, you may hear the word *sensory*, which means that something relates to or

loose parts theory A theory suggesting that children be given open-ended materials to be used alone or with other materials, without specific directions, which they can move, carry, combine, redesign, line up, take apart, and put back together in multiple ways, offering many opportunities to be creative.

intelligent materials Open-ended creative resources that are full of potential to express children's creativity.

Loose parts and materials in the environment.

Angela Brant and Fox Hollow Child Care Centre

provokes the senses. Use a search engine and type in "sensory activities in early learning"—you will find many links with suggestions. Reviewing the list will reveal that touch is a common sense for children to explore in early learning environments, but the more senses that are involved in an experience, the higher the potential is for learning. There are five physical senses, as illustrated in Figure 9.5.

Figure 9.5 The five senses

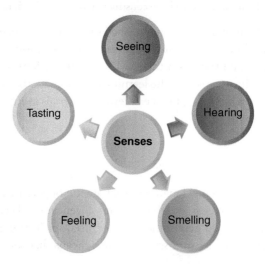

Children exploring in the garden.

Angela Brant and Fox Hollow Child Care Centre

In addition to being sensorial, intelligent materials have potential to communicate—to be expressive. They need to speak in languages or "alphabets." Look at the photo on this page. How might children explore the sensory experience? What senses may they potentially use in their exploration? Why?

MATERIALS AS LANGUAGES

When children encounter materials and begin to explore them, they build awareness of what can happen. Early learning students and professionals can be there to observe and support. It is through interactions between a child and a material that a language is developed. "As children use their minds and hands to act on a material using gestures and tools and begin to acquire skills, experience, strategies, and rules, structures are developed within the child that can be considered a sort of alphabet or grammar" (Gandini, 2005, p. 13). The child discovers the language of the material through experimentation and by observing and interacting with others (Gandini, 2005). Think about a ball made of elastic bands as an example of a material. Figure 9.6 on the next page depicts the types of knowledge that can be acquired by acting on this particular material.

A material's language can be thought of as the combination of the features of a particular material with the relationship that emerges in the interaction that the child has with the material. It is during this process that the possibilities for modification, transformation, and structuring of the material become apparent. It then becomes a "conduit for expression that communicates the child's thoughts and feelings" (Gandini, 2005, p. 13). Throughout the experience, the child is "acquiring knowledge about the material itself" (Gandini, 2005, p. 14).

Look around you and take in whatever objects are in your environment. Start to think about these ordinary objects as intelligent materials. Reggio educators give the example of a paper napkin:

A paper napkin is an anonymous object camouflaged by daily use and presence. A customary material which, when explored, reveals many properties. It is white, lightweight, soft and delicate

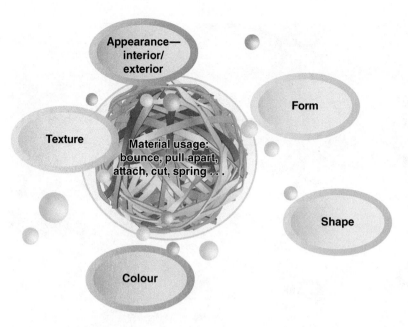

Figure 9.6 The language of a ball of elastic bands

and just slightly rough to the touch. In layers it obscures light but when unfolded it is almost transparent. Hands, perceptions, mind and material come together to know each other. Children's gestures build the first shapes. Research is being done on a "grammar" for the material, alphabets and compositions that will carry traces of the children's thinking and the identity of the material used. Compositions are placed next to each other and made to merge. They become extended and re-combined into one large final composition searching for balance between different gestures, different way of thinking. (Cavallini, Filippini, Vecchi, & Trancossi, 2011, p. 74)

Everyday objects have the potential to spark curiosity. These materials can become part of the indoor or outdoor environments. When early learning students and professionals offer children intelligent materials that can be expressive in many ways, they are creating material-rich environments. Think about the outdoor environment during the fall. What types of intelligent materials can students and children gather from their play spaces or within the community? How do the beautiful leaves or pine cones offer children different ways of thinking? What new languages might children express as a result of using these materials? What happens when you make resources available, such as magnifying glasses, paper, and paint?

MATERIAL-RICH ENVIRONMENTS

By creating and sustaining environments that are rich with materials, early learning professionals provide opportunities for children to be expressive and acquire knowledge and skills while thinking creatively and designing their own play experiences and representations. Many questions can be asked about adding materials to the environment:

- Will the material be used in many ways, or does the material dictate a particular use?
- Will many children use the material, or does the material have limited usage?
- Does the material lend itself to a variety of different kinds of explorations?
- How could the material be introduced to the children to allow for the greatest number of possibilities?
- Is the material better suited for indoor or outdoor exploration? Why?

OPEN-ENDED MATERIALS AND FLEXIBLE FURNISHINGS

Carter and Curtis (2003) suggested that when children are offered furnishings that are flexible and that can be moved in combination with open-ended materials, they engage in a range of activities that foster development and learning. **Open-ended materials** stand in contrast to closed-ended materials, which are limited in their use. Consider a puzzle piece—it is closed-ended if it can be used only as a part of a puzzle. The piece fits in one particular space. What happens when a puzzle piece goes missing? Early learning professionals have choices to make. If they choose, puzzle pieces can become loose parts and have open-ended possibilities as they are added to the imaginative creations that children construct. Another possibility is for children to have an opportunity to solve a problem, as illustrated in this story of an early learning professional and a missing puzzle piece experience: http://bit.ly/1boztSE. Consider the choices made and relate this story to the thinking lens framework.

open-ended materials Materials that can be used in many possible ways.

When children have ample opportunities to engage in experiences with materials in environments that are not static but flexible, they "become more competent in their physical abilities and develop self-confidence and independence. They develop specific skills, self-awareness, and an alertness and respect for others around them. Open-ended materials encourage children to become flexible thinkers and responsive playmates" (Carter & Curtis, 2003, p. 57). Figure 9.7 illustrates the many ways children respond to open-ended materials and flexible furnishings.

As children manipulate and build with materials, they may need an area in the room to be expanded to accommodate larger groups of children or larger construction projects. Being able to push furnishings back to increase the floor space is beneficial. Depending on the group of children, they may need smaller spaces within larger ones for cozier gatherings. Portable screens or dividers can be used to give children the opportunity to "work" in smaller spaces. With two-tiered steps and risers placed against walls, children can use open-ended materials to create different arrangements and scenes (Carter & Curtis, 2003).

Creating arrangements and scenes are a way for children to engage in **small world play**, a type of imaginative play that uses figurines and loose parts or materials, giving children an opportunity to mix and match as well as improvise to create their own symbolic scenarios. Think about the possibilities when children are provided with small animals and other creatures, such as farm, zoo, and domestic animals; prehistoric animals; and sea creatures. They can create a pond, beach, swimming pool, snow, swamp, forest, hills, mountains, valleys, and space scene. The children can put together a parking lot, airport, railroad, roads, or fields. By adding figurines of people and/or vehicles such as cars, trains, planes, and buses, they can make their play scenes more complex. Rocks, blocks, pebbles, boxes, tins, cones, shells, and pieces of fabric, carpet, or paper will add to the possibilities as the children create their small world play scenes. During small world play, children get the chance to be in control of their environment—to make things happen how and when they choose (Bromley & Scott, 2004). For more information on small world play, go to http://bit.ly/14tpyaF.

small world play The manipulation of small materials and toys to act out stories and to develop ideas.

Building   Manipulating
Problem solving
Representing
Creating
Investigating
Communicating
Moving

Figure 9.7 Children's response to open-ended materials and flexible furnishings

THE BEAUTIFUL STUFF OF CHILDHOOD

In 1999, Cathy Weisman Topal and Lella Gandini wrote *Beautiful Stuff! Learning with Found Materials*, chronicling the experience of early learning professionals who were inspired by the Reggio Emilia educators to explore the potential of materials in learning environments for young children. In the introduction to the book, they described the wonder of materials:

> To the young child the world is full of materials to touch, discover, and explore. To find, collect, sort and use materials is to embark on a special kind of adventure. For adults, gathering materials means rediscovering the richness and beauty in natural, unexpected, and recyclable objects that are all around us, but not often noticed. One way to rediscover our own creative impulses is to see possibilities in material. Children possess a natural openness to the potential of materials. When adults become aware of this process, they find ways to watch and listen to children. Children and adults become collaborators as they discover, collect, sort, arrange, experiment, create, construct, and think with materials. The goal is to allow children to become fluent with materials—as if materials were a language. (Topal & Gandini, 1999, p. 1)

Taking the view that materials are a language will also help early learning professionals to see the potential of materials as a way of thinking. Gandini and Topal (1999) suggested that bringing materials into the environment and "discovering their potential for learning will involve many of the same process skills used in math and science and interpreting literature. It's a way of thinking about things" (p. 98). Materials are thinking tools for children and adults.

MATERIAL CHOICES

Schwall (2005) offered ideas for the material choices in the learning environment. For example, in open jars, baskets, or trays that are placed on accessible shelves, early learning professionals can supply children with collections of shells, leaves, folded paper strips, and small wood and metal items that contrast and complement one another. Think about offering baskets of various wires, beads, nuts and bolts, and materials for twisting, such as foil paper and screen door mesh. When the materials are presented in an enticing and inviting manner, they "send a message of complexity, connection, and openness" (Schwall, 2005, p. 22). This supports children in gaining an appreciation for their environment and a sense of intrigue about how the materials may be used in their play and learning experiences.

Early learning students and professionals benefit from thinking deeply about possible materials that they can supply to children that will facilitate opportunities to explore, discover, and create. In order to think deeply about possibilities, you need practice. In addition to the materials suggested by Schwall (2005), Dietze and Kashin's list (2012) in Table 9.2 suggests many different objects, often reclaimed and repurposed, that can spark the creativity and curiosity of children, giving them chances for playful expression in many languages. Keep in mind that these materials are suggested for you to mess about and explore with. Some of these materials, such as Styrofoam, may be restricted in some areas and for some ages because of choking hazards.

MATERIALS AS THINKING TOOLS

An excellent source for learning about how important materials are to the early learning environment, written by British pedagogical consultant Debi Keyte-Hartland, can be found at http://bit.ly/12V9H0f. In an artful way, this presentation demonstrates how the materials offered in the learning environment create the context of learning and shows that there is an interrelationship between the use and types of materials offered and the ethics, values, and knowledge of the early learning professional.

Light as a material choice.

Angela Brant and Fox Hollow Child Care Centre

Table 9.2 Material Possibilities

REPURPOSED	FOUND	ACQUIRED
Straws	Driftwood	Metal materials
Clothespins & fasteners	Rocks	Blocks
Rulers	Pebbles	Magnets
Wood	Beach glass	Glass & plastic lenses
Corks & straws	Dirt	Levers & pulleys
Pegboard	Sand	String, ribbon, rope
Wire	Water	Clay & molding materials
Flashlights	Shells	Lids
LED lights	Sticks	Tubing
Squirt bottles	Seeds	Popsicle sticks
Sieves	Leaves	Electronics
Bottles & jars	Plants	Measuring cups
Batteries	Pine cones	Air pumps
Styrofoam	Dried plants & flowers	Tools: shovels, hammers, screwdrivers

Source: Based on Table 8.2 from Playing and Learning in *Early Childhood Education*, 1e by Dietze, p. 243. Copyright (©) 2012 by Pearson Canada.

Early learning professionals make ethical choices in the materials they choose to offer children. Ethically, do you think that it is appropriate to give children food as materials? How do you feel about children picking flowers to bring into the early learning environment? Early learning students and professionals keep environmental responsibility in mind. For more on environmental education in early learning, follow this link: http://bit.ly/150y00a. Consider your own values and beliefs regarding materials and their usage. How do your ideas connect with environmental perspectives? What might you need to explore further? Your knowledge about materials and the environment indoors and outdoors will increase the likelihood that you will make appropriate material choices.

THE HAWKINS THEORY OF MESSING ABOUT

Hawkins (2000) maintained that adults need time to play with materials in order to realize their potential for learning. By experimenting, you might realize that when you combine different materials what you are really doing is exploring concepts such as balance, aerodynamics, and velocity, for example. When you then offer these materials to children, you will be more confident in scaffolding their understanding and experimentation with these concepts. Hawkins understood the importance of offering materials to adults and children as a way to learn. Hawkins saw nature as a significant source of materials. For this "eminent mathematician and philosopher of science, the ideal location for messing about is a pond" (Kellogg, 2010).

> For Hawkins, mathematics is the language of nature. The heart of his ideas about education lay in his passion for the workings of the natural world and for the beauty of the patterns of the rhythms of the attendant mathematics and physics. This world seemed to furnish an infinity of paths to be explored, discovered and rediscovered. He seemed to feel himself as part of the pulse. (Kellogg, 2010, p. 60)

In the 1970s, David Hawkins and his wife, Frances, engaged with a group of young children and their teachers in the study of a pond (Kellogg, 2010). A pond can be an environment rich with intelligent natural materials to be explored. Think about how we have described investigative triggers, and then ponder ideas about what you might find in a pond.

To understand materials as tools for expression, you need to experiment, explore, and investigate the different material choices in order to discover their possibilities. Hawkins (2000) suggested that you "mess about" with materials; you will not know how to support aspects of learning unless you "have been encouraged to explore and appreciate the manifold ways these simple materials of childhood play are related, as subject matter, to the style and character and history of the great world around us" (p. 52). We encourage exploring materials indoors and outdoors. We invite you to play with others in your experimentations and record your discoveries before offering children those very same materials.

OUTDOOR AND INDOOR MATERIALS

Although the types of experiences and curiosity triggers may differ between indoor and outdoor environments, they are equally important to children and should be given equal consideration in design and materials. The early learning program philosophy influences the accessibility that children have to the outdoor environment and, in turn, to materials. One of the major differences between the indoor and outdoor environment is that the outdoor environment may have natural attributes that add materials. For example, when children have access to grass, pine cones, mud, and plants, as well as weather combinations, the experiences may lead them to have specific questions, such as where the rain comes from or

Eolithism - begins with a child's existing curiosity and content and engages a sense of wonder from the exhibit Cultivate the Scientist in Every Child http://bit.ly/1uYydQx.

Diane Kashin

Table 9.3 Levels of Complexity of Materials

Simple Units	Complex Units	Super-Complex Units
Refers to single-use materials to manipulate or create, such as a swing, tricycle, or slide.	Refers to two different kinds of materials that children may manipulate together, such as clay and scissors.	Refers to three or more kinds of materials that children may combine, such as sand, water, and digging tools.

Source: Adapted from Kritchevsky et al., 1977.

what makes clouds. As with the indoor environment, early learning students and professionals ensure that there are various types of materials outdoors to support children in wanting to explore and wonder, while stimulating them to seek answers to their questions in various ways.

Kritchevsky, Prescott, and Walling (1977) noted that early learning students and professionals benefit from considering the levels of complexity of various materials. Table 9.3 outlines the levels of complexity. Early learning students and professionals examine their environments to ensure that materials are available to support each level. Super-complex units offer children many opportunities to explore a variety of ideas, sometimes at great depth, because of the open-ended nature of the materials.

PROGRAM DESIGN FOR CHILDREN

Early learning professionals' work can include a wide range of children. The developmental profile of an infant is different from that of a child of three or a child of six years of age. When designing a program that is rich with materials, age and development must be considered. In Table 9.4 on the next page, we offer a way to bring materials into the learning environment for three age groups: infancy, early childhood, and middle childhood.

Table 9.4 Ways of Bringing Materials into the Learning Environment

INFANCY

Program Suggestion	Description	Big Ideas
Treasure Baskets  Diane Kashin	An excellent way to introduce materials to very young children is with a treasure basket. This gives early learning students and professionals an opportunity to collect age-appropriate, safe materials for infants in a way that is aesthetically pleasing and accessible.	Look closely and observe the interactions that infants and toddlers have with materials. How do they react to the different materials? How would you interpret the learning involved? Have the children discovered properties of materials? What other materials could be added to enhance the learning?

EARLY CHILDHOOD

Program Suggestion	Description	Big Ideas
Marble Run  Diane Kashin	Creating ramps and pathways for balls or marbles will help young children create, construct, and combine materials for a purpose. For more on marble runs, see http://bit.ly/12CRzgJ.	Document the children's progress as they are building their ramps and pathways for marbles and balls. What big ideas are they discovering? Are they grappling with balance, size, and velocity? What other materials can you offer that will scaffold their learning?

MIDDLE CHILDHOOD

Program Suggestion	Description	Big Ideas
Building Down 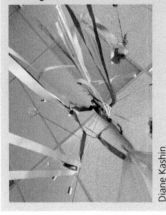 Diane Kashin	Older children can use materials suspended from a ceiling indoors or a tree branch outdoors to build down instead of the more common experience of building up. Children can use pipe, loose parts, and other materials to build down.	Building down affords children the opportunity to explore big ideas such as weight, balance, and aerodynamics. What materials could be added to enhance the experience?

PROGRAM DESIGN FOR FAMILIES

Families can be given the opportunity to engage with their children and materials in a collaborative way. At the Acorn School (www.acornschool.ca) in Ontario, a beautiful stuff project was launched with an invitation to families to collect materials at home in a paper bag. Lined up in the cubby area of the kindergarten room, the bags of beautiful stuff left the children overcome with excitement as the time came closer for them to unveil the materials that they had collected with their families. When the materials were emptied from the bags, they became a provocation for children to observe and compare, sort and classify. The materials became a provocation for the child to observe and compare, sort and classify as depicted in the accompanying photo.

Beautiful stuff organized by colour.

Diane Kashin

ROLES AND RESPONSIBILITIES OF EARLY LEARNING PROFESSIONALS

Think back to the child's story at the beginning of the chapter. If Maddie and Bailey approached you asking questions about the materials that were added to the outdoor play area, what would you say? What would you do? Your role and responsibility as an early learning professional is to enhance learning in a way that is meaningful for children. By applying the thinking lens previously discussed in the chapter, early learning students and professionals can take on the child's perspective and consider the following, based on Carter and Curtis (2003), as well as the idea of investigative triggers and trial balloons.

- What is drawing the attention of Maddie and Bailey, and what are they excited about?
- What might the children want to accomplish with the materials they observed in the outdoor play space?
- How might the children interact with others using this material and different materials in the outdoor play area?
- What developmental themes, ideas, or theories might the children be exploring during this time?
- What trial balloons may be used to trigger play?
- What types of materials or experiences may be introduced as part of an investigative trigger?

Found materials that the children have collected can also be added to other open-ended objects or be used by the children on their own. When such materials are found outdoors, you can take inspiration from the famous British artist Andy Goldsworthy, who creates huge pieces of land art in the environment using natural objects, such as pebbles, twigs, branches, pine cones, mud, leaves, and petals. Type the words "images of Andy Goldsworthy art with children" into a search engine to see examples of art created by children using these natural, loose, beautiful parts of the outdoor environment. We introduce nature art in Figure 9.8's programming bubble.

Nature Art
Providing children with baskets and bags in which to collect materials while exploring the outdoors will offer the opportunity to collect natural loose parts. Sharing the inspiration of the artist with children can elicit their own interpretations and representations of outdoor art. For more information, check
http://bit.ly/11TICkp
http://bit.ly/16GhoKp.

Figure 9.8 Programming bubble: nature art inspired by Goldsworthy

FEATURED RESEARCH

David Hawkins was a philosopher, mathematician, historian, physicist, educator, and essayist. His wife, Frances P. Hawkins, was an early learning professional and writer. Together they made many contributions to the early learning sector (New, Cochran, & Franzosa, 2006). David spent many years as a teaching professor at the University of Boulder in Colorado. He was the recipient of numerous awards for his work in philosophy and early science education. Frances taught for many years and was a thoughtful and passionate observer of young children in action. In the 1970s, David and Frances founded and directed a centre in Colorado for professional learning, providing workshops "notable for [the] inclusion of the voices of teachers writing about teaching and learning in their classrooms" (New et al., 2006, p. 409). When David visited Reggio Emilia, he became friendly with Loris Malaguzzi. Malaguzzi referenced Hawkins as a source of his understanding of teaching and learning, and Hawkins wrote about this experience of meeting Malaguzzi (Hawkins, 1998). As proponents of free play as a significant element of scientific exploration, David and Frances made a substantial contribution to early learning. They are truly role models for early learning students and professionals, as they were also activists who believed strongly in peace and social justice (New et al., 2006). For more information on the lives, writings, and theories of David and Frances Hawkins, see www.hawkinscenters.org.

PEDAGOGICAL TOOLS

We suggest early learning students and professionals take inspiration from the ideas of this chapter and consider using play as a pedagogical tool. Play with materials and play with each other are ways for you to realize the significance of play, the importance of materials, and the benefits of experiential learning. The opportunities for play and learning for early learning students and professionals have expanded. To be professionally literate means more than reading professional literature presented in traditional print format. It can include multiple literacies: playing online, while searching, collecting, archiving, curating, and sharing professional resources. For early learning students and professionals, this can be a playful experience.

PROFESSIONAL CASE STUDY

Marelli, James, Jill, and Joel were employed at an early learning centre for six years. They considered the early learning centre to be a traditional centre. Over the years the owner had purchased most of the play materials from a supply catalogue for early childhood programs. For example, the materials for the art centre were displayed in colourful plastic tubs. Sometimes when they looked at the environment, it was like viewing the colours in a kaleidoscope.

Marelli, James, Jill, and Joel have now purchased the early learning centre. One of their goals is to reconfigure the environment so that it is engaging for the children. For example, they want to remove as much plastic as they can from the environment. They want to bring natural products in, and they want the materials to have meaning for the children. As they think about making this shift, they feel overwhelmed. Many questions have surfaced and need answers. How will they know if and when the materials are suitable for children? What signs will give them clues that the materials are supporting children's curiosity? Should they establish ways to use trial balloons or wonder walls? How will they know if the environment is right for the children?

REFLECTION QUESTIONS FOR SELF-LEARNING

In this case study, Marelli, James, Jill, and Joel ask themselves many questions as they think about reconfiguring the early learning environment. Think about the following questions. How would you respond?

1. What advice would you give them on the types of materials they may wish to incorporate into the environment?
2. What suggestions would you have in relation to bringing cultural materials into the environment?
3. How might they know if the environment is supporting children's sense of wonderment and curiosity?
4. How might their program philosophy require adjustment? Why?

BIG IDEAS FOR DIALOGIC LEARNING

Materials within the indoor and outdoor play spaces are key contributors to supporting children's sense of wonderment, exploration, and curiosity. Think about early learning environments where you have visited or worked. When you think about the intelligent materials, loose parts, and open-ended materials, how do you visualize displaying them? What natural materials would you bring to the environment? How would those natural displays change with the seasons? What natural materials would you bring to the environment to support local cultures and family cultures? Now think about a potential trial balloon that you might want to share with the children. Why use trial balloons? How are trial balloons different from provocations? How do the two concepts differ? What are their similarities? How do you bring materials into the environment that will trigger children to have big ideas?

Use the following questions to consider environmental factors and the big ideas of providing materials that support children's curiosity and learning.

1. You are required to prepare a curiosity basket that will be placed in an outdoor snowbank. What natural items will you put in the basket? Why?
2. In small groups, share ideas of interesting items from the hardware store that you could put together to create a display that may spark big ideas with children.

3. Examine the Acorn School story of beautiful stuff. In small groups, create an idea for a bag of beautiful stuff. What would your group put in the bag? Create the bag and share with your colleagues. Listen to the language, and think about questions that could extend the level of exploration or curiosity.

4. While each group presents its beautiful stuff bag, think about how this sparks your interest to explore. How does this inform your practice?

VISION

It is our vision that early learning students will develop an understanding of the potential of materials to be vehicles for children to express themselves in multiple ways. By claiming your curiosity and exploring opportunities to experiment with learning through play as an adult learner, you will be able to realize value and apply high-level thinking about pedagogy in professional practice. The importance of materials cannot be underestimated. Playing with social media is one way to express your understanding. We invite you to begin by creating a social poster as described in Making Connections that reflects your beliefs about materials.

MAKING CONNECTIONS

Technology is a process and a tool that can be used to enhance professional learning (Dietze & Kashin, 2013) and to advocate for children's right to material-intensive learning environments that keep them engaged, playful, and cognitively challenged. By connecting with others through social media, you can make a case for material-intensive play environments. Take on a technological and cognitive challenge to develop a social poster that depicts your values and beliefs about materials. Figure 9.9 depicts two examples of social posters that can also be found at http://checkthis.com/user/dianekashin.

The steps to making a social poster are not difficult. You need to think of a title and perhaps a subtitle. Then you will need some content. Make sure to reference your content. You can include images, video, and links to other sites. Once you are satisfied that your social poster is an excellent representation of your beliefs and professionalism, make it public. You are now a connected professional!

Figure 9.9 Social posters about materials

Source: Diane Kashin

KEY TERMS

Affinity spaces 207
Curiosity 204
Intelligent materials 213
Investigative triggers 210

Loose parts theory 213
Open-ended materials 217
Small world play 217

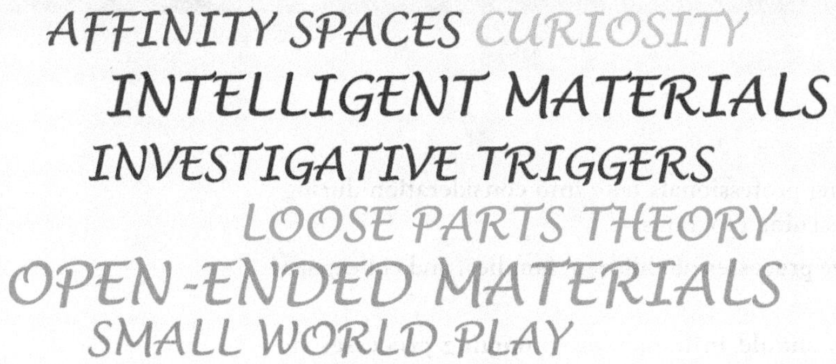

AFFINITY SPACES CURIOSITY
INTELLIGENT MATERIALS
INVESTIGATIVE TRIGGERS
LOOSE PARTS THEORY
OPEN-ENDED MATERIALS
SMALL WORLD PLAY

Figure 9.10 Key terms wordle

SUMMARY

This chapter reflects on the relationship of spaces and materials to children's sense of curiosity, wonderment, and experimentation. Early learning students can benefit from thinking about what makes them curious and how that sense of curiosity can be extended to their practice. Think about the learning outcomes and reflect upon the following:

1. Materials in the environment, including intelligent materials, have a major influence on children's play, learning, and desire to engage with the people, things, and opportunities within the environment.

2. *Loose parts* and *open-ended* are terms that relate to the process of building curiosity and supporting children's play. When early learning students and professionals apply a thinking lens to reflect on the process, the importance of these materials becomes more apparent.

3. When early learning students and professionals see materials as intelligent and as having their own language, they too become a thinking tool to embed theory into practice.

4. The Hawkins theory of messing about provides another way for adults to see the importance of open-ended materials in the lives of children. By looking at both the indoor and outdoor environments and considering strategies for enhancing children's curiosity, early learning students and professionals can realize the potential of materials.

"Cultivate the Scientist in Every Child: The Philosophy of Frances and David Hawkins" is an educational exhibit created by the Hawkins Centers of Learning as a tribute to the work of this couple. Their work has a very timely message about the importance of incorporating materials both as a vehicle for children's learning and as a tool for early learning professionals to mess about with, so as to be better able to enrich unstructured learning experiences for the children with whom they work. The exhibit is travelling through the United States and spent a year in Canada. For more information about the exhibit, go to www.hawkinscenters.org/exhibit.

For Further Thought

Chapter 10
The Programming Process

LEARNING OUTCOMES

After exploring this chapter, you should be able to

1. Discuss the factors that early learning professionals take into consideration during the programming process for early learning programs.

2. Outline the relevancy of collaborative processes of children, families, and colleagues to program planning.

3. Discuss how current developments should influence programming processes in early learning programs.

4. Describe the relationship of theory to practice in early learning programs.

5. Explain the roles and responsibilities of early learning professionals in the planning process.

6. Discuss processes that may be used to develop a program plan that supports children in their play and learning.

A CHILD'S STORY   Kamil

Yesterday when our teachers took us outside, I found something that I had never ever imagined before. It all started when I went to the shed to get that big wagon so that I could haul some wood stumps to the area where my friends Alex and Ahmed and I were making a theme park. I got the wagon out. I started to move the wood stumps but my wagon starting rolling backwards. I couldn't stop it. My teacher Annie stopped it with her feet. She asked me, "What can you do so that it won't roll backwards?" I told her, "I don't know." Then, I thought about moving the wagon in front of the stumps. That worked. As I was about to move one of the stumps, I found a lot of bugs. They were red and yellow and green. I called Alex and Ahmed over to look at the bugs. Alex said, "They are yucky," but I didn't think so. Annie came over to see what I had found.

I showed her all the colours on the bugs. We didn't know what kinds of bugs they were. Annie asked me if I wanted to take a photo of them so we could investigate them on the internet. I liked taking the photo. After my rest, Annie, Ahmed, and I looked for the bugs on the internet. We found a big picture of a bug that looked just like mine. I went outside with the picture from the internet, a magnifying glass, and the camera to see if my bugs really looked like the ones in the picture. My bugs were not there anymore, so we had to go look for them. We found more under another stump. I think they live under the stump. Annie said, "Maybe we can confirm that once we determine if we have the right bug information from the internet." I think we do. I am going to pick up a bug and take it home to show my daddy.

Children's environments influence their level of exploration.

Kelly McPherson

CHAPTER PREVIEW

*We grant space and time to young plants and animals because
we know that, in accordance with; the laws that live in
them, they will develop properly and grow well; young
animals and plants are given rest, and arbitrary interference
with their growth is avoided, because it is known that the
opposite practice would disturb their pure unfolding and
sound development; but the young human being is looked
upon as a piece of wax, a lump of clay which man can mold
into what he pleases.*

—FRIEDRICH FROEBEL (1782–1852)

The programming process is foundational to this textbook, with all the previous chapters setting the stage for Chapter 10. **Programming** describes the approach to education in the early learning environment. Early learning professionals use the term interchangeably with **curriculum** (Dietze & Kashin, 2012). Traditionally, curriculum in early learning was seen as a plan of activities carried out by educators in order for children to acquire predefined developmental or subject skills (Bennett, 2000). With the term *curriculum* being associated with traditional prescribed methodologies used in the past, we view *programming* as an alternative postmodern term that allows for the voices of others within a broad focus.

The program in an early learning environment integrates all elements of professional practice. Programming incorporates an early learning professional's philosophy, values, and beliefs, while demonstrating theory in practice. The early learning program communicates the professional's understanding of the players within the learning environment. Effective programming should incorporate all the players, reflecting a variety of interests and strengthening relationships while respecting each member of the learning community.

programming The approach to education in the early learning environment. The term is used as an alternative to *curriculum* in play-based learning environments.

curriculum A plan of activities carried out to meet predetermined goals and outcomes.

>> Box 10.1 **Claim Your Voice and Ability to Articulate**

Chepko Danil/Fotolia

CLAIM YOUR VOICE and your ability to articulate by providing experiences for children to learn through multiple languages.

articulation The process of formulating and expressing the programming approach with clarity and effectiveness.

Programming is a process; it is the approach to education used by the professional. It cannot be done in isolation. Instead, a mindful professional collaborates with children, families, and colleagues to create and deliver effective learning experiences for all concerned. Early learning professionals use their voice to ensure that the voices of others are heard in the early learning environment. They provide multiple means of expression so that children may learn through many languages. We encourage you to claim your voice as an essential part of your professional practice (see Box 10.1).

Articulating the teaching and learning process is congruent with being able to explain your programming process. **Articulation** is a skill that allows an early learning professional to help others understand the non-prescriptive approach to process in non-traditional programming. The word *traditional* implies that the approach is long established and generally teacher directed. The children's parents and family members may not be accustomed to the kind of programming where children, teachers, and families collectively have input into the types of experiences and materials that are available in the environment at any one time. By making a child's learning visible and articulating the process, early learning professionals can help others see beyond the traditional. This is a fundamental role of the early learning professional in the programming process.

This chapter will guide early learning students and professionals in developing the skills to plan and deliver effective programming that supports children's multiple languages. Any of the curriculum frameworks described in Chapter 5 can be used as resources for programming. Overwhelming evidence within these curriculum framework documents shows that the approach to education in early learning environments should be process related. Traditional prescribed activities are being replaced in practice by

emergent programming—a process-related approach where the program emerges from the children with input from adults.

When your approach is process related and socially constructed within a community of learners, it can be described as an emergent curriculum. To avoid confusion with the traditional meaning of *curriculum*, we recommend that early learning students use emergent *programming* instead. This approach assumes a non-traditional stance, much like that taken by Reggio Emilia educators.

emergent programming An approach to planning where the program is process related and co-constructed by children and adults.

BRINGING THE PLAYERS TOGETHER

In order to incorporate your voice and the voice of others within a program, you will need to practise the skill of collaboration. Collaborating in designing or planning a program and delivery is a part of emergent programming. To be effective as a collaborator, early learning students and professionals must recognize the need for continuous reflection in their practice. Reflection does not take place once a month at a planning meeting with others. Rather, Curtis, Lebo, Cividanes, and Carter (2013) strongly recommended that a stand be taken for the "right to exercise creative, critical, and reflective thinking" in professional practice (p. 3). This requires everyday reflection.

Various approaches, as described in Chapter 4, are designed to be collaborative, including the project approach and the Reggio Emilia approach. These are emergent programming examples. In learning from these approaches, early learning students and professionals benefit from engaging in critical reflective practice. Moving toward an emergent, evolving-process program should be a transformative experience for all the players in the early learning environment, with learning and development demonstrated (MacNaughton, 2009). Critical reflection processes help early learning professionals identify and determine many aspects of their practice. For example, through critical reflection, early learning professionals can analyze the results of programming in which the role of the educator is to transmit knowledge to the learner. In the process of reflecting, early learning professionals may realize that when early learning professionals assume a power dynamic, this does not allow the voices of the other players to be integrated into the program.

Educators who use the theme approach are trying to transmit information to children and can become the focus of the program. Even when they attempt to assume a more transformative approach that uses project-based learning, it is possible that educators will continue to transmit rather than stretch to embrace how children can lead the curriculum through experiential learning. Follow this link to an article about emergent programming http://bit.ly/1KsuYbl. It describes the experiences of four early learning professionals who strove to incorporate projects into their programs. Their stories indicate that a pivotal time in the programming process is when the project topic, title, or direction is established. If the project topic, title, or direction reflects a learning question rather than a one-word statement such as "cars," "trees," or "shapes," the voices of others are more likely to be heard. Examples of learning questions include

- What makes the wheels of a car move?
- Why do trees lose their leaves in the winter?
- Where are the shapes in our world?

The richest learning questions to lead the program are established by involving the other players. Starting an investigative project without a question that reflects the players is a common pitfall and may result in a transmission-of-information approach that is neither authentic nor emergent. Other common pitfalls to avoid when using projects include

- predetermining interests in a non-collaborative way without documented evidence to support that the interests are authentic and meaningful;
- taking over and deciding the direction of the program and the materials that will be made available to the children without collaboration; and
- directing and controlling the experiences and environment in a non-collaborative way by starting a project with the materials and resources that the teacher has collected and providing connecting activities (Kashin, 2011).

collaboration The act of working together with others, especially in the intellectual endeavours of playing and learning.

The essential element of an emergent program is **collaboration**—working together with children to plan learning experiences. What does it mean to collaborate with all the players? Follow this link to gain further information on ways to collaborate with children for effective programming: http://bit.ly/17KvAUh.

FROM THE INFORMATION AGE TO THE CONCEPTUAL AGE

There is no denying that we have entered a new age, a time that Pink (2006) suggested would be dominated by conceptual work requiring right-brain thinking. **Right-brain thinking** reflects a more artistic and creative side than the more logical left-brain thinking. Scientific research suggests that this conceptualization is not accurate, but we have included it as a prompt for your whole-brain thinking. For the latest science, see http://bit.ly/1juKDYg.

right-brain thinking Thinking characterized as intuitive, thoughtful, and subjective; left-brain thinking is usually more logical, analytical and objective.

The progression from the agricultural age to the conceptual age through the centuries is illustrated in Figure 10.1. In your learning experiences, we encourage you to practise your conceptualization skills, which we have been fostering throughout the textbook. Thinking deeply and considering multiple perspectives about complex professional issues helps you

Figure 10.1 Moving into the twenty-first century

develop the disposition to be reflective and to conceptualize. It will also help you to reconceptualize. You will be developing skills that will benefit you in this conceptual age. Early learning professionals have a responsibility to help children develop the skills essential to this new age, including digital literacy, creativity, and the ability to collaborate. These skills align more appropriately with emergent programs than those with a prescribed traditional curriculum. Still, many programs resist the move into the twenty-first century.

Systems that reinforce an academic-focused curriculum for the early years prevail. Instead of allowing for flexibility according to the context of the program, there are calls for testing and stringent accountability measures. In this way, the traditional structure of curriculum in the early years, such as the theme approach, has been "sanctified and maintained in these new times" (Yelland & Kilderry, 2005, p. 2). As emergent programming approaches spread and postmodern views continue "seeping into social and educational thinking whereby many have begun to question" (Yelland & Kilderry, 2005, p. 2) practices, it is difficult to understand why, with the knowledge that we have about how children learn, the theme approach is still used. Assume your position in this postmodern world and learn to question and think critically about your beliefs and values.

PROGRAMMING IN THE TWENTY-FIRST CENTURY

To make decisions about designing a program, you need to know the children you work with and apply your observational and documentation skills. You have to begin somewhere by planning an experience that ignites an initial spark of interest. We have used trial balloons as an example of how to trigger or capture children's interest in a way that can be expanded to create a meaningful, authentic program. We extend our concept of trial balloons to include bubbles. Bubbles are transient objects that last a brief moment in time. By bringing together wondrous materials in an inspiring environment that acts as a third teacher, trial balloons can produce bubbles of programming experiences to support children's learning and development, as illustrated in the accompanying photos.

Balloons and bubbles pop. They have a life that brings joy, ignites wonder, and sparks curiosity; they pop to further provoke minds and expand learning. It is a playful process that requires professional attention to generate bigger balloons, bubbles, and ideas. Include the voice of all the players in the environment by continually encouraging the expression of children and their families, as well as your own expression. Be mindful that every individual in the learning environment has a right to feel a sense of belonging—to feel included and to have his or her voice heard. Everyday moments with ethical encounters guide professional practice. Within those moments you can include, when appropriate, inquiry that leads to learning. The "popping" process is featured in Table 10.1 on the next page.

Trail balloons, the "popping process" can lead to everyday moments for children's exploration.

(L) Falcon Eyes/Fotolia; (R) Diane Kashin

Table 10.1 Program Popping

Program Design		Professional Responsibilities
P	Provocations for play	Set the stage and provide children with the bubbles and balloons to begin the playful process.
O	Observation, documentation, and interpretation	Own your voice as the professional engaging with children in this playful process.
P	Keeping a project/ inquiry, or multiple projects/ inquiries, going	Based on observation, documentation, and interpretation, build your program in collaboration with others while you continue to observe, document, and interpret.
P	Planning for future experiences	Conceptualize learning questions that will lead the inquiry and identify the project to be undertaken. Consider the whole of the project through its title. Have it reflect its collaborative nature.
I	Identifying interests	As part of the interpretative process, identify the interests of the children, but be careful not to trivialize (Hawkins, 2002). Look for authentic and meaningful interests that can provide future experiences.
N	Next steps	Like a bubble, the project or inquiry cannot last forever. A balloon cannot stay inflated forever. Plan for the transition. What are your next steps?
G	Group growth	Document your group and community experiences, including the growth and development of all the players.

THE PROGRAM DESIGN

Bubbles and balloons are iconic features of childhood. We suggest that they be used metaphorically to trigger, prompt, provoke, or spark curiosity and learning. Bubbles and balloons make up the program's design. When you launch a trial balloon with children that engages and inspires learning, programming bubbles up. Figure 10.2 illustrates the bubble metaphor with a spiral backdrop to indicate that purposeful, intentional triggers can spiral

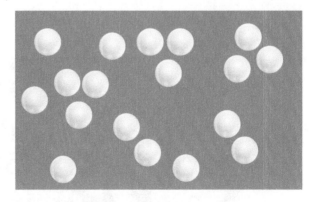

Figure 10.2 **The bubble and spiral metaphor of program design**

into learning that has no beginning or end, much like Malaguzzi's metaphor of a tangle of spaghetti (Malaguzzi, 1998), as described in Chapter 8.

THE PROGRAMMING PROCESS

A focus on inquiry requires a program that is conscious of twenty-first-century skills, including technology integration and creativity. Using projects is a way to frame a program to ensure that children are engaged and collaborative in deciding future directions. Reflection is so important throughout the process of program design that we have devoted our two final chapters to professional reflection and research.

Belonging, Being and Becoming: The Early Years Learning Framework for Australia (Australian Government Department of Education, Employment and Workplace Relations [DEEWR], 2009) recommends a four-quarter planning cycle of questioning, planning, acting, and reflecting (see Figure 10.3).

When an early learning professional questions an idea, an observation, or the content of dialogue, the process for programming begins. You start by asking questions about your observations and analysis. What learning is taking place and how is it meaningful? The responsibility lies with you to recognize children's strengths and interests, both as a group and as individuals. It is also your role to seek answers to what others recognize about their strengths and interests, including children, their families, and your colleagues (DEEWR, 2009).

The next part of the cycle involves thinking about what other experiences are possible, and if or how individuals and groups may learn from the experience. Will it involve individual learning or learning together? The planning needs to include all the players. During the planning process, the early learning professional reflects about how potential experiences and materials may contribute to supporting children to learn and develop. It is recommended that outcomes be set at this time. We will explain how to write outcomes for programming later in the chapter. For those of you living in provinces or territories with

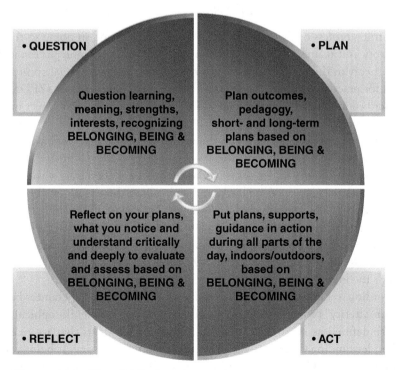

Figure 10.3 The EYLF planning cycle

Source: Australian Government Department of Education, Employment and Workplace Relations, 2009.

a curriculum framework, we encourage you to begin to practise writing outcomes based on your framework. Program planning includes creating plans for individuals and groups, transitions or routines, experiences, and interactions that can take place indoors or outdoors. When you plan, you consider both short-term and long-term programming. Short-term programming would involve plans that extend over the course of a morning, afternoon, or day or two. Long-term plans extend well beyond that.

The third quadrant in the cycle involves acting. When you act, you are responding to what you know, what you observe, and what you have planned for. This is where you put your plans into action and support your colleagues, the families, and the children in order to enact a plan that engages children in learning and development. During the process, the Australian early years learning framework recommends that the practices and principles of the framework guide the way. This part of the process requires you to respond to the outcomes that were set at the beginning. If the outcomes were met, how were they met? If the outcomes were not met, why not?

During the reflection phase, early learning professionals reflect upon outcomes and take their reflection further by considering what they have noticed, understood, planned, and have questions about, as well as "aha" moments. This calls for critical reflection. How did the children and their families respond to your plans? What were the benefits? While dialogic learning is recommended throughout the cycle, during the reflection stage it is essential to meet with others to discuss, debate, talk, and review observations, perspectives, and questions that evolved (DEEWR, 2009). We recommend that you do this in person or through social media. Also in this part of the cycle, you will evaluate what has occurred and assess children's learning. Assessment is an important part of the cycle, but it is also a topic that garners debate and discussion. You will find more on assessment in programming in Chapter 11. For a printout of the Australian early years learning framework planning cycle, see http://bit.ly/1eWOxfA.

THEORY TO PRACTICE IN PROGRAMMING

Early learning professionals bring ethics to their practice, and in doing so think deeply about theory as it relates to their role. If you agree that early learning professionals should consider theory in their practice, there is a need to conceptualize social constructivism as the basis for practice, particularly the **zone of proximal development (ZPD)**, which we have described in previous chapters and will return to here, as it has a direct influence on the programming process.

The ZPD is "the distance between the actual developmental level as determined by independent problem solving and the level of potential development as determined through problem solving under adult guidance, or in collaboration with more capable peers" (Vygotsky, 1978, p. 86). Thinking deeply about the theory of ZPD tells us that what children can achieve through the assistance of more knowledgeable others in a social construct is greater than what they can do on their own (Vygotsky, 1978). The term **more knowledgeable other (MKO)** is self-explanatory and can include any adult or child with more knowledge or experience. ZPD and MKO are considered the two main principles of Vygotsky's theories.

According to Parkes (2000), viewing the ZPD as a strategic encounter between the "self" and "alterity" provides the basis for ethical practice. The philosophical term *alterity* can be defined as meaning "otherness," and it reminds us that we need to work toward understanding Others. If you bring this theory to practice, it helps you to grasp the otherness of the Other (outlined in Chapter 7) at the same time that it provides a strategy for programming. Your programming process involves problem solving together with the children, and it is in this process that you demonstrate your commitment to ethical programming.

zone of proximal development (ZPD) The difference between what a child can achieve on his or her own and what he or she can achieve with guidance and encouragement from a skilled partner.

more knowledgeable others (MKO) Someone who has a better understanding or a higher ability level than the child when involved with a particular task, process, or concept.

The role of the early learning professional in the programming process also involves extending opportunities for children to solve problems in a social context where they may cross their zone of proximal development. These opportunities can exist among the children and between the children and adults. The zone of proximal development theory helps students and professionals to be active and accountable. Your role is not to stand back or to be a silent observer while children play. In order for learning to happen, according to this theory, a collaborative play and learning environment must be created and be always growing among the players.

NEGOTIATED LEARNING

Forman and Fyfe (1998) referred to what happens in Reggio Emilia as **negotiated learning** because it is based on helping children to "study their ways of making meaning, their negotiations with each other in a context of symbolization, communication, narrative, and metaphor" (p. 240). To practise negotiated learning as an early learning student, you begin by analyzing the "children's interest, the source of their current knowledge, and their level of articulation about its detail" (Forman & Fyfe, 1998, p. 240). To do this, we encourage you to go beyond just "simply identifying children's interests" (Forman & Fyfe, 1998, p. 240). Listening to the children, speaking with the children, observing children, and using the process of trial balloons help early learning professionals to devise an open-ended environment that supports negotiated learning.

negotiated learning Involves uncovering children's beliefs about topics to be investigated.

The programming role of the early learning professional doesn't end with establishing a particular interest. The process continues with further dialogue, discourse, documentation, and analysis. The continuous process of programming is supported by the use of the zone of proximal development as it applies to each child within the learning environment on a day-to-day basis. The program is socially constructed. At a "**metalinguistic** level, the children talk about how they represent what they know" (Forman & Fyfe, 1998, p. 240). Teachers, children, and families "discuss the social and symbolic processes by which meanings are negotiated, toward some level of shared understanding" (Foreman & Fyfe, 1998, p. 240). Aspects of the discussions are then incorporated into the program and become transparent in various parts of the early learning environment.

metalinguistic Refers to talking about talking and is similar to the term *metacognition*, which is thinking about thinking.

The potential of dialogue and documentation is rich when children have the freedom to explore.

Bora Kim

According to Forman and Fyfe (1998), the program is neither child centred nor teacher directed; instead, the program is "child-originated" and "teacher-framed" (p. 240). Negotiated learning as fundamental to program planning creates a "dynamic system of causes, effect, and counter-effects" characterized by three components: "design, documentation and discourse" (Forman & Fyfe, 1998, p. 240). Design refers to anything the child does, whether it involves a drawing or a sketch that can guide the construction of items. Discourse involves a desire to understand the words and intentions of the children. It involves intentionally constructive confrontation with others. It can involve conflict in the struggle to understand. Documentation is what makes the learning and the process visible. "Design and documentation serve to focus, maintain, and improve the discourse during the negotiated process of learning" (Forman & Fyfe, 1998, p. 241). The program that emerges from this dynamic process of negotiated learning doesn't happen by accident. It involves planning and design.

PROGETTAZIONE

progettazione An Italian term used by Reggio Emilia educators to describe flexible program planning.

The Italian word **progettazione** means "planning and design" and is used by Reggio Emilia educators to describe flexible program planning (Gandini, 1998). We first introduced you to this term in Chapter 7. In the book *Art and Creativity in Reggio Emilia: Exploring the Role and Potential of Ateliers in Early Childhood Education*, Vecchi (2010) made a distinction between the word *progettazione* and another Italian word, *programmazione*:

> In Italian, the verb *progettare* has a number of meanings: to design, to plan, to devise, to project (in a technical-engineering sense). The use of the noun *progettazione*—translated in this book as "project"—by Reggio educators, however, has its own special meaning. (p. xiii)

hypothesis A proposed explanation made on the basis of evidence that is a starting point for further investigation.

For Reggio educators, *progettazione* stands in opposition to *programmazione*, which implies a predefined program. *Progettazione* is more flexible and global, where original **hypotheses**, or proposed explanations of children's interests and ideas based on evidence, are subject to modifications and changes in direction. When visualizing *progettazione*, it is impossible to see it in a linear way. It grows in many directions without an overarching principle to the order (Vecchi, 2010) because there are many influences on the programming process.

PROGRAMMING FLOWCHART

The process of programming is uncharted, and you can know the direction to go in only once you have begun the journey. It may be helpful to see the process in a flowchart format, depicted in Figure 10.4, as it provides a visual that illustrates where you begin.

PROGRAM FORMATTING AND DOCUMENTATION

This section focuses on creating the format for your program. We provide only a few examples because we think that designing your own format or template for programming is an excellent exercise in applying design thinking. There are many examples that will help you find a format that works for you and that you can work with effectively. You use a documentation format that will be evidence of your accountability to your professional practice to create, design, plan, and implement your program.

We recommend that as early learning students, you begin to apply your own voice in order to create a framework that is authentic. The framework is most effective when it is based on your context, practice, and experience. Effective frameworks are dynamic, fluid, and reflective of the children and families in the early learning space. Use design thinking to design your own format. Consider examples of programming formats that early learning

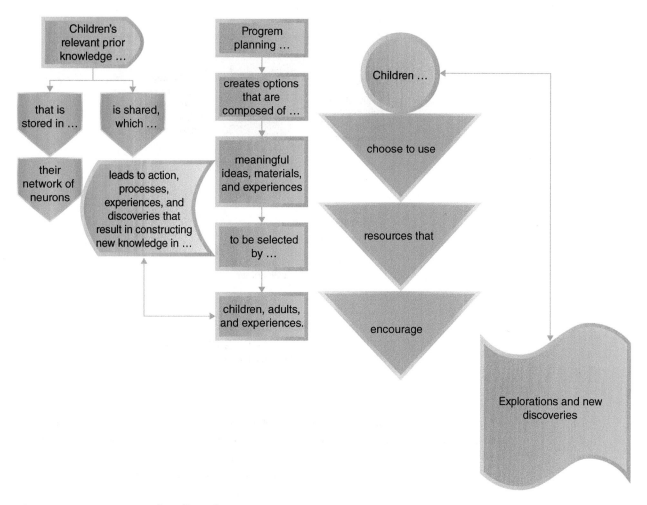

Figure 10.4　**Programming flowchart**

professionals currently use. The following links illustrate some sample formatting templates used by early learning professionals. After you connect to these links, think about why planning formats are important. Think of as many reasons as you can for using them.

1. From Australia: http://bit.ly/1ffXDOT.

2. From American author and educator Ann Pelo: http://bit.ly/1c3jnNB.

3. From Ontario—a kindergarten teacher's inquiry planning form: http://bit.ly/16swm62.

ROLES AND RESPONSIBILITIES OF EARLY LEARNING PROFESSIONALS

As noted in Chapter 3, many provinces across Canada have developed or are in the process of developing curriculum frameworks to guide early learning professionals in the process of program planning and implementation. The quality of the programming process and the work environment for early learning professionals directly links to the quality of the early learning environment (Carter & Curtis, 2010; Goleman, 2000). Programming is not a simple process—it needs to be examined from a variety of perspectives. As illustrated in Figure 10.5 on the next page, we will introduce you to five core roles and responsibilities of early learning professionals in the programming process.

Figure 10.5 **Roles and responsibilities of early learning professionals in programming**

Know Your Vision

Early learning professionals continually seek out ways to develop programming processes that illustrate the fundamental values of the philosophy and the families that are part of the early learning centre. They develop their vision for programming by thinking about such topics as what they believe about children, play, learning, environments, families, and experiential learning. A programming vision is personal to every individual because life experiences, beliefs, values, creative thinking, and inspirations about what is possible influence one's vision. Early learning professionals require a vision of what programming is and what it could be, because visions provide teachers with a "sense of purpose" (Hammerness, 2003, p. 45). According to Block (1987),

> A vision exists within each of us, even if we have not made it explicit or put it into words. Our reluctance to articulate our vision is a measure of our despair and a reluctance to take responsibility for our own lives, our own unit, and our own organization. (p. 107)

Early learning professionals' visions are concrete, provide direction, and help to guide what and how they offer overall programming to children. Individuals who establish a vision for practice have a sense of what inspires them, providing an underlying motivation for their practice. They observe and listen to the children and reflect upon their practice to guide their programming model. They examine their vision to gain a deeper understanding of their practice and to identify gaps between what they hope their programming offers children and their practice (Hammerness, 2003).

Engaging in a visioning process for programming, early learning professionals think deeply about what the experiences might look like for children. They may consider what roles the children should have in programming, and what experiential learning opportunities might bubble up. They may think about their roles and potential ways of extending the experiences so that children gain a sense of intrigue and wonder. They may think about how the programming looks within certain environments. What types of experiences or activities may be occurring at any one time indoors and outdoors? How might the two areas differ in programming? They may ask themselves about particular conflicts and contradictions or things they had not considered when thinking about the programming.

Enable Children to Recognize Their Knowledge and Learning

Early learning professionals and children work together in collaborative play environments. Through observations and pedagogical documentation, children and early learning professionals discuss their interests and what types of ideas or experiences they need for their play. Engaging children in conversation and encouraging them to discuss what they know about a particular topic is a form of children's self-assessment. Discussing children's learning with them, giving them feedback, and working with them to map out their next steps if they have aspirations to continue exploring an interest but don't know how to proceed are part of the active role early learning professionals play with children.

An effective way to model the learning process to children is through small-group discussion and interactions among the children and early learning professional. The early learning professions frames the dialogue with the child on what they know, or how they know what they have completed or need to explore further (Blandford & Knowles, 2011). The HighScope curriculum process focuses on children discussing their child-initiated experiences through a plan-do-review process. The benefits of this review process are that children and the early learning professional discuss their discoveries, and children have voice and power (Blandford & Knowles, 2011). This review is essential to the programming planning and implementation process, as early learning professionals use the information to scaffold children's experiences so that they move from simple to more complex discoveries, reflecting the zone of proximal development concept discussed earlier.

Programming to meet the children's needs occurs in environments that promote sustained **shared thinking**. Siraj-Blatchford, Sylva, Muttock, Gilden, and Bell (2002) described sustained shared thinking as "an episode in which two or more individuals work together in an intellectual way to solve a problem, clarify a concept, evaluate activities, extend a narrative etc. Both parties must contribute to the thinking and it must develop and extend" (p. 489). There are many benefits to adopting a shared-thinking process as part of the programming framework because it helps the key players work together to think about how to solve a problem or explore an area of interest to them.

shared thinking A process of two or more people working together to think about how to solve a problem or explore an area of interest to them.

A shared-thinking process helps early learning professionals to be continuously aware of children's interests, allowing them to introduce new materials and experiences that reflect children's expressed interests. Shared thinking is most effective when early learning professionals practise formulating questions that help children to articulate their thoughts and knowledge while empowering them to follow their interests and learning. This collaborative process supports children in developing self-competence.

Children and professionals who have shared common interests ultimately influence the program direction. According to Hawkins (1974), the process of teaching and learning can be represented in an instructional diagram represents a triangle of "I," "Thou," and "It." The "I" is the teacher, "Thou" is the child, and "It" represents the shared interest.

Children benefit from a model of practice where early learning professionals support children in collaborating in experiences, sharing their knowledge, and acquiring information that they need. This type of programming model encourages individuals and groups to discuss resources and ways that the resources may be used in the play episode.

Create Inclusive Programming

With continued recognition of the importance of diverse families and staff in early learning programs, early learning professionals ensure that their program-planning and implementation process are inclusive. The meaning of *inclusive programming* is broad, requiring early learning professionals to think about each aspect of their programming. For examples of how inclusive programming can have a wide effect, take a look at the Reflective Moment

What do you think a gender-neutral play zone would look like? How might you encourage girls to use hockey sticks in their play and boys to use pots and pans?

How might you respond to a mother or father who expresses concern because their son is playing house?

box to think about how the programming process can promote gender equity. This means that early learning professionals ensure that their programming process "counteract[s] the traditional gender patterns and gender roles and make[s] it possible for children to gain access to alternative ways of being girls and boys without gender limitations" (Arlemalm-Hagser, 2010, p. 515). Arlemalm-Hagser (2010) reminds us of the importance of viewing gender equity as a key component in programming. As shown in Figure 10.6, early learning professionals can advance gender equity in programming by constantly examining practices.

Video recordings and observations of practice help early learning professionals review their interactions and programming related to gender equity. Early learning professionals have a role in examining the types of materials, experiences, and practices extended to children to determine if and how they can extend their play space to be gender neutral. For example, think about the indoor environment. Where do the boys play? Are those play spaces different from where the girls play? Who plays together outdoors? Early learning professionals share their knowledge and understanding about gender equity and weave it into their programming practice.

Early learning professionals also have a strong interest in creating early learning places for play that support diverse learning styles among the children, as well as their linguistic and cultural requirements. This requires early learning professionals to hear the voices of children and their families. Take a reflective moment to think critically and challenge the concept of quality programming—you can be more open to the voices of others.

Children's play and learning are influenced by multiple intersecting internal and external factors. Behavioural challenges, emotional issues, and family issues are considered by early learning professionals in their programming models, and when observing the ways in which children execute their play experiences. Hatch (2010) has suggested that "early childhood education needs teachers who have the capabilities and dispositions to focus on

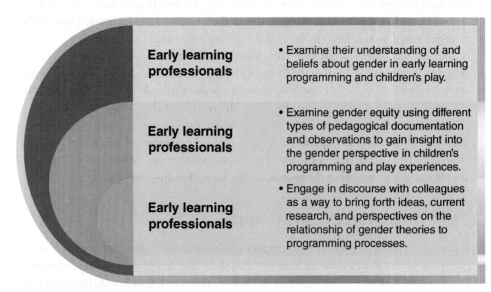

Early learning professionals
- Examine their understanding of and beliefs about gender in early learning programming and children's play.

Early learning professionals
- Examine gender equity using different types of pedagogical documentation and observations to gain insight into the gender perspective in children's programming and play experiences.

Early learning professionals
- Engage in discourse with colleagues as a way to bring forth ideas, current research, and perspectives on the relationship of gender theories to programming processes.

Figure 10.6 Roles of early learning professionals in advancing gender equity in children's programming

Critical commentators (Grieshaber, 2002; Novinger & O'Brien, 2003) suggest that "quality programming" is a problematic social construct that cannot be defined or measured. They note that this leads to a more prescribed program model and observational processes. How do you respond to this perspective? Why?

children's learning" (p. 266). Children benefit when early learning professionals examine the children's level of engagement and response to programming options.

Engage in Collaboration

Collaboration among children, families, and colleagues contributes to the vision of experiences incorporated into the programming model. The richness that occurs from collaboration enables a partnership approach to programming that encourages creative problem solving, generates options for programming, examines "what-ifs," and facilitates discussions that help early learning professionals examine their beliefs, values, practices that address children's needs, and programs that are supportive of the whole child (Anderson, 2013).

Working with colleagues in examining programming direction creates environments that reflect children's divergent learning styles. The collaborative process is essential for early learning professionals for "sharing information, validating each other's roles, and providing input around which strategies promote positive outcomes for all children" (Anderson, 2013, p. 25). The collaborative process further supports individual teachers and groups of teachers to always be aware of the context of programming and to develop new ways of thinking about programming so that there are increased options for children's experiences. A model of practice that has shared thinking as the core helps to reduce "silo" or rigid programming.

Listening to children, families, and colleagues has been a consistent theme throughout this text. This is one of the most important components that guide the programming process.

Creating spaces that encourage collaboration is part of the programming process.

Angela Brant and Fox Hollow Child Care Centre

Colleagues must have a voice and listen to the voices of others. Failure to listen and to understand one another's ideas, ideals, and perspectives, or failure to take advantage of the knowledge, skills, and dispositions that colleagues, children, and families bring to the environment, disadvantages children and the potential experiences that may be extended to them.

Effective early learning programming connects children to their communities. Early learning professionals extend their collaboration to include organizations, agencies, families, and businesses that can spark children's curiosity, support children in acquiring new information, or give exposure to new experiences within the community. For example, in some places, children from early learning programs participate with community groups to plant springtime flowers in local gardens. Throughout the summer, the children return to the areas to view the flowers, take photos of the gardens, and learn about the bugs, butterflies, or birds that the flowers have attracted. In the fall, the children work with the staff to prepare the flower beds for the winter. Such experiences bring intergenerational learning to programming, while developing relationships among children and community partners.

Follow Regulatory Requirements

Early learning professionals are guided by provincial regulatory systems. This requires program-planning and implementation processes to meet at least the minimal standards as set forth by government regulations and, in some provinces, curriculum frameworks. Early learning professionals use the regulatory documents to guide their practice and to self-evaluate their programming methods and beliefs in combination with a code of ethics from a provincial association or national association (Fenech, Robertson, Sumsion, & Goodfellow, 2007). The more innovative the teachers, children, and families become in exploring, experimenting, and wondering, the more flexible and exciting materials and possibilities for discovering become. Programming is richest when the experiences are a response to observations, pedagogical documentations, and listening.

Conduct Observations

Early learning professionals observe children at play from a variety of perspectives. They consistently seek to gain insight into children's interests and sense of wonderment. The process of observation is more than watching children, as shown in Figure 10.7.

Early learning professionals examine the type of observation that they wish to complete by first asking the questions "Why am I observing this child or group of children?" and "What do I hope to gain from the observation?" Once those questions are answered, the observation method is determined. As identified in Table 10.2, early learning professionals who use a constructivist approach in their philosophical orientation are drawn to observation strategies that celebrate the strengths and interests of children. They use these

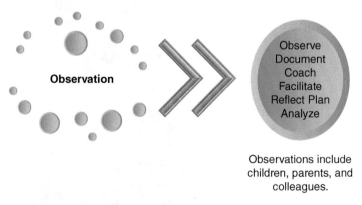

Figure 10.7 The observation process

Table 10.2 Observation Strategies

Type of Observation Strategy	Benefits of Observation Strategy
Video Recordings	Video recordings capture children's play experiences. Early learning professionals gain insight into all aspects of development and interests that children have on particular topics. Video recordings provide opportunities for children and early learning professionals to discuss their perceptions of what they see and what it means to them.
Portfolios	The portfolio is an active, living document that is a collection of observations, stories, photos, drawings, and creative expressions of an individual child or group of children. Early learning professionals, children, and families collectively examine and discuss the contents of the portfolio. If children express an interest in revisiting experiences or building upon experiences, opportunities are incorporated into the program plan.
Photographs	Photographs capture particular moments in time. Children, parents, and early learning professionals use the photos to revisit previous play and learning experiences, reflect upon the experiences, and potentially discuss how new experiences may evolve.
Learning Stories and Journeys	Early learning professionals and children use learning stories to document a particular activity or experience. Children and early learning professionals may create them in conjunction with videos or photographs. Early learning professionals listen to the children's stories and seek out potential areas of interest that may be incorporated into the program.

findings to gain insight into the children's interests and to enhance the types of experiences that are incorporated into the program.

Observing children occurs during play experiences in both the indoor and outdoor environments because early learning professionals gain different types of information about children and with children in these different environments (Dietze & Kashin, 2012). Children's play is more active outdoors, they exhibit different strengths and language outdoors, and they engage in levels of risk-taking that are not possible indoors. Observing children using various methods, such as video recordings and photographs, is crucial to creating effective program plans. Various observation methods help early learning professionals understand children's play interests and determine the types of environments that may support them in being able to explore, wonder, experiment, discover, and tell their stories (Bowne, Cutler, DeBates, Gilkerson, & Stremmel, 2010).

SCHEDULING THE PROGRAM

The program schedule reflects the program philosophy and the vision that early learning professionals have for and with the children. For example, a program philosophy that states children learn through play will be reflected in early learning professionals' acknowledging and maintaining flexibility in the schedule. They will ensure that there are large blocks of time and materials available to children so that they may design their play and carry it out.

They do not disrupt or rush play episodes in order to arbitrarily move from one activity to the next. Children require a balanced and flexible indoor/outdoor schedule that provides them with active and quiet options based on their expressed needs.

Early learning professionals take their lead from the children. They create a set of events throughout the day that become time markers for children, as these markers help them to predict what will happen next. For example, mealtimes, nap times, going home times, and, in some centres, group discussion times become strategic events that children use to gauge the day.

As part of the scheduling of programming, early learning professionals consider the types of transitions that are in the children's lives. Depending on the professionals' vision for children and programming, transition time may be either a joyful experience or, regrettably, one with stress and chaos for children and staff. Early learning professionals observe and work with children and their families to learn about the experiences and environments that are most helpful in transitioning children from one event to another. For example, in a centre in Nova Scotia, children are given the opportunity to engage in outdoor play upon arrival at the centre. This play option has supported the children with their transition from their family to the centre, reducing incidents of tantrum-like behaviours.

PLANNING GUIDELINES

Many planning guidelines are used in program planning. Programs that follow a constructivist approach plan their programs so that children engage in play for the process of play and learning. Each child is viewed as an individual. Therefore, the program-planning process ensures that the ideas and experiences flow from the children and the staff. This approach does not support programming that includes pre-cut materials, predetermined crafts, or pre-set curriculum themes as experiences with the children (Carter & Curtis, 2010).

Early learning professionals work with families and children to guide ideas about intended experiences and learning, and these become a framework for program planning. Some programs use learning outcomes, other programs use objectives, and still others use concept maps or a combination of maps and outcomes/objectives as part of their planning process.

Using objectives to guide practice dates back to 1949, when Tyler (1949) explained the importance of objectives by suggesting that if a program "is to be planned and if efforts for continued improvement are to be made, it is very necessary to have some conception of the goals that are being aimed at. These educational objectives become the criteria by which materials are selected, content is outlined, instructional procedures are developed" (p. 3). Tyler suggested that when using objectives as the planning framework, "only those objectives which might result from learning and which are educationally obtainable should be included" (p. 37). Meanwhile, in Mager's (1962) seminal work on objectives, he maintained the need for objectives to state what the learner will be able to do after the learning experience that was not possible before engaging in the experience or activity. Today, objectives are used in early learning programs to help professionals, children, and parents think about what the intent of the experience could be and the potential for where the experience may go. For example, think of a group of children who have expressed an interest in playing with balls. Teachers may think about programming objectives related with balls. The objectives may include the following:

At the end of the play experience with balls, children should be able to

1. choose the type of ball that best suits the play experience—e.g., large balls for ball races, small balls for playing "hole in one";

2. name the type of ball that has the most bounce; and

3. highlight five ways that the ball may be used.

Learning outcomes differ from objectives. Whereas objectives outline what the expected performance is and the actions that may occur to reach that performance, learning outcomes focus on what a child knows or may be able to do as a result of an experience. Learning outcomes consider the levels of play that children may participate in and the types of potential for extending language, thinking critically, synthesizing ideas and information, and drawing knowledge from previous experiences to incorporate into the play. Learning outcomes are more fluid than objectives (Allan, 2006). For instance, think about early learning programs that are focusing on active play and movement with children. Early learning professionals will be able to create learning outcomes for and with children that have a focus on children's understanding of the various ways they can use balls—big balls, medium balls, small balls, bouncy balls, and rolling balls—in their play. Assume you allow the children to experience using balls in the rain or in puddles during their play. The children may note that the ball gets stuck in the mud in the puddles, they may not like the feel of the ball when it is wet, or they may experience making sounds of splashing with the ball as they throw it into the puddle. They may create games in which they can use the ball. What types of outcomes may evolve from the ball-play experience? Think about what children will have learned or do differently after playing with the various types of balls and using balls in the rain. Children may learn about how some balls float and others sink in the puddles; they may seek answers as to why some balls get stuck in the puddles; they may learn about spatial awareness as they play various games using the balls. Learning outcomes are rich when they evolve from the changes you observe in children as they experience their world. They are not necessarily predetermined.

PROGRAM DESIGN FOR CHILDREN

Throughout the previous chapters we have given examples of programs for children from infants to school age. In this chapter, we are supporting the role of the early learning professional to give voice to the children in the learning environment. In an exercise suggested by Curtis and colleagues (2013), we have used digital technology to crop and enlarge the photos in Table 10.3 to expose more detail. As you study these images, try to give voice to

Table 10.3 Program Design for Children

INFANCY

Everyday Example	Description	Sample Learning Outcome
	A young toddler holding a brush in each hand, one dipped in green paint and the other in blue, is using broad brush strokes to create colour, line, shape, dimension, movement, and space. An early learning professional can consider extending experiences connected to colour mixing to this child by providing paint that the child may mix together to create colours for using at the easel.	Through exploration of colour mixing, the child may discover that by mixing blue and green, the colour turquoise will appear.

EARLY CHILDHOOD

Everyday Example	Description	Sample Learning Outcome
	A three-year-old extends his arms around a tree while playing outdoors. He is connecting to the tree physically by way of touch, texture, smell, and sight. An early learning professional can consider extending experiences connected to tree explorations focusing on a variety of barks and textures.	Through exploration of the tree with various materials, the child may discover that the layers of tree bark can be separated, cut, and marked on.

(continued)

Table 10.3 *(continued)*

MIDDLE CHILDHOOD

Everyday Example	Description	Sample Learning Outcome
 Diane Kashin	A child in grade 1 adds colour to a sketch of a rainbow done earlier in the day. She draws large arches and shows deliberation in spacing the rainbow beams so the colours remain fixed, showing spatial awareness. An early learning professional can consider extending experiences connected to space and design.	Through exploration with modelling clay, the child can create a rainbow that supports experimenting with space, colour sequences, and design.

the children by reflecting on what the children are seeing every day during play experiences and using this information to further the program. We give you three examples in the table. Each example is described and a sample learning outcome is listed so you can see how this exercise can be used as part of program design.

PROGRAMMING BUBBLE

As advocates for integrating technology as a tool to support children's play and learning and as a professional learning tool for teachers, we view technology as an important component of early learning. We believe that technology has a place in play-based programs. Using technology with children in their active play can change, for the better, the way they engage in play and exploration, as well as their overall learning experiences (McManis & Gunnewig, 2012; Parikh, 2012; Shifflet, Toledo, & Mattoon, 2012). We introduce technology in the programming bubble in Figure 10.8. Notice that this programming bubble is an extension of the nature art depicted in Chapter 9.

Technology and Play
Providing children with a variety of natural materials, in combination with technology tools such as cameras, video recorders, and tablets with access to the internet, advances children's abilities to reflect upon their play and learning and add new information from their research to their play. For an example, see http://thiskindylife.blogspot. ca/2013_05_01_archive.html.

Figure 10.8 Programming bubble: technology and play

FEATURED RESEARCH

Social constructivism is a learning theory. It is an explanation about how learning happens by joining new knowledge to pre-existing patterns in the mind. Read educational blogger Tom Taylor's post on social constructivism to learn about the theory and the importance of the ZPD. He makes the argument for seeing social constructivism as more than an approach or strategy, so as not to assume a position of either, as it is his position that Vygotsky did not prefer one approach over the other: http://bit.ly/1dcgQVm.

PEDAGOGICAL TOOLS

There is an ongoing concern about how children gain information and store it. According to Paivio (1991), information is processed and stored in one's memory in two forms: a linguistic form derived from words or statements, and a visual form that is created from mental pictures or physical sensations (Birbili, 2006). Children benefit from being in environments where new information is presented in a combination of words and visual representation, as the visual representation increases the activity in the brain, resulting in a deeper process of exploration for children (Birbili, 2006).

Concept maps (similar to webbing) that are created by early learning professionals, children, and families offer a visual that clearly articulates the children's knowledge and experiences relevant to a potential experience being proposed. The creation of concept maps encourages children to think about what they know about a topic, see how their peers' ideas connect to or are different from theirs, and develop more in-depth thinking as they try to connect new information with their previous ideas. As a result of combining dialogue with a concept map, the children may suggest how they envision exploring and engaging in play. Often, early learning professionals and children add to the concept map as they "mess about" and discover new information that can provide the direction for future programming. Early learning students and professionals can also use concept maps as a tool for planning.

Concept maps, when used for the planning process, can be a combination of words and pictures. Concept mapping is "particularly effective in helping children see and externalize the relationships among concepts" (Birbili, 2006, p. 3). Revisiting the concept maps during the play process can help to bridge children's ideas with current knowledge and new discoveries. Early learning professionals cross-link the new discoveries with more complex options for exploration (Hay, 2007). Using Vygotsky's (1978) zone of proximal development process, early learning professionals seek out information about children's play experiences so that they can further create play options that will stretch children's thinking, exploration strategies, and boundaries. This helps children to combine past learning with new situations and then construct new knowledge, as illustrated in Figure 10.9.

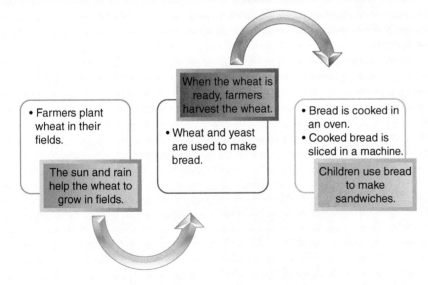

Figure 10.9   A concept map example

Concept maps, whether simple or complex, should consist of the concepts and the relationships among them. When children and early learning professionals revisit the concept map on an ongoing basis for the purpose of adding ideas to it, it becomes a useful tool in documenting children's experiences and learning. For example, early learning professionals ensure the following:

1. Early learning professionals model and support children in using concept maps as a way of thinking about concepts presented.

2. Early learning professionals encourage children to link words with pictures as a way to help them make connections (Sparks Linfield & Warwick, 2003).

3. Early learning professionals combine real objects with words and diagrams to support young children in bringing meaning to concepts presented.

4. Early learning professionals work with children to scaffold concept maps from simple to more complex hierarchical relationships of concepts (Sparks Linfield & Warwick, 2003).

As children and early learning professionals create concept maps, they develop a plan of action for play and learning. Although it is a plan, it is just that. The implementation of the experience may differ from the plan as children execute the plan based on their life experience, materials available to them, and the overall feeling tone within the environment.

PROFESSIONAL CASE STUDY

When Myrna decided to become an early learning professional, she had imagined creating learning spaces, places, and programming with her colleagues where children would become so engaged in the program that the professionals would be there as facilitators of children's play, not directors. Myrna had been working at a specialized early learning program for five years. For the past three years, she struggled with how to align her philosophy with the centre and with her colleagues. Although she continually tried to dialogue with her colleagues about visioning and thinking about big ideas, Myrna had begun to think that with no collegial support, and no resources that reflected intelligent materials, natural materials, or beautiful things, the programming experiences for the children were becoming humdrum. Myrna discussed her feelings with her colleagues, but they seemed fine with the program. They said they didn't have time and were not paid to do any more than what they could accomplish during the day. Myrna began to think about her philosophy and wondered if she was too idealistic. She wondered if perhaps she should go with the flow and adjust her dreams of children, play, and engagement. Maybe she needed to rethink her career.

Myrna decided that before pursuing another career, she would search out positions in other early learning programs to see if there might be an early learning centre with a philosophy similar to her own, or a centre with such intriguing programming processes that she could rekindle her aspirations of working with young children and creating places where children's spirits and curiosity could be expressed and celebrated.

The valuable lessons Myrna learned through her reflection and inquiry process led her to employment in a new early learning environment. She has been at her new centre for six months and feels for the first time an incredibly deep commitment to children and families. She values the fact that their early learning centre programming model is guided by the children. She celebrates that when you walk into their indoor and outdoor learning spaces, you see children being self-directed, investigating ideas that have evolved from them or the teachers. She appreciates that staff are open to new ideas and working with children to extend their ideas and inquiry. Programming trial balloons, bubbles, and popping the bubbles make visions reality, and then, as a group, bigger ideas are thought about so that the children and staff are always stretching their realities, their discoveries, and their wonderment.

REFLECTION QUESTIONS FOR SELF-LEARNING

Thinking about the case study about Myrna, you can see that she engaged in an exploratory and reflective process when she got to a point where she had lost her spirit. Thinking deeply about this situation, answer the following questions:

1. What advice would you give Myrna and other colleagues when they become concerned about the programming that is being offered to children?

2. Why should that be a concern?

3. What suggestions would you make in relation to bringing the staff together to review programming?

4. How might they know if the programming is meeting the needs of the children?

5. How can you determine if the experiences offered to the children are supporting their sense of wonderment and curiosity?

6. Do you think that Myrna will experience the same feelings as in her previous centre in a few months? Why or why not? What might the differences be in this new setting?

BIG IDEAS FOR DIALOGIC LEARNING

Effective program planning sets the stage for children's play and learning. Think about how you acquire information to cultivate a place of rich play and learning for and with the children. How does the environment interact with the ideas that children bring forth? How do early learning professionals listen to the children and their families and then use that information to think about the materials within the indoor and outdoor play spaces? How can you ensure that your program-planning process reflects children's ideals, is fluid rather than rigid, and celebrates the diversity of the children within the environment? How can your program-planning process encourage children to reflect upon their experiences and consider where they may want to take their play next? What types of provocations do we incorporate into the planning process? Do provocations work best when planned or should they be spontaneous? How do you devise a program-planning process that honours and celebrates the children? How does it reflect your philosophy?

Consider the following questions about program planning that reflects big ideas.

1. You are required to prepare a program-planning model that reflects a constructivist philosophy of how children learn and play. What would the model look like? Why?

2. In small groups, share ideas about how you would gain information from children about their interests and how you would illustrate this in a program plan.

3. Examine the concept map presented in Figure 10.9. Think about two children who have expressed an interest in worms. How would you transfer that interest to a concept map?

4. While each group presents their concept map, compare the similarities and differences. How might these differences be viewed in an early learning program? How does this inform your practice?

VISION

It is our vision that early learning students will develop program-planning processes that reflect the children's interests and sense of curiosity while expanding their opportunities for learning and discovery. By claiming your voice, creating programming options that are multi-faceted, and providing children with environments that are intriguing and reflective of multiple languages, you enhance children's opportunities to experience curiosity and exploration. Just as the importance of material cannot be underestimated, program plans created from multiple resources, including children, observations, families, and colleagues, are vital to the quality of children's play and learning. Early learning students and professionals "mess about" with program planning in their quest to find a process that is both collaborative and reflective of program philosophies and individual visions and beliefs. We encourage you to create a program-planning model that reflects you and your beliefs about how children learn through their play.

MAKING CONNECTIONS

Early learning professionals who are connecting using social media have discovered a forum for collaboration that supports professional growth and development. You can find some examples of conversations that are taking place between professionals on Twitter by searching by these hash tags: #kinderchat or #ReggioPLC. When you are on Twitter, put these hash tags into the search bar to get a list of past tweets from members of these professional learning networks. By reviewing past tweets from this group of early learning professionals who are connecting with each other from all parts of the country and the world, you will see how they offer each other virtual programming support. We encourage you to establish your own professional learning community or network.

KEY TERMS

Articulation   230
Collaboration   232
Curriculum   229
Emergent programming   231
Hypothesis   238
Metalinguistic   237
More knowledgeable others
   (MKO)   236

Negotiated learning   237
Progettazione   238
Programming   229
Right-brain thinking   232
Shared thinking   241
Zone of proximal development
   (ZPD)   236

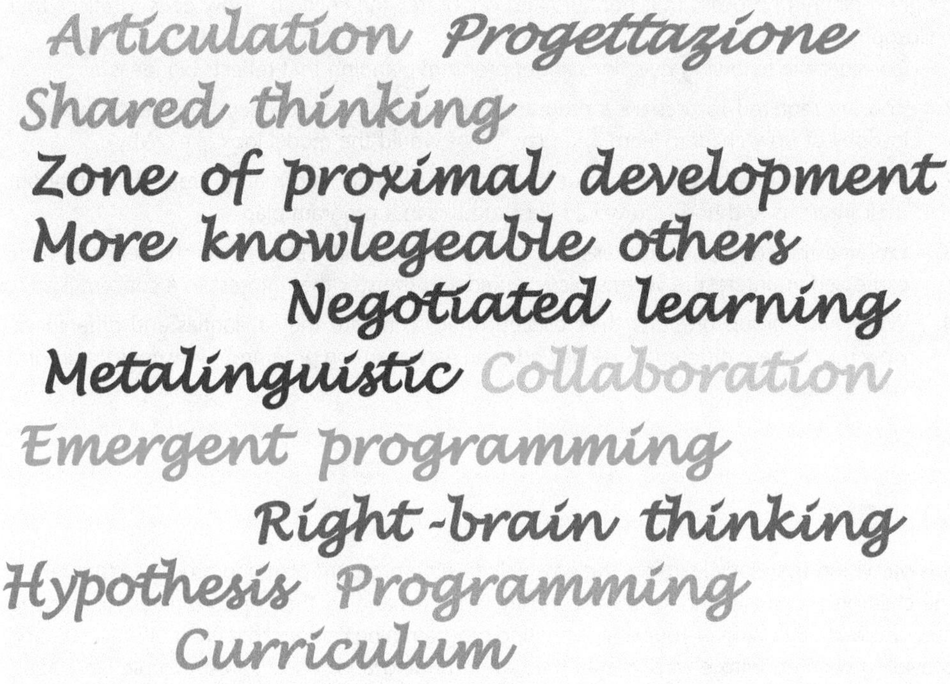

Figure 10.10 Key terms wordle

Articulation Progettazione
Shared thinking
Zone of proximal development
More knowlegeable others
Negotiated learning
Metalinguistic Collaboration
Emergent programming
Right-brain thinking
Hypothesis Programming
Curriculum

SUMMARY

Early learning students entering into the process of programming are required to determine the direction of the learning based on multiple considerations and in collaboration with others, including children, families, and colleagues. In the process of programming, both students and professionals should be aware of current developments in early learning in order to help children build skills necessary for a new age. Early learning professionals recognize that there are multiple factors to take into consideration during the programming process.

1. Collaborative processes with children, families, and colleagues is a necessary step to program planning.

2. New technologies and expectations are changing the ways of the world and should influence the programming processes in early learning programs.

3. Bringing theory into practice is one of the responsibilities of the early learning professional, who must consider many factors in order to support children in their play and learning.

4. It is the role of the early learning professional to collaborate during the planning process and consider what is necessary to support children in their play and learning.

For more information on David Hawkins's instructional strategy of "I, Thou, It," we encourage you to read the original 1974 article, which can be found by linking to this address: http://bit.ly/1eGY9Vr.

For Further Thought

Chapter 11
The Reflective Process

LEARNING OUTCOMES

After exploring this chapter, you should be able to

1. Discuss the concept of spirituality as it relates to children and early learning programming, and the role of early learning professionals in promoting spirituality.
2. Explain the relationship that reflection and spirituality have with the programming process.
3. Describe how early learning professionals use pedagogical documentation to make learning visible, guide programming, and conduct research.
4. · Define authentic assessment and authentic learning.
5. Reflect on learning stories and pedagogical documentation as examples of authentic assessment.
6. Describe how early learning professionals design programs for children that support reflection and spirituality while creating intentions for children to observe their world around them.

A CHILD'S STORY   Everly

I am excited today because my group of friends and I will be making bread with our teacher, Nancy, and then we are going to serve it for a snack! Yesterday, we looked at bread recipes and we all decided that we would make the whole-wheat honey bread. Then, we went to the organic store at the corner to buy the flour, milk, and honey. When we got back, we took pictures of all the things we bought and posted them on our board, and we wrote how much we needed of each item. Nancy said it was like making a recipe card.

When Nancy said it was time to make the bread, my friend and I brought the recipe from yesterday to the kitchen. We all got to add ingredients to the bread. We had to stir and stir and stir. Then, Nancy showed us how we had to knead the bread. We covered the bread and put it in a warm place. Later, Jana came to me when I was playing and said, "Come look at the bread bowl. It is getting bigger and bigger and bigger." Nancy gathered our group and we had to punch the bread down . . . and it got bigger and bigger again. We cut the bread dough into four parts and we each put one in a pan and baked it. It smelled so good. When it came out of the oven, we let it cool and Nancy helped us cut it. We took it to our tables and shared it. I asked Sara, the teacher at my table, and the other children to guess what made the bread sweet. Reese said sugar, Marina said salt, and Andi said molasses. I didn't even know what molasses was. Sara said, "I wonder if it might be maple syrup." I told them it is something that our favourite storybook bear eats!

Cutting bread.

Rosalba Bortolotti

> *The voyage of discovery is not in seeking new landscapes, but
> in having new eyes.*
>
> —MARCEL PROUST (1871–1922)

The strengths of early learning programs lie in the people, space, human experiences, and relationships among the players in the environment (Bone, 2007; Goodliff, 2013). Early learning professionals continuously think about, assess, and reflect upon their professional skills, experiences, and knowledge as a way to bring meaning to their perceptions, feelings, and attitudes, and to determine how those ideas guide their interactions and programming experiences with children and families. Schön (1987) suggested that as part of the reflective process, professionals should think about what needs to be different and how to apply new learning to a variety of situations. This helps to transfer reflection to practice.

Social practices involving children, families, and early learning professionals contribute to the awakening of one's spirituality. Spirituality can be viewed as "an inherent property of

Box 11.1 **Claim Your Spirituality**

Chepko Danil/Fotolia

CLAIM YOUR SPIRITUALITY by examining your identity that incorporates your personal and professional passions into practice.

the human being" (Zhang, 2012, p. 39). Many researchers suggest that spirituality correlates to quality of life in terms of social, emotional, and physical well-being; relationships; and social inclusion (Johnstone, Glass, & Oliver, 2007).

From a social-cultural construct of the child and childhood, Vygotsky's (1978) work suggested the importance of recognizing children's ability from birth to construct meaning through the process of being part of a community and actively participating as a member of that community (Rogoff, 1990). As identified by Goodliff (2013), children use cultural tools in their play with peers to mediate their learning (Vygotsky, 1978) and their language, both spoken and unspoken. These cultural tools, combined with play and experiences, influence how children develop "a mode of deep thinking and reflective consciousness to which expressions of creativity and spirituality (Nye, 1996) are tangible outcomes" (Goodliff, 2013, p. 1055). The more intriguing the environments, the more opportunities children have to express their creativity and spirituality in a variety of play experiences. Think about children, think about environments, and then, as outlined in Box 11.1, think about how you claim and share your spirituality in your practice.

The concept of spirituality is interwoven in a number of philosophies and pedagogies. For example, within the pedagogy of Reggio Emilia, the "pedagogy of relationships and listening" (Rinaldi, 2005, p. 19) reflects the view of the child as a social being. This is further illustrated in Rinaldi's (2005) description of the "rich child, an active subject with rights and extraordinary potential and born with a hundred languages" (p. 17). Children flourish in environments where they have opportunities to influence their environments and spaces, and where they can exhibit their "being" without judgment or prejudice.

Bronfenbrenner's (1979) ecological theory emphasized the "bi-directional" and reciprocal influences that ensue as children engage in their play and with the people in their environment. These influences reinforce the importance of environments to children's meaning-making process, and, as identified in Chapter 2, the benefits of children sharing power with adults in the environment. All children have a unique "ecological niche" that is influenced by those around them (Goodliff, 2013). Although other people in the lives of children have influence, the children themselves also "actively influence their 'ecological niche'" (David, 1998, p. 18). Children's spirituality, then, is influenced by their environments, their experiences, and their meaning making within their play environments.

The importance of nurturing the child's spirit is well documented in the literature on indigenous children. According to Ball (2012), one of the key goals that most Aboriginal parents have for their children is for them to "develop a sense of one's spirit and their relationship with one's ancestors and with a benevolent Creator" (p. 289). Many Aboriginal parents view the development of a strong sense of one's spiritual identity as a way to help children in times of difficulty. It provides grounding for them. Spirituality is fostered in many ways in Aboriginal families, including "sharing what they have with others, being respectful, and serving other community members, especially babies" and elders (Ball, 2012, p. 289). Aboriginal families encourage the child-to-child caregiving process as a way to build "empathy and social responsibility and a sense of self-value within the family" (Ball, 2012, p. 289).

SPIRITUALITY IN CHILDREN

The concept of spirituality in early learning programs is a way of thinking among staff, children, and families. It requires the key players to be comfortable expressing different perspectives on "how our knowledge about the world and about each other gets constructed and negotiated" (Bruner, 2006, p.172). Family considerations, community values, and early learning program philosophies are incorporated into the holistic approach to spirituality.

Think about the children making bread. How did that experience relate to building spirituality? What were some of the core attributes of that experience that would build a sense of community? How does the ritual of snack and food relate to spirituality?

Children are spiritual beings. They are born with "spiritual competence" that supports them in having an inner ability to develop faith (Hawkins, 1996, as cited by Mountain, 2005, p. 295). Children's ability to express spirituality is influenced by the adults in their lives and the ability of the children to understand them (Mueller, 2010). Children's sense of wonder and curiosity and their ability to spark connections with families and friends are intuitive strategies that children exhibit in providing aspects of spirituality to their community (Yust, 2003). In essence, children express their spirituality through their behaviours.

Children's spirituality in the early years is a fairly new area of research in North America. One challenge that is consistent in the literature is that the term **spirituality** has a different meaning for each person because of lived experiences, philosophy of life, and perspectives on daily living (Erickson, 2008). Hooks (2003) identified a spiritual dimension to education, especially in environments where children and teachers are connecting to explore, experiment, and nurture one another. Meanwhile, Frankl (1987) defined *spirituality* as a need and a process undertaken to find meaning and purpose to life. Reed (1992) viewed spirituality as the source of connectedness or interconnectedness within oneself and with others. According to Sewell (2009), "spirituality refers to having a deep sense of identity and authenticity (Palmer, 1998), from which individuals

spirituality The process of finding meaning about and purpose in life. The process of spirituality requires opportunities to explore, experiment, and connect with things, space, place, and people.

connect with others, both unselfconsciously and selflessly" (p. 6). Spirituality is distinct from religion.

Mueller (2010) made a distinction between religion and spirituality. She identified religion as "a structured, formalized expression of faith by a community of people. Religion captures memories, stories, images, ethical teachings, and rituals in the expression of spirituality. Spirituality is more like the fabric itself, rather than the design or pattern of the garment" (p. 197). Mueller drew upon the work of Benson (2003) and Borgman (2006) to further define spirituality. She identified spirituality as "self-transcendence in which self becomes embedded in something greater than self, including the sacred, leading to connectedness, meaning, purpose, and contribution" (p. 197). This reinforces the importance of early learning programs creating play and learning communities, because children need to develop the ability to create meaning, to feel purposeful, and to feel that they are contributing to the various communities of which they are a part.

From an early learning perspective, spirituality becomes part of the process of creating a sense of wholeness for children and a sense of who they are. Early learning professionals structure their practice around the concepts of the early learning environment; the children, families, and communities; and the spirit of the individuals who interact within the space. Children develop their powers to express themselves by having experiences and in expressing their voice and hearing the voices of others in early learning programs.

Spirituality can be "massively present in the lives of children" (Hay & Nye, 2006, p. 9), especially in environments where early learning professionals nurture a pedagogy of connectedness. Spirituality occurs in children when they have the ability and desire to invest energy in goals, activities, or projects with others that go beyond the self (Csikszentmihalyi, 2002).

Children require an environment that will free them from routine.

Angela Brant and Fox Hollow Child Care Centre

For example, a child may choose to help another child in building a large block structure rather than continue with a particular project of interest, purely so that a playmate will be successful in creating a structure.

Children's spiritual development mirrors cognitive, emotional, and moral developmental theories, as well as theories of acculturation. The developmental theories of Piaget and Erikson described children's cognitive and emotional development as a series of stages that each person works through, scaffolded from simple to more complex. Kohlberg's (1981) theory of moral development and Erikson's (1963) theory of psychosocial development brought forth the notion of faith development theory. Faith theory is defined as "the body of truths combined with an integration of implied values lived out in a way consistent with those beliefs and values" (Mueller, 2010, p. 197). Fowler (1981), in his studies of faith development and spirituality, suggested that children develop spirituality in stages. Based on Fowler's spirituality stages, Table 11.1 on the next page outlines children's developmental characteristics with spirituality stages.

Spiritual experiences derive from repetitive group rituals that children participate in and that spark new and authentic connections and relationships among the players. These connections build a sense of a community of learners. As children acquire life experience, they become capable of increasingly abstract, reflective thought processes that relate to spirituality.

There are many advantages to children being part of healthy, active communities of learners. One of the most significant benefits for children is gaining positive feelings associated with learning to care for others and being part of a group where others care for them. Through learning communities, children develop reciprocal relationships (Brown & Campione, 1998). This is the basis for developing a sense of spirituality because as children and teachers explore, experiment, and discover together, they are engaged in new knowledge construction, which occurs from sharing ideas and skills and figuring out answers to questions. These acts evoke the spirit (Sewell, 2009). The more children

Table 11.1 Spiritual Stages

Ages	Developmental Characteristics	Stage of Spirituality
Infancy (0 to 1½)	• Behaviour is reflective. • Bonding occurs with primary caregivers. • Infant learns to feel safe and develop trust if expressed needs are met.	Undifferentiated faith/infancy phase • Spirituality develops when infant has positive interactions with caregivers that create feelings of trust, courage, and love.
Early childhood (2 to 6)	• Mobility occurs. • Specific and purposeful behaviours are reproduced. • Child learns to understand words and language. • Autonomy and self-confidence evolve.	Stage I: intuitive-projective faith (rise of imagination and formation of images) • Spirituality develops through experiences such as storytelling and children speaking about their feelings, actions, and events of the day.
Childhood (7 to 12)	• Concrete mental operations and organized, logical thought develop. • Classifying and organizing objects in logical categories occurs. • Concrete problem solving is evident.	Stage 2: mythic-literal faith (rise of narrative and stories of faith) • Spirituality develops as children seek answers to understand "how things are." They require clarity on what is real and what is real to them. • Stories, beliefs, and observances of their ideals and those around them are taken literally and are one-dimensional.
Adolescent (13 to 21)	• Thoughts become abstract. • Principles of logic are used for decision making. • Children generate abstract propositions, hypotheses, and outcomes.	Stage 3: synthetic-conventional faith (reflective construction of ideology) • Spirituality evolves from having the desire to know what they want of themselves and their lives. • Children require the ability to understand that there are expectations and judgments of others that need to be considered while they develop the ability to express their independent perspective through self-examination.

Source: Adapted from Fowler, 1981.

learn together, the greater the connection they make to the people in the space and the environment in which they are together. Spiritual experiences evolve because the act of learning is transformative when connections are made among individuals in the same environment (Tisdell, 2003).

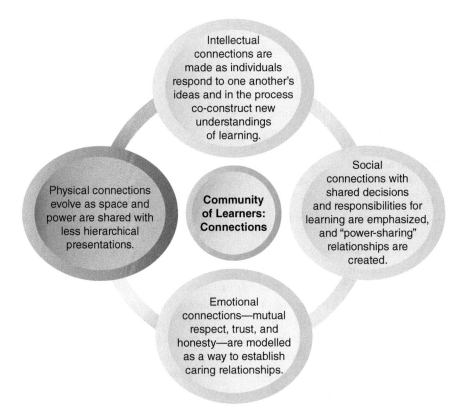

Figure 11.1 Connections within communities of learners

Sewell (2009) suggested that when there is a healthy sense of community, four core connections are made, as outlined in Figure 11.1. Reciprocal connections among children, early learning professionals, visitors, and parents increase children's confidence and competence, which in turn creates opportunities for new connections to be made that contribute to advancing physical and spiritual qualities (Sewell, 2009). Early learning professionals recognize that spirituality flourishes in environments where it is modelled. It is more than a private inner experience (Bone, 2008). Bone (2008) suggested that spirituality is part of early learning programs. She maintained that spirituality can be examined in terms of relational space, as shown in Figure 11.2.

Early learning professionals who view spirituality as part of their daily practice weave the spiritual dimension into all aspects of the program. Bone (2008) reinforced the importance of early learning professionals examining how a spiritual approach to pedagogy can be made transparent in the early learning space and in relationships among staff, children, families, and community.

Spiritual withness

- *Relational space that happens between people who often describe feeling a strong sense of connection to others.*

Spiritual in-betweenness

- *Space constructed in certain environments and supported by specific rituals and events.*

Spiritual elsewhere

- *Space inhabited by children as they connect to everything around them in the world of dreams and the imagination.*

Figure 11.2 Spirituality and Relational Space

Source: Adapted from Bone, 2008.

ROLES AND RESPONSIBILITIES OF EARLY LEARNING PROFESSIONALS

Early learning professionals work with and communicate to children in many ways. Children are influenced more by what adults do than by what they say, but mostly by what they are (Palmer, 1999). Early learning professionals have an important role in nurturing and nourishing the spirituality of young children. Before reaching out to children, they benefit from first understanding the concept of spirituality, and then fostering that within themselves and among their team members. Critical friends, as described in Chapter 1, can be very helpful in supporting, coaching, or nurturing aspects of personal development that will expand the understanding of holistic early learning programming. Spiritual environments for children require early learning professionals to integrate identity with personal and professional passions.

Early learning professionals who recognize the relationship of spirituality to children's growth and development view part of their role as creating environments and implementing teaching and learning processes to nurture spiritual growth reflective of "relational practice" (Darling-Hammond, 1997). Relational practice further requires early learning professionals to recognize the needs and interests of individual children and groups of children so that the environment meets children's "needs for compassion, connection and unity" (Fraser, McGee, & Thrupp, 2008, p. 264). This requires early learning professionals to consistently work with children to find their voices. Take a look at the accompanying Reflective Moment box and consider how early learning professionals might promote a sense of spirituality in their work with children. These professionals encourage and model to children the benefits of sharing ideas and perspectives that may support others in their quest to develop knowledge or skills, rather than encouraging children to be passive followers of an adult's instructions.

Early learning professionals and children collectively establish rituals that support children in being able to express aspects of their lives that reflect compassion for others. In some early learning programs, the adults and children establish a talking-stick ritual. During this time, those who wish to be part of the talking time come together for discussion and connection. Such rituals bring together the children and early learning professionals as valuable members of the community. The intent of talking-stick time is for children to share any information they wish. The ritual may be led by children or teachers, resulting in a power-neutral zone; a co-construction of experiences can occur. Spirituality evolves through the ordinary conversations that take place in the environments every day (Bone, 2005).

Spirituality flourishes in environments where early learning professionals establish pedagogical connectedness in their practice that encourages children and colleagues to

- explore and discover by co-facilitating and co-constructing ideas and processes;
- share and celebrate discoveries and new ways of using knowledge gained;
- model respect and caring for those in the learning community and their families;
- express values and make value judgments;

≫ A Reflective Moment

Review the following situations and think about how the sense of spirituality might influence them.

1. Think about a child or teacher who has just experienced the death of a pet. How can compassion and caring be extended to the person who is dealing with the loss of the pet?

2. Think about a teacher who has broken his leg and is required to use crutches. How might children express their spirituality in this situation?

- have access to programs that encourage creative expression—e.g., through art, dance, songs, and movement;
- create environments that model collaboration, negotiation, co-responsibility, laughter, and humour (Mata, 2006);
- provide space, time, and appreciation for quiet reflection and creativity, and for children to be alone; and
- give spirituality expression.

Early learning professionals build strategies within their practice to understand the backgrounds of children and families. Observations of children's behaviours guide early learning professionals in understanding the attitudes, values, and needs of children. For example, if there is a change in a child's eating or sleeping patterns, or greater use of silence or aggressive behaviour, these may be indicators of spiritual distress. As well, if children feel

Think about the following:

1. How do my work and practice with children reflect who I am?

2. To what extent do I feel I am a contributing member to my community of practice?

3. How do I empower children to embrace their own ideas and spiritual development?

isolated from their friends or undergo a stressful family or personal situation, there may be similar or other distinctive signs of spiritual distress (Mueller, 2010).

Good teaching is more than a technique to support children in their explorations and learning (Palmer, 1998). It is having a passion for connecting with children, wanting to be with children, and knowing how to create environments that offer options in daily routine. The teachers' roles and the approaches they use are rooted in their identity and integrity. The quality of children's experiences is influenced greatly by the inner qualities of the early learning professional (Palmer, 1998). Early learning professionals who take a holistic approach to their work regularly examine children's experiences and environments—all developmental domains, including the spiritual dimension (Zhang, 2012). This perspective challenges early learning professionals who have typically focused on cognitive development to take on a role that "fosters wholeness and well-being, and nurtures deep and enduring personal relationships between individuals and communities" (Zhang, 2012, p. 42). Early learning professionals and children collectively support and nurture individuals within their environments.

There are many ways to support children in their spiritual development. Early learning professionals acknowledge children's inner thoughts, expressions of feelings, and meaning making relevant to family and culture. They provide children with culturally meaningful learning environments and experiences that support and incorporate children's heritage, language, and culture into programming (Hare, 2011). When children, families, and early learning professionals are partners in programming, there is an enhanced opportunity for children to be in environments that are open to their expression of spirituality. This requires environments where children and adults feel trust and openness, enabling children to "weave together the threads of meaning, and to quest for authentic ways of being in the world" (Hyde, 2008, p. 126). Early learning professionals need to create appropriate spaces in which to nurture spirituality. Connecting to the spiritual self involves reflection. Early learning students and professionals are capable of reflection, and children, too, have the capacity to be reflective. We offer you another Reflective Moment box to consider and help you reflect upon your role as an early learning professional.

REFLECTION IN PROGRAMMING

Reflection and spirituality are closely connected. Reflection is an integral part of the programming process. It is an important way for early learning professionals to be in touch with their spiritual self. Reflection is an ongoing part of the programming process. There isn't really a beginning or an end—it is cyclical. In previous chapters, we have discussed reflective practice, and in this chapter we focus on the vital role reflection plays in providing optimal learning environments for children and their families. In the visualization of a cycle, it is difficult to conceptualize a point of entry. If you were to start reflecting, where would you begin?

The starting reflection point for optimal programming that speaks to children across many domains and in many languages, including their spiritual self, is context. **Context** is the features related to the early learning environment, such as the economic, political, and

context The features related to the early learning environment, such as the economic, political, and social context, which place the program within a broader societal context.

Figure 11.3 **Reflection and the programming process**

social context, which place the program within a broader societal context. Every early learning program has a context. Reflecting on the broader community and the program's place within it can define the broad **intentions**, or deliberate, purposeful, and thoughtful decisions and actions that fuel the programming process as it evolves. What are the areas of meaning to the players within the learning environment and the surrounding community? Beginning with families, early learning professionals develop programs based on identified intentions that may include having natural, environmental, or democratic experiences. These then lead into the cycle that is illustrated in Figure 11.3.

Based on pedagogical documentation created from the triggers that lead to the children's explorations and discoveries, early learning professionals reflect deeply, both individually and in dialogue with others. In order to build understanding and gain perspective, reflection should be critical. Early learning professionals critique and engage in discourse. From this experience, when all the players are considered during the reflective phase, new intentions may be formed. Epstein (2007) referred to educators who think deeply about programming as *intentional teachers*. According to the Australian Early Years Framework, "intentional teaching is the opposite of teaching by rote or continuing with traditions simply because things have 'always' been done that way" (Australian Government Department of Education, Employment and Workplace Relations, 2009, p. 15).

There are many early learning professionals and early learning programs that consider contextual elements and intentional teaching in their programs. At Petaluma Village Preschool in California, educators are deliberate in their choices in order to create learning opportunities for children that connect to their context. Petaluma Village Preschool's website, which can be found at http://bit.ly/1geNxOn, explains that the intention is to engender lifelong civic responsibility and engagement. This goal is at the heart of the preschool's "service learning project," which gives children the opportunity to make connections between activities that serve others and their own knowledge. The educators created a list of five elements that define this intention to provide experiences for children that help them reflect on the context of their world:

1. *Curricular connections.* The service activity has connections to the current program and the children's skills.

2. *Child voice and choice.* Beyond being actively engaged in the project itself, children have the opportunity to help select, implement, and evaluate their service activity. This encourages relevancy and sustained interest.

intentions The deliberate, purposeful, and thoughtful decisions and actions early learning professionals use to develop programs.

3. *Reflection*. Opportunities are created to talk, draw, engage in related dramatic play, and document the service activity. The reflection activities give children awareness of the value and impact of the service.

4. *Community partnerships*. Ideally, the project will involve collaboration with a community member or agency to help identify genuine needs and contribute the assets and/or expert knowledge needed for the project.

5. *Authentic assessment*. As part of the reflection process, the project's elements and outcomes will be assessed by the children, teachers, families, and community members involved.

PEDAGOGICAL DOCUMENTATION

If pedagogy is the study of teaching and learning, and documentation serves as a record, then pedagogical documentation is the recording of the teaching and learning. It is not a straightforward listing of daily events, but rather a study of those events as they relate to teaching and learning. Educators from Reggio Emilia make records of the events that take place and use the documentation as a tool for research. This has come to be known as *pedagogical documentation*, and it has an important role in supporting reflective practice (Dahlberg, Moss, & Pence, 1999).

Pedagogical documentation involves making records of events as they intersect with people, places, and other events. As noted in Chapter 6, meaningful relationships are essential in order to gain the depth of analysis required to create pedagogical documentation. Building relationships will enhance your capacity to gain a deeper understanding of the meaning of the teaching and learning. This process allows for the creation of authentic relationships, which in turn can lead to authentic assessment. For more information on pedagogical documentation and how it can be used to support the reflective and programming process, see http://bit.ly/19S2T9O.

Pedagogical documentation communicates a variety of messages to children and families.

Diane Kashin

Making Learning Visible

Pedagogical documentation is **making learning visible** and can be seen in many places. It can be found in the images children create and their representations of their learning. These can be posted on the walls of indoor or outdoor learning environments or on social media platforms such as Facebook, Twitter, and Pinterest.

Harvard University has supported the practice of pedagogical documentation for a number of years through the Project Zero initiative, started by the contemporary theorist Howard Gardner and inspired by his experience with Reggio Emilia educators. The official Project Zero website and the companion Making Learning Visible website provide ample resources, as well as numerous examples of pedagogical documentation from educators around the world. For more information, see the following links: http://bit.ly/1411FZ6 and http://bit.ly/1geOk1M.

making learning visible The process of early childhood professionals seeing learning through the lens of children, and children seeing early childhood professionals as guides to their ongoing exploration and learning.

A Pedagogical Documentation Example

Zooms is a process developed by a group of teachers and a program director who were inspired by Reggio Emilia and the Making Learning Visible project. The process leads to the creation of documentation panels, which are snapshots of pedagogy. It is an example of teacher research. In Chapter 12, we will devote more space to discussing the role of the early learning professional in relation to research. The objective of the process is to "generate new insights about teaching and learning" (Mardell et al., 2009, p. 1). Specifically, a Zoom is

> a three-by four-foot documentation panel that offers a close look, as with a zoom lens, at the children's and teachers' responses and understandings of their classroom's research question. Zoom is both a verb and a noun. The dual usage encompasses a way of zooming in (verb) and creating a snapshot of particular moments of classroom life, and it refers to a specific type of documentation—a Zoom panel (noun). (Mardell et al., 2009, p. 4)

The goal is to capture key aspects of the "larger picture of unfolding relationships and understandings between the teacher and the children as they consider the inquiry question in small groups" (Mardell et al., 2009, p. 4). A Zoom panel may include photographs and quotes from discussions between children and their teachers, as well as the children's artwork representing their ideas. Some Zoom panels may also include comments from parents and visitors who view the panels.

Key to this process of pedagogical documentation is that the educators incorporate their analysis of the documented small-group sessions and try to interpret what these data say about the inquiry question. This process is designed to be long term. The educators involved read about the topic and have discussions about the inquiry question, both formally at meetings and informally between the teachers. Toward the end of the project, an episode is selected that accurately represents what has been learned about the inquiry question and a Zoom is created (Mardell et al., 2009). For more information, see http://bit.ly/16uuNsJ.

AUTHENTIC ASSESSMENT

Authentic assessment refers to the process that early learning professionals establish with the children and families to engage in ongoing observation, documentation, and interpretation of what they are seeing, hearing, and understanding from the children. It is aligned with authentic learning, which refers to learning experiences that are contextualized in realistic situations (Gulikers, Bastiaens, & Kirschner, 2007). Authentic learning in early learning programs occurs as a result of the combination of intriguing materials, experiences, people, and places, and children's freedom to explore individually and in groups. As identified in Figure 11.4, authentic learning is connected to programming.

authentic assessment The process that early learning professionals establish with children and families to engage in ongoing observation, documentation, and interpretation of what they are seeing, hearing, and understanding from the children.

Figure 11.4 Authentic learning and assessment

Diane Kashin

Observation and documentation are integral to supporting and guiding early learning professionals in their program planning and to the types of experiences that are extended to children. The National Association for the Education of Young Children (NAEYC), an association for early learning, has consistently identified that quality programs begin with professionals creating "thoughtful, appreciative, systematic observation and documentation of each child's unique qualities, strengths, and needs" (NAEYC, 2001, p. 33). Through observation and documentation, early learning professionals gain insight into how children use the environment, engage in the environment, and support their peers within the environment. They see the children's interests, the ways in which children problem solve, their learning styles, accomplishments, obstacles, and aspects of temperament (Forman & Hall, 2005; Kline, 2008).

Authentic assessment occurs through the process of ongoing observation, documentation, and interpretation of what early learning professionals are seeing, hearing, and understanding from the children. This is how they gain insight into children's thinking and use their findings to directly influence the programming process (Jablon, Dombro, & Dichtelmiller, 2007).

Early childhood professionals balance potential experiences with materials that support and build on children's strengths and push them to use new ideas or critical-thinking skills in their exploration and execution of play. Early learning professionals observe and document children engaging in learning experiences that provide insight into what they investigate, what they can do, and what they know.

There is a difference between traditional observation strategies and authentic assessment. Traditional observation, as shown in Table 11.2, focuses on requesting children to conduct particular activities so the teacher can determine what the child can and can't do in relation to developmental norms that have been set for children of similar ages. Authentic assessment differs in that the early learning professional is taking the lead from the children and observing them in their environment and in their experiences. The observer is looking at the strengths and skills that children exhibit.

Table 11.2 Traditional versus Authentic Assessment

Traditional Assessment	Authentic Assessment
Children are asked questions and are required to provide the correct response.	Children perform a task in a real-life situation as would normally occur during routines.
Teachers determine experiences to observe.	Observations of real-life play occur.
Children are required to recall/recognize specific information.	Construction/application activities are observed.
Activities are teacher directed.	Activities are child centred.
Teacher interpretations are given.	Direct evidence is assessed.

Authentic assessments are based on documentation of the children's journey of learning using a variety of observations, conversations with children, and extensive types of evidence-based record keeping (Kline, 2008). There is no single correct answer, nor are comparisons made among the children. Rather, early learning professionals use the information that they have gathered about children to plan experiences and programming that support them in their quest for knowledge (Jablon et al., 2007). Early learning professionals identify each child's zone of proximal development so that the programming offered to the children stretches their experiences and options for new knowledge development.

Authentic assessment has been strongly influenced by documentation processes practised in schools in Reggio Emilia, Italy. Gandini (1993) identified that many teachers are in the practice of taking notes, photographs, and audio recordings intended to capture group discussions and children's play experiences throughout the day. In Reggio Emilia schools, observations and pedagogical documentation are used as a way to try to see, understand, and bring meaning to what is going on in the work and what the child is capable of, without preset expectations or norms (Dahlberg et al., 1999). The documentation tells a story that helps early learning professionals develop programming that is flexible and respectful of the children in the learning community (Kline, 2008).

There are many advantages to authentic assessment and the use of documentation as a way to bring meaning to children's work. When the documentation is transparent and available to the children, it can become a trigger for them to continue to explore a particular area of interest while building their self-confidence and celebrating their accomplishments (Malaguzzi, 1998).

Early learning professionals have an important role in working with the children to document the children's learning and the teacher's learning. By creating ways to engage in authentic assessment, early learning professionals and children collaborate to look at and reflect upon new knowledge and plan for future investigations. Documentation then offers early learning professionals tools for their own research, reflection, collaboration, and decision making, while capturing children's play, learning, and teachable moments.

Authentic assessment requires evidence. One way to authentically assess is through the use of photography. "Photography is a language of inquiry through which teachers construct new understanding and communicate, because it conveys and provokes meaning" (Kline, 2008, p. 72). Another way of documenting learning is to encourage children to present their learning in ways that have meaning for them. This may include models, paintings, design of a construction area or dramatic centre, or the telling of stories. However children choose to represent their learning becomes authentic assessment. The early learning professional and children continuously examine the artifacts. This is a way to seek information about children's potential next phase of exploration.

Early learning professionals ensure that their authentic assessment strategies are conducted in a natural environment; use multiple methods of gathering information; gather multiple types of information; involve families in the process (Bredekamp & Copple, 1997); and make a connection between the intent of the assessment process and the use of the information gained from the process (Grisham-Brown, Hallam, & Brookshire, 2006). To be truly authentic, the assessment process builds on children's strengths and interests.

PROGRAM DESIGN FOR CHILDREN

Children's books are resources to trigger imagination and creativity in programming. They can be used to provoke a topic for inquiry or to support an inquiry question already established. In designing programs for children that support reflection and spirituality, early learning professionals can be guided by context to create intentions for children that have them stop and look closely at the world around them. By doing so, they will be able to take the time to inquire, reflect, and learn. The Looking Closely series by author Frank Serafina is designed for children to take a closer look at their surroundings. While intended for beginning readers, the series can be used with much younger children, as illustrated in Table 11.3. Hopefully, even the youngest child has access to a garden to look closely.

Table 11.3 Program Design for Children

INFANCY

Looking Closely	Experience	Interpretations and Wonderings
Diane Kashin	Bringing infants and toddlers to a garden provides an experience rich in potential for inquiry. Early learning professionals can provide opportunities for smelling, tasting, touching, listening, and seeing the wide range of plant life and animal life that can be found in a garden.	Early learning professionals can interpret the experience. Did the children respond to different smells, textures, and tastes? What did they seem to wonder about? What engaged the children? How did they respond? Why were they engaged? How can the experience be extended indoors?

EARLY CHILDHOOD

Looking Closely	Experience	Interpretations and Wonderings
Diane Kashin	As children become more mobile, excursions can be made to forested areas to look closely at the plant and animal life there. In the forest, children can notice colours and shapes all around them.	Children can interpret their surroundings to understand scientific principles about the life cycle, ecology, and the environment. They may wonder about what makes everything in the forest grow, leading to further investigations and ideas.

Looking Closely	Experience	Interpretations and Wonderings
 Diane Kashin	As children develop a global awareness, they can examine life in a desert. Early learning professionals can provide simulated experiences of desert life for exploration and discovery.	Children can compare and contrast the desert to their local forested space to become aware of the differences. They may wonder why there are stark contrasts.

PROGRAMMING BUBBLE

Early learning professionals are using yoga with children to help them make deeper spiritual connections. Yoga is an ancient form of movement that involves breathing, meditation, and a variety of poses. Poses can be modified to meet the motor development of the children. There are many benefits to yoga, as it promotes a less stressful and healthier lifestyle. We introduce yoga in the programming bubble illustrated in Figure 11.5.

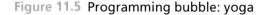

Yoga

By providing yoga books for children, as well as yoga mats, calming music, and posters illustrating children posing in yoga positions, early learning professionals can trigger the interest of the children to engage in this healthy form of exercise.

For more information check out http://playfullearning.net/2012/08/introducing-children-to-yoga-through-storytelling.

Figure 11.5 Programming bubble: yoga

A child enjoying a yoga experience.

Rosalba Bortolotti

FEATURED RESEARCH

Inspired by the educators from Reggio Emilia, *Visible Learners* is a book written to promote the approach for use with learners of all ages. Follow this link to read more about how the authors are working on promoting Reggio-inspired approaches in all schools: http://visiblelearningplus.com/about-us.

PEDAGOGICAL TOOLS

Vivian Paley (1979, 1981) is an inspirational example of an early learning professional who has "made extensive use of narrative in order to share her ethnographic observations of children" (Dunphy, 2008, p. 25). Over two decades, Paley has published her stories of practice that illustrate how a professional can reflect and modify teaching in response to observations of children. Carr (2001) and her colleagues created the learning stories approach to assess outcomes and as a means to strengthen the use of documentation as a pedagogical tool (Carter, 2010).

Carr (2000) describes learning stories as "structured observations, often quite short, that take a 'narrative' or story approach. They keep the assessment anchored in the situation or action" (p. 32). According to Dunphy (2008), the key point about this pedagogical tool is that the learning stories are "accounts of specific instances of learning that capture its complexity and richness. The stories make both early learning and the assessment of that learning visible" (p. 26). For examples of learning stories, see the following links:

- From educator Tom Drummond: http://bit.ly/14PFeIY.
- From Margie Carter of Harvest Resources: http://bit.ly/16slPei.
- From the blog Technology Rich Inquiry Based Research: http://bit.ly/1amnQN6.

PROFESSIONAL CASE STUDY

Madel is a three-and-a-half-year-old child who has been at the early learning centre since she turned two. She usually bounces into the early learning program daily. She plays with her peers on a regular basis and consistently tells early learning professionals stories about what she, her mummy and daddy, and Teddy Molly do on the weekends. For example, two weeks ago, as she and her mother were preparing to leave the centre, she told the staff that she and Teddy Molly were going on a plane.

When Madel returned to the centre, she did not seem herself. The early learning staff assumed during the first few days that it was due to making the adjustments back to the centre after having been away with her family. Sara, the early learning professional, attempted on a few occasions to begin conversations with Madel about her vacation, but Madel said little and continued to be much quieter than before the vacation. Sara noticed Madel in the hammock by herself late one afternoon. She went over and said in a soft, calm tone, "Madel, you don't seem to be very happy right now. Is something wrong?" Madel began to cry. Sara held her hand and stroked her hair, trying to imagine what was bothering Madel. Finally Madel said, "Teddy Molly is lost and Mummy says she is never coming back." Sara said, "Did Mummy say anything about why Molly would not be coming back?" "She said Molly is lost in the Vancouver airport and that she will never be found."

REFLECTION QUESTIONS FOR SELF-LEARNING

Sara was concerned that Madel had lost some of her spirituality upon her return from her vacation. As she tried to support Madel, she reflected upon the process of spirituality, observations, and programming. She further thought about her role in supporting children when life experiences occur that can influence children's spirituality. Thinking about this situation, answer the following questions:

1. What response would best support Madel in dealing with her lost teddy, Molly? What would you say to her about Molly?

2. What would you suggest she do to support her memories of Molly? How would you encourage discussion on what it might feel like to be a lost teddy?

3. How might you know that Madel is gradually accepting the loss of Teddy Molly? How might you include aspects of this situation in programming?

4. How would you support Madel in talking about the importance of Molly to her?

5. How can you determine if the experiences offered to all the children are supporting their sense of spirituality?

6. What does Sara need to work through in relation to her spirituality? Why?

BIG IDEAS FOR DIALOGIC LEARNING

Through spirituality, children find meaning in their lives and make meaning of their experiences. Think about the opening vignette. How was spirituality present in the experience of making bread, serving the bread, and having the children and staff try to name the ingredient that was put in the bread to make it sweet? How is food used in your family as a ritual of coming together, to renew connections and engagement? How do those experiences contribute to your growth as an individual? How do these social practices contribute to children participating in new or different ways of learning together (Bone, 2005)? What other types of rituals and early learning curriculum processes encourage harmony, new directions, change, a balance of power among the players, and, most importantly, honouring the spirit of the child?

Consider the following questions about spiritual curriculum and authentic assessment:

1. You are required to prepare a ten-minute presentation for parents who are considering enrolling their children at your centre. How would you describe spiritual curriculum and authentic assessment? How would you distinguish spiritual curriculum from programming with religious aspects?

2. In small groups, share ideas of what you might observe in an early learning program that is using authentic assessment processes with children. What might be visible in the early learning space? Make a list of strategies that your group would use to begin authentic assessment in your practice.

3. In small groups, create a concept map that outlines the connectors of spiritual curriculum and authentic assessment.

4. As each group presents their concept map, compare the similarities and differences. What aspects of the concept maps presented would you like to transfer to your practice? Why?

VISION

It is our vision that early learning students enter practice with a keen interest in working with children and families to help shape the children's minds and love for life. A curriculum that is designed for and with children is transformational and holistic, within which "all young children explore their personal and social journeys of meaning-making and celebrate their unique socio-emotional, spiritual, physical, ethnic, intellectual, and linguistic characteristics" (Harris, 2007, p. 272). By claiming your voice and viewing spiritual curriculum as a rainbow that adds colour, then changes its colours, form, and shape when new light appears as children gain new knowledge and shift their thinking, you create critical thinkers and visionaries. Early learning students and professionals create curriculum and a feeling tone within the environment that gives children a sense of hope. They provide environments that support children's need to explore, "mess about," and discover, rather than an environment with a power imbalance that requires children to ask permission. Ideally, the early learning environment is constantly changing, and adults and children together build and encourage a collaborative learning community among the partners.

MAKING CONNECTIONS

The concept of communities of practice arises from the work of Wenger (1998) and describes an environment where mutual engagement, joint enterprise, and shared repertoire "hold the key to real transformation" (p. 85). Miller and Shoptaugh (2004) developed a Reggio-inspired professional learning program aimed at building communities of practice where professionals connect through dialogue without judgment and question each other with respect in a non-threatening environment. The study documents powerful stories of transformation as a result of being part of community of practice.

Establishing communities of practice where early learning professionals engage together in research can be an empowering means to improve and to avoid top-down models of professional development, in which adults are viewed as implementers of externally driven change (Wood & Bennett, 1999). Wood and Bennett's (1999) seminal study of nine early learning professionals and their road toward change exemplifies the value of establishing communities of practice in which communities generate their own professional discourses. We encourage all early learning students and professionals to create their own communities of practice. We recommend the workbook for developing communities of practice at http://amzn.to/1f3GtJS.

The conceptualization of the teacher as collaborator and researcher reflects a theoretical shift from a view of learning as primarily individual centred to one that is fundamentally socially and culturally situated (Kashin, 2009). In Chapter 12, we will explore in more depth he role of the early learning professional as a collaborative researcher.

KEY TERMS

Authentic assessment   267

Context   264

Intentions   265

Making learning visible   267

Spirituality   257

Figure 11.6   Key terms wordle

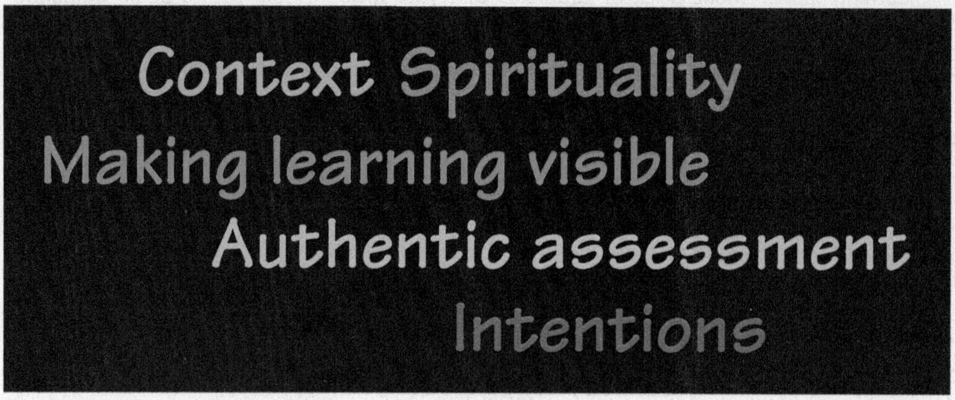

Context Spirituality
Making learning visible
Authentic assessment
Intentions

SUMMARY

In summary, early learning students can see the connection between spirituality and programming.

1. Early learning professionals can articulate their role in making the connection between spirituality and the programming process.

2. Pedagogical documentation as a vehicle for making learning visible guides programming and serves as a tool for research.

3. Early learning professionals can reflect on the connection between spirituality and authenticity, both in assessment and learning. Learning stories are an effective means of authentic assessment, as is pedagogical documentation.

4. Early learning professionals can plan programs for children that support reflection and spirituality while creating intentions for children to observe the world around them.

5. Through observation and reflection of children's learning processes, early learning professionals support children in developing reflective skills and their own spirituality.

Kagan and Bowman's (1997) work on leadership continues to be relevant and refers to five faces of leadership for early learning professionals: (1) administrative leadership, (2) pedagogical leadership, (3) community leadership, (4) conceptual leadership, and (5) advocacy leadership. Developing these kinds of leadership could be an effective way to develop the skills of early learning professionals. For more on leadership and learning from Kagan and Bowman see: http://bit.ly/1tziJ1X.

Li (2010) defined leadership as being able to connect with the people. "The more you share with them, the vision, strategy, and motivation to be able to understand what the strategy is, the stronger the authority is." Therefore, sharing in the workplace forms relationships between leaders and their followers.

For Further Thought

Democratic, open leadership is having the confidence to give up the need to be in control while inspiring commitment from people to accomplish goals. For more information on democratic leadership see: http://bit.ly/144Wquy.

Another approach to leadership that early learning students and professionals may find interesting is the social leadership model, which can be found at www.pinterest.com/pin/71142869087067765. It supports a collaborative approach that uses socially collaborative technologies (Stodd, 2013).

Chapter 12
Teacher as Researcher

LEARNING OUTCOMES

After exploring this chapter, you should be able to

1. Discuss the key concepts of research and how research may influence the growth of early learning professionals and the programming offered to children and families.

2. Describe what is meant by qualitative and quantitative research and how each supports professional learning.

3. Explain relationship of pedagogical documentation and research.

4. Outline how a narrative inquiry or action research model may be implemented in early learning environments to research core questions that evolve from working with children, families, or programming models.

5. Describe how early learning professionals incorporate research into practice.

A CHILD'S STORY   Azril

Amy and Daddy asked me if I wanted to be part of a searching project for the next two weeks with my teacher Mila. Daddy said, "It will just be like other days, but at the end Mila will talk to us about what we do when we play." I said, "Okay," but I don't know what I will be searching for. Amy and Daddy said they didn't know all the details. They said this was important to my teacher because she is doing something like action search. They told me that after the action search was done with the children, my teacher was going to interview them. Daddy said it was important to remember to take with us the piece of paper that he signed saying that I could be part of the searching project.

When I got to school, I heard Daddy and Mila talking about the search project, but then I forgot about it. A few days later, Daddy asked me how the search project was. I had forgotten all about it and said, "I don't know." I haven't been searching for anything—just playing with my friends and Mila took pictures of us.

A few weeks later, Amy and Daddy and I and my friend Josh's daddies got to look at a whole bunch of pictures of us playing together. Mila talked to us about our play. Mila said this was part of her searching project and she appreciated our conversations with her. She said it was important for her action search and that she was going to write about it.

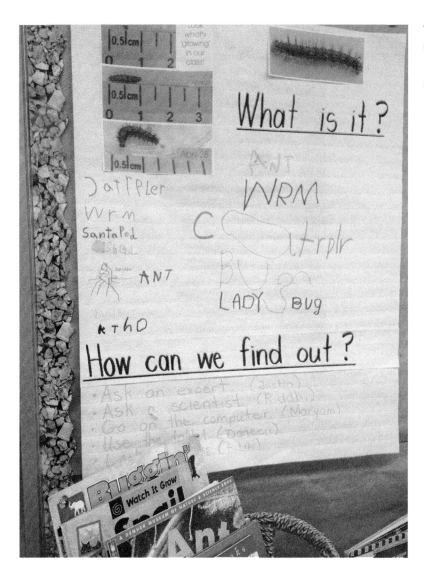

The early learning professional presents to the children what she has written about their play.

Diane Kashin

We sometimes talk as if "original research" were a peculiar prerogative of scientists or at least of advanced students. But all thinking is research, and all research is native, original, with him who carries it on, even if everybody else in the world already is sure of what he is still looking for. It also follows that all thinking involves a risk. Certainty cannot be guaranteed in advance.

—John Dewey (1859–1952)

Research is the framework of a profession. Research with children and for children differs from discussions with or listening to children (Kellett, 2011). Research is a process used to examine questions and produce outcomes that form findings, which will advance knowledge, skills, or abilities about a particular issue or practice (Kellett, 2011). Engaging in ongoing research supports professionals in finding their voice and in integrating findings into their practice. Having

Box 12.1 **Claim Your Potential**

CLAIM YOUR POTENTIAL as a researcher capable of taking action to improve practice.

strong links between research and practice strengthens programming and the children's experiences, while positioning early childhood education to be viewed with an enhanced professional status. Conducting research in early learning programs supports early learning professionals and children in their quest for daily inquiry, problem solving, and the desire to gain different kinds of insights into children and programming (Moore & Gilliard, 2008).

We encourage early learning students to claim their potential to conduct research. We believe that you are capable of taking action to improve your practice. As depicted in Box 12.1, we ask that you claim your potential as a teacher-researcher capable of the type of in-depth analysis of your practice that can lead to change.

According to Rolfe, MacNaughton, and Siraji-Blatchford (2010), "research is best conceptualized simply as a tool that helps us answer important questions about early childhood" (p. 3). When you claim your potential as a researcher, you will find that some questions have complex answers that lead to more questions. However, if you had not engaged in the research process, these questions would remain unanswered. "Research is about uncovering and enabling the emergence of new understandings, insights and knowledge" (Rolfe et al., 2010, p. 3).

For Reggio educators, "an element that has been fundamental to our experience is the concept of the teacher as a researcher" (Rinaldi, 2003, p. 1). These educators find joy in searching and researching; they see the value of research. Research has been a long-standing tradition within the educational domain, aimed at improving social contexts (Ampartzaki, Kypriotaki, Voreadou, Dardioti, & Stathi, 2013; Levine, 2002). Research remains less visible or explored in the early childhood field (Moore & Gilliard, 2008), despite research on children dating back to the late nineteenth century. At that time, the research grew out of an interest in gaining information about child health and well-being. In the 1930s, the number of psychologists, psychiatrists, and social workers working with children and families increased. This societal change prompted research about children, primarily with a focus on children's development (Kellett, 2011). During that time, children were viewed as objects of research. The researcher had the voice and the power and set the framework in which the questions were asked and experiments were conducted. A large percentage of the research focused on children's cognitive development.

Kellett (2011) noted that research "on" children persisted late into the twentieth century. At that time, sociologists began questioning the assumptions that had been made about children and their role in society. Discussions around children and research were expanded to include an examination of the roles of children and their rights to be involved in research. Kellett (2011) suggested "a rights-based perspective prompted expectations that children should be active participants in this process. Research 'with' rather than research 'on' children became a dominant discourse" (p. 3). This redirection also emphasized the importance of children's voices being heard, respected, and incorporated into the research agenda.

Another major influence in the late twentieth century was the ratification of the United Nations Convention on the Rights of the Child (1991). Article 3 states, "The best interests of children must be the primary concern in making decisions that may affect them. All adults should do what is best for children. When adults make decisions, they should think about how their decisions will affect children." For many researchers and institutions, the UN's Article 3 serves to guide ethical principles and practices associated with research in early childhood education. Whether intentional or not, there has been further acknowledgment of and movement toward having children and families as partners in research during the first decade and a half of the twenty-first century. When given the opportunity, children have the skills and abilities to identify areas of research that they would like to pursue.

RESEARCH ETHICS

Early learning students and professionals work with young children. As research participants, children are considered highly vulnerable. "Researchers must understand and address ethical issues that arise in research" (Rolfe et al., 2010, p. 4). If the benefits to the research reflect more the researcher's interests than the participants', there could be an ethical issue. Early learning professionals who engage in research must "protect the interests and ongoing welfare of the research participants" (Rolfe et al., 2010, p. 4). Most academic institutions and many community organizations have research **ethics** policies, or a set of moral rules of conduct that researchers must adhere to. Ethics are an important consideration in research, as "researchers must not put their need to carry out their study above their responsibility to maintain the well-being of the study participants" (Mills, 2011, p. 25). As early learning students, you will benefit from becoming aware of the research ethics policies of your institution and how they may influence your ability to conduct research with children and families.

Rolfe and colleagues (2010) stressed that high-quality research in the early years is

ethics A set of moral rules of conduct that researchers must adhere to.

- ethical;
- purposeful;
- well designed;
- transparent;
- contextualized;
- credible;
- careful;
- imaginative; and
- equitable.

When research is guided by the above principles, there are many possible benefits for both the researcher and the research subjects—the children. "Research can make a positive difference in the lives of children" (Rolfe et al., 2010, p. 4). At the core of any research process is the need for an ethical professional who is respectful of children's rights in the collection of data.

Research involves the collection of **data** and data analysis. Early learning students and professionals collect data when they observe and document children's play and learning experiences. The documentation is the data. When the documentation is analyzed and interpreted, the documenter is involved in research. We encourage professionals and students to include "researcher" among the roles they take on, because the process of research examines and improves practice.

RESEARCH CATEGORIES

There are two basic categories of research—qualitative and quantitative—and within them, many methods may be used by children and adults to conduct the research. **Quantitative research** requires some form of measurement. Data are assigned a numerical value to the subject being researched. This type of research "seeks not only to understand but also to explain" (Rolfe et al., 2010, p. 5). Research that seeks to understand and describe in an effort to seek knowledge from complex and diverse data often is achieved by the researcher using a quantitative approach.

Qualitative research generates data that provide descriptors or stories in response to the questions being explored. In this chapter, we focus on qualitative inquiry because of its relationship to constructivism, and how it complements themes, ways of knowing, and experiences. Qualitative researchers focus on answering the *why* questions that surface through observations, pedagogical documentation, and conversations with children and families. The settings for the research are usually ones that are known and familiar to those involved in the research. The words or stories provide the richness of the research. The researcher analyzes the data by making comparisons within the data and coding emergent themes and categories. As patterns emerge, new discoveries are made, which often leads to knowledge creation and new ways of modelling professional practice.

THE RATIONALE FOR RESEARCH

As noted throughout the text, we encourage early learning professionals to view children and their families as active participants and contributors to their early learning programs. This means that both children and adults become valuable partners in "generat[ing] a body of children research knowledge" (Kellett, 2011, p. 1). Kellett (2011) explained that when early learning professionals engage in research with, for, and by children, there are complementarities that inform and interact with each other.

As this is the final chapter of a textbook designed to support early learning students in preparing to launch their careers, we end with a focus on you. The first five chapters provided you with foundational professional knowledge. Chapters 6 through 11 focused on applying professional knowledge to practice, beginning with relationships as the ultimate starting point for considering programming in the early years. In Chapters 6 to 12, each chapter represented "meta-knowledge" or the application of your professional knowledge to your professional practice. We provided you with an invitation to claim an aspect of your professional practice, ending with the final call for you to claim your potential. We believe in the capacity of early learning students and in the limitless potential of the early learning professional.

In Figure 12.1, we bring all the claim invitations into one wordle. When you view yourself in the role of a researcher, you can claim your voice, spirituality, curiosity, knowledge, and potential. Claiming your potential as a researcher helps you to participate in a reflective process, apply knowledge, change practice, and create new knowledge. The application of knowledge is an important element in teaching and learning today.

data In research, that which is collected, observed, or created for purposes of analysis or to produce original research results.

quantitative research The collection of data in numerical form; it involves careful experimental design and control to determine relationships between variables.

qualitative research The collection of data that are not in numerical form. This method involves an inductive research process to seek understanding.

Figure 12.1 Claims wordle

PROFESSIONAL KNOWLEDGE IN THE TWENTY-FIRST CENTURY

According to Kereluik, Mishra, Fahnoe, and Terry (2013), under the auspices of twenty-first-century learning, the issue of what knowledge learners "should" have has received attention. The educational demands of this century require new ways of thinking and learning (Ampartzaki et al., 2013; Gardner, 2008; Pink, 2006). We've seen an increased demand for new knowledge frameworks, suggesting that the way education was viewed in the twentieth century is no longer sufficient for today's learners (Kereluik et al., 2013). Follow this link to a research study that analyzed existing frameworks and researched available literature to arrive at the framework depicted in Figure 12.2: http://bit.ly/1apkYfK.

We view research as an opportunity for early learning professionals to act upon their knowledge in a way that can be collaborative, creative, and critical. The research process

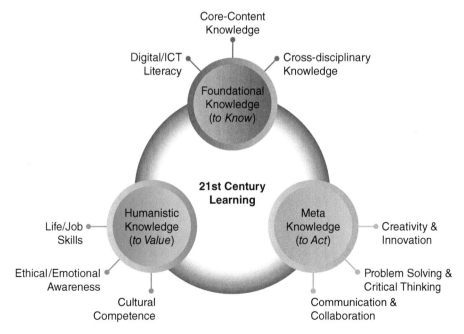

Figure 12.2 Twenty-first-century knowledge framework

Source: Kereluik et al., 2013.

supports lifelong learning and professional skills, while strengthening ethical and emotional awareness, as well as cultural competence. We are committed to research in our practices. Collectively, through the qualitative process of narrative inquiry, we have collaborated on research projects that have informed our practice and generated new knowledge that, when shared, advanced and continues to advance the early childhood education field.

Early learning programs are perfect "incubators of inquiry" (Pelo, 2006, p. 50). Bringing children, families, and early learning professionals together to engage in investigations and respond to questions such as "what if," "why," or "if" leads to a culture of inquiry (Pelo, 2006). The process of investigating creates curiosity, a sense of wonderment, and intellectual stimulation, all of which help early learning professionals to stretch their knowledge, engage in discourse, and take risks to try new strategies and processes in their practice.

Wien, Guyevskey, and Berdoussis (2011) described early learning professionals who engage in pedagogical documentation as researchers. Pedagogical documentation is considered as a form of research because it is a "research story, built upon a question of inquiry 'owned by' the teachers, children, or others, about the learning of children" (p. 1). The authors suggested that pedagogical documentation "reflects a disposition of not presuming to know and of asking how the learning occurs" (p. 1). Pedagogical documentation is a way in which early learning professionals make sense of what they wonder about, what they question, what they think they see, and how they work through the questions that evolve in their practices from the experiences they have with children and families.

Wien and colleagues (2011) suggested that when early learning professionals engage in interpreting pedagogical documentation, the method should be consistent with the qualitative ethnographic research method. This means the researcher should complete analysis and interpretation from observational data gathered from field notes, discussions, and visual materials. Pedagogical documentation processes may also reflect aspects of the qualitative narrative inquiry research method, as described in the next section.

NARRATIVE INQUIRY RESEARCH

Narrative inquiry is a qualitative research method that involves bringing meaning to experiences through storytelling (Meier & Stremmel, 2010). However, narrative inquiry is much more than just telling stories. Narrative inquiry is a research method that supports reflecting on and bringing meaning to practice. Sharing stories is a way to compare experiences, bring new meaning to situations, and understand practice.

Early learning professionals and students may use narrative inquiry to challenge their practice, seek clarity about questions, and make sense of values, beliefs, and new ways of thinking. Sharing stories is one way to address ideas or ways of knowing and, in the process, may increase the culture of inquiry and collaborative learning. Narrative inquiry is rich when collaborators share experiences, learning, and practices with peers or colleagues. As identified by Bresier (2013), "in the context of research, the idea of interaction between 'outside' and 'inside' and the possibility of dialogic connection are supported by the postmodern attention to researchers' interactions with participants and in settings" (p. 27). For us, the authors, by sharing our stories we have experienced many "aha!" moments through our discourse and collective exploration of questions or practices we have struggled with. Research findings become stimulants for the big ideas that shape professional practice and create supportive learning communities.

As we tell each other stories of practice and act as mentors and critical friends, we challenge ourselves to think deeply to test our theories and expand our questions (Pelo, 2006). This process further develops research themes and leads to knowledge creation. Mentors and critical friends have different roles. Figure 12.3 provides an overview of the differences between a mentor and a critical friend.

There are roles for both mentors and critical friends in early learning programs and in research environments. Healy and Welchert (1990) defined the *mentoring process* as "a dynamic, reciprocal relationship in a work environment between an advanced career incumbent (mentor) and a beginner (protégé), aimed at promoting the career development of both" (p. 16). Lea and Leibowitz (1983) defined *mentoring* as an integrative process that includes "teaching, guiding, advising, counselling, sponsoring, role modelling, validating, motivating, protecting and communicating" (p. 26). The mentoring process is a way to create informal links between the protegé and organizational expectations.

The term *critical friend* has its origins in critical pedagogy. One of the most widely used definitions of a critical friend was outlined by Costa and Kallick (1993). They suggested that

> a critical friend can be defined as a trusted person who asks provocative questions, provides data to be examined through another lens, and offers critiques of a person's work as a friend. A critical friend takes the time to fully understand the context of the work presented and the outcomes that the person or group is working toward. The friend is an advocate for the success of that work. (p. 14)

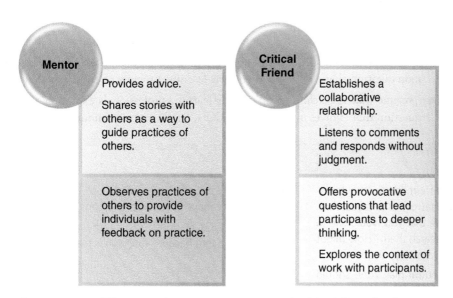

Figure 12.3   Differences between mentor and critical friend roles

Critical friends and mentors provide constructive feedback about strengths, weaknesses, problems, and opportunities for further development. For more information on critical friends, go to http://bit.ly/PqSxIR.

ACTION RESEARCH

Research is undertaken as a way to discover new knowledge. It almost always begins with a question and with what has been gained or discovered from previous research. We think of research in early childhood learning as being similar to constructing a house out of blocks. Each time a new block is positioned on the structure, it must be done so by first looking and thinking about what has already been done, the current position of blocks, and the intent of the placement of the new block. When stepping back and looking at what has been accomplished, what is known, and what questions remain, a knowledge base for success is attained. There are many qualitative methods that may be used in research in addition to narrative inquiry. We introduce you to another method: action research.

Kurt Lewin (1890–1947) is often credited with coining the term **action research** (Mills, 2011). The concept of "teacher as researcher" and the practice of action research call for those who work with children to research issues related to their practice. Piggot-Irvine (2003) stated that "the word 'action' in action research is key. It is about making or implementing change, rather than investigating an issue. It is an approach that always involves participants making or implementing change, rather than investigating an issue" (p. 28). Action research helps early learning students and professionals connect with their practices and critically reflect upon how their practices are influenced by their beliefs and values.

Action research is an approach that supports early learning teachers and children in examining core questions through a systematic, thoughtful, and reflective process (Moore & Gilliard, 2008). Through research, we gain ideas "to improve the lives of children and to learn about the craft of teaching" (Mills, 2011, p. 7) while contributing to the knowledge base that informs and guides programming processes and practices. By reading the Reflective Moment box and thinking about research questions that relate to your practice, you can start visualizing yourself as a researcher. This is the beginning of the action research process. This professional learning process may be completed individually or collectively, where teachers systematically reflect on their practice and work, seek support and feedback from colleagues, identify options for new practices, and make changes in their practice (Borgia & Schuler, 1996; Moore & Gilliard, 2008).

Ferrance (2000) categorized action research as

- *individual teacher research*: early learning professionals investigating a single question that evolves from a child or an early learning program situation;

- *collaborative action research*: a group of early learning professionals examining a common question that evolves from an early learning program or child experience; and

- *program-wide research*: a group of early learning professionals exploring a common question that evolves from children, adults, family, or programming process.

action research A form of self-reflective inquiry that early learning professionals can use to understand practice and improve social and professional practices.

A Reflective Moment

Think about the observations you have made in early learning environments. Now put your hat on as a researcher. What types of questions do you have that you would like to research? Why would you like to research them? How might you use action research to seek answers to your questions?

What do you think a gender-neutral play zone should look like?

How might you encourage girls to use hockey sticks in their play, and boys to use pots and pans?

How might you respond to a mother or father who expresses concern because their son is playing house?

Borgia and Schuler's (1996) seminal work illustrates how action research changes practices. They provided an example of early learning professionals who use ineffective traditional rituals and practices, such as daily rote exercises involving calendar and weather, holiday curricula, learning "a letter a week," and isolated skill-and-drill, in lieu of methods that result in meaningful learning. "While it might be difficult to stop such practices from the outside, a teacher is likely to discover their futility upon closer investigation, made possible through action research" (p. 1). Much can be gained by examining this teacher-centred approach to programming through the lens of action research. Action research can bring forth a number of new perspectives. For example, what if the researcher poses the question, "How might children discover information about holidays, names of days, and weather in their day-to-day play?" In that exploration, the researcher may begin to think about the relationship between his or her philosophy about how children learn and the programming and practices the children are exposed to. Also, through action research, the researcher may gain insight into ways in which people, learning environments, and practices can affect and change program directions and experiences to reflect children's play and learning.

Action research is linked to social constructivism. When communities of learners share ideas or knowledge about early learning practices, new knowledge is created that changes practice (Moore & Gilliard, 2008). "Social constructivism emphasizes education for social transformation and reflects human development theory within a sociocultural context" (Moore & Gilliard, 2008, p. 46). Early learning professionals focus on the social constructs of the environment to support how programming is designed and implemented with children.

Early learning professionals engage most successfully in action research when they have participated in professional learning that focuses on action research, so that they are familiar with the steps. As outlined in Figure 12.4, using an organized process when embarking on action research makes the results much richer and more reliable than trying to do research with an informal plan of action. Thinking about questions of inquiry

Figure 12.4 The action research process

and why they are questions helps the professional formulate the foundation for research. This process generally leads professionals to identify their willingness to commit to investigating a "problem" that needs to be explored, which should lead to the creation of a list of potential data sources that will support the investigation of the problem. After ethics approval has been obtained, early learning professionals determine how and what data to collect. This could include recording instances of children's inattention to the daily rituals of the calendar. It could also involve keeping a journal of experiences or exchanging stories of practice. Then, early learning professionals could also record their perspectives, questions, and ideas of future exploration in their reflective journals. Reflections may describe what the researchers observed, the comfort or concerns about what evolved, new perspectives that have evolved, questions that remain prominent regarding practice, and what they question or have learned about their practice. This process supports researchers in focusing on programming processes, teaching and learning methods, and the responses that children make to their environments and programming experiences. We invite you to think about questions by taking a look at the Reflective Moment box that focuses on getting started in action research. The final step is to take action. The teacher engaged in action research would then go back to the first step and begin the cycle again. According to Borgia and Schuler (1996),

> educators who have used action research say that it becomes a way of life in their work. Classroom practice and children's experiences are changed, and in the process, there is improvement in learning. Professional development becomes an ongoing process in which educators and children are concurrent learners and teachers. Action research is a positive, supportive, proactive resource for change. (p. 3)

Carr and colleagues (2007) determined that action research is more than a strategy for early learning professionals to solve problems that they experience. "Action research is a form of active learning: in essence, planned or studied enactment" (McKernan, 1991, p. 43). Others, such as Atweh, Kemmis, and Weeks (1998) suggested that action research be participatory among key partners because this promotes a social process, participation, and a collaborative model of practice. When action research is participatory, it has the potential to also be emancipatory, whereby "people explore the ways in which their practices are shaped and constrained by the wider social structures" (pp. 23–24).

Early learning professionals frame open-ended questions so that potential possibilities emerge. Questions that begin with "how" or "why" or "under what conditions" often lead to richer, more useful information. They should not be aimed at quick-fix solutions to situations in the learning environment, and ones that involve understanding children and teaching in profound ways amplify the benefits of research.

McNiff, Whitehead, and Laidlaw (1996) described four important points about action research. They determined that an early educator should be able to state,

- I am the central person in my research.
- I am asking a real question about a real issue, and I am hoping to move toward a possible solution.

A Reflective Moment

What are the questions you would like to explore? Why?

What knowledge do you already have about your question?

What have you noticed about this question with the children?

What are you learning about the topic from your critical friends?

- I am starting from where I am.
- I am trying to bring about some improvement to my practice that has been identified through research (remember, any improvement is still improvement, no matter how small).

Action research occurs in our daily environments and is something you do with, rather than "on," the children and environments in which you practice.

Critical friends are important in action research because they support you (the researcher) in having an open mind through the process. They may also become a sounding board when you uncover new findings or become challenged by some of your previous beliefs and practices.

TEACHER AS RESEARCHER

In the Reggio Emilia approach, the meaning of teacher as researcher complements the process of action research. Research is a routine and expected function of teachers' lives in the classroom (Hill et al., 2005). In a Reggio-inspired classroom, teachers learn and relearn with children through observation, reflection, speculation, questioning, and theorizing. The teacher learns alongside the children, and is a teacher-researcher—a resource and a guide to lend expertise (Malaguzzi, 1998). Within such a teacher-researcher role, educators listen, observe, and document children's work and the growth of community in their classroom. They provoke, co-construct, and stimulate thinking based on a process of reflection about their own teaching and learning (Organisation for Economic Co-operation and Development, 2004). Similarly, when emergent curriculum teachers "make the problem the project" (Hill et al., 2005, p. 47), they are becoming teacher-researchers, as the documentation cycle involves the process of action research.

To move to a position of teacher as researcher, the act of research needs to be redefined as something teachers do as part of their teaching (Hill et al., 2005). This requires a broad view of research that expands beyond the testing of a hypothesis. The growing acceptance of qualitative research methods has helped expand the education community's understanding and acceptance of less empirical methods.

Taking a teacher-researcher stance can have implications for the early learning professional. Evidence suggests that teachers who have been involved in research may become more reflective, more critical, and more open and committed to professional learning (Hansen, 1997; Keyes, 2000; Oja & Pine, 1989). Wood and Bennett (1999) described a research study that examined early childhood teachers' theories of play and the relationship of those theories to practice. An unintended outcome of involvement in the research process was that all the teachers changed their theories, practice, or both. Stremmel (2002b) maintained that teachers who participate in teacher research become more deliberate in their decision making and actions in the classroom. Stremmel (2002b) also stated,

> The real value of engaging in teacher research at any level is that it may lead to rethinking and reconstructing what it means to be a teacher or teacher-educator and, consequently, the way teachers relate to children and students. Distinct from conventional research on teaching, teacher research is transformative, enabling the teachers to develop a better understanding of themselves, their classrooms, and their practice through the act of reflective inquiry. (p. 64)

Geertz (1973) noted that when educators become researchers, research becomes a permanent and enduring part of practice and intellectual challenge. As early learning professionals grow and develop, so too does their meaning making about their practice and aspirations for future development and practice.

The Hawkins room for messing about at Seneca College Newnham Lab School.

Louise Jupp

CONTINUOUS PROFESSIONAL LEARNING

Across Canada, each province and territory has identified the professional learning requirements necessary for early learning professionals to practise. There are also associations that identify standards of practice, which may include additional professional learning requirements.

Continuous professional learning can be defined in many ways. For example, we view continuous professional learning as an organized approach that individuals and organizations adopt to support early learning professionals in maintaining competence in their practice, acquiring new knowledge, and redefining practices that reflect evidence-based practices. It is a career-long process. Continuous professional learning evolves from many types of learning experiences, some of which are formal and structured, while others may be informal, self-planned, and self-directed. Establishing learning communities within the early learning environment increases the transfer of learning to practice.

Vescio, Ross, and Adams (2006) suggested learning communities should be grounded in two assumptions: "First, it is assumed that knowledge is situated in the day-to-day lived experiences of teachers and best understood through critical reflection with others who share the same experience" (Buysse, Sparkman, & Wesley, 2003, p. 81). Second, "it is assumed that teachers who are actively engaged in professional learning communities will increase their professional knowledge and enhance student learning" (p. 3). Meanwhile, Ellström, Ekholm, and Ellström (2007) suggested that professional learning be viewed in two ways. The first way is to view professional learning as an adjustment to practice, and the second is to view it as development. Ellström and colleagues determined that when professional learning is examined in this dual way, it allows one to consider (1) the relationship between the individual and the context in which learning takes place, and (2) how learning options can provide individuals and colleagues with opportunities to examine practice and identify ways to improve practice.

There are many benefits to early learning programs when there is a continuous learning model in which all early learning professionals participate (Meier & Stremmel, 2010). For example, early learning professionals take an active role in, and ownership of, defining a strategy that will provide them with ways to have access to learning that supports their desired outcomes (Harris & Jones, 2010). Individuals and groups benefit when they determine their own learning strategy and how the change process will occur.

According to the Association of Early Childhood Educators Ontario (2013), there are direct and indirect benefits to early learning professionals being active, continuous learners. They include the following:

- critically identifying, evaluating, challenging, and reflecting upon daily practice;
- posing questions about values and beliefs and being accountable for current practices;

- examining how new and relevant ideas, topics, and research can be transferred to practice;
- promoting ongoing learning using a broad range of formal and informal strategies; and
- promoting internal and external collaborative partnerships among early learning professionals.

Continuous learning, combined with action research, supports early learning professionals to understand the complexity of the early learning field of practice and all the intricacies that affect the quality of the children's experiences. Professional learning experiences and professional learning communities facilitate collaborative inquiry, whereby teachers explore new ideas, examine current practices, and engage in discourse that may lead individuals and groups to think about practices from a new perspective (Vescio, Ross, & Adams, 2008).

Carter and Curtis (2010) suggested that when we have a vision of early childhood programs as places for children to thrive and as learning communities for adults and children, that vision influences the organizational culture. Early learning professionals grow in environments that challenge them and cause them to think, cultivate new ideas, provoke new ways of thinking, and break through barriers that restrict children's options for learning.

ROLES AND RESPONSIBILITIES OF EARLY LEARNING PROFESSIONALS

Continuous learning and research are important roles and responsibilities that early learning professionals incorporate into their practice. Early learning professionals should view research as an aspect of their development that is just as important as the colleagues with whom they would share their questions and findings. Without continuous research and development, early learning professionals may negatively influence their personal development and career options.

Early learning professionals incorporate their values, beliefs, and strategies for conducting research into their practice. Although we have introduced you to narrative inquiry and action research, many other research methods are suitable for use with children and in early learning programs. Hansen (1997) reminds early learning professionals that "a teacher researcher, among other things, is a questioner. Her questions propel her forward" (p. 1). Early learning professionals observe their environments, listen to the children, and use their questions or areas of interest to figure out what is happening in their environment and to develop their goals for their practice.

As early learning professionals combine continuous learning with research, posing questions about practice forms the foundation for one's research agenda. Early learning professionals are proactive in carving out their research and continuous learning journey, as this keeps motivation and passion higher than if such professional practices are assigned to them.

Early learning professionals model behaviours, such as curiosity, intrigue, and exploration, that they hope children will also have and act upon. Effective modelling begins with early learning professionals asking themselves questions such as, "What do I believe and why do I believe that?" and "How do I support the children?" Research studies in the early learning sector are plentiful. In designing your own professional research experiences, you are cultivating a climate of inquiry. By reviewing examples of research studies conducted by others, you can begin to think about your own research process. Research provides the framework for professional decisions about supporting children in building and designing co-constructed programming inquiry and play experiences. Table 12.1 on the next page provides research study examples for infancy, early childhood, and middle childhood.

Figure 12.5, on page 291, provides our final, all-encompassing programming bubble for this text. Using an inquiry approach to play will provide much potential for research. Inquiry-based learning is an approach to teaching and learning that places questions, big ideas, and observations at the centre of the learning experience, to create a culture of inquiry and research among the children and early learning professionals (Scardamalia, 2002).

Table 12.1 Program Design for Children

INFANCY

Research Study Example	Research Themes	Insights for Programming
This action research study took place in a university lab school and focused on relationships. Relationships between the children over the course of a year were carefully examined, and over time, teachers cultivated these connections, focusing on building relationships between the infants and the toddlers/two-year-olds.	The research pointed to the importance of the following to relationship building: • how the environment was arranged; • opportunities to play with materials and dolls; • giving older children a role in caregiving assistance; • planned play opportunities between the children; • support of spontaneous interactions.	The findings back the idea that children, with support, can be quite capable of interacting with one another. The result of the project was that the early learning professionals supported relationships in a way that created richer interactions and closer relationships (McGaha, Cummings, Lippard, & Dallas, 2011). For more information on this research study, see http://ecrp.uiuc.edu/v13n1/mcgaha.html.

EARLY CHILDHOOD

Research Study Example	Research Themes	Insights for Programming
This action research study focused on story dictation. After noticing that when children dictated and dramatized stories they tended to use gender stereotypes and segregate themselves by gender, the research study, which lasted over a year, began. Data were collected through the transcription of the children's stories as they were dictated. The study involved over one hundred children ranging in age from thirty-three months to children in grade 2.	Reflection was an important part of this study, and after analysis of the stories via print, audio, and video data, the research themes that emerged focused on preconceived notions of gender, as in "girl stories" about princesses and/or fairies and "boy stories" about combat and/or superheroes.	When children were engaged in discussion about gender stereotypes, they were more able to negotiate identities, potentially expanding their conceptions of gender. Rather than ignoring gender stereotypes emerging in the stories, the research study found that "teachers can help children construct more open views and actions about gender through the storytelling/dramatizing process, an engaging and collaborative activity that invites children into discussion about their beliefs" (Daitsman, 2011, p. 11). For more on this research study, see www.naeyc.org/files/naeyc/file/vop/VOP_Daitsman_Final(1).pdf.

MIDDLE CHILDHOOD

Research Study Example	Research Themes	Insights for Programming
This research study examined critical inquiry with young children. It was initiated after an episode occurred with five- and six-year-olds in a summer program. The children, who were headed to sit on a bench outdoors, were told that the bench was for teachers only. The teacher who engaged in this research "decided to create the time and space where the children were comfortable enough to discuss what had happened" (Kuby, 2013, p. 4). The discussions were focused on the history of the civil rights movement in the United States, particularly the famous story of Rosa Parks.	Data were collected during planned and incidental interactions through video and audio recordings, photography, children's artifacts, program plans, parent newsletters and questionnaires, as well as a personal professional journal to help understand ponderings about critical inquiry in early childhood.	Beliefs about young children's capacity to discuss injustices and consider multiple viewpoints were reinforced. The teacher-researcher discovered that while social justice curriculum can be appropriate for young children, it is important to be careful about using language when discussing injustice. Social action can be part of relationships in the early years. Critical inquiry teaching using events and questions from children's lives was the springboard for curriculum. To see this study, go to www.naeyc.org/files/naeyc/file/Voices/Voices_Kuby_v8n1pdf.pdf.

Inquiry and Play
Inquiry is an approach to learning that is driven by the natural curiosity of children to question, explore, and make sense of their world. When this takes place in a play-based program, rich in materials for exploration, children will naturally wonder. For more information, see http://rec.ohiorc.org/orc_documents/orc/recv2/briefs/pdf/0008.pdf.

Figure 12.5 Programming bubble: inquiry and play

Children express their sense of "I wonder."

Diane Kashin

FEATURED RESEARCH

C Rinaldi is a professor and pedagogical consultant to Reggio Children. Reggio Children (www.reggiochildren.it/?lang=en) is an organization that was founded in 1994 to promote the rights of children and to organize the exchanges between Reggio Emilia's municipal early learning programs and teachers, academics, and researchers worldwide. In 2003, Rinaldi spoke at length about the concept of the teacher as researcher. Being "open towards others and towards everything that is produced by the encounter with others" attests to the teacher as researcher and the school as a place of research (Rinaldi, 2003, p. 3). For Rinaldi, "the school of research is a school of participation" (p. 3). A recent report from Rinaldi (2013) on reimagining childhood provides a testament to this concept with a visual impact. In this media-rich flipbook, Rinaldi (2013) speaks to the teacher who sees him- or herself as a learner and as a researcher, calling for us to make endless efforts because together with our children, we could "understand and live learning as an act of love" (p. 61). To read more from Rinaldi, see www.reggioalliance.org/downloads/researcher:rinaldi.pdf and www.thinkers.sa.gov.au/rinaldiflipbook.

PEDAGOGICAL TOOLS

In Chapter 2, we introduced the mosaic approach in the Featured Research section. In this final chapter, we return to this method of teacher research in more depth to illustrate how it can be used as a pedagogical tool (Clark, 2011). Clark and Moss (2011) determined that using the mosaic approach not only encourages early learning professionals to give children a voice, but it also provides a framework for teacher research. In the mosaic approach, participatory tools such as cameras, book-making, tours, and map-making support children in creating and documenting their perspectives. When children and adults reflect on the materials produced, children have an opportunity to share their thoughts.

The mosaic approach employs a specific methodology for exploring practice and learning environments in order to understand the perspectives of others. It has multiple components, as listed in Table 12.2. The mosaic approach is a way for early learning professionals to view themselves as researchers exploring environmental perspectives of those within the community. It helps programs to become "living spaces" for children and adults, where each is attuned to the other person's capabilities and needs (Clarke & Moss, 2011).

Table 12.2 The Mosaic Approach

Method	Description
Observation	Narrative accounts.
Child conferencing	A short, structured interview, one on one or in a group.
Using cameras	Children using cameras to take photographs of important things.
Tours	Tours directed and recorded by the children.
Map-making	2D representations of the site using children's own photographs and drawings.
Interviews	Informal interviews with practitioners and parents.

Source: Clarke & Moss, 2011.

PROFESSIONAL CASE STUDY

Two years after becoming a college lab school, the early childhood education faculty of the college and the early learning professionals working in the lab school identified the need to engage in some form of research. The early learning professionals were "newbies" to action research, but they were searching for a way to bring clarity to their practice. They recognized that they had been in their positions for more than five years and were feeling some comfort in their roles, but they also had some disequilibrium because they felt they were becoming complacent in their practice. Their leader arranged for them to participate in on-site professional learning on action research. They became intrigued with how they could engage in conducting action research at their site. Collectively, they determined that they had questions about their programming. One of their key questions was whether children were being provided with the freedom to choose their play experiences during the morning portion of their programming. With the help of an external coach, they made the commitment to learn about action research and implement an action research project.

The team developed an action research model, whereby each early learning professional took on one of their core questions to explore. As they engaged in the process, they realized within two weeks of the project that they were gaining incredible insights into their personal practices and the practices of their colleagues. As a professional group, they began to have deep, reflective discussions about their practices and personal philosophies, and those of the lab school. They began to seek out research from other sources to compare and contrast what other researchers had discovered on similar topics. As they embraced the learning that occurred from action research, the lab school professionals recognized that their success in embarking on action research had been supported by the professional learning process, the use of critical friends, their individual and collective reflective experiences, and their desire to share their learning experiences with other professionals. In combination, all of these factors had increased the quality of the children's play and learning experiences.

The process of action research changed the workplace at the lab school. The lab school had been transformed into a place of inquiry among staff and children. The early learning professionals heard the voices of their colleagues, children, and families. They wrote about what they saw and did to improve their practice. They determined that not only did action research help them improve their practice, but the process also supported them in becoming professionals and becoming researchers.

REFLECTION QUESTIONS FOR SELF-LEARNING

The early learning professionals at the lab school took an incredible risk in moving from a place of comfort in their practice to a place of uncertainty. They engaged in professional learning, they embraced action research, and they transformed their practice to include action research. Ask yourself the following questions when discussing action research or being a critical friend with colleagues during an action research project:

1. What advice would you give to other colleagues who would like to engage in action research? How would you suggest they begin the process?

2. How might you recommend a director manage the process if some professionals wish to engage in action research and others do not?

3. How might you get children involved in action research? Are there risks for children and families when professionals begin the process of action research?

4. Do you think that all staff members have the ability to engage in action research? Why or why not?

5. What types of information would you share with parents when an early learning professional begins action research?

6. How might action research make a difference to children's experiences and those of early learning professionals?

BIG IDEAS FOR DIALOGIC LEARNING

Action research and professional learning can be enriched with the everyday actions, documents, and artifacts that are created to support children in their play and learning. Think about engaging in an action research project that focuses on how to trigger children's interests in the use of block play among the children. How might you set up the research question? Why is this a question? How might you acquire information about the children's use of blocks currently? How might you seek out information from the children about block play?

How might previous pedagogical documentations help you in seeking answers to the question? What types of questions and conversations might you have with your critical friends? Think about how you can place materials or "plant seeds of ideas" with the children that may spark a sense of curiosity in using blocks in their play. How do you determine if the question is worth researching? How might the question be related to an early learning professional's philosophy?

Consider the following questions about program planning that reflects big ideas:

1. You are required to think about an early learning program that you have observed. Identify a core question that you would like to explore. What is the question and why is it important to you?

2. In small groups, share ideas about how you, as a group of early learning professionals, could proceed to use action research to seek answers to your question.

3. Examine the cycle of action research in Figure 12.4 on page 285. Use that process to determine areas that you are comfortable with and areas in which you would require further professional development. How might you gain professional learning in the areas that require further development?

4. Assume you are required to implement your first action research project next week. Write a reflective note to your critical friend describing your feelings, concerns, and questions about the process. How might this support your understanding of action research? How might discussions with your critical friend support you?

VISION

It is our vision that early learning students will develop the skills to design and implement action research strategies in their practice. Action research is one way to examine practice, use research to inform practice, and seek answers to questions. Claiming your voice, exploring the questions that surface in your practice, seeking answers and perspectives on data that evolve from your research, and sharing your new knowledge with critical friends and colleagues all will increase the quality of the environments and the experiences extended to children. The process of research informs the growth and development of teachers and children (Moore & Gilliard, 2008). Without growth, teachers are at risk of becoming complacent, less curious, and less motivated to support children in their quest to question, explore, and discover. We believe that action research offers early learning professionals many options in their daily practice. It sets the stage for listening to the children and for promoting inquiry and problem solving of questions that evolve from the members of the learning community. Early learning students and professionals use action research as a way to further their practice and to create new knowledge that will advance the profession of early childhood education. We encourage you to embrace action research as a model of practice that will be instrumental for you in making decisions about your daily practice and your personal philosophy about how children learn through their play.

MAKING CONNECTIONS

Throughout the textbook, we have encouraged early learning students and professionals to make connections using technology as a tool. The concept of the connected educator supports the idea of the teacher as a researcher. It allows for the embracing of many perspectives as attempts are made to reach out through technology to children, families, and other educators. We encourage you to visit this site for support on surviving and thriving in a connected world: http://connectededucators.org/cem/cem-getting-started.

KEY TERMS

Action research 284
Data 280
Ethics 279
Qualitative research 280
Quantitative research 280

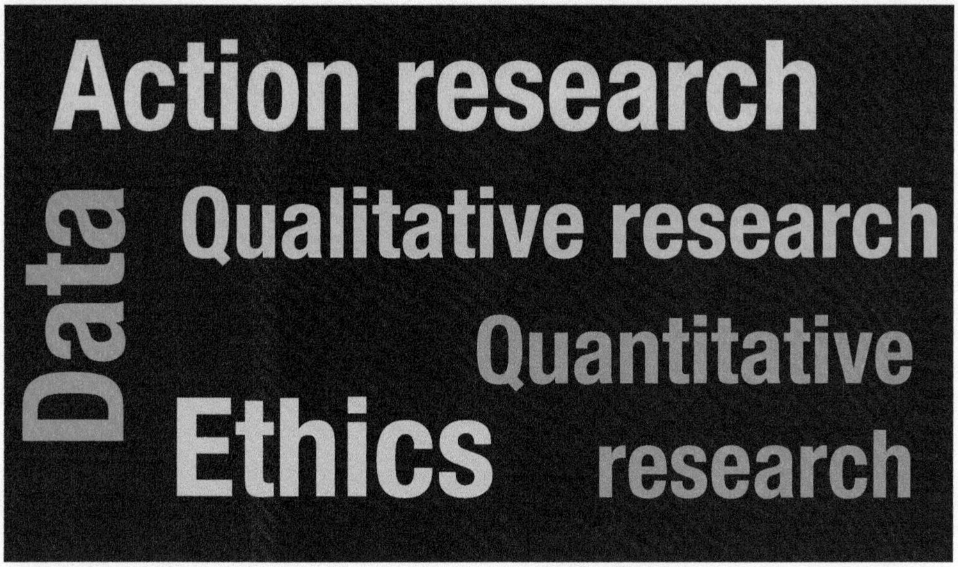

Figure 12.6 Key terms wordle

SUMMARY

This chapter has introduced the concept of research as an essential part of practice for early learning professionals, who can reflect on how research informs practice by thinking about and discussing the following:

1. Early learning professionals are acknowledging the importance of engaging in research to inform their practice. They have dual roles as both teacher and researcher.
2. There are two types of research methods: qualitative and quantitative. The type of research question that early learning professionals wish to explore determines the research method used.
3. Pedagogical documentation complements qualitative research methods, such as action research and narrative inquiry methods.
4. Conducting action research or narrative inquiry in early learning programs supports teachers in gaining new learning that may be transferred to their practice and ultimately to the children through programming, environmental designs, and relationships.
5. Being involved in research influences the growth and development of early learning professionals, in addition to contributing to the effectiveness of programming.

For Further Thought

Embrace your self-image as a researcher and visit these sites for additional support on action research and the value of teacher research: www.sagepub.com/upm-data/27030_2.pdf and http://www.naeyc.org/files/naeyc/file/vop/Voices-Stremmel%281%29.pdf.

References

Ainsworth, M. (1979). *Patterns of attachment*. New York, NY: Halsted Press.

Allan, J. (2006). Learning outcomes in higher education. *Studies in Higher Education, 21*(1), 93–108.

Alsop-Shields, L., & Mohay, H. (2001). John Bowlby and James Robertson: Theorists, scientists and crusaders for improvements in the care of children in hospital. *Journal of Advanced Nursing, 35*(1), 50–58. doi:10.1046/j.1365-2648.2001.01821.x.

Ampartzaki, M., Kypriotaki, M., Voreadou, C., Dardioti, A., & Stathi, I. (2013). Communities of practice and participatory action research: The formation of a synergy for the development of museum programmes for early childhood. *Educational Action Research, 21*(1), 4–27.

Anderson, E. (2013). Preparing the next generation of early childhood teachers: The emerging role of interprofessional education and collaboration in teacher education. *Journal of Early Childhood Teacher Education, 34*(1), 23–25.

Ang, L. (2010). Critical perspectives on cultural diversity in early childhood: Building an inclusive curriculum and provision. *Early Years, 30*(1), 41–52.

Arce, E. M. (2000). *Curriculum for young children*. Albany, NY: Delmar.

Arlemalm-Hagser, E. (2010). Gender choreography and microstructures: Early childhood professionals' understanding of gender roles and gender patterns in outdoor play and learning. *European Early Childhood Education Research Journal, 18*(4), 515–525.

Arnone, M., Small, R., Shauncey, S., & McKenna, H. P. (2011). Curiosity, interest and engagement in technology-pervasive learning environments: A new research agenda. *Education Tech Research Development, 59*, 181–198.

Asanova, J. (2008). Educating ethnic minority children: The case in Canada. *The Education of Diverse Student Populations, 2*, 65–77.

Association of Early Childhood Educators Ontario. (2013). *Discussion paper: A dialogue on professional learning for registered early childhood educators*. Retrieved from www.aeceo.ca/files/user_files/AECEO%20professional%20learning%20discussion%20paper%20June%202013.pdf.

Atweh, B., Kemmis, S., & Weeks, P. (1998). *Action research in practice: Partnerships for social justice*. London, England: Routledge.

Australian Government Department of Education, Employment and Workplace Relations. (2009). *Belonging, being and becoming: The early years learning framework for Australia*. Sydney, Australia: Commonwealth of Australia.

Avis, J., & Bathmaker, A. (2004). Critical pedagogy, performativity and a politics of hope: Trainee further education lecturer practice. *Research in Post-Compulsory Education, 9*(2), 301–316.

Babalis, J. (2013). *Transforming our learning environment into a space of possibilities: Illuminating the path of inquiry-based learning for others working with young children*. Toronto, ON: York University.

Ball, J. (2012). Identity and knowledge in Indigenous young children's experiences in Canada. *Childhood Education, 88*(5), 286–291.

Barratt Hacking, E., Barratt, R., & Scott, W. (2007). Engaging children: Research issues around participation and environmental learning. *Environmental Education Research, 13*(4), 529–544.

Barrera, I., & Corso, R. M. (2003). *Skilled dialogue: Strategies for responding to cultural diversity in early childhood*. Baltimore, MD: Paul H. Brookes.

Bassett, C. (2005). Emergent wisdom: Living a life in widening circles. *ReVision: A Journal of Consciousness and Transformation, 27*(4), 6–11.

Beach, J., & Friendly, M. (2013). *The state of early childhood education and care in Canada 2010: Trends and analysis*. Childcare Resource and Research Unit. Retrieved from www.childcarecanada.org/sites/default/files/state_ecec_canada_2010_CRRU.pdf.

Belenky, M. F., Clinchy, G., Goldberger, N., & Traule, J. (1986). *Women's ways of knowing: The development of self, voice, and mind*. New York, NY: BasicBooks.

Bennett, J. (2000). *Goals, curricula and quality monitoring in early childhood systems*. Organisation for Economic Co-operation and Development, consultative meeting on international developments in ECEC, Paris, France.

Bennett, J. (2005). Curriculum issues in national policy-making. *European Early Childhood Education Research Journal, 13*(2), 5–23.

Bennett, J., & Leonarduzzi, S. (2004). *Starting strong: Curricula and pedagogies in early childhood education and care*. Paris, France: Organisation for Economic Co-operation and Development.

Benson, P. (2003, November 10). *Spirituality: Its role in child and youth development*. Presented at Tufts University, Medford, MA.

Bergen, D. (2002). The role of pretend play in children's cognitive development. *Early Childhood Research and Practice, 4* (1), 1–13.

Berk, L. E. (2006). *Child development* (7th ed.). Toronto, ON: Pearson.

Berlyne, D. E. (1954). A theory of human curiosity. *British Journal of Psychology, 45*(3), 180–191.

Berlyne, D. E. (1960). *Arousal, conflict and curiosity*. New York, NY: McGraw-Hill.

Berlyne, D. E. (1978). Curiosity and learning. *Motivation and Emotion, 2*(2), 97–175.

Best Start Expert Panel on Early Learning. (2007). *Early learning for every child today: A framework for Ontario early childhood settings*. Toronto, ON: Ontario Ministry of Education.

Bhabha, H. K. (2004). *The location of culture*. London, England: Routledge.

Biesta, G. J. J., Lawy, R., & Kelly, N. (2008). Understanding young people's citizenship learning in everyday life: The role of contexts, relationships and dispositions. *Education Citizenship and Social Justice, 4*(1), 5–24.

Bilton, H. (2002). *Outdoor play in the early years: Management and innovation.* London, England: David Fulton.

Birbili, M. (2006). Mapping knowledge: Concept maps in early childhood education. *Early Childhood Research and Practice,* 8(2), 1–10.

Blandford, S., & Knowles, C. (2011). Assessment for learning: A model for the development of a child's self-competence in the early years of education. *Education 3–13, 40*(5), 487–499. doi:10.1080/03004279.2010.548818.

Blank, J. (2010). Early childhood teacher education: Historical themes and contemporary issues. *Journal of Early Childhood Teacher Education, 31*(4), 391–405.

Block, P. (1987). *The empowered manager: Positive political skills at work.* San Francisco, CA: Jossey-Bass.

Bodrova, E., & Leong, D. J. (1996). *Tools of the mind: The Vygotskian approach to early childhood education.* Upper Saddle River, NJ: Merrill Prentice Hall.

Bodrova, E., & Leong, D. J. (2008). Developing self-regulation in kindergarten: Can we keep all the crickets in the basket? *Young Children on the Web, 63*(2), 56–58.

Bolduc, Y., Schneider, J., Gerlach, A., & Gray Smith, M. (2009). *Creating pathways—an Aboriginal early years five year strategic plan.* Victoria, BC: Little Drum Consulting.

Bone, J. (2005). An ethical journey: Rights, relationships and reflexivity. *Australian Journal of Early Childhood, 30*(1), 1–6.

Bone, J. (2007). *Everyday spirituality: Supporting the spiritual experience of young children in three early childhood education settings* (Ph.D. thesis). Massey University, Palmerston North, New Zealand.

Bone, J. (2008). Breaking bread: Spirituality, food and early childhood education. *International Journal of Children's Spirituality, 10*(3), 307–317.

Borgia, E., & Schuler, D. (1996). *Action research in early childhood education.* Retrieved from ERIC database, (ED401047).

Borgman, D. (2006). Bridging the gap: From social science to congregations, researchers to practitioners. In E. Roehlkeopartain, P. King, L. Wagener, & P. Benson (Eds.), *The handbook of spiritual development in childhood and adolescence* (pp. 435–445). Thousand Oaks, CA: Sage.

Bowlby, J. (1973). *Attachment and loss: Separation.* New York, NY: Basic Books.

Bowne, M., Cutler, K., DeBates, D., Gilkerson, D., & Stremmel, A. (2010). Pedagogical documentation and collaborative dialogue as tools of inquiry for pre-service teachers in early childhood education: An exploratory narrative. *Journal of the Scholarship of Teaching and Learning, 10*(2), 48–59.

Boyer, W. (2009). Crossing the glass wall: Using preschool educators' knowledge to enhance parental understanding of children's self-regulation and emotion regulation. *Early Childhood Education, 37,* 175–182.

Boyle, L. (2006). Environmental experiences in child care. *National Childcare Accreditation Council (NCAC), 19,* 14–17.

Bredekamp, S. (1987). *Developmentally appropriate practice in early childhood programs serving young children from birth through age 8* (expanded ed.). Washington, DC: National Association for the Education of Young Children.

Bredekamp, S., & Copple, C. (1997). *Developmentally appropriate practice in early childhood education.* Washington, DC: National Association for the Education of Young Children.

Bresier, L. (2013). Embodied narrative inquiry: A methodology of connection. *Journal of Digital Learning in Teacher Education, 29*(4). doi:10.1177/1321103X06027010201.

Bromley, H., & Scott, P. (2004). Fifty exciting ideas for small world play. Birmingham, England: Lawrence Educational Publications.

Bronfenbrenner, U. (1979). *The ecology of human development: Experiments by nature and design.* Cambridge, MA: Harvard University Press.

Bronson, M. B. (2000). *Self-regulation in early childhood: Nature and nurture.* New York, NY: The Guilford Press.

Brookfield, S. (2006). *The skillful teacher.* San Francisco, CA: Jossey-Bass.

Brown, A. L., & Campione, J. C. (1998). Designing a community of young learners: Theoretical and practical lessons. In N. M. Lambert & B. L. McCombs (Eds.), *How students learn: Reforming schools through learner centred education* (pp. 153–186). Washington, DC: American Psychological Association.

Bruce, T. (2005). *Early childhood education.* London, England: Hodder & Stoughton.

Bruner, J. (1978). The role of dialogue in language acquisition. In A. Sinclair, R. J. Jarvelle, & W. J. M. Levelt (Eds.), *The child's concept of language.* New York, NY: Springer-Verlag.

Bruner, J. (2004). Life as narrative. *Social Research, 71,* 691–710.

Bruner, J. (2006). *In search of pedagogy: The selected works of Jerome S. Bruner* (Vol. 2). London, England; New York, NY: Routledge.

Bullough, R., Knowles, G., & Crow, N. (1991). *Emerging as a teacher.* New York, NY: Routledge.

Burgess, J., & Fleet, A. (2009). Frameworks for change: Four recurrent themes for quality in early childhood curriculum initiatives. *Asia-Pacific Journal of Teacher Education, 37*(1), 45–61.

Burke, C. (2007). Inspiring spaces: Creating creative classrooms. *Creative Spaces for Learning, 5*(2), 35–37.

Burke, R. W. (1999). Diverse family structures: Implications for P-3 teachers. *Journal of Early Childhood Teacher Education, 20*(3), 245–251.

Buysse, V., Sparkman, K., & Wesley, P. (2003). Communities of practice: Connecting what we know with what we do. *Exceptional Children, 69*(3), 263–277.

Buysse, V., & Wesley, P. W. (2006). Evidence-based practice: How did it emerge and what does it really mean for the early childhood field? In V. Buysse & P. W. Wesley (Eds.), *Evidence-based practice in the early childhood field* (pp. 1–34). Washington, DC: Zero to Three.

Cadwell, L. B. (2003). *The Reggio approach to early childhood education: Bringing learning to life.* New York, NY: Teachers College Press.

Caldwell, B. (2004). What's in a name? ChildCare Exchange.com. Retrieved from www.childcareexchange.com/resources/free_resources.php.

Campbell, K., Jamsek, M., & Jolley, P. D. (2005, Fall). Planning holiday celebrations: An ethical approach to developing policies and practices. *Texas Child Care,* 24–31.

Canadian Association for Young Children. (2006). *Young children have the right to learn through play* (position statement). Retrieved from www.cayc.ca/node/140.

Cannella, G. S. (1997). *Deconstructing early childhood education: Social justice and revolution*. New York, NY: Peter Lang.

Carr, M. (2000, July 9–12). *Let me count the ways (to do assessment)*. Proceedings of the Practice, Policy and Politics Conference, Victoria University of Wellington, New Zealand: New Zealand Educational Institute.

Carr, M. (2001). *Assessment in early childhood settings: Learning stories*. London, England: Paul Chapman.

Carr, M., Cowie, B., Gerrity, R., Jones, C., & Pohio, L. (2001). Democratic learning and teaching communities in early childhood: Can assessment play a role? In B. Webber & I. Mitchell (Eds.), *Early childhood education for a democratic society* (pp. 27–36). Wellington, New Zealand: New Zealand Council for Educational Research.

Carr, M., May, H., Podmore, V., Cubey, P., Hatherly, A., & Macartney, B. (2007). Learning and teaching stories: Action research on evaluation in early childhood in Aotearoa-New Zealand. *European Early Childhood Education Research Journal, 10*(2), 115–125.

Carter, M. (2010, November/December). Using learning stories to strengthen teachers' relationships with children. *Child Care Exchange*, 40–43.

Carter, M., & Curtis, D. (2003). *Designs for living and learning*. St. Paul, MN: Redleaf Press.

Carter, M., & Curtis, D. (2007). *Learning together with young children*. St. Paul, MN: Redleaf Press.

Carter, M., & Curtis, D. (2010). *The visionary director: A handbook for dreaming, organizing and improvising in your center*. St. Paul, MN: Redleaf Press.

Cavallini, I., Filippini, T., Vecchi, V., &Trancossi, L. (2011). *The wonder of learning*. Reggio Emilia, Italy: Reggio Children.

Center for Applied Special Technology. (2002). Universal design for learning. Retrieved from www.cast.org/udl.

Center for Universal Design. (2008). About UD. Retrieved from www.ncsu.edu/ncsu/design/cud/about_ud/about_ud.htm.

Chak, A. (2007). Teachers' and parents' conceptions of children's curiosity and exploration. *International Journal of Early Years Education, 15*(2), 141–159.

Chakraborty, A., Patrick, L., & Lambri, M. (2013). Racism and mental illness in the UK. In R. Woolfolk & L. Allen (Eds.), *Mental disorders—theoretical and empirical perspectives* (pp. 119–155). Retrieved from http://dx.doi.org/10.5772/46217.

Child Care Human Resources Sector Council. (2010). *Occupational standards for early childhood educators*. Ottawa, ON: Author.

Childcare Resource and Research Unit. (2013). *The state of early childhood education and care in Canada 2010: Trends and analysis*. Toronto, ON: Author.

Church, E. (2007). Exploring children's big questions. *Scholastic Early Childhood Today, 21*(4), 44–45.

Clark, A. (2011). Ways of seeing: Using the Mosaic approach to listen to young children's perspectives. In A. Clark, A. Kjorholt, & P. Moss (Eds.), *Beyond listening: Children's perspectives on early childhood services* (pp. 29–49). Bristol, England: Policy Press.

Clark, A., & Moss, P. (2011). *Listening to young children: The Mosaic approach* (2nd ed.). London, England: National Children's Bureau.

Clark, A., Kiorholt, A. T., & Moss, P. (2005). *Beyond listening: Children's perspectives on early childhood services*. Bristol, England: Policy Press.

Clarkin-Phillips, J., & Carr, M. (2012). An affordance network for engagement: Increasing parent and family agency in an early childhood education setting. *European Early Childhood Education Research Journal, 20*(2), 177–187.

Cochran-Smith, M., & Lytle, S. (1991). Learning to teach against the grain. *Harvard Educational Review, 61*(3), 279–310.

Coffin, G., & Williams, M. (1989). *Children's outdoor play in the built environment*. London, England: The National Children's Play and Recreation Unit.

Conn-Powers, M., Cross, A. F., Traub, E. K., & Hutter-Pishgahi. (2006, September). The universal design of early education: Moving forward for all children. *Beyond the Journal: Young Children on the Web*. Retrieved from www.iidc.indiana.edu/styles/iidc/defiles/ECC/ECC_Universal_Design_Early_Education.pdf.

Cope, B., Kalantzis, M., & Lankshear, C. (2005). A contemporary project: An interview. *E-learning, 2*, 192–207.

Corsaro, W. (2000). Early childhood education, children's peer cultures, and the future of childhood. *European Early Childhood Education Research Journal, 8*(2), 89–102.

Corsaro, W. (2003). *We're friends, right? Inside kids' culture*. Washington, DC: Joseph Henry Press.

Corsaro, W. A., & Johannesen, B. (2007). The creation of new cultures in peer interaction. In J. Valsiner & A. Rosa (Eds.), *The Cambridge handbook of sociocultural psychology* (pp. 444–459). Cambridge, NY: Cambridge University Press.

Cortazzi, M., & Jin, L. (2007). Narrative learning: EAL and metacognitive development. *Early Childhood Development and Care, 177*, 645–660.

Costa, A., & Kallick, B. (1993). Through the lens of a critical friend. *Educational Leadership, 51*(2), 49–51.

Craig, C. J., & Deretchin, L. F. (2010). *Cultivating curious and creative minds: The role of teachers and teacher educators. Teacher education yearbook*. Lanham, MD: Rowman & Littlefield.

Crossley, B., & Dietze, B. (2002). Opening the door to the outdoors. Retrieved from http://childcare.basecorp.com/siteuploads/document/Opening%20the%20Door%20to%20the%20Outdoors.pdf.

Crowther, I. (2003). *Creating effective learning environments*. Scarborough, ON: Thomson Nelson.

Csikszentmihalyi, M. (2002). The good work. *The North American Montessori Teachers' Association Journal, 27*(3), 67–82.

Cuffaro, H. (1995). *Experimenting with the world: John Dewey and the early childhood classroom*. New York, NY: Teachers College Press.

Curtis, D., Lebo, D., Cividanes, W., & Carter, M. (2013). *Reflecting in communities of practice: A workbook for early childhood educators*. St. Paul, MN: Redleaf Press.

Dahlberg, G. (2003). Pedagogy as a loci of an ethics of an encounter. In M. Bloch, K. Holmlund, I. Moqvistamd, & T. Popkewitz (Eds.), *Governing children, families and education: Restructuring the welfare state* (pp. 3–35). New York, NY: Palgrave Macmillan.

Dahlberg, G., & Moss, P. (2005). *Ethics and politics in early childhood education*. London, England: RoutledgeFalmer.

Dahlberg, G., Moss, P., & Pence, A. (1999). *Beyond quality in early childhood education and care: Postmodern perspectives*. London, England: Falmer Press.

Dahlberg, G., Moss, P., & Pence, A. (2006). *Beyond quality in early childhood education and care: Postmodern perspectives* (2nd ed.). London, England: Falmer Press.

Daitsman, J. (2011). Exploring gender identity in early childhood through story dictation and dramatization. *Voices of Practitioners*, 6(1). Retrieved from www.naeyc.org/files/naeyc/file/vop/VOP_Daitsman_Final(1).pdf.

Daniels, E., & Gamper, C. (2011). The yin and yang of Montessori and Waldorf in early childhood education. *Commongroundmag*, 62–63. Retrieved from http://learningcompanion.files.wordpress.com/2010/12/commonground-decjan-nlcarticle_page_4.jpg.

Darling-Hammond, L. (1997). Quality teaching: The critical key to learning. *Principal*, 77(1), 5–11.

David, T. (1998). Changing minds: Young children and society. In L. Abbott & A. Langston (Eds.), *Birth to three matters supporting the framework of effective practice* (pp. 16–25). Maidenhead, England: Open University Press.

Davis, B. (2000). *A body of writing 1900–1999*. Walnut Creek, CA: AltaMira Press.

Davis, J. (1998). Young children, environmental education, and the future. *Early Childhood Education Journal*, 26(2), 117–123.

Day, C. (2000). Effective leadership and reflective practice. *Reflective Practice*, 1(1), 113–127.

Department of Education and Early Childhood Development. (2009). *Victorian Early Years Learning and Development Framework for all children from birth to eight years*. Melbourne, Australia: State Government of Victoria.

Derman-Sparks, L., & Edwards, J. O. (2010). *Anti-bias education for young children and ourselves*. Washington, DC: National Association for the Education of Young Children.

Derman-Sparks, L., & Ramsey, P. G. (2005). What if all the children in my class are white? Anti-bias/multicultural education with white children. *Young Children*, 60(6), 20–27.

Deviney, J., Duncan, S., Harris, S., Rody, M., & Rosenberry, L. (2010a). *Inspiring spaces for young children*. Silver Springs, MD: Gryphon House.

Deviney, J., Duncan, S., Harris, S., Rody, M. A., & Rosenberry, L. (2010b). *Rating observation scale for inspiring environments: A companion observation guide for inspiring spaces for young children*. Silver Springs, MD: Gryphon House.

Dewey, J. (1903). Democracy in education. *The Elementary School Teacher*, 4(4), 193–204.

Dewey, J. (1913). *Interest and effort in education*. Boston, MA: Houghton Mifflin.

Dewey, J. (1934). *Art as experience*. New York, NY: Minton, Balch.

Dewey, J. (1966). *Democracy and education*. New York, NY: Free Press. Original work published 1916.

Dickson, B. (2007). Defining and interpreting professional knowledge in an age of performativity: A Scottish case-study. *Australian Journal of Teacher Education*, 32(4), 1–15.

Dietze, B. (2006). *Foundations of early childhood education: Learning environments and child care in Canada*. Toronto, ON: Pearson.

Dietze, B. (2013). How accessible and usable are our neighbourhood playgrounds for children who have mobility restrictions or use mobility devices? *Canadian Children*, 38(2), 14–20.

Dietze, B., & Kashin, D. (2012). *Playing and learning in early childhood education*. Toronto, ON: Pearson.

Dietze, B., & Kashin, D. (2013). Shifting views: Exploring the potential for technology integration in early childhood education programs/Changementd'opinion: Exploration du potentield'intégration de la technologiedans les programmesd' éducation de la petite enfance. *Canadian Journal of Learning and Technology/La revue canadienne de l'apprentissage et de la technologie*, 39(4).

Dillabough, J. (1999). Gender politics and conceptions of the modern teacher: Women, identity, and professionalism. *British Journal of Sociology of Education*, 20(3), 373–394.

Dolby, R. (2007). *The Circle of Security: Roadmap to building supportive relationships. Research in Practice Series*, 14(4). Watson, Australia: Early Childhood Education Australia.

Doyle, W. (1990). Themes in teacher education research. In W. R. Houston, M. Haberman, & J. Sikula (Eds.), *Handbook of research on teacher education* (pp. 3–24). New York, NY: Macmillan.

Driscoll, A., & Nagel, N. (2005). *Early childhood education: Birth–8: The world of children, families, and educators*. Boston: Allyn & Bacon.

Driscoll, E., & Lownds, N. (2007). The garden wonder wall: Fostering wonder and curiosity on multi-day garden field trips. *Applied Environmental Education & Communication*, 6(1), 105–112.

DuCette, J. P., Sewell, T. E., & Shapiro, J. P. (1996). Diversity in education: Problems and possibilities. In F. B. Murray (Ed.), *The teacher educator's handbook: Building a knowledge base for the preparation of teachers* (pp. 136–155). San Francisco, CA: Jossey-Bass.

Duhn, I. (2012). Making place for ecological sustainability in early childhood education. *Environmental Education Research*, 18(1), 19–29.

Dunphy, E. (2008). *Supporting early childhood development through formative assessment: A research paper*. Dublin, Ireland: National Council of Curriculum and Assessment.

Edwards, C., Gandini, L., & Forman, G. (1998). *The hundred languages of children: Advanced reflections*. Norwood, NJ: Ablex.

Edwards, S., & Nuttall, J. (Ed.). (2009). *Professional learning in early childhood settings*. Rotterdam, The Netherlands: Sense.

Edyburn, D. (2010). Would you recognize universal design for learning if you saw it? Ten propositions for new directions for the second decade of UDL. *Learning Disability Quarterly*, 33, 33–40.

Ellis, A. (2004). *Exemplars of curriculum theory*. New York, NY: Eye on Education.

Ellström, E., Ekholm, B., & Ellström, P. E. (2008). Two types of learning environments: Enabling and constraining a study of care work. *Journal of Workplace Learning*, 20(2), 84–97.

Epstein, A. (2007). *The intentional teacher: Choosing the best strategies for young children's learning*. Washington, DC: National Association for the Education of Young Children.

Erickson, D. (2008). Spirituality, loss and recovery in children with disabilities. *International Journal of Children's Spirituality*, 13(3), 287–296.

Erikson, E. (1963). *Childhood and society* (2nd ed.). New York, NY: W. W. Norton.

Evans, G. (2006). Child development and the physical environment. *The Annual Review of Psychology, 57*, 423–451.

Fagan, W. (2011). Politics and education: Decision making. *Morning Watch*. Retrieved from http://bit.ly/188p5yg.

Feeney, S. (2012). *Professionalism in early childhood education: Doing our best for young children*. Upper Saddle River, NJ: Pearson.

Fenech, M., Robertson, G., Sumsion, J., & Goodfellow, J. (2007). Working by the rules: Early childhood professionals' perceptions of regulatory requirements. *Early Child Development and Care, 177*(1), 93–106.

Fenech, M., & Sumsion, J. (2007) Early childhood teachers and regulation: Complicating power relations using a Foucauldian lens. *Contemporary Issues in Early Childhood, 8*(2), 109–122.

Ferrance, E. (2000). *Action research. Themes in education series*. Providence, RI: Brown University. Retrieved from www.brown.edu/academics/education-alliance/sites/brown.edu.academics.education-alliance/files/publications/act_research.pdf.

Fiala, R. (2007). Educational ideology and the school curriculum. In A. Benavot & C. Braslavsky (Eds.), *School knowledge in comparative and historical perspective: Changing curricula in primary and secondary education* (pp. 15–34). Dordrecht, The Netherlands: Springer.

Findlay, L., & Kohen, D. (2010). Child care for First Nations children living off reserve, Métis children, and Inuit children. *Canadian Social Trends, 90* (Catalogue No. 11-008-X).

Fjortoft, I. (2001). The natural environment as a playground for children: The impact of outdoor play activities in pre-primary school children. *Early Childhood Education Journal, 29*(2), 111–117.

Flanagan, K. (2011). *PEI early learning framework: Relationships, environments, experiences. The curriculum framework of the preschool excellence initiative*. Prepared for PEI Department of Education and Early Childhood Development. Retrieved from www.gov.pe.ca/photos/original/eecd_peielf2012.pdf.

Fleer, M., & Robbins, J. (2006). Diversity in the context of universal early childhood education: Family involvement or family exclusion? In M. Fleer, S. Edwards, M. Hammer, A. Kennedy, A. Ridgway, et al. (Eds.), *Early childhood learning communities: Sociocultural research in practice* (pp. 57–69). Sydney, Australia: Pearson Education.

Fleet, A. (2002). Revisiting adult work in early childhood settings: Shifting the frame. *Australian Journal of Early Childhood, 27*(1), 18–23.

Florez, I. R. (2011). Developing young children's self-regulation through everyday experiences. *Young Children, 66*(4), 46–51.

Follari, L. (2011). *Foundations and best practices in early childhood education: History, theories, and approaches to learning*. Boston, MA: Pearson.

Forman, G., & Fyfe, B. (1998). Negotiated learning through design, documentation, and discourse. In C. Edwards, G. Forman, & L. Gandini (Eds.), *The hundred languages of children* (2nd ed., pp. 239–260). Westport, CT: Ablex.

Forman, G., & Hall, E. (2005, Fall). Wondering with children: The importance of observation in early childhood education. *Early Childhood Research and Practice, 7*(2). Retrieved from http://ecrp.uiuc.edu/v7n2/forman.html.

Foucault, M. (1971). The order of discourse. In R. Young (Ed.), *Untying the text* (pp. 52–64). Boston, MA: Routledge & Kegan Paul.

Foucault, M. (2002). *The archaeology of knowledge*. London, England: Routledge.

Foucault, M. (1988). *Politics, policy, culture: Interviews and other writings 1977–1984* (L. Kritzman, Ed.). London, England: Routledge.

Fowler, J. W. (1981). *Stages of faith: The psychology of human development and the quest for meaning*. New York, NY: HarperOne.

Frankl, V. (1987). *Man's search for meaning*. London, England: Hodder & Stoughton.

Fraser, D., McGee, C., & Thrupp, M. (2008). Current and future issues. In C. McGee & D. Fraser (Eds.), *The professional practice of teaching* (pp. 255–273). Melbourne, Australia: Cengage.

Fraser, S. (2000). *Authentic childhood: Experiencing Reggio Emilia in the classroom*. Scarborough, ON: Nelson.

Fraser, S. (2011). *Authentic childhood: Experiencing Reggio Emilia in the classroom* (3rd ed.). Scarborough, ON: Nelson.

Fraser, S., & Gestwicki, C. (2012). *Authentic childhood: Experiencing Reggio Emilia in the classroom*. Toronto, ON: Delmar & Thomson Learning.

Freire, P. (1970). *Pedagogy of the oppressed*. New York, NY: Herder & Herder.

Fromberg, D. P. (1997). The professional and social status of the early childhood educator. In J. P. Isenberg & M. R. Jalongo (Eds.), *Major trends and issues in early childhood education: Challenges, controversies and insights* (pp. 188–204). New York, NY: Teachers College Press.

Frost, J., Wortham, S., & Reifel, S. (2005). *Play and child development* (2nd ed.). Upper Saddle River, NJ: Pearson/Merrill Prentice Hall.

Frost, J. L., Brown, P. S., Suttenby, J., & Thorton, C. (2004). *The department benefits of playgrounds*. Olney, MD: Association for Childhood Education International.

Frost, J. L., Wortham, S., & Reifel, S. (2012). *Play and child development* (4th ed.). New York, NY: Pearson.

Fu, V. R. (2002). The challenge to reinvent the Reggio Emilia approach: Pedagogy of hope and possibilities. In V. R. Fu, A. J. Stremmel, & L. T. Hill (Eds.), *Teaching and learning: Collaborative exploration of the Reggio Emilia Approach* (pp. 23–35). Upper Saddle River, NJ: Merrill Prentice Hall.

Galinsky, E. (2010). *Mind in the making: The seven essential life skills every child needs*. New York, NY: HarperCollins.

Gandini, L. (1993). Fundamentals of the Reggio Emilia approach to early education. *Young Children, 49*(1), 4–8.

Gandini, L. (1998). Educational and caring spaces. In C. Edwards, L. Gandini, & G. Forman (Eds.), *The hundred languages of children: The Reggio Emilia approach—advanced reflections* (pp. 161–178). Greenwich, CT: Ablex.

Gandini, L. (2004). Foundations of the Reggio Emilia approach. In J. Hendrick (Ed.), *First steps toward teaching the Reggio way: Accepting the challenge to change* (pp. 13–26). Upper Saddle River, NJ: Pearson.

Gandini, L. (2005). From the beginning of the *atelier* to materials as languages. In L. Gandini, L. Hill, L. Cadwell, & C. Schwall (Eds.), *In the spirit of the studio: Learning from the atelier of Reggio Emilia* (pp. 6–15). New York, NY: Teachers College Press.

Gardner, H. (1999). *Intelligence reframed: Multiple intelligences for the 21st century*. New York, NY: Basic Books.

Gardner, H. (2008). *The 25th anniversary of the publication of Howard Gardner's frames of mind: The theory of multiple intelligences*. Retrieved from www.old-pz.gse.harvard.edu/PIs/MIat25.pdf.

Geertz, C. (1973). *The interpretation of cultures*. New York, NY: Basic Books.

Gibbs, J. (2006). *Tribes learning communities*. Windsor, CA: Center Source.

Gill, T. (2006). *Providing for children and young people's play and informal recreation: The London plan—draft supplementary planning guidance*. London, England: The Mayor of London.

Gillen, J., & Hall, N. (2003). The emergence of early childhood literacy. In N. Hall, J. Larson, & J. Marsh (Eds.), *Handbook of early childhood literacy* (pp. 369–378). London, England: Sage.

Gillespie, L., & Seibel, N. (2006). Self-regulation: A cornerstone of early childhood development. *Young Children, 61*, 34–39.

Giroux, H. (1988). *Teachers as intellectuals: Toward a critical pedagogy of learning*. Westport, CT: Greenwood.

Goffin, S. G. (2000, August). *The role of curriculum models in early childhood education*. Retrieved from ERIC database (ED443597).

Goffin, S. G., & Wilson, C. (2001). *Curriculum models and early childhood education: Appraising the relationship* (2nd ed.). Upper Saddle River, NJ: Merrill Prentice Hall.

Goldberger, J., LueberingMohl, A., & Thompson, R. (2009). Psychological preparation and coping. In R. H. Thompson (Ed.), *The handbook of child life: A guide for pediatric psychosocial care* (pp. 160–198). Springfield, IL: Charles C. Thomas.

Goleman, D. (2000). Emotional intelligence: Issues in paradigm building. In D. Goleman & C. Cherniss (Eds.), *The emotionally intelligent workplace: How to select for, measure, and improve emotional intelligence in individuals, groups, and organizations*. San Francisco, CA: Jossey-Bass. Retrieved from www.eiconsortium.org/pdf/emotional_intelligencedigm_building.pdf.

Gonzalez-Mena, J., & Bhavnagri, N. P. (2000). Diversity and infant/toddler caregiving. *Young Children, 55*(5), 31–35.

Gonzalez-Mena, J., & Eyer, D. W. (2012). *Infants, toddlers, and caregivers: A curriculum of respectful, responsive, relationship-based care and education*. Whitby, ON: McGraw-Hill.

Goodliff, G. (2013). Spirituality expressed in creative learning: Young children's imagining play as space for mediating their spirituality. *Early Child Development and Care, 183*(8), 1054–1071.

Gordon, A. M., & Browne, K. W. (2011). *Beginning essentials in early childhood education*, Belmont, CA: Wadsworth.

Gorman, N., Lackney, J. A., Rollings, K., & Huang, T. (2007). Designer schools: The role of school space and architecture in obesity prevention. *Obesity, 15*, 2521–2530. doi:10.1038/oby.2007.300.

Government of British Columbia. (2008). *British Columbia early learning framework*. Victoria, BC: Ministry of Health and Ministry of Children and Family Development.

Government of Manitoba. (2011). *Early returns: Manitoba's early learning and child care curriculum framework for preschool centres and nursery schools*. Retrieved from www.gov.mb.ca/fs/childcare/pubs/early_returns_en.pdf.

Government of New Brunswick. (2008). *Early learning and child care curriculum*. Fredericton, NB: Department of Social Development.

Government of Quebec. (2007). *Meeting early childhood needs: Québec's educational program for childcare services*. Quebec City, PQ: Ministry of Family and Children.

Government of Saskatchewan. (2008). *Play and exploration: Early learning program guide*. Regina, SK: Ministry of Education.

Grace, C. (1992). The portfolio and its use: Developmentally appropriate assessment of young children. Retrieved from ERIC database, (ED351150).

Graetz, K. A., & Goliber, M. J. (2003). Designing collaborative learning places: Psychological foundations and new frontiers. In N. Van Note Chism & D. J. Bickford (Eds.), *The importance of physical space in creating supportive learning environments: New directions in teaching and learning, 92* (pp. 13–22). San Francisco, CA: Jossey-Bass.

Greenfield, C. (2003). Outdoor play: The case for risks and challenges in children's learning and development. *Safekids News, 21*, 5.

Greenman, J. (1988). *Caring spaces, learning places: Children's environments that work*. Redmond, WA: Exchange Press.

Greenman, J. (2005). Places for childhood in the 21st century: A conceptual framework. *Young Children on the Web*, 1–8.

Greenman, J. (2006). The importance of order. *Exchange*, 53–55.

Grieshaber, S. J. (2002). A national system of childcare accreditation: Quality assurance or a technique of normalization? In G. S. Cannella & J. L. Kincheloe (Eds.), *Kidworld: Childhood studies, global perspectives, and education* (pp. 161–180). New York, NY: Peter Lang.

Grisham-Brown, J., Hallam, R., & Brookshire, R. (2006). Using authentic assessment to evidence children's progress toward early learning standards. *Early Childhood Education Journal, 34*(1), 45–51.

Gulikers, J., Bastiaens, T., & Kirschner, P. (2007). Authentic assessment, student and teacher perceptions: The practical value of the five-dimensional framework. *Journal of Vocational Education & Training, 58*(3), 337–357.

Gurland, S. T. & Grolnick, W. S. (2008). Building rapport with children: Effects of adults' expected, actual, and perceived behaviour. *Journal of Social and Clinical Psychology, 27*(3), 226–253.

Hall, E. L., & Rudkin, J. (2011). *Seen and heard: Children's rights in early childhood education*. New York, NY: Teachers College Press.

Hall, E. T. (1966). *The hidden dimension*. New York, NY: Doubleday.

Hammerness, K. (2003). Learning to hope, or hope to learn? The role of vision in the early professional lives of teachers. *Journal of Teacher Education, 54*(43), 43–56.

Hansen, J. (1997). Researchers in our own classrooms: What propels teacher researchers? In D. Leu, C. Kinzer, & K. Hinchman (Eds.), *Literacies for the 21st century: Research and practice* (pp. 1–14). Chicago, IL: National Reading Conference.

Hare, J. (2011). Learning from Indigenous knowledge in education. In D. Long & O. P. Dickason (Eds.), *Visions of the heart: Canadian Aboriginal issues* (3rd ed., pp. 90–112). Oxford, England: Oxford University Press.

Harris, A., & Jones, M. (2010). *Professional learning communities in action*. London, England: Leannta Press.

Harris, K. (2007). Re-conceptualizing spirituality in the light of educating young children. *International Journal of Children's Spirituality, 12*(3), 263–275.

Harry, B. (2002). Trends and issues in serving culturally diverse families of children with disabilities. *The Journal of Special Education, 36*(3), 131–147.

Hatch, J. A. (2010). Rethinking the relationship between learning and development: Teaching for learning in early childhood classrooms. *The Educational Forum, 74*(3), 258–268.

Hawkins, D. (1974). *The informed vision.* Edison, NJ: Agathon.

Hawkins, D. (1998). Remarks: Malaguzzi story, other stories. In C. Edwards, L. Gandini, & G. Forman (Eds.), *The hundred languages of children: The Reggio Emilia Approach—advanced reflections* (2nd ed., pp. xix–xii). Westport, CT: Ablex.

Hawkins, D. (2000). *The roots of literacy.* Boulder, CO: University of Colorado Press.

Hawkins, D. (2002). *The informed vision: Essays on learning and human nature.* New York, NY: Algora.

Hawkins, J. (Ed.). (1996). *The spirituality of children.* London, England: The Way Publications.

Hay, D. (2007). Using concept maps to measure deep, surface and non-learning outcomes. *Studies in Higher Education, 32*(1), 39–57.

Hay, D., & Nye, R. (2006). *The spirit of the child.* London, England: Jessica Kingsley.

Health Canada. (2004). *Aboriginal Head Start On Reserve Program, Phase I—Evaluation—February 2003.* Retrieved from www.hc-sc.gc.ca/ahc-asc/performance/eval/index-eng.php#a4-5.

Healy, C. C., & Welchert, A. J. (1990). Mentoring relations: A definition to advance research and practice. *Educational Researcher, 19,* 17–21.

Heick, T. (n.d.). Five learning strategies that make students curious. TeachThought. Retrieved from www.teachthought.com/learning/5-learning-strategies-that-make-students-curious.

Helsby, G., Knight, P., McCulloch, G., Saunders, M., & Warburton, T. (1997, January). *Professionalism in crisis: A report to participants on the professional cultures of teacher's research project.* Lancaster, England: Lancaster University.

Helvacioglu, E., & Olgunturk, N. (2011). Colour contribution to children's wayfinding in school environments. *Optics & Laser Technology, 43,* 410–419.

Hendrick, J. (2004). Reggio Emilia and American schools: Telling them apart and putting them together: We can do it! In J. Hendrick (Ed.), *Next steps toward teaching the Reggio way: Accepting the challenge to change* (pp. 39–49). Upper Saddle River, NJ: Pearson Prentice Hall.

Hendrick, J., & Weissman, P. (2006). *The whole child* (8th ed.). Upper Saddle River, NJ: Prentice Hall.

Henninger, M. L. (2002). *Teaching young children: An introduction.* Upper Saddle River, NJ: Merrill Prentice Hall.

Hewett, V. M. (2001). Examining the Reggio Emilia approach to early childhood education. *Early Childhood Education, 29*(2), 95–100.

Hill, L. T., Stremmel, A. J., & Fu, V. R. (2005). *Teaching as inquiry: Rethinking curriculum in early childhood education.* Boston, MA: Pearson.

Holland, D., Lachicotte, D., Skinner, D., & Cain, C. (1998). *Identity and agency in cultural worlds.* Cambridge, MA: Harvard University.

hooks, b. (2003). *Teaching community: A pedagogy of hope.* New York, NY: Routledge.

hooks, b. (2010). *Teaching critical thinking: Practical wisdom.* New York, NY: Routledge.

Howe, N., Jacobs, E., & Fiorentino, L. M. (2000). The curriculum. In L. Prochner & N. Howe (Eds.), *Early childhood care and education in Canada* (pp. 11–65). Vancouver, BC: University of British Columbia Press.

Howes, C., & Tsao, C. (2012). Introducing a conceptual framework of professional development in early childhood education. In C. Howes, B. Hamre, & R. Pianta (Eds.), *Effective early childhood professional development: Improving teacher practice and child outcomes* (pp. 1–11). Baltimore, MD: Paul H. Brooks.

Hyde, B. (2008). The identification of four characteristics of children's spirituality in Australian Catholic primary schools. *International Journal of Children's Spirituality, 13*(2), 117–127.

Irwin, L., Siddiqui, A., & Herzman, C. (2007). *ECD: A powerful equalizer. Final report for the WHO Commission on the Social Determinants of Health.* Geneva, Switzerland: WHO.

Isbell, R., & Raines, S. (2003). *Creativity and the arts with young children.* New York, NY: Thompson Delmar Learning.

Jablon, J. R., Dombro, A. L., & Dichtelmiller, M. L. (2007). *The power of observation for birth through eight* (2nd ed.). Washington, DC: Teaching Strategies.

Jaeger, M., & Holm, A. (2007). Does parents' economic, cultural and social capital explain the social class effects on educational attainment in Scandinavia? *Social Science Research, 36,* 719–744.

Jenkins, H. (2006). *Convergence culture: Where old and new media collide.* New York, NY: New York University Press.

Jenkins, H., Clinton, K., Purushotma, R., Robinson, A. J., & Weigel, M. (2006). Confronting the challenges of participatory culture: Media education for the 21st century. Chicago, IL: The John D. and Catherine T. MacArthur Foundation. Retrieved from www.newmedialiteracies.org.

Jensen, B., & Mehlbye, J. (2009). *Indkredsningafcentralebegreber. I:Socialtudsatteboern I dagtilbud—indsatsog effect. Sammenfattende rapport.* Copenhagen, Denmark: AKF, DPU, NIRASKonsulenterne, Udviklingsforum.

Jenson, B. (2009). A Nordic approach to early childhood education (ECE) and socially endangered children. *European Early Childhood Education Research Journal, 17*(1), 7–21.

Jessee, P. O., & Gaynard, L. (2009). Paradigms of play. In R. H. Thompson (Ed.), *The handbook of child life: A guide for pediatric psychosocial care* (pp. 136–159). Springfield, IL: Charles C. Thomas.

Johnstone, B., Glass, B., & Oliver, R. (2007). Religion and disability: Clinical, research and training considerations for rehabilitation professionals. *Disability and Rehabilitation, 29*(15), 1153–1163.

Jones, E., & Nimmo, J. (1994). *Emergent curriculum.* Washington, DC: National Association for the Education of Young Children.

Jones, M., & Shelton, M. (2011). *Developing your portfolio: Enhancing your learning and showing your stuff.* New York, NY: Routledge.

Kagan, S. L., & Bowman, B. T. (Eds.). (1997). *Leadership in early care and education.* Washington, DC: National Association for the Education of Young Children.

Kagan, S. L., & Kauerz, K. (2012). *Early childhood systems: Transforming early learning*. New York, NY: Teachers College Press.

Kamii, C., & Devries, R. (1993). *Physical knowledge in preschool education: Implications of Piaget's theory*. New York, NY: Teachers College Press.

Karsten, L. (2005). It all used to be better? Different generations on continuity and change in urban children's daily use of space. *Children's Geographies, 3*(3), 275–290.

Kashin, D. (2009). *Reaching the top of the mountain: The impact of emergent curriculum on the practice and self-image of early childhood educators*. Koln, Germany: Lambert Academic.

Kashin, D. (2011, January/February). From theme based to emergent curriculum: Four teachers learn about themselves, the children and authentic practice. *Exchange Magazine*, 45–48.

Katz, L. (1993). Dispositions as educational goals. *ERIC Digest*. Champaign, IL: ERIC Clearinghouse on Elementary and Early Childhood Education. Retrieved from ERIC database (EDO-PS-93-10), http://ceep.crc.uiuc.edu/eecearchive/digests/1993/katzdi93.html.

Katz, L. G. (1994). The project approach. *ERIC Digest*. Champaign, IL: ERIC Clearinghouse on Elementary and Early Childhood Education. Retrieved from ERIC database (ED368509), http://ecap.crc.illinois.edu/eecearchive/digests/1994/lk-pro94.html.

Katz, L., & Chard, S. (1989). *Engaging children's minds: The project approach*. Norwood, NJ: Ablex.

Katz, L., & Chard, S. (2000). *Engaging children's minds: The project approach* (2nd ed.). Norwood, NJ: Ablex.

Kellett, M. (2011). *Researching with and for children and young people*. Centre for Young People background briefing series (No. 5). Lismore, Australia: Centre for Children and Young People, Southern Cross University.

Kellogg, E. T. (2010). *David Hawkins and the Pond Study: David and Frances Hawkins and the Mountain View Center for Environmental Education, Books One and Two*. Bloomington, IL: XLibris.

Kennedy, E., Dunphy, E., Dwyer, B., Hayes, G., McPhillips, T., Marsh, J., O'Conner, M., & Shiel, G. (2012). *Literacy in early childhood and primary education (3–8 years)* (Research Report No. 15). Dublin, Ireland: National Council for Curriculum and Assessment.

Kereluik, K., Mishra, P., Fahnoe, C., & Terry, L. (2013). What knowledge is of most worth: Teacher knowledge for the 21st century. *Journal of Digital Learning in Teacher Education, 29*(4), 127–140.

Keyes, C. (2000). The early childhood teacher's voice in the research community. *International Journal of Early Years Education, 8*(1), 3–13.

Kilderry, A. (2004). Critical pedagogy: A useful framework for thinking about early childhood curriculum. *Australian Journal of Early Childhood, 29*(4), 33–37.

Kirova, A. (2010). Children's representations of cultural scripts in play: Facilitating transition from home to preschool in an intercultural early learning program for refugee children. Diaspora, indigenous, and minority education. *Studies of Migration, Integration, Equity, and Cultural Survival, 4*(2), 74–91.

Kline, L. (2008). Documentation panel: The "making learning visible" project. *Journal of Early Childhood Teacher Education, 29*(1), 70–80.

Knowles, M. (1990). *The adult learner: A neglected species* (4th ed.). Houston, TX: Gulf.

Kohlberg, L. (1981). *Essays on moral development*. San Francisco, CA: Harper & Row.

Kohlberg, L., & Mayer, R. (1972). Development as the aim of education. *Harvard Educational Review, 42*, 449–496.

Kounin, J., & Sherman, L. (1979). School environments as behaviour settings. *Theory into Practice, 18*(3), 145–151.

Kritchevsky, S., Prescott E., & Walling, L. (1977). *Planning environments for young children: Physical space* (2nd ed.). Washington, DC: National Association for the Education of Young Children.

Kuby, C. R. (2013, March). Critical inquiry in early childhood education: A teacher's exploration. *Voices of Practitioners, 8*(1). Retrieved from www.naeyc.org/files/naeyc/file/Voices/Voices_Kuby_v8n1pdf.pdf.

Lackney, J. (2005). New approaches for school design. In F. W. English (Ed.), *The Sage handbook for educational administration* (pp. 506–537). Los Angeles, CA: Sage.

Langford, R. (2007). Who is a good early childhood educator? A critical study of differences within a universal professional identity in early childhood education preparation programs. *Journal of Early Childhood Teacher Education, 28*, 333–352.

Langford, R. (2010). *Innovations in provincial early learning curriculum frameworks* (Occasional Paper No. 24). Toronto, ON: Childcare Resource and Research Unit.

Lea, D., & Leibowitz, Z. B. (1983). A mentor: Would you know one if you saw one? *Supervisory Management, 28*(4), 32–35.

Leach, J., & Moon, B. (2008). *The power of pedagogy*. London, England: Sage.

Lenz Taguchi, H. (2010). *Going beyond the theory/practice divide in early childhood education: Introducing an intra-active pedagogy*. New York, NY: Routledge.

Levine, M. (2002). Why invest in professional development schools? *Educational Leadership, 59*(8), 65–68.

Lewin, K. (1997). *Resolving social conflicts and field theory in social science*. Washington, DC: American Psychological Association. Original work published 1951.

Li, C. (2010, April 26). *Making the case for open leadership* [video file]. Retrieved from http://vimeo.com/11241081.

Lim, C., & Able-Boone, H. (2005). Diversity competencies within early childhood teacher preparation: Innovative practices and future directions. *Journal of Early Childhood Teacher Education, 26*, 225–238.

Lindon, J. (2012). *Reflective practice and early years professionalism*. London, England: Hodder Education.

Lotherington, H., Holland, M., Sotoudeh, S., & Zentena, M. (2008). Project-based community language learning: Three narratives of multilingual story-telling in early childhood education. *The Canadian Modern Language Review, 65*(1), 125–145.

Loughran, J. (2006). *Developing a pedagogy of teacher education: Understanding teaching and learning about teaching*. New York, NY: Routledge.

Lyon, A. (2009, Summer). Teaching others: Preservice teachers' understandings regarding diverse families. *Multicultural Education*, 52–55.

Macfarlane, K., & Cartmel, J. (2008, June). Playgrounds of learning: Valuing competence and agency in birth to three-year-olds. *Australian Journal of Early Childhood, 33*(2), 41–48.

MacNaughton, G. (2009). *Shaping early childhood: Learners, curriculum and contexts.* Berkshire, England: Open University Press.

Mager, R. (1962). *Preparing instructional objectives* (2nd ed.). Belmont, CA: David Lake.

Maher, F. (2001). John Dewey, progressive education, and feminist pedagogies: Issues in gender and authority. In K. Wiler (Ed.), *Feminist engagements: Reading, resisting, and revisioning male theorists in education and cultural studies* (pp. 13–32). New York, NY: Routledge.

Malaguzzi, L. (1998). History, ideas and basic philosophy: An interview with LellaGandini. In C. Edwards, L. Gandini, & G. Forman (Eds.), *The hundred languages of children: The Reggio Emilia approach advanced reflections* (2nd ed., pp. 49–97). Greenwich, CT: Ablex.

Malaguzzi, L. (2001, October). Introduction to the hundred languages of children. *Rechild Newsletter, 5*(12). Reggio Emilia, Italy: Reggio Children. Retrieved from www.reggiochildren.it/wp-content/uploads/2012/08/rechild05.pdf.

Mannheim, K. (1959). *Ideology and utopia: An introduction to the sociology of knowledge. Harvest books HB 3.* New York, NY: Harcourt Brace. Original work published 1936.

Marbina, L., Church, A., & Taylor, C. (2011). *Victorian Early Years Learning and Development Framework evidence paper: Practice Principle 6: Integrated teaching and learning approaches.* Melbourne, Australia: Department of Education and Early Childhood Development.

Mardell, B., LeeKeenan, D., Given, H., Robinson, D., Merino, B., & Liu-Constant, Y. (2009). Zooms: Promoting schoolwide inquiry and improving practice. *Voices of Practitioners, 4*(1), 1–15.

Marsh, J. (2004). The techno-literacy practice of young children. *Journal of Early Childhood Research, 2*(1), 51–66.

Maslow, A. (1987). *Motivation and personality* (3rd ed.). New York, NY: Harper & Row.

Masney, D., & Cole, D. R. (Eds.). (2009). *Multiple literacies theory: A Deleuzian perspective.* Rotterdam, The Netherlands: Sense.

Mata, J. (2006). Nurturing spirituality in early childhood classrooms: The teacher's view. Retrieved from www.inter-disciplinary.net/wp-content/uploads/2011/02/jmataspaper.pdf.

Maybin, J., & Woodhead, M. (Eds.). (2003). *Childhoods in context.* Chichester, England: Wiley.

Maynard, T. (2007). Forest schools in Great Britain: An initial exploration. *Contemporary Issues in Early Childhood, 8*(4), 320–331. Retrieved from http://dx.doi.org/10.2304/ciec.2007.8.4.320.

Maynard, T., & Waters, J. (2007). Learning in the outdoor environment: A missed opportunity? *Early Years, 27*(3), 255–265.

McCain, M., & Mustard, F. (1999). *Reversing the real brain drain: Early years study final report.* Toronto, ON: Ontario Children's Secretariat.

McCain, M., Mustard, F., & Shanker, S. (2007). *Early years study 2: Putting science into action.* Toronto, ON: Council for Early Childhood Development.

McCain, M., Mustard, F., & McCuaig, K. (2011). *Early years study 3: Making decisions, taking action.* Toronto, ON: Margaret and Wallace McCain Family Foundation.

McCelland, D. C. (1987). *Human motivation.* Cambridge, NY: Cambridge University Press.

McGaha, C. G., Cummings, R., Lippard, B., & Dallas, K. (2011). Relationship building: Infants, toddlers and 2-year-olds. *Early Childhood Research and Practice, 13*(1). Retrieved from http://ecrp.uiuc.edu/v13n1/mcgaha.html.

McKernan, J. (1991). *Curriculum action research.* London, England: Kogan Page.

McManis, L., & Gunnewig, S. (2012). Finding the education in educational technology with early learners. *Young Children, 67*(3), 14–24.

McNiff, J., Whitehead, J., & Laidlaw, M. (1992). *Creating a good social order through action research.* Bournemouth, England: Hyde.

Meier, D. R., & Stremmel, A. J. (2010). Reflection through narrative: The power of narrative inquiry in early childhood teacher education. *Journal of Early Childhood Teacher Education, 31*(3), 249–257.

Millei, Z. (2011). Governing through early childhood curriculum, "the child," and "community." *European Education, 43*(1), 33–55.

Miller, P., Ostrosky, M., Laumann, B., Thorpe, E., Sanchez, S., & Fader-Dunner, L. (2003). Quality field experiences underlying performance mastery. In V. D. Stayton, P. S. Miller, & L. A. Dinnebeil (Eds.), *DEC personnel preparation in early childhood special education: Implementing DEC recommended practices* (pp. 113–138). Longmount, CO: Sopris West.

Miller, S. M., & Shoptaugh, S. (2004). Reflections on a journey of inspiration: Teacher change in public education. In J. Hendrick (Ed.), *Next steps toward teaching the Reggio way: Accepting the challenge to change* (pp. 241–256). Upper Saddle River, NJ: Pearson Prentice Hall.

Mills, G. E. (2011). *Action research: A guide for the teacher researcher.* Boston, MA: Pearson.

Ministry of Education. (1996). *Te Whariki: Early childhood curriculum.* Wellington, New Zealand: Learning Media.

Mitchell, S., Foulger, T. S., & Wetzel, K. (2009, September). Ten tips for involving families through internet-based communication. *Young Children,* 46–49.

Moomaw, S., & Jones, G. (2005, Winter). Native curriculum in early childhood classrooms. *Childhood Education,* 89–94.

Mooney, C. G. (2000). *Theories of childhood: An introduction to Dewey, Montessori, Erikson, Piaget and Vygotsky.* St. Paul, MN: Redleaf Press.

Moore, R. A., & Gilliard, J. L. (2008). Preservice teachers conducting action research in early education centers. *Journal of Early Childhood Teacher Education, 29*(1), 45–58.

Morgan, A., & Clark, B. (1987). *Sadie and the snowman.* New York, NY: Scholastic.

Moss, P. (2005). It is your choice. *Nursery World, 24,* 26–27.

Moss, P. (2006). Early childhood institutions as loci of ethical and political practice. *International Journal of Education Policy, Research and Practice, 7,* 127–136.

Moss, P. (2007). Bringing politics into the nursery: Early childhood education as a democratic practice. *European Early Childhood Education Research Journal, 15*(1), 5–20.

Moss, P. (2011). Democracy as first practice in early childhood education and care. In *Encyclopedia on early childhood development*. Retrieved from www.child-encyclopedia.com/Pages/PDF/MossANGxp1.pdf.

Moss, P., & Petrie, P. (2002). *From children's services to children's spaces: Public policy, children and childhood*. London, England: RoutledgeFalmer.

Mountain, V. (2005). Prayer is a positive activity for children: A report on recent research. *International Journal of Children's Spirituality, 10*(3), 291–305.

Mueller, C. (2010, July/August). Spirituality in children: Understanding and developing interventions. *Pediatric Nursing, 36*(4), 197–208.

Mustard, J. F. (2006). *Early childhood development and experience-based brain development: The scientific underpinnings of the importance of early childhood development in a globalized world*. Washington, DC: The Brooking Institute.

Muttart Foundation. (2010). *In the best interests of children and families: A discussion of early childhood education and care in Alberta*. Edmonton, AB: The Muttart Foundation. Retrieved from www.muttart.org/sites/default/files/report/ECEC%20Discussion%20Paper%201011_0.pdf.

Nair, P., Fielding, R., & Lackney, J. (2009). *The language of school design: Design patterns for 21st century schools*. Minneapolis, MN: DesignShare.Com.

National Association for the Education of Young Children. (2001). *Standards for early childhood professional preparation*. Retrieved from www.ncate.org/standard/new%20program%20standards/naeyc%202001.pdf.

National Association for the Education of Young Children. (2012). *Technology and interactive media as tools in early childhood programs serving children from birth through age 8* (Position statement).

National Playing Fields Association. (2000). *Best play: What play provisions should do for children*. London, England: National Playing Fields Association, Children's Play Council, & PLAYLINK.

National Research Council. (2012). *Education for life and work: Developing transferable knowledge and skills in the 21st century*. Washington, DC: The National Academies Press.

New, R. (2000). Reggio Emilia: Catalyst for change and conversation. *ERIC Digest*. Champaign, IL: ERIC Clearinghouse on Elementary and Early Childhood Education. Retrieved from ERIC database (ED447971).

New, R. (2003). Reggio Emilia: New ways to think about schooling. *Educational Leadership, 60*(7), 34–38.

New, R. S., Cochran, M., & Franzosa, S. D. (2006). Early childhood education: An international encyclopedia. *Education Faculty Book and Media Gallery*. Book 5. Retrieved from http://digitalcommons.fairfield.edu/education-books/5.

Newman, L., & Pollnitz, L. (2002). *Ethics in action: Introducing the Ethical Response Cycle*. Watson, Australia: Australian Early Childhood Association.

Nguyen, M. (2011). Closing the education gap: A case for Aboriginal early childhood education in Canada, a look at the Aboriginal Headstart program. *Canadian Journal of Education, 34*(3), 229–248.

Nicholson, S. (1971). How not to cheat children: The theory of loose parts. *Landscape Architecture, 62*(1), 30–35.

Nieto, S. (2005). *Why we teach*. New York, NY: Teachers College Press.

Nixon, H. (2011). From bricks to clicks: Hybrid commercial spaces in the landscape of early literacy and learning. *Journal of Early Childhood Literacy, 11*(2), 114–140.

Novinger, S., & O'Brien, L. (2003). Beyond "boring, meaningless shit" in the academy: Early childhood teacher educators under the regulatory gaze. *Contemporary Issues in Early Childhood, 4*(1), 3–31. Retrieved from http://dx.doi.org/10.2304/ciec.2003.4.1.4.

Nye, R. (1996). Childhood spirituality and contemporary developmental psychology. In R. Best (Ed.), *Education, spirituality and the whole child* (pp. 108–120). London, England: Cassell.

Oberhuemer, P. (2005). Conceptualising the early childhood pedagogue: Policy approaches and issues of professionalism. *European Early Childhood Education Research Journal, 13*(1), 5–16.

O'Brien, L., Novinger, S., & Leach-Bizari, A. (2007). What does it mean to be a "good" early childhood teacher? An analysis of themes in application essays submitted to two early childhood education teacher certification programs. *Journal of Early Childhood Teacher Education, 28*(3), 205–217.

O'Connor, A., & Diggins, C. (2002). *On reflection: Reflective practices for early childhood educators*. Lower Hutt, Aotearoo, New Zealand: Open Mind.

Office of Childcare. (2004). *NSW Curriculum framework for children's services: The practice of relationships. Essential provisions for children's services*. New South Wales, Australia: NSW Department of Community Services.

Oja, S. N., & Pine, G. J. (1989). Collaborative action research: Teachers' stages of development and school contexts. *Peabody Journal of Education, 64*(2), 96–115.

Ollin, R. (2008). Silent pedagogy and rethinking classroom practice: Structuring teaching through silence rather than talk. *Cambridge Journal of Education, 38*(2), 265–280.

Organisation for Economic Co-operation and Development. (2004). *Early childhood education and care policy: Canada country note*. OECD Directorate of Education. Retrieved from www.oecd.org/canada.

Osgood, J. (2006). Deconstructing professionalism in early childhood education: Resisting the regulatory gaze. *Contemporary Issues in Early Childhood, 7*(1), 5–14.

Pacini-Ketchabaw, V., & Pence, A. (2005). Contextualizing the reconceptualist movement in Canadian early childhood education. In V. Pacini-Ketchabaw & A. Pence (Eds.), *Early childhood education in motion: The reconceptualist movement in Canada* (pp. 5–20). Ottawa, ON: Canadian Child Care Federation.

Paivio, A. (1991). Dual coding theory: Retrospect and current status. *Canadian Journal of Psychology, 45*(3), 255–287.

Paley, V. (1979). *White teacher*. Cambridge, MA: Harvard University Press.

Paley, V. (1981). *Wally's stories: Conversations in the kindergarten*. Cambridge, MA: Harvard University Press.

Palmer, P. J. (1998). *The courage to teach: Exploring the inner landscape of a teacher's life*. San Francisco, CA: Jossey-Bass.

Palmer, P. J. (1999). Evoking the spirit in public education. *Educational Leadership, 6*, 6–12.

Pantaleo, S. (2007). Interthinking: Young children using language to think collectively during interactive read-alouds. *Early Childhood Education, 34*(6), 439–447.

Parikh, M. (2012). Technology and young children: New tools and strategies for teachers and learners. *Young Children*, 67(3), 10–11.

Paris, A. H., & Paris, S. G. (2007). Teaching narrative comprehensions strategies to first graders. *Cognition and Instruction*, 25(1), 1–44.

Parker, A., & Neuharth-Pritchett, S. (2006). Developmentally appropriate practice in kindergarten: Factors shaping teacher beliefs and practice. *Journal of Research in Childhood Education*, 21(1), 65–78.

Parkes, R. J. (2000). *On the subject of pedagogies: Contributions of Vygotskian theory to radical pedagogy as a postmodern practice.* Retrieved from www.academia.edu/908476/On_the_subject_of_pedagogies_Vygotskian_contributions_to_a_postmodern_approach_to_critical_pedagogy.

Pascal, C. (2009). *With our best future in mind: Implementing early learning in Ontario.* Report to Government of Ontario. Retrieved from www.ontario.ca/education-and-training/early-learning-report.

Pascal, C., & Bertram, T. (2008). Listening to young citizens: The struggle to make real a participatory paradigm in research with young children. *European Early Childhood Education Research Journal*, 17(2), 249–262.

Pedraza, L. (2006). *"Because they are spiritually discerned": Spirituality in early childhood education* (Electronic thesis). Retrieved from https://etd.ohiolink.edu.

Pelo, A. (2006, November/December). Growing a culture of inquiry: Observation as professional development. *Exchange*, 50–53.

Pelo, A. (2008, Fall). Embracing a vision of social justice in early childhood education. *Rethinking Schools Online*, 23(1). Retrieved from www.rethinkingschools.org/restrict.asp?path=archive/23_01/embr231.shtml.

Penn, H. (2005). *Understanding early childhood: Issues and controversies.* New York, NY: Open University Press.

Perry, B. (2001). Incubated in terror: Neurodevelopmental factors in the cycle of violence. Retrieved from www.childtrauma.org/CTAMATERIALS/incubated.asp.

Perry, B. (2004, September 23). *Maltreatment and the developing child: How early childhood experience shapes and child and culture.* Inaugural lecture, Margaret McCain Lecture Series. Retrieved from www.lfcc.on.ca/mccain/perry.pdf.

Peterson, R. (1992). *Life in a crowded place: Making a learning community.* Portsmouth, NH: Heinemann.

Phillips, M. B., & Hatch, J. A. (2000). Practicing what we preach in teacher education. *Dimensions in Early Childhood Education*, 28, 24–30.

Piaget, J. (1952). *The origins of intelligence in children.* New York, NY: International Universities Press. Original work published 1936.

Pieterse, J. (2004). *Globalisation and culture: Global mélange.* Lanham, MD: Rowman & Littlefield.

Piggot-Irvine, E. (2003, November 29). *The nuts and bolts of action research.* Presentation to NZARE Conference, Auckland, New Zealand.

Pink, D. H. (2006). *A whole new mind: Why right-brainers will rule the world.* New York, NY: Riverhead Trade.

Prochner, L. (2000). A history of early education and child care in Canada: 1820–1966. In L. Prochner & N. Howe (Eds.), *Early childhood care and education in Canada* (pp. 11–65). Vancouver, BC: University of British Columbia Press.

Public Health Agency of Canada. (2004). *AHS program overview.* Ottawa, ON: Government of Canada. Retrieved from www.phac-aspc.gc.ca/dca-dea/programs-mes/ahs_overview_e.html.

Pushor, D. (2007a, January 18–20). *Parent engagement: Creating a shared world.* Paper presented at the Ontario Education Research Symposium, Toronto, Ontario.

Pushor, D. (2007b). Welcoming parents: Educators as guest hosts on school landscapes. *Education Canada*, 47(4), 6–11.

Pye, K. (2013). *Child care practitioners' perceptions of risk-taking in early learning programs* (Unpublished dissertation). Mount Saint Vincent University, Halifax, Nova Scotia.

Pyle, R. (2002). Eden in a vacant lot: Special places, species and kids in community of life. In P. H. Kahn & S. R. Kellert (Eds.), *Children and nature: Psychological, sociocultural and evolutionary investigations* (pp. 305–328). Cambridge, MA: MIT Press.

Raines, S. C. (1997). Developmental appropriateness: Curriculum revisited and challenged. In J. P. Isenberg & M. R. Jalongo (Eds.), *Major trends and issues in early childhood education: Challenges, controversies and insights* (pp. 71–89). New York, NY: Teachers College Press.

Rankin, B. (2004). Dewey, Piaget, Vygotsky: Connections with Malaguzzi and the Reggio approach. In J. Hendrick (Ed.), *Next steps toward teaching the Reggio way: Accepting the challenge to change* (pp. 27–35). Upper Saddle River, NJ: Pearson Prentice Hall.

Read, M., & Upington, D. (2009). Young children's color preferences in the interior environment. *Early Childhood Education Journal*, 36, 491–496.

Reed, P. G. (1992). An emerging paradigm for the investigation of spirituality in children. *Research in Nursing and Health*, 15(2), 213–230.

Reio, T. G., Petrosko, J. M., Wiswell, A. K., & Thongsukmag, J. (2006). The measurement and conceptualization of curiosity. *The Journal of Genetic Psychology*, 167(2), 117–135.

Renninger, K. A., Sansone, C., & Smith, J. (2004). Love of learning. In C. Peterson & M. E. P. Seligman (Eds.), *Character strengths and virtues: A classification and handbook.* New York, NY: Oxford University Press.

Reynolds, P. (2003). *The dot.* Cambridge, MA: Candlewick Press.

Rimm-Kaufman, S., Nathanson, L., Brock, L. L., Curby, T. W., & Grimm, K. J. (2009). The contribution of children's self-regulation and classroom quality to children's adaptive behaviors in the kindergarten classroom. *Developmental Psychology*, 45(4), 958–972.

Rinaldi, C. (1998). Projected curriculum constructed through documentation-*progettazione*: An interview with LellaGandini. In C. Edwards, L. Gandini, & G. Forman (Eds.), *The hundred languages of children: The Reggio Emilia approach to early childhood education* (pp. 113–125). Norwood, NJ: Albex.

Rinaldi, C. (2003). The teacher as researcher. *Innovations in early education: The International Reggio Exchange*, 10(2), 1–4.

Rinaldi, C. (2005). Documentation and assessment: What is the relationship? In A. Clark, A. T. Kjorholt, & P. Moss (Eds.), *Beyond listening: Children's perspectives on early childhood services* (pp. 17–28). Bristol, England: The Policy Press.

Rinaldi, C. (2006). *In dialogue with Reggio Emilia: Listening, researching and learning.* London, England: Routledge-Falmer.

Rinaldi, C. (2013). *Re-imagining childhood: The inspiration of Reggio Emilia education principles in South Australia.* Adelaide, Australia: Government of South Australia.

Roberts, R. (2002). *Self-esteem and early learning.* London, England: Paul Chapman Educational.

Robinson, H. F., & Schwartz, S. (1982). *Designing curriculum for early childhood.* Boston, MA: Allyn & Bacon.

Robinson, L. (2012). *The development of rapport with children and families in hospital settings* (Master's thesis). Mount Saint Vincent University, Halifax, Nova Scotia.

Rogoff, B. (1990). *Apprenticeship in learning.* New York, NY: Oxford Press.

Rogoff, B., Paradise, R., Arauz, R. M., Correa-Chavez, M., & Angelillo, C. (2003). Firsthand learning through intent participation. *Annual Review of Psychology, 54,* 173–203.

Rolfe, S., MacNaughton, G., & Siraji-Blatchford, I. (2010). *Doing early childhood research: International perspectives on theory and practice.* New York, NY: Open University Press.

Roskos, K., & Neuman, S. (2011). The classroom environment. *The Reading Teacher, 65*(2), 110–114.

Ryan, S., & Grieshaber, S. (2005). Shifting from developmental to postmodern practices in early childhood teacher education. *Journal of Teacher Education, 56*(1), 34–45.

Saffigna, M., Franklin, D., Church, A., & Taylor, C. (2011). *Victorian Early Years Learning and Development Framework evidence paper: Practice Principle 4: Equity and Diversity.* Melbourne, Australia: Department of Education and Early Childhood Development.

Samuelson, A. (2010, August). Best practices for parent education and support programs. *What Works Wisconsin—Research to Practice Series, 10,* 1–8.

Sandseter, E. B. (2007). Categorizing risky play: How can we identify risk-taking in children's play? *European Early Childhood Education Research Journal, 15*(2), 237–252.

Sareen, H., Visencio, D., Russ, S., & Halfon, N. (2005). The role of state early childhood comprehensive systems in promoting cultural competence and effective cross-cultural communication. In N. Halfon, T. Rice, & M. Inkelas (Eds.), *Building state early childhood comprehensive systems series, No. 8.* Los Angeles, CA: National Center for Infant and Early Childhood Health Policy at UCLA.

Scardamalia, M. (2002). Collective cognitive responsibility for the advancement of knowledge. In B. Smith (Ed.), *Liberal education in a knowledge society* (pp. 67–98). Chicago, IL: Open Court.

Schön, D. (1983). *The reflective practitioner: How professionals think in action.* New York, NY: Basic Books.

Schön, D. (1987). *Educating the reflective practitioner.* San Francisco, CA: Jossey-Bass.

Schunk, D. H., & Zimmerman, B. J. (Eds.). (1998). *Self-regulated learning: From teaching to self-reflective practice.* New York, NY: The Guilford Press.

Schwall, C. (2005). The *atelier* environment and materials. In L. Gandini, L. Hill, L. Cadwell, & C. Schwall (Eds.), *In the spirit of the studio: Learning from the atelier of Reggio Emilia* (pp. 16–31). New York, NY: Teachers College Press.

Schweinhart, L. J., & Weikart, D. P. (2010). The High Scope model of early childhood education. *Approaches to early childhood education,* 217–240.

Scott, S., McGuire, J., & Foley, T. (2003). Universal design for instruction: A framework for anticipating and responding to disability and other diverse learning needs in the college classroom. *Equity & Excellence in Education, 36*(1), 40–49.

Sewell, A. (2009). Evoking children's spirituality in the reciprocal relationships of a learning community. *International Journal of Children's Spirituality, 14*(1), 5–16.

Shah, B. (2007). Being young, female and Laotian: Ethnicity as social capital at the intersection of gender, generation, "race" and age. *Ethnic and Racial Studies, 30*(1), 28–50.

Shifflet, R., Toledo, C., & Mattoon, C. (2012). Touch tablet surprises: A preschool teacher's story. *Young Children, 67*(3), 36–41.

Shulman, L., & Shulman, J. (2004). How and what teachers learn: A shifting perspective. *Journal of Curriculum Studies, 36*(2), 257–271.

Siegler, R. (2005, November). Children's learning. *American Psychologist, 60*(8), 769–778.

Siraj-Blatchford, I., Sylva, K., Muttock, S., Gilden, R., & Bell, D. (2002). *Researching effective pedagogy in the early years* (Research Report No. 356). Oxford, England: Department of Educational Studies, University of Oxford.

Smith, A. P. (2007). Children's rights and early childhood education. *Australian Journal of Early Childhood, 32*(3), 1–8.

Souto-Manning, M., & Hermann-Wilmarth, J. (2008). Teacher inquiries into gay and lesbian families in early childhood classrooms. *Journal of Early Childhood Research, 6,* 263. doi:10.1177/1476718X08094450.

Sparks Linfield, R., & Warwick, P. (2003). "Is it like the school bus?" Assessment in the early years. In D. Whitebread (Ed.), *Teaching and learning in the early years* (2nd ed., pp. 117–136). London, England: RoutledgeFalmer.

Spodek, B. (1973). *Early childhood education.* Englewood Cliffs, NJ: Prentice Hall.

Spodek, B., & Saracho, O. (2003). On the shoulders of giants: Exploring the traditions of early childhood education. *Early Childhood Journal, 31*(1), 3–19.

Stankovic, D. (2011). The environmental revitalization of the space for children. *Architecture and Civil Engineering, 9*(3), 481–489.

Statistics Canada. (2009). Population and dwelling count highlight tables, 2006 census. Retrieved from www12.statcan.ca/census-recensement/2006/dp-pd/hlt/97-550/Index.cfm?Page=INDX & LANG=Eng.

Steinberg, S. (2011). *Kinderculture: The construction of childhood.* Boulder, CO: Westview Press.

Stephen, C. (2010). Pedagogy: The silent partner in early years learning. *Early Years: An International Research Journal, 15*–28.

Stephenson, A. (2003). Physical risk-taking: Dangerous or endangered? *Early Years, 23*(1), 35–43.

Sternberg, R. J. (2004). What is wisdom and how can we develop it? *The Annals of the American Academy of Political and Social Science, 591,* 164–174.

Stine, S. (1997). *Landscapes for learning.* New York, NY: John Wiley & Sons.

Stodd, J. (2013, October 16). The narrative of social leadership. Retrieved from http://julianstodd.wordpress.com/2013/10/16/the-narrative-of-social-leadership.

Stremmel, A. J. (2002a). The cultural construction of childhood: United States and Reggio perspectives. In V. R. Fu, A. J. Stremmel, & L. T. Hill (Eds.), *Teaching and learning: Collaborative exploration of the Reggio Emilia approach* (pp. 37–49). Upper Saddle River, NJ: Merrill Prentice Hall.

Stremmel, A. J. (2002b). Teacher research: Nurturing professional and personal growth through inquiry. *Young Children, 57*(5), 62–70.

Suárez-Orozco, C., & Suárez-Orozco, M. (2001). *Children of immigration*. Cambridge, MA: Harvard University Press.

Swedish National Agency for Education (Skolverket). (2006). *Curriculum for the pre-school. Lpfo 98*. Fritzes, Stockholm: Skolverket.

Taggart, G. (2011). Don't we care? The ethics and emotional labour of early years professionalism. *Early Years, 31*(1), 85–95.

Tanner, L. (1997). *Dewey's Laboratory School*. New York, NY: Teachers College Press.

Thornburg, D. D. (2001, June). Campfires in cyberspace: Primordial metaphors for learning in the 21st century. *Ed at a Distance, 15*(6). Retrieved from http://tcpd.org/Thornburg/Handouts/Campfires.pdf.

Thornton, L., & Brunton, P. (2007). *Bringing the Reggio approach to your early years practice*. London, England: Routledge.

Tisdell, E. J. (2003). *Exploring spirituality and culture in adult and higher education*. San Francisco, CA: Jossey-Bass.

Topal, C. W., & Gandini, L. (1999). *Beautiful stuff: Learning with found materials*. Worcester, MA: Davis.

Tough, P. (2009, September 25). Can the right kinds of play teach self-control? *New York Times Magazine*, p. MM31.

Tyler, R. (1949). *Basic principles of curriculum instruction*. Chicago, IL: University of Chicago Press.

UNICEF. (2009). *Children in immigrant families in eight affluent countries: Their family, national and country context*. Retrieved from www.unicef.org.uk/Documents/Publications/immigrant_children09.pdf.

United Nations Convention on the Rights of the Child. (1991). Retrieved from www.unicef.org.uk/unicefs-work/our-mission/un-convention.

United Nations Convention Related to the Status of Refugees. (1951). Retrieved from www2.ohchr.org/english/law/refugees.htm.

University of East London, Cass School of Education, & University of Ghent, Department for Social Welfare Studies. (2011). *CoRe: Competence requirements in early childhood education and care: A study for the European Commission Directorate-General for Education and Culture. Final report*. Ghent, Belgium: Centre for Innovation in the Early Years.

Vartuli, S., & Rohs, J. (2006). Conceptual organizers of early childhood curriculum content. *Early Childhood Education Journal, 33*(4), 231–237.

Vecchi, V. (2010). *Art and creativity in Reggio Emilia: Exploring the role and potential of ateliers in early childhood education*. New York, NY: Routledge.

Vescio, V., Ross, D., & Adams, A. (2006, January). *Review on professional learning communities: What do we know?* Paper presented at the NSRF Research Forum. Retrieved from www.nsrfharmony.org/research.vescio_ross_adams.pdf.

Vescio, V., Ross, D., & Adams, A. (2008). A review of research on the impact of professional learning communities on teaching practice and student learning. *Teaching and Teacher Education, 24*, 80–91.

Victorian Curriculum and Assessment Authority. (2008). *Analysis of curriculum/learning frameworks for the early years (birth to age 8)*. East Melbourne, Australia: Department of Education and Early Childhood Development.

Vygotsky, L. S. (1978). *Mind in society: The development of higher psychological processes*. Cambridge, MA: Harvard University Press.

Vygotsky, L. S. (1981). The development of higher forms of attention in childhood. In J. V. Vertsch (Ed.), *The concept of activity in Soviet psychology* (pp. 189–240). Armonk, NY: Sharpe.

Wake, S. (2004). Think global, act local: A model for learning-informed design of children's gardens. *Landscape Review, 9*(1), 222–224.

Waller, T., Sandseter, E. B., Wyver, S., Arlemalm-Hagser, E., & Maynard, T. (2010). The dynamics of early childhood spaces: Opportunities for outdoor play? *European Early Childhood Education Research Journal, 18*(4), 437–443.

Warden, C. (2007). *Nurture through nature*. Perthshire, Scotland: Mindstretchers. Retrieved from www.mindstretchers.co.uk/product.cfm/product_ID/496/title/Nurture-Through-Nature.

Warden, C. (2010). *Nature's kindergartens and forest schools*. Perthshire, Scotland: Mindstretchers.

Weikart, D. P., Rogers, L., Adcock, C., & McClelland, D. (1971). *The cognitively oriented model: A framework for preschool teachers*. Urbana, IL: University of Illinois Press.

Welch, P. (Ed.). (1995). *Strategies for teaching universal design*. Boston, MA: Adaptive Environments.

Wells, G. (2007). Semiotic mediation, dialogue and the construction of knowledge. *Human Development, 50*, 244–274.

Wells, N. M., & Evans, G. W. (2003). Nearby nature a buffer of life stress among rural children. *Environment and Behavior, 35*(3), 311–330.

Wenger, E. (1998). *Communities of practice: Learning, meaning and identity*. Cambridge, England: Cambridge University Press.

Wheatley, M., & Kellner-Rogers, M. (1996). *A simpler way*. San Francisco, CA: Berrett Kochler.

Whitebook, M., Kipnis, F., Sakai, L., & Austin, L. (2012). Early care and education leadership and management roles: Beyond homes and centers. *Early Childhood Research and Practice, 14*(1), 1–13.

Whitty, P. (2009). Towards designing a post foundational curriculum document. In L. O. Iannacci & P. Whitty (Eds.), *Early childhood curricula: Reconceptualist perspectives* (pp. 35–59). Calgary, AB: Detselig Enterprises.

Wien, C. A. (1995). *Developmentally appropriate practice in real life: Stories of teacher practical knowledge*. New York, NY: Teachers College Press.

Wien, C. A. (2004). From policing to participation: Overturning the rules and creating amiable classrooms. *Young Children, 59*(1), 34–40.

Wien, C. A., Guyevskey, V., & Berdoussis, N. (2011). Learning to document in Reggio-inspired education. *Early Childhood Research and Practice, 13*(2), 1–12.

Wilkoff, W. L., & Abed, L. (1994). *Practicing universal design: An interpretation of the ADA*. New York, NY: Van Nostrand Reinhold.

Wilson, T. L. (1991). Let's join hands for human understanding. In J. D. Quisenberry, E. A. Eddowes, & S. L. Robinson (Eds.), *Readings from childhood education* (pp. 183–192). Wheaton, MD: Association for Childhood Education International.

Wojtasik, S. P., & White, C. (2009). The story of child life. In R. H. Thompson (Ed.), *The handbook of child life: A guide for pediatric psychosocial care* (pp. 3–22). Springfield, IL: Charles C. Thomas.

Wood, E., & Bennett, N. (1999). Changing theories, changing practice: Exploring early childhood teachers' professional learning. *Teaching and Teacher Education, 16*, 635–647.

Woolley, H. (2008). Watch this space! Designing for children's play in public open spaces. *Geography Compass, 2*(2), 495–512.

Yelland, N. J., & Kilderry, A. (2005). Against the tide: New ways in early childhood education. In N. J. Yelland (Ed.), *Critical issues in early childhood* (pp. 1–13). Buckingham, England: Oxford University Press.

Yust, K. (2003). Toddler spiritual formation and the faith community. *International Journal of Children's Spirituality, 8*(2), 133–149.

Zhang, K. (2012). Spirituality and early childhood special education: Exploring a "forgotten" dimension. *International Journal of Children's Spirituality, 17*(1), 39–49.

Index

Page numbers followed by "*f*" indicate figures, and those followed by "*t*" indicate tables.

C

campfire archetype, 192
cave space archetype, 192
ceremonies, 68–69
challenges, 36t
child care facilities, 120
child care programs, 89
childhood, 260t
child life programs, 89
children
  behaviour, and environment, 191t
  and behaviourist approach, 27–28
  as being, 131
  as citizens, 32–35
  curiosity, and children's spaces, 207–208
  curiosity, exhibited in, 207t
  early childhood, 247t, 260t, 270t, 290t
  and ecological theory, 28–30, 28f, 37, 257
  and environmental design, 194
  experiences and outcomes for, 140t
  and feeling of comfort, 67, 138, 183
  image of, 157–159
  as learners, 30–32
  middle childhood, 248t, 271t, 290t
  play, importance to, 171, 171f
  as players, 26–27, 27f, 131, 229, 231–232
  program design for, 139–141, 167–169t, 221–222t,
    247–248, 270–271
  and psychological construct, 28
  rights of, 27
  and self-regulation, 69, 137–139,
    137f, 141
  self-worth, and children's spaces, 132f
  skills for, 35–36t
  and social construct, 28
  socially endangered children, 69–70
  and spirituality, 257–261
  voice, of, 33–35, 163–164
children disadvantaged by poverty, 69
children's literature, 64–65, 65f, 270
children's portfolios, 145
children's spaces, 132f, 207–208
Circle of Security, 145
citizens
  children as, 32–35
  early learning professionals as, 44
  families as, 40–43
citizenship, 32–33
City and Country, 91t
clarity to practice, 3f
classical theorists, 81f
classical tradition, 80
code of ethics. See also ethics
  ethical practice, 134–135
  and professional practice, 7–8, 8f, 244
cognitive engagement, 208, 208f
collaboration
  defined, 232
  and emergent programming, 231–232
  as professional responsibility, 243–244

collaborative learning, 13–14
colours, and environment, 183
Comenius, John Amos, 81f
commercial programs, 89
common-law families, 37t
commune, 37t
communication
  skills, of children, 36t
  skills, of early learning professionals, 26
  technologies used for. See technologies
communities of practice, 45, 274
community
  building a learning community, 66–69
  connections, 261, 261f
  defined, 67
  and democratic values, 69
  and ecological theory, 69–70
  as value-based framework, 66–67
competencies, of professionals, 14–15
complex thinking, 3
concept maps, 249–250
confidentiality, 13
connections
  communities of practice, 274
  community of learners, 261, 261f
  International Dot Day, 200
  making, 22–23, 49, 74, 127, 147–148, 174,
    252, 294
  social poster, 106, 226
constructivism
  defined, 11, 87
  discovery gardens, 185
  and environments, 178
  and modern tradition, 80
context, 264–265
continuous professional learning, 288–289
Creating Pathways: An Aboriginal Early Years
  Five Year Strategic Plan, 60, 121
Creative Curriculum, 90t
critical friend, 262
  defined, 9
  and democratic practice, 164
  vs. mentor, 283–284, 283f
critical pedagogy, 134–135
critical reflection, 3–4
critical thinking, 11–12, 36t
cross-cultural/religious families, 37t
crowded space, 67
cultural competency, 63
cultural transmission ideology, 86
culture
  cultures in-between, 58–59
  defined, 58
  within early learning sector, 53–55
  and narrative learning, 63–66
  peer culture, 62–63
  and postmodern perspective, 71–72f
  and programming, 59–62
cultures in-between, 58–59
curate, 92

professional responsibilities
  and assessment, 103
  building capacity for relationships, 142–144
  child–adult learning relationship, 44–45
  and collaboration, 243–244
  and continuous professional learning, 288–289
  and cultural diversity, 59
  and curiosity, 223
  and curriculum frameworks, 123–124
  defined, 13
  and environment, 195–197
  and program accountability, 102–103
  in the programming process, 170–171, 237,
    239–245, 240f
  and reflective process, 262–264
professional roles
  and contexts, 6
  and continuous professional learning,
    288–289
  and curiosity, 289
  defined, 4–5
  and environment, 195–197
  in programming process, 170–171, 239–245,
    240f, 242f
  in reflective process, 262–264
  relationship building, 142
professionals. *See also* early learning professionals
  continuous professional learning, 288–289
  defined, 6
  learning community for, 288
  skills and competencies, 14–15
professional self, 12
professional skills and competencies, 14–15
progettazione, 158–159, 238
program design
  for children, 139–141, 167–169t, 221–222t, 247–248,
    270–271
  dimensions of quality, 139t
  and the environment, 141, 170, 195t
  for families, 141, 170, 222
  outcomes, 236, 247
  quality, in early learning, 139–140
  using bubbles and balloons, 233–234, 234t
programmazione, 238
programming. *See also* program design;
    programming process
  and Aboriginal families, 59–60
  arts-based programming, 97–98
  and children's literature, 64–65, 65f
  vs. curriculum, 18, 229
  defined, 18–19, 229
  and diversity, 56–57
  emergent programming, 231–232
  gender equity, 242–243, 242f
  and immigrant families, 60–62
  inclusive programming, 241–243
  learning stories, 170
  and narrative learning, 63–66
  and play, 170–171, 171f
  reflection in, 264–266, 265f
  reforming approach, 161

  and refugee families, 60–62
  and social justice, 166–167
  storyboards, 65
  teacher scripts, 168, 168f, 169t
  theories to practice in, 236–237
  traditional, 230
  transformative approach, 161
  in the twenty-first century, 232f, 233
programming bubble
  dramatic play, 143f
  great artists, 196f
  inquiry and play, 291f
  loose parts, 32f
  nature art, 224f
  play, 171f
  technology and play, 248, 248f
  yoga, 271, 271f
programming flowchart, 238, 239f
programming process. *See also* programming
  formatting and documentation, 238–239
  four-quarter planning cycle of, 235–236, 235f
  HighScope, 241
  inclusive programming, 241–243
  from information age to conceptual age, 232–233
  more knowledgeable other (MKO), 236
  planning guidelines, 246–247
  professional roles and responsibilities in, 170–171, 237,
    239–245, 240f
  programming flowchart, 238, 239f
  regulatory requirements, 244
  scheduling the program, 245–246
  zone of proximal development (ZPD), 63,
    236, 249
program popping, 234t
programs
  auspice, 89
  Bank Street, 90t
  child care programs, 89
  child life programs, 89
  City and Country, 91t
  commercial programs, 89
  Creative Curriculum, 90t
  documentation of, 238–239
  exemplars, 90t–91t
  formalized, 88–89, 88f
  formatting, 238–239
  for-profit programs, 89
  Head Start, 91t
  history of, 88–90
  not-for-profit programs, 89
  outdoor programs, 101–102
  Tools of the Mind, 91t
progressive stream, 86
progressivism, 87f
project approach, 95–96, 231–232
Project Zero, 267
provocations, 206
proxemics, 178
psychological construct, 28
psychological region, 207, 208
psychosocial theory, 132, 259